# Pauper po

MANCHESTER
1824

Manchester University Press

# Pauper policies

## Poor law practice in England, 1780–1850

SAMANTHA A. SHAVE

Manchester University Press

Published by Manchester University Press
Altrincham Street, Manchester M1 7JA
www.manchesteruniversitypress.co.uk

*British Library Cataloguing-in-Publication Data*
A catalogue record for this book is available from the British Library

*Library of Congress Cataloging-in-Publication Data applied for*

ISBN 978 0 7190 8963 3 hardback

First published 2017

ISBN 978 1 5261 3567 4 paperback

First published 2018

Typeset
by Out of House Publishing

Printed in Great Britain
by Lightning Source

For Mum and Dad

# Contents

# Figures

# Tables

# Acknowledgements

I would like to thank the ESRC for the 1+3 Open Competition Award that gave me the opportunity to continue studying and undertake this research (PTA-030-2005-00267). The work was researched in many different archives and libraries across the south of England. Thank you to everyone who helped me gain access to large numbers of documents, especially to the staff at the Dorset History Centre, Hampshire Record Office, Somerset Record Office, West Sussex Record Office, Wiltshire and Swindon Archives and The National Archives. I am grateful to Lord Egremont for his permission to use the Petworth House Archives, and to Alison McCann for her assistance in accessing these papers. The Hartley Library at the University of Southampton provided me with a peaceful environment to study, and I wish to thank the librarians who dealt with my copious requests for obscure publications.

Bernard Harris was a patient and encouraging supervisor at Southampton. He has continuously provided me with insights and guidance, for which I am very grateful. Many others have also offered their support and interest in this research in different ways, including Heather Buckingham, David Green, Steve Hindle, Tim Hitchcock, Lesley Hoskins, Joanna Innes, Malcolm Lill, Chris Kempshall, Jane McDermid, Susannah Ottaway, Alastair Owens, Vincent Quinn, Jonathan Reinarz, Christine Seal, Anna Winterbottom, Nicky Marsh and the late Leonard Schwarz, to name a small number. I am especially grateful to Keith Snell for his interest in this project as well as my development into a welfare historian. I was recently appointed as an Honorary Visiting Fellow at the Centre for Medical Humanities at the University of Leicester. The Centre provided me with a valuable environment to complete the work, and met the costs associated with the reproduction of Figure 5.1. I would like to thank the Director, Steve King, for his support. I have appreciated the questions and enthusiasm of all the audiences at the various papers I presented on this subject. I am thankful for the advice offered by Manchester University Press and the constructive comments of several anonymous reviewers throughout the preparation of this book.

I am especially indebted to my friends and my family – my partner Tom and his parents Elizabeth and Andrew, my grandparents Mary, Kenneth, Ruby and Robert, my siblings Sarah-Jayne, Scott and Stephen, and my parents Julie-Anne and Trevor – for their love, support and encouragement.

# Permissions

Figure 1.1 has been reproduced and redrawn from figure 1.9 in W. Parsons, *Public Policy: An Introduction to the Theory and Practice of Policy Analysis* (Cheltenham: Edward Elgar, 1995), p. 14, with the permission of the author. Figure 2.4 has been reproduced from A. Young, *General View of the Agriculture of the County of Sussex* (London, 1818), between pp. 439 and 440. Figure 5.1 has been reproduced with the permission of The National Archives. Chapter 2 incorporates material and ideas from S.A. Shave, 'The welfare of the vulnerable in the late 18th and early 19th centuries: Gilbert's Act of 1782', *History in Focus*, 'Welfare' edition (2008). Online: www.history.ac.uk/ihr/Focus/welfare/articles/shaves.html (last accessed 11 December 2016). Chapter 3 was originally published as: S.A. Shave, 'The impact of Sturges Bourne's poor law reforms in rural southern England', *Historical Journal*, 56 (2013), 399–429; Corrigendum, 57 (2014), 593. This is reprinted with permission from the copyright holders Cambridge University Press. Part of Chapter 5 was originally published as: S.A. Shave, '"Immediate death or a life of torture are the consequences of the system": the Bridgwater Union Scandal and policy change', in J. Reinarz and L. Schwarz (eds.), *Medicine and the Workhouse* (Rochester, NY: University of Rochester Press, 2013), pp. 164–91.

# Abbreviations

RECORD OFFICES

| | |
|---|---|
| BCRO | Bristol City Record Office |
| DHC | Dorset History Centre |
| ESRO | East Sussex Record Office |
| HRO | Hampshire Record Office |
| PCRO | Portsmouth City Record Office |
| PHA | Petworth House Archives |
| SCRO | Southampton City Record Office |
| SHC | Surrey History Centre |
| SRO | Somerset Record Office |
| TNA | The National Archives |
| WSA | Wiltshire and Swindon Archives |
| WSRO | West Sussex Record Office |

GOVERNMENT PAPERS

| | |
|---|---|
| BPP | British Parliamentary Papers |
| HO | Home Office |
| MH | Ministry of Health |
| PLC | Poor Law Commission |

All quotations are taken directly from documents and contain the same wording and spelling as the original. Any alterations to the originals have been placed in square brackets.

# Introduction: pauper policies

> I am sorry to receve such a measage from you that I am to have four Shillans of my Pay taken of I hope you will not be so hard harted as to take it from me as I stand in more need of having some. Ann Dunster

Ann Dunster was unemployed and living on Exmoor. In 1821 she wrote to the parish officers outlining her circumstances, arguing that she needed poor relief to keep her children, and herself, from going hungry. Ann argued that she had little control over her situation: '[i]t is not by Idleness' or misbehaviour 'that I am forst to come to you but it is by Death'. Ann knew where her status as a widow placed her entitlement according to the law. As 'aloud by the Justice of Peace', it was the duty of the parish to send money to maintain the fatherless children until 'they are abel to do for them selves'.[1] The main purpose of her letter was not to obtain poor relief for the first time, or to ask for an increase in the value of a payment, however. Ann had written to her parish officers to remonstrate against a reduction in her out-door relief. Her letter was one of thousands that were sent from relief claimants to the overseers during the poor laws. Whilst there was no such thing as a typical relief claimant, Ann's case does typify the complex interactions between policy, practitioners and paupers from the mid eighteenth century. This book examines the social policies developed during this period of poor relief transition, the sorts of policies that had affected individuals, such as Ann, and their families.

## The poor and poor relief in crisis

England witnessed both industrial and agricultural revolutions during the late eighteenth and early nineteenth centuries, provoking great social and economic change. Employment in agriculture, forestry and fishing fell from constituting 35.9 per cent of the workforce in 1700 to 21.7 per cent by 1851, whilst those employed in manufacturing, mining and industry increased from 29.7 to 42.9 per cent.[2] Due to mechanisation and cheaper costs of production in large-scale factories, cottage industries declined, something that had a dramatic impact upon many rural communities.[3] In the countryside, the quickening of the capitalist imperative essentially divided rural societies into three main groups: landlords, tenant farmers and agricultural labourers.[4] The widespread enclosure of commons and open fields allowed landlords to make efficiency savings as well as to capitalise on a long-term rise in rents. The labouring poor, conversely, almost invariably lost out, as the increased employment to which proponents of enclosure pointed rarely made up for the loss of any common and wasteland access.[5] The economic effects of the Napoleonic Wars further exacerbated these problems, causing a further decline in real wages and acting to intensify structural unemployment. Although labour shortages between 1793 and 1815 reduced unemployment rates, unemployment increased dramatically after 1815.[6] This, combined with a decline of live-in service that tended to reduce marriage ages, created an ever-increasing underemployed population.[7]

By the nineteenth century, rural society in England had polarised. Wealthy landowners and tenant farmers were at the thick end of the wedge and the 'landless agricultural labourers' were at the other, heading families that were unable to supplement the household budget with cottage industry or able to subsist on a male wage alone.[8] In their ground-breaking book, *The Village Labourer*, published over a century ago, the Hammonds describe the transformation as follows: 'The labourers, stripped of their ancient rights and their ancient possessions, refused a minimum wage and allotments, were given instead a universal system of pauperism. This was the basis on which the governing classes rebuilt the English village.' The shift led to what Dunbabin controversially claimed to be the creation of 'the only real Marxian proletariat that England ever had'.[9] Whilst some historians have charted the impact of enclosure on the labouring class, historians of protest have examined how their grievances came head-to-head with authority in the Swing Riots of 1830–31, a series of connected events considered to be the last time England came close to a revolution.[10]

It is little wonder therefore that poor law historians agree that poor relief was essential to the survival of the labouring classes by the beginning of the nineteenth century.[11] Yet, those in need of assistance needed to navigate the system of the 'Old Poor Law', a system that originated in punitive statutes. The Webbs, whose forensic research cemented the theme of welfare firmly into the discipline of English economic and social history, described the 'The Old Poor Law' in the first volume of their *English Poor Law History* as 'The Relief of Destitution within a Framework of Repression'. The earliest group of laws (1350s) relating to the poor (Statutes of Labourers) had 'forbade the freeman from wandering out of his own parish, from asking for more than the customary wage, from spending money on fine clothes or on the education of his children, and generally from demeaning himself otherwise than as a poor and dependent person'. The Webbs argued that the laws created a way 'of thrusting the free labourer back into the serfdom out of which, in one way or another, they had escaped'.[12] And so the pattern of control and deterrence in the 'poor laws' was set. Indeed, the Acts passed infrequently in the late fifteenth and sixteenth centuries, such as those of 1495 and 1531, gave local magistrates the power to punish vagrants as well as to issue begging licences to confine their movements.[13]

The statutes 'which defined the Old Poor Law', according to Paul Slack, an authority on this period, were the Acts of 1598 and 1601 at the end of Queen Elizabeth's reign. The Act for the Relief of the Poor, and its revised version in 1601, stipulated that the parish was the unit from which poor relief would be both funded and distributed. To raise funds for relief, the parish had to organise the charging and collection of a new parish-based tax, the poor rate, which was levied in correlation to property ownership. In addition, the legislation demanded that the impotent should be given relief, the able-bodied should be set to work and children should be apprenticed. In charge of administering these laws were churchwardens and overseers. Magistrates maintained a 'supervisory' role over the endeavours of individual parishes, ensuring that parish officials had been elected fairly, and relief provision was operating within the confines of the new legislation.[14] Magistrates also listened to individuals' appeals against parish relief decisions and overruled them whenever they believed it was appropriate. As a consequence, when the poor were at odds with their treatment they could successfully mobilise the magistracy to 'defend their interests'.[15]

Slack has posited that '[i]n all essentials ... the poor law was complete in 1601', but, as others have already highlighted, a variety of
Acts were passed in the seventeenth century.[16] These Acts enabled
parishes to identify who their poor were and to whom relief should
be provided. The Settlement Act of 1662, although not considered
to be a poor law per se, allowed parish officials to quiz individuals
who they thought were 'likely to be chargeable' to the parish and
(with the approval of two justices) return the paupers to their place
of settlement. Whilst this legislation reinforced parish boundaries'
social and cultural importance within communities, another piece of
legislation (passed in 1697) allowed parish officers to literally label
their poor with the parish name.[17] There were various interpretations
of this Act, such as how and when the badge should be worn and
what types of relief should be given to its wearers, and it has been a
source of intrigue as to whether badging was a stigmatising practice
or whether it reinforced individuals' entitlement to relief. Whatever
the intentions of the parish officers using this policy, however, the
practice persisted into the 1790s.[18]

In the meantime, providing relief by way of admittance into parish-
funded accommodation became increasingly popular. Although
numerous parishes had decided to pay individuals' house rents, or had
hired or bought a house for the reception of their poor as allowed
under Elizabeth's Act of 1601, many parish officers decided to establish institutions.[19] There were two main types. First, Local Act workhouses (also known as 'incorporation' workhouses), which allowed a
set of parish officials, with the consent of the wider community, to
provide a workhouse with rules agreed in a piece of legislation. And
second, the parochial workhouse, the adoption of which was concen-
trated in the 1720–30s, not least due to the passage of Knatchbull's
Act (1723), an 'enabling' or 'non-compulsory' piece of legislation that
allowed parishes to build, alone or in collaboration with other parishes, a workhouse for the receipt of the poor. The workhouse movement lost momentum by the 1740s, but in the 1777 parliamentary
enquiry into institutions, a total of 1,916 workhouses were identified
in England, housing over 90,000 paupers.[20]

The old poor laws created a remarkably flexible system. In the
first instance, parishes could adopt Acts and develop practices that
best suited their local contexts and, second, relief provision could be
tailored to suit the needs of the individual claimants' situation. This

optimistic perspective led Blaug to call the last few decades of relief under the old poor laws 'a welfare state in miniature', as it had managed 'elements of wage escalation, family allowances, unemployment compensation, and public works'.[21] Indeed, the south of England saw the growth of Speenhamland-style practices, whereby relief was allocated according to family size, as well as parish employment-linked relief and allotment provision. In addition, parish-funded medical attendance was common, and those in need of specialist treatments were sent to hospitals, to reside with medical men and to take a change of air. The parish would also pay for, or subsidise, food, clothing and tools to enable people to work.[22]

But just as the relief system was flexible, it was also open to corruption. It is to the widespread adoption of allowances as well as employment-linked relief provision that historians have attributed some of the causes of agricultural unrest in the 1830s.[23] Regardless of the mesmerising levels of flexibility on offer in the old poor law system, when the social and economic conditions of the late nineteenth century had led the labouring class to the vestry door, parish ratepayers saw their poor rate bills escalate. The £2 million spent on relief in England and Wales in 1783–85 had doubled by 1802–03 and continued to grow to £8 million by 1818. When accounting for population growth, there was still a significant increase in the average annual cost of poor relief, from 4s per head in 1776 to 13s in 1818.[24] Parish officials, not least in southern England, faced a seemingly insurmountable challenge: to provide poor relief whilst endeavouring to keep the rates stable. Steven King found 249 pamphlets and open letters written by the landed gentry and other interested parties on the subject of the old poor law, dating between 1700 and 1820.[25] Arthur Young's *Annals of Agriculture* (published in 45 volumes from 1784), contained contributions from people from across the country on the topic of poor relief and wages in the English countryside.[26] These are indicators of the energy that characterised an age of 'debates, experiments and reforms'.[27]

Opinion moved in favour of long-term, government-led policy change, culminating in the Poor Law Amendment Act 1834. The Royal Commission, after researching the practices of the old poor laws, and under the influence of political economists, believed that the deterrent workhouse system would be the best option for the relief of the poor. Not only would this put a stop to the allowance system, but also would suppress other perceived 'evils' that the flexible old system had brought on, including unrest. As Anthony Brundage wrote, 'lurking behind the financial concerns of peers and squires was the spectre of social disintegration'.[28] Whilst the Amendment Act of 1834 did not make the creation of workhouse-centred unions compulsory, in practice the zealous activities of the Poor Law Commission – the London-based welfare authority responsible for the central administration of the New Poor Law – meant that few places fell outside their control by the late 1830s. Although there were pockets of resistance to the Act throughout England, the pro-reform sympathies of many local elites and the middle classes had ensured its implementation.[29] The Commission instructed that parishes form into unions, ideally around a market town or city, to provide a central union workhouse. These policies meant that the Act has been viewed by historians as detrimental to relief recipients and yet significant in the history of welfare provision. The Hammonds argued that the situation of the labouring classes had changed from bad to worse: they were 'stripped of their ancient rights and their ancient possessions' and were given 'instead a universal system of pauperism'.[30] The Victorian workhouse is the most reviled institution of the British working class, although it is now disappearing from living memory. At the same time, academics taking a longue durée perspective of the development of the modern welfare state have often heralded the Amendment Act as the most significant social policy of the nineteenth century.[31] For the first time a central authority, albeit arguably a weak one, was responsible for overseeing poor relief provision.

### Context: southern England

Behind the account of the poor laws provided above was a complex web of negotiations between and within central and local welfare authorities, and between welfare providers and recipients. This book unpicks these in order to expose the dynamism of pauper policies: how they emerged, were taken up, implemented and developed in the late eighteenth and early nineteenth centuries. Such a perspective requires a locality within which to examine these themes, therefore giving access not only to the typical records of governance used, but to local vestry and union minute books and a variety of other documents that did not come from administrative processes.

The geographical focus of the book is the agrarian counties of the south of England, namely Dorset, Hampshire, Somerset and Wiltshire (or Wessex) and the neighbouring area of West Sussex.[32] There several reasons leading to this exact region, although the south of England in general has been selected for one main reason: it was the place that the Royal and then the Poor Law Commission hoped the Amendment Act would change the most. As one of the Assistant Poor Law Commissioners reported to the Commission in 1834, 'pauperism … [is] influenced by uncertainty in employment, and the degree in which the population depend on their daily labour'.[33] Snell's comparison of male agricultural weekly rates of wages in the early nineteenth century demonstrates that wages had remained high and stable in the north of England compared to wages in the south. This maps onto King's national study of poor relief provision that showed the southern and eastern regions of England provided more poor relief compared to the north and west. By the end of the eighteenth century allowances of 2–3 shillings per week were common, supplemented by an average of a further 30 per cent through payments in cash and kind. Elsewhere in England, an average of 2s per week was granted with other payments supplementing incomes by 10 to 20 per cent.[34] Green argues that poor relief expenditure comparisons should be used with caution, not least as expenditure figures often included the costs of establishing and running workhouses.[35] Nevertheless, the low wages and widespread unemployment experienced in the south of England necessarily meant that parish vestries in southern England had to provide more substantial amounts of relief to their parishioners.

Unfortunately our perspectives on southern England have been skewed by a disproportionate number of studies about the operation of the poor laws in the south-east, especially Kent, East Sussex and Essex. There is little mystery as to why this has been the case. Of the counties that experienced the most dramatic decline in wages, the majority were located within the south-east, where labourers were often ready to protest against their impoverishment.[36] That the Swing Riots started, and were most intense, in Kent is no coincidence.[37] King has made the point that there is 'need for greater spatial balance and new perspectives on the character and role of poor relief outside the south-east' to stress that more detailed studies of the north are needed.[38] But this bias towards the south-east also suggests that poor relief in the south-central and western counties also deserve to be explored. Indeed, the bias has caused problems in King's own regional work because the south-east is the main source for the south in north–south comparisons, and Wessex straddles both the south and far west regions he creates, which receive the descriptions of 'generous' and 'narrow and inflexible' relief provision respectively.[39]

The Wessex and West Sussex area provide fresh ground as well as a diverse socio-economic context within which to examine the dynamics of pauper policies.[40] Wessex had a varied rural economy, a result of the varied landscape, featuring the Quantocks and Mendips in Somerset to the west – cooler, more economically marginal landscapes from which to make a living – to the Blackmore Vale in Wessex's centre – predominantly pasture and woodland – to the chalk arable lands of Wiltshire and Hampshire in the east. Wessex was therefore an area of mixed farming, including the production of corn and barley and the rearing of livestock, mainly cattle, sheep and pigs. Work in Wessex was created in the production of high-quality dairy foods, as well as wool that was turned into products such as broadcloth, cassimere (lighter twilled cloth), linsey (a cloth of linen and wool) and carpets within many of the small market towns in the region. These products were sold to buyers in the local vicinity as well as in large urban centres, such as Bristol and Salisbury, and transported to London. Glove-making ('gloving') and silk production were also very common employments in market towns stretching from south Somerset to Hampshire, and the production of cotton was common in several Somerset towns before a decline associated with the end of the East India Company's monopoly. Wessex was rich in natural resources, with particularly the mining of coal in Somerset and stone in Dorset presenting employment opportunities. The proximity of waterways and the sea also brought work. Bridgwater thrived on building material production including glass, bricks, tiles and clay pipes; the latter were used to drain the Somerset Levels. Many coastal populations fished, or made boats and various sailing and fishing equipment. Not only was there local demand for such products, but coastal towns and villages, such as those in Dorset, exported vast quantities of sailing and fishing equipment as far as Newfoundland and the West Indies. In Hampshire, many places such as Gosport had similar trades, supplying the demands of the naval dockyard at Portsmouth. The towns and villages along Sussex's coastline had similar industry, although the landscape offered some further diversity of agriculture. The South Downs were suitable for mixed farming and sheep walks, and at their foot arable and livestock farming. The High and Low Weald also featured mixed farming and cattle and dairy farming, although the High also featured hop fields and orchards.[41] Such crops offered many communities more autumnal work than they could undertake, and so temporarily attracted many families from further afield.

Despite what appears to be a bountiful array of employments, demand for labour in many of the manufacturing districts in Wessex and West Sussex declined by the 1830s and gaining subsistence from the boat-building and mining industries had become more marginal. Yet for the agricultural labourer the rot had already set in. From the late eighteenth-century labourers faced under- and unemployment, and wages that did not rise commensurately with the cost of grain. As Wilson writes, in Wiltshire families experienced '50 years of subsistence living and often actual hunger', but this could be extended across the whole geographical focus in this book.[42] Supplementing the household budget through the cottage industries had long been difficult. For instance, in Dorset the piecework women and children received in the north of the county in the production of the Dorset Button declined due to the manufacture of cheaper pearl buttons.[43] In communities along the coast, including Bridport and Poole, Okeden reported to the Commission that 'there is no employment for women and children but in the field'.[44] He also reported that in Shaftesbury, a hill-top town with limited water supply before the mid nineteenth century, the poor carried water on their heads or on their horses.[45] Perhaps such small tasks could still be gained, but the overall number of chances to supplement incomes was declining.

It is not surprising that the area was the inspiration for many poor law innovations, including the first Local Act establishing a 'Corporation of the Poor' in Bristol in 1696. But it was rural poverty in the late eighteenth and early nineteenth centuries that sparked the desire for reform of the poor laws amongst many members of the elite, including the third Lord Egremont, George O'Brien Wyndham, who resided at Petworth House in West Sussex. The west of Sussex witnessed a high concentration of large landowners who exerted, according to Verdon, 'huge influence' over the parishes of the county.[46] Egremont was known for engaging in philanthropic activities throughout his life, and with 110,000 acres to his name he was keen to experiment with new poor relief policies.[47] He implemented an optional poor law called Gilbert's Act (1782), which enabled him to establish workhouses for the vulnerable poor, in and around the parishes he controlled. This move was replicated in other parts of the county. The politician William Sturges Bourne served as a chairman on the Hampshire Quarter Sessions (1817–22) at exactly the same time as he chaired the Select Committee into the reform of the poor laws that resulted in the two enabling Acts of 1818 and 1819. New and powerful nineteenth-century organisations had connections in the region too, including the British Medical Association, which was established in 1832 with the name the Provincial Medical and Surgical Association. The Associated gave support to, and was supported by, several medical men in Somerset during a New Poor Law scandal, and thereafter became very active in national poor law reform. As such, there is no doubt that this region was a fertile ground of policy innovation, making it a suitable place to examine neglected aspects of the poor laws.

Through a series of thematic chapters, this book aims to expose the complicated nature of social policies under the poor laws. This book therefore presents not simply a description of the poor, policies and the government, but a lens through which to view the processes linking the poor, policies and the government. The book does this using a 'policy process' approach developed by social scientists, which allows for an understanding of the dynamism of policy, as well as identification and examination of distinct parts of the policy process. Essentially I have used it to highlight and examine aspects of the poor laws that have hitherto received little attention. As such the book does not directly follow the tide of recent research about individuals' experiences of welfare receipt. Rather, it makes a case for the continued study of relief administration, in a way that at times must include the close reading of lived experiences. As the next chapter illustrates, when existing knowledge is examined from this perspective, it appears that significant parts of the history of the poor laws have been left unexamined. This has largely been due to several questions that have dominated poor law history: whether the architects of the Amendment Act were correct in their judgements of past welfare provision (i.e. the allowance system) and whether the centralised authorities were subsequently 'successful' in their implementation of the Amendment Act. Although studying these sorts of questions about the Amendment Act has resulted in very active debate and a multiplicity of new perspectives, their dominance of the field has somewhat overshadowed other pauper policies and other dynamics of pauper policies, including those developed throughout the New Poor Law. A policy process lens reveals these areas, and this book seeks to address them in turn.

Before 1834 policy was based on the development and implementation of a series of permissive Acts. Chapters 2 and 3 will show how this process worked through an examination of the adoption and implementation of two sets of enabling Acts that have hitherto received little attention. The first is Thomas Gilbert's Act of 1782 and the second Sturges Bourne's Act of 1819. In both instances, it is shown that the adoption of both so-called 'enabling' Acts was far more common than has previously been considered. In addition, their application diverted from the initial intentions of their makers. Gilbert's Act was passed with the intention that those parishes adopting it would place the 'vulnerable' sections of the poor within a workhouse and allocate employment and distribute outdoor relief to the able-bodied. The Act also had intended to promote industry and good morals amongst the poor, allowing parish officers to work the poor within the workhouse and embark on teaching programmes for children. Yet, as the eighteenth century drew to a close, and the pursuit of more economical modes of relieving the poor became ever more important, the Act was adapted in ways that could have actually contradicted Gilbert's intentions. Sturges Bourne's Acts permitted parishes to employ an assistant overseer, whose main tasks were inspecting the poor and distributing relief, and to appoint a select vestry to take charge of policy decisions and relief claimants. Whilst the retrenchment of relief provision was an inevitable consequence of the Act, the sheer variety of ways in which it was implemented is interesting. Sturges Bourne allowed parish officials to return to the clear-cut decision-making that had originated with the Elizabethan poor law – individuals were identified as either 'deserving' of poor relief, or not.

Chapter 4 takes a different angle. It sets out to develop an understanding of how social policies were disseminated between welfare officials. The first half demonstrates that, before the creation of the Poor Law Commission, there was no central welfare authority to suggest ways in which parishes could cope with the increasing demand on poor relief, resulting in parish officials seeking solutions from one another. The information they passed originated at a specific location, but it was presented and promoted as 'best practice'. Knowledge was transferred between officials in a number of ways: they conducted correspondence, went on trips to workhouses and published, read and referred to pamphlets detailing workhouse practice. Locally derived knowledge was not insignificant after the passage of the Amendment Act. The Commission was proactive in seeking local precedents and encouraging Boards of Guardians to adopt particularly beneficial practices. In addition, regardless of the presence of a central welfare authority, evidence can be found of officials continuing the tradition of conferring with one another, without the interference of the Commission. In short, the policy process was not constrained by parish boundaries before 1834, nor controlled by the Commission thereafter.

The penultimate chapter examines the role of welfare scandals in policy-making after the passage of the Amendment Act. The post-1834 relief system opened the policy-making process to a number of other stakeholders to express their own requirements from the relief system, such as the medical profession. These 'stakeholders', and notable 'key actors' from the anti-New Poor Law movement, shaped the direction of social policies during the early years of the New Poor Law, not the Commission alone. The existence of a central authority, to hold the local authorities to account, ensured that policies developed in ways that would resolve the problems happening within the unions. This meant that the experiences of the poorest played a role in the policy-making process when their voices were carried to the ears of authority. There was, essentially, a feedback mechanism between the policy implementation and policy evaluation and change stages of the policy process under the New Poor Law. Essentially, the creation of a centralised welfare authority brought with it centralised accountability for local relief administration.

This book demonstrates that social policies under the poor laws were not stable, stationary entities, simply appearing within the policy landscape. Rather, social policies were a myriad of laws and practices that were conceived and exchanged between those in positions of power. Social policies were also applied on the ground sporadically and multifariously, both converging and diverting from the initial intentions of their makers. And even those who appeared to lack any power, that is, individuals not in formal positions of authority, were still able to influence both the policy process and its outcomes. As such, in response to the recent trends in poor law literature, the administration of poor relief should not always be viewed as a system apart from welfare recipients' experiences.

## Notes

1 Ann Dunster to Mr Allen (Cannington), [no day or month] 1821, Cannington, Overseers' Correspondence, SRO D\P\Can13/13/6.

2 N. Tranter, 'The labour supply 1780–1860', in R. Floud and D. McCloskey (eds.), *The Economic History of Britain since 1700*, Volume 1, second edition (Cambridge, 1994), pp. 204–26, cited in B. Harris, *The Origins of the British Welfare State: Social Welfare in England and Wales, 1800–1945* (Basingstoke, 2004), p. 29.

3 P. Sharpe, *Adapting to Capitalism: Working Women in the English Economy, 1700–1850* (London, 1996); B. Reay, *Microhistories: Demography, Society and Culture in Rural England, 1800–1930* (Cambridge, 1996); B. Reay, *Rural Englands: Labouring Lives in the Nineteenth Century* (Basingstoke, 2004).

4 E. Hobsbawm and G. Rudé, *Captain Swing* (London, 1969).

5 J.L. Hammond and B. Hammond, *The Village Labourer* (1911, London, 1978); J.M. Neeson, *Commoners: Common Right, Enclosure and Social Change in England, 1700–1820* (Cambridge, 1993); J. Humphries, 'Enclosure, common rights, and women: the proletarianization of families in the late eighteenth and early nineteenth centuries', *Journal of Economic History*, 50 (1990), 85–149.

6 K.D.M. Snell, *Annals of the Labouring Poor: Social Change and Agrarian England 1660–1900* (Cambridge, 1985), pp. 65–6.

7 Snell, *Annals of the Labouring Poor*, pp. 67–103. For further debate surrounding this issue, see D.A. Baugh, 'The cost of poor relief in southeast England, 1790–1834', *Economic History Review*, 28 (1975), 50–68; M. Blaug, 'The myth of the Old Poor Law and the making of the New', *Journal of Economic History*, 23 (1963), 151–84; M. Blaug, 'The Poor Law Report re-examined', *Journal of Economic History*, 24 (1964), 229–45; J.P. Huzel, 'Malthus, the poor law, and population in early-nineteenth century England', *Economic History Review*, 22 (1969), 430–52; J.P. Huzel, 'The demographic impact of the Old Poor Law: more reflexions on Malthus', *Economic History Review*, 33 (1980), 367–81; S. Williams, 'Malthus, marriage and poor law allowances revisited: a Bedfordshire case study, 1770 – 1834', *Agricultural History Review*, 52 (2004), 56–82.

8 R. Wells, 'The development of the English rural proletariat and social protest, 1700–1850', in M. Reed and R. Wells (eds.), *Class, Conflict and Protest in the English Countryside, 1700–1880* (London, 1990), p. 29.

9 J. Dunbabin, *Rural Discontent in Nineteenth Century Britain* (London, 1974), p. 248.

10 For the most comprehensive account of Swing, see C.J. Griffin, *Rural War: Captain Swing and the Politics of Protest* (Manchester, 2012).

11  J.P. Huzel, 'The labourer and the poor law, 1750–1850', in G. Mingay (ed.), *The Agrarian History of England and Wales, Volume 6: 1750–1850* (Cambridge, 1989), p. 755.

12  S. Webb and B. Webb, *English Poor Law History, Part 2: The Last Hundred Years* (1929, London, 1963), p. xi.

13  P. Slack, *The English Poor Law, 1531–1782* (1990, Cambridge, 1995), p. 9; Harris, *Origins of the British Welfare State*, p. 40.

14  Slack, *The English Poor Law*, p. 11.

15  S. Hindle, *On the Parish? The Micro-Politics of Poor Relief in Rural England c.1550–1750* (Oxford, 2004), p. 406.

16  Slack, *The English Poor Law*, p. 11; Harris, *Origins of the British Welfare State*, p. 41.

17  K.D.M. Snell, 'The culture of local xenophobia', *Social History*, 28 (2003), 8. Those in receipt of regular parish relief were to 'openly wear upon the shoulder of the right sleeve a badge or mark with a large Roman P, and the first letter of the name of the parish', cited in S. Webb and B. Webb, *English Poor Law History, Part 1: The Old Poor Law* (1927, London, 1963), p. 151. The Act itself was, however, thought to have been inspired by 'the military institution, when the nobility distinguished their followers with peculiar ensigns'; T. Ruggles, 'On the police and situation of the poor', in A. Young (ed.), *Annals of Agriculture and Other Useful Arts*, Volume 18 (London, 1792), p. 338.

18  S. Hindle, 'Dependency, shame and belonging: badging the deserving poor, c. 1550–1750', *Cultural and Social History*, 1 (2004), 6–35; Hindle, *On the Parish?*, pp. 433–49. For an in-depth study of how seventeenth- and early-eighteenth-century policies impacted on the experiences of claiming and receiving poor relief, see J. Healey, *The First Century of Welfare: Poverty and Poor Relief in Lancashire, 1620–1730* (Woodbridge, 2014).

19  43 Eliz. c.2, V.

20  T. Hitchcock, 'Paupers and preachers: the SPCK and the parochial workhouse movement', in I. Davison, T. Hitchcock, T. Keirn and R.B. Shoemaker (eds.), *Stilling the Grumbling Hive: The Response to Social and Economic Problems in England, 1689–1750* (London, 1992), pp. 145–6.

21  Blaug, 'The Poor Law Report re-examined', p. 229.

22  R. Wells, *Wretched Faces: Famine in Wartime England 1763–1803* (Gloucester, 1988).

23  Snell, *Annals of the Labouring Poor*, p. 27; Hobsbawm and Rudé, *Captain Swing*, p. 47.

24  Harris, *Origins of the British Welfare State*, p. 43.

25  S. King, *Poverty and Welfare in England, 1700–1850* (Manchester, 2000), p. 32.

26  J. Innes, *Inferior Politics: Social Problems and Social Policies in Eighteenth-Century Britain* (Oxford, 2009), p. 152.
27  A. Brundage, *The English Poor Laws, 1700–1930* (Basingstoke, 2003), p. 67.
28  A. Brundage, *The Making of the New Poor Law: The Politics of Inquiry, Enactment, and Implementation, 1832–1839* (London, 1978), p. 15.
29  W. Apfel and P. Dunkley, 'English rural society and the New Poor Law: Bedfordshire, 1834–47', *Social History*, 10 (1985), 37–68; B. Harris, 'Charity and poor relief in England and Wales, circa 1750–1914', in B. Harris and P. Bridgen (eds.), *Charity and Mutual Aid in Europe and North America since 1800* (London, 2007), pp. 20–3.
30  Hammond and Hammond, *The Village Labourer*.
31  A. Digby, *British Welfare Policy: Workhouse to Workfare* (London, 1989), p. 31; D. Englander, *Poverty and Poor Law Reform in Nineteenth Century Britain, 1834–1914* (Harlow, 1998), p. 1; A. Kidd, *State, Society and the Poor in Nineteenth Century England* (Basingstoke, 1999), p. 4; Harris, *Origins of the British Welfare State*, p. 49.
32  The Reform Act (1832) divided Sussex into the eastern and western portions, but only after the Local Government Act (1888, implemented in 1889) did East Sussex and West Sussex become two separate counties. The West Sussex area I refer to and use throughout this book relates to this nineteenth-century version of West Sussex, rather than the modern-day equivalent.
33  BPP 1834 (44) XXVIII, Report from His Majesty's Commissioners for Inquiring into the Administration and Practical Operation of the Poor Laws. Appendix A. Reports from Assistant Commissioners. Part 1. Report 15. Captain Chapman, p. 424.
34  King, *Poverty and Welfare*, p. 257.
35  D. Green, *Pauper Capital: London and the Poor Law, 1790–1870* (Farnham, 2010), p. 5.
36  Snell, *Annals of the Labouring Poor*, pp. 130–1.
37  See Griffin, *Rural War*.
38  S. King, 'Reconstructing lives: the poor, the poor law and welfare in Calverley, 1650–1820', *Social History*, 22 (1997), 319; also see King, *Poverty and Welfare*, p. 8.
39  King, *Poverty and Welfare*, pp. 262, 264.
40  On Wessex, see J. Bettey, *Rural Life in Wessex 1500–1900* (Bradford-on-Avon, 1977); J. Bettey, *Wessex from AD 1000* (London, 1986).
41  N. Philbeam and I. Nelson, *Mid Sussex Poor Law Records 1601–1835* (Lewes, 2000), pp. 7–9.
42  A.R. Wilson, *Forgotten Labour: The Wiltshire Agricultural Labourer and His Environment, 4500 BC–AD 1950* (East Knoyle, 2007), p. 189.

43  BPP 1834 (44) XXVIII, Report from His Majesty's Commissioners for Inquiring into the Administration and Practical Operation of the Poor Laws. Appendix A. Reports from Assistant Commissioners. Part 1. Report 3. D.O.P. Okeden, p. 11. Also see N. Verdon, *Rural Women Workers in Nineteenth-Century England: Gender, Work and Wages* (Woodbridge, 2002), pp. 47, 53, 55, 65, 67, 133, 196; Reay, *Rural Englands*, p. 63; M. Bright, *Buttony: The Dorset Heritage* (Lytchett Minster, 1971); M.A. Jackson, *The History of the Dorset Button* (Romsey, 1970).

44  BPP 1834 (44) XXVIII, Report from His Majesty's Commissioners for Inquiring into the Administration and Practical Operation of the Poor Laws. Appendix A. Reports from Assistant Commissioners. Part 1. Report 3. D.O.P. Okeden, p. 11.

45  BPP 1834 (44) XXVIII, Report from His Majesty's Commissioners for Inquiring into the Administration and Practical Operation of the Poor Laws. Appendix A. Reports from Assistant Commissioners. Part 1. Report 3. D.O.P. Okeden, p. 25.

46  N. Verdon, 'Hay, hops and harvest: women's work in agriculture in nineteenth-century Sussex', in N. Goose (ed.), *Women and Work in Industrial England: Regional and Local Perspectives* (Hatfield, 2007), p. 79.

47  C. Rowell, 'Wyndham, George O'Brien, third earl of Egremont (1751–1837)', *Oxford Dictionary of National Biography* (Oxford, 2004; online edition, May 2006). Online: www.oxforddnb.com/view/article/30141 (last accessed 18 January 2016).

# A policy process approach to the poor laws

The curtailment of Ann Dunster's outdoor relief mirrors the experiences of many other claimants after the late eighteenth century when relief provision became subject to different rules and expectations. Foregrounding the experiences of relief recipients has, however, only been a recent trend in poor law studies. The first section of this chapter outlines the recent trend in welfare history to examine the 'welfare process'; that is, the process by which people negotiated welfare provision, and the agency of those claiming welfare, which includes how they asked for assistance and from whom they sought this help. Although this 'experiential turn' in poor law research has resulted in a much greater understanding of the impact of poor law, administrative aspects of the poor laws have become neglected. The chapter then makes a case for a new approach to understanding the poor laws, one informed by the social science concept of the 'policy process'. After a description of this concept, I apply the 'policy process' model to the current, mainly administrative, literature on the poor laws in the late eighteenth and early nineteenth centuries. This highlights several aspects of poor law administration that are currently not well understood, each one subsequently examined in further chapters in this book. A final section outlines the sources used in order to examine the poor laws according to this policy process approach.

## The 'welfare process' and agency

In the late 1990s Lyn Hollen Lees argued that '[t]he heart of the welfare process lay in the contacts between the pauper and administrator'.[1] Both had predetermined aims and desired outcomes and engaged in a negotiation before any poor relief would be offered. This idea served as inspiration for other academics writing about welfare, as it drew the focus away from the welfare outcome – the relief itself – and towards the welfare process. Indeed, the term 'welfare process' was adopted by other historians, notably Steve Hindle who, in his research into relief in early modern England, argues that the 'welfare process' was embedded in a complex web of interactions 'between the various participants – the labouring poor, the parish officers, the county magistrates, the itinerant judiciary'. People were not necessarily the passive recipients or administrators of relief, but actively entangled in the 'micro-politics' of poor relief provision. As such, we have now learnt that the 'welfare process' involved many 'protracted and often antagonistic negotiations'.[2] With these understandings, historians started to research and analyse the negotiations between relief recipients and relieving officers.

Research that explored a more active relationship between poor individuals, policy and those in power started to gain attention at the same time that historians became interested in how the poorest in societies got by on an everyday basis. Although the phrase 'economies of makeshift' was first coined by Olwen Hufton to describe poor people's strategies in eighteenth-century France, it has been adopted by historians throughout Europe to capture the 'disparate nature of income for poor households' in the past.[3] Twenty years ago, a volume entitled *Chronicling Poverty* brought together different pieces of research into the diverse strategies of the poor in England.[4] According to its editors, its purpose was to 'explore an important and little-regarded aspect of social history, contributing to a fuller and more nuanced "history from below"'.[5] In particular, these analyses have demonstrated that the poor should not be defined solely by their association with statutory forms of relief provision. Indeed, the collection of articles demonstrated an understanding that individuals did claim poor relief, but that they also utilised a variety of other options. The poor mobilised the resources of voluntary organisations, whether large, such as the London Foundling Hospital, or small, such as a parish-based Penny Clothing Club.[6] Private organisations offered important sources of support for the poor, especially the provision of credit in shops and pawnshops.[7] The varied ways in which individuals got by were subsequently captured in a further collection of essays entitled *The Poor in England, 1700–1850: An Economy of Makeshifts*.[8]

This approach has influenced the perspectives taken in more recent studies of the 'household economy' of the labouring class. Alannah Tomkins has sought to examine the alternative sources of support beyond the parish relief, such as using charities and pawnbrokers, in eighteenth-century urban England.[9] Samantha Williams examined household budgets in Bedfordshire to illustrate how proportions of income, parish relief and 'charity cash' varied over time during the formative years of the New Poor Law.[10] She also acknowledges more informal inputs into the household economy, such as acting as a costermonger and taking in lodgers.[11] Work undertaken by historians such as Tomkins and Williams has, therefore, provided us with a detailed picture of the overlapping practices of statutory relief alongside charity, mutual aid and the private sector.

Although the focus on 'strategy' has opened up the alternative forms of welfare the poor used to get by, it has also made poor law historians question the ways in which statutory relief could be used and even manipulated to an individual's advantage during tough times. Outdoor relief during the old poor laws was more necessary for certain periods of the life-course than others, as my own previous research has shown, as well as the work of Wales, Stapleton, King, Williams and, most recently, French.[12] Demographic factors, especially the number of family members, therefore impacted upon the use of outdoor relief. Because parishes, under the 1662 Settlement Act, only had to provide relief to their own parishioners – as stipulated by various settlement criteria such as birth, marriage, work and tax – a settlement examination, like an interview, would be conducted with people who started claiming relief, or whom the parish believed would start to claim for relief. Snell, in *Annals of the Labouring Poor*, found that in England men aged about 34 years old with an average of 2.1 or 2.6 children were given a settlement examination between 1700 and 1834. This pinpoints one moment in the life-course when most labouring families needed parish assistance.[13] But periods of relief receipt and non-relief came at different times for different individuals, as my own research has demonstrated. Combining a microhistorical and biographical approach, I traced eight individuals' life-courses, detailing their relief receipt and demographic events. Most individuals received outdoor relief to get by during times of hardship, but it was the parish vestry that judged these requests and tailored relief to suit individuals' circumstances.[14] Of course, the *use* of the statutory welfare system extended into the realms of indoor relief – it is clear that individuals may not have entered workhouses because of their poverty exclusively. Hitchcock draws our attention towards the functions of London workhouses in the mid eighteenth century, examining how women entered the Chelsea workhouse to receive medical treatment and to give birth. Mothers and fathers also left their children in this workhouse upon accepting an offer of employment.[15] Harley has recently extended this thesis with a case study of the Beaminster workhouse in Dorset. Here he demonstrates how new entrants were able to strategise and therefore negotiate with authority for the safe storage, and even use, of their possessions in the institution.[16]

These studies demonstrate that relief claimants were able to assert their own agency, and therefore express their needs, in the 'welfare process'. They could present their cases to the parish officers in particular ways, and once in receipt of relief they could negotiate for particular types of outdoor relief, use parish relief from a palette of welfare resources and alter the conditions of their indoor relief. Yet, the agency of the poor is only one side of the 'welfare process', the negotiation between relief claimants and relief providers. And it was relief providers who had overwhelmingly more power within this negotiation. To 'get at' these negotiations, research has turned away from records detailing welfare administration to those containing 'pauper narratives'. Pauper narratives, i.e. words thought to be written or influenced by the poor, have been found in a vast variety of archives, as Alysa Levene's five-volume collection of sources, *Narratives of the Poor in Eighteenth-Century England*, illustrates. The collection contains a host of sources hitherto neglected by historians, including pamphlets, short stories, ballads, the notes left with children in London's Foundling Hospital and a very rich source of information about the lives and negotiations of statutory relief claimants: 'pauper letters'.[17] Pauper letters are pieces of correspondence written by, or for, individuals and families asking for relief from their parish of settlement when they were unable to make a claim in person. Alannah Tomkins first demonstrated how a series of 'pauper letters' from an individual could reveal both the changing circumstances of a relief claimant and how they varied their negotiations.[18] Thomas Sokoll's *Essex Pauper Letters* was the first substantial collection of letters from a whole county, a total of 758, to be transcribed and published.[19]

Many other transcriptions of pauper letters have been published by both academic and local history publications, and it is clear the analysis of this correspondence has blossomed over the last 15 years. The source has helped historians analyse the process and experience of obtaining poor relief, the complexities of being poor and many other aspects of relief claimants' identities. James Taylor recognised four different 'voices' from the authors, each category with varying formality and insistence that their need for relief was urgent.[20] Steven King has produced several articles that explore the language individuals used to secure payments when ill.[21] In 2009 both King and Peter Jones each examined how the poor were able to secure entitlement to clothing. Jones detailed how the poor used specific tropes in letters (such as 'barefooted' and 'naked') to express their need, and King noted that the poor and welfare officials shared an understanding of minimal clothing needs.[22] They both suggest, therefore, that there is a shared 'linguistic register', as King puts it, for 'linking clothing and deservingness'.[23] As Keith Snell expresses, in his own research using the source to examine notions of 'home' and 'friendship', '[a]longside oral history, they [pauper letters] are *the* most authentic source for "history from below"'.[24] The field is moving at a rapid pace, and expanding beyond England and Wales, as the recently published edited collection about European pauper narratives and sickness testifies.[25]

There has, however, been little research on pauper letters written after the passage of the 1834 Amendment Act. This is largely due to the fact that the many surviving letters are held in unwieldy volumes of correspondence at The National Archives, rather than, as per the older letters, in small parish correspondence bundles in county and city record offices. Research has, however, examined individuals' agency in the context of the New Poor Law Union workhouse. Through an examination of workhouse offences and prison committals, Green has demonstrated that the early-nineteenth-century workhouse was a 'deeply contested site of resistance in which paupers and poor law officials negotiated' relief provision.[26] He is extending this research by examining the kinship and criminal connections between individuals entering the workhouse system. As illustrated in this work, sometimes it was one candid individual who could make a difference to their conditions, but there have also been studies revealing the very overt collective action in nineteenth-century workhouses. Anna Clark examined a riot in the South Dublin workhouse in 1860 that was started by 16-year-old girls, whilst Virginia Crossman examined the 1887 workhouse riot of New Cross (Wexford), which was started by female inmates, women and girls, and led to an assault on the workhouse master.[27] Both of these historians were concerned with how these one-off riots reflected the broader political issues of the day, not necessarily the workhouse system actually being resisted.

### A 'preoccupation' with administration?

There is no doubt that a plethora of new research questions has blossomed in the field of poor law studies because of the experiential turn. We are learning much more about the lives of those in – and out – of poverty and the agency of the poor in shaping their welfare provision. Several prominent academics interested in these questions have, though, been forthright in setting out their aims, in contrast to a tradition of understanding the poor laws from an administrative perspective. Hitchcock *et al.* wrote in the introduction to *Chronicling Poverty* that previous work that had examined more administrative aspects of poor relief was 'clearly important', especially the ways in which social historians have unearthed the '"social control" strategies and ideological edifices of the propertied' and the abuse of positions of power 'to make and justify policies that furthered their diverse interests'. Yet, they argued that despite the calls to write histories 'from below', academics had not been doing so. There had been a growing literature about collective action during the eighteenth and nineteenth centuries on a par with E.P. Thompson's own work, but little about the *everyday* actions of the poor. 'Historians', they contended, had not looked beyond 'the abundance of readily available sources detailing the attitudes of the rich towards the poor', sources that led to histories being written which 'tended to portray the poor mainly as passive objects, victims of actions of the rich'.[28]

Hitchcock has continued to be the most forthright proponent of the approach, insisting that a more 'democratic' history from below should be created, where the labouring class should no longer be allowed 'the smallest walk-on parts' in our accounts of poverty and its relief.[29] There is an element of disapproval towards work that continues to analyse the perspectives of the middling sort and upper classes on the poor, through their policies and pamphlet cultures, because it takes up time and space that could be used to explore the worlds, lives and opinions of the poor themselves. Some even stronger positions have been forged on this topic. Peter Jones writes that he has analysed pauper narratives 'despite an ongoing historical preoccupation with all aspects of its administration', a 'preoccupation' that has endured at the expense of research on 'how paupers actually interacted with' and 'were able to influence' poor relief provision.[30] What do we mean by 'administration'? According to dictionary definitions, this word denotes the 'performance', 'execution' or 'management' of a duty or of business.[31] Stating that historians have been 'preoccupied' with the administrative aspects of the poor laws suggests, therefore, that we now know enough about the ways in which the poor laws were put into practice. Perhaps a more moderate position has been more carefully reached by a group of poor law historians in their introduction to a collection of essays using pauper narratives: that the 'discovery' of sources containing narratives and the thriving nature of this field 'has led welfare and other historians to balance their questions about the administration and organisation of welfare, the supply of resources and the political, religious and philosophical rationale for particular welfare structure, with wider consideration of issues' about pauper experience and agency.[32]

Whilst such a perspective brands administrative questions as outdated, creating an administration–experience divide causes at least three, albeit related, problems in the field of poor law history. First, the position ignores the extent to which information about paupers' own experiences is often derived from administrative records, or from records directly associated with administrative processes. For instance, pauper letters are the result of the Settlement Acts and outdoor relief policies. But they have to be used *interpretatively*, i.e. with an understanding of 'their context, production and consumption'.[33] As Steedman suggests, these are not simply the words of the poor, but 'enforced narratives' constructed through an administrative process.[34] It is therefore essential to know about the administrative context in which these records and processes occurred, in order to have some understanding of why particular things are said and then recorded, and how they are said and recorded.

Related to this is a second issue. It is impossible to isolate agency and strategy from the context in which individuals employed them. In *Down and Out in Eighteenth-Century London*, Hitchcock contextualises accounts of pauper agency with administrative information. For instance, he states that '[t]he system of poor relief' in this context 'was extensive, expensive and remarkably comprehensive'.[35] Thereafter he refers to several pieces of research about London's relief provision, including the types of institutions that served the city's poor. These stories could be interpreted rather differently if the poor of London had to search far and wide for a parish institution within which they could take shelter or receive emergency medical treatment. This highlights a broader point: it is impossible to detach people's lives from the social, cultural, political and economic contexts in which they live. Whether we like it or not, the middling sort and upper classes had the most power in this context, even in the 'welfare process': they were the very individuals who were able to decide on policies, and how and when to allocate particular relief to particular people. As Green has been careful to acknowledge, 'paupers and poor law officials negotiated, albeit from very different power bases'.[36] By ceasing to research the location and nature of power in this way, we could fail to appreciate just how uneven the playing field on which negotiations took place really was.

This leads to a third issue. By focusing on the experience of individual claimants themselves, and ignoring the administrative context, historians could unintentionally underplay the role that welfare claimants themselves played in particular aspects of the administration of the poor laws, such as the development of pauper policies. Hitchcock and Shoemaker have addressed this point in their recent volume on life in eighteenth-century London. This new work, they state, 'is about the hundreds of thousands of Londoners who, although they were obliged to negotiate from positions of weakness with overseers and constables, magistrates and judges, helped shape social policy'.[37] The challenge embraced in their work is to trace the impact of agency and experiences on how policies were made, implemented and changed, a technique that weaves together information about both individual and context. Overall, it would seem that the continued examination and understanding of the administrative aspects of poor relief provision is vital to the history of British poverty, poor laws and our understandings of the experience of being poor in the past.

As such, there is a need for a dynamic approach to understanding the administration of the poor laws, an approach that also lets the experiences of the poor in. This leads me to discuss the approach I have taken in this book. The administrative nature of policy has been conceptualised within the social sciences, and is commonly known as the 'policy process'. Compared to the 'welfare process', which I contend is a term developed by historians to describe the interactions of welfare claimants, their allies and welfare providers, the 'policy process' is a model that has been applied to aid the analysis of more recent innovations in British social policy. By applying the 'policy process' to the literature on the poor laws, significant gaps in our understandings of how the poor laws operated administratively can be revealed, and at the same time it provides us with a framework for exploring less tangible, and therefore less obvious, developments in pauper policies from the late eighteenth to the mid nineteenth centuries.

## The policy process

Before addressing the 'policy process' itself, it is important to define 'policy'. Parsons contends that policy is broadly 'a course of action ... an attempt to define and structure a rational basis for action or inaction'.[38] There have, however, been many different definitions of the term, and social scientists have tended to disagree over its exact usage. Spicker has put forward the clearest working definition of policy. He states that it is 'a decision about a course of action, but it is also supposed to represent a set of decisions, interrelated and consistent with others'.[39] *Social* policy also has contested meanings, and has been the subject of considerable definitional debate.[40] In its broadest sense it can be clarified by Baldock *et al.* as 'the principles and practice of state activity – including state policy for private or voluntary action – relating to redistribution in pursuit of ... welfare outcomes'.[41] Spicker's and Baldock *et al.*'s definitions allude to the idea that policy is not simply an individual decision, but a decision embedded within a framework of other decisions and within a context of particular principles. According to Lorie Charlesworth in her socio-legal account of the poor laws, there were several 'legal imperatives'. Charlesworth argues that 'it was not social altruism and custom that motivated the provision of poor relief, rather long-standing legal "rules"'.[42] However, poor relief was allocated not according to the statute alone, but according to policies that were also developed both *before* and *beyond* the auspices of the law. With this more general understanding of policy from the social sciences, we can see how poor relief policies were forged from conscious and unconscious decisions – which may or may not have been documented, and may or may not have formed any enduring pattern. Indeed, many pauper policies were customs and practices. Medical relief, for instance, was organised for poor parishioners by the vestries of many parishes for perhaps as long as two centuries before it was officially acknowledged as a state responsibility towards the poor in a General Order formulated by the Poor Law Commission in the 1840s.[43] Dorothy Marshall, in her 90-year-old text on the eighteenth-century poor laws, constantly informed us that there was nothing new about many of the policies that were later legitimised in statues – from workhouses to badging claimants entitled to relief. Most of the supposedly new policies had been drawn up and implemented previously.[44] This thesis has been developed by Joanna Innes, who has explored the origins of a broad range of social policies in Britain. Her introduction bolsters my point about policies developing beyond the law. Innes argues that misrepresentations of these origins of social policies may be because founding texts on welfare and governance, such as those written by the Webbs, led their followers to believe that 'significant social policy must be devised and implemented by a powerful executive'.[45] As, for instance, the existence of controversial labour-based poor relief schemes such as the Speenhamland system demonstrates, this is not the case. As such, social policies and, specifically for this research, pauper policies must include an understanding of the workings of the law, but statutes alone will not create the full picture.

As the multiple definitions and applications of the term 'policy' testify, policies are very complicated. As Spicker outlines: '[i]t is often difficult to find out what a policy is, who has made decisions, and where policy has come from. By the same token, it can be difficult to reform policy, or to manage change'.[46] A 'policy process' approach tries to reduce this confusion by viewing 'policy making and implementation as a continuous process'.[47] There are two fundamental stages to the policy process: policy-making and policy implementation. Others have preferred to view these two stages as interlinked, rather than linear, because policy implementation can have an impact on further policy-making. Parsons has illustrated the concept of the 'policy life-cycle' (see Figure 1.1). The cycle demonstrates a connection from the identification of a problem, to the evaluation of options available to rectify the problem and the selection of a policy, then the implementation and evaluation of the policy. This policy may undergo further development, or have unforeseen repercussions. In these cases,

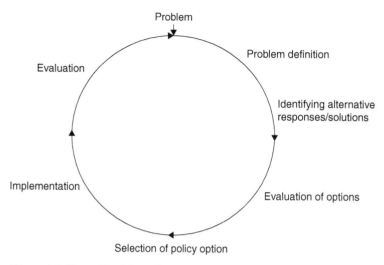

**Figure 1.1** The policy life-cycle

it could either create a new 'problem' or exacerbate the 'problem' that provoked the policy in the first instance. Others have broken down the policy process into even more stages, including Bridgman and Davis who have identified eight stages for those working in the Australian policy-making system, namely: identify issues, policy analysis, policy instruments, consultation, coordination, decision, implementation and evaluation.[48]

Although it is useful to outline parts of the policy process as 'a sequence of ordered stages', which serves as a guide to those currently working with policies, the reality is far more complex. Spicker lists several examples: '[p]olicy instruments are likely to be refined and developed as time goes on; consultation may not go to schedule; coordination and partnership work is likely to be continuous; policy analysis can be undertaken at any stage of the process'.[49] In addition, 'governments inevitably must consider the means of implementation before establishing policies'.[50] The complications of this process are numerous. As Parsons puts it, 'phases and stages tend to blur, overlap and intermingle'.[51] Nevertheless, as Hill argues, 'there are clearly advantages in separating different aspects of the process'.[52] One advantage is to use these stages to address the ways in which policies should be made and implemented: for instance, as Bridgman and Davis suggest, by placing a model in a handbook. As Spicker contends, the model and its stages can act as a 'checklist' for those working in the field of policy.[53] Another advantage is that it provides us with some categories within which we can encapsulate, and therefore evaluate, the knowledge of the 'policy process' in any area of social policy.

The rest of this chapter draws upon the policy process model's three main stages – policy-making, policy implementation and policy development and change – to assess what we know about pauper policies between the 1780s and 1850, a period of immense transformation in poor relief history. From these assessments, several key gaps in our knowledge are revealed and details about how each will be examined in this book will be outlined. The final section of this chapter will note the national and local sources that have been used to research these pauper policies.

## Policy-making

As mentioned already, policy-making can occur in two main ways: 'bottom-up' and 'top-down'. 'Bottom-up' policy-making occurs when officials develop 'practical ways of responding to issues', which are then 'imitated by others' and acknowledged and 'taken up by decision makers at the local or national level. Hence, it becomes a general policy'.[54] 'Top-down' policy-making originates with central, governmental decisions. Although the history of the poor laws demonstrates the difficulty of drawing a clear distinction between the two approaches, as shall be demonstrated below, by applying these understandings to the literature we can illustrate which aspects of policy-making have been researched thus far.

Spicker suggests that there is one obvious example of 'bottom-up' policy-making during the nineteenth century: the influence of the Nottinghamshire reformers' deterrent workhouse system upon the genesis of the New Poor Law workhouse.[55] Reverends J.T. Becher and Robert Lowe, from the parishes of Southwell and Bingham respectively, had initially forged the 'anti-pauper system', covering 49 parishes and containing two workhouses (Southwell and Upton), in the face of what were escalating poor rates. The parishes were united under Gilbert's Act, but rather than offering a sanctuary for the poor the workhouse was used as a deterrent to relief claimants. It was only after the arrival of George Nicholls to the Southwell workhouse that the Nottinghamshire plans reached a wider audience.[56] Nicholls, author of numerous poor law pamphlets, discussed his ideas with the creators of the 1834 Poor Law Report, and was also friends with Robert Peel. He subsequently influenced Nassau Senior, who devised and authored the Poor Law Amendment Act alongside Edwin Chadwick, to appoint Nicholls as a Poor Law Commissioner. Overall, local practices gained wider attention and, therefore, provided the context within which Chadwick, and other key figures in the Royal Commission, framed their ideas.[57]

This 'bottom-up' perspective is clearly a useful way to understand some other features of the policy process during the last decades under the old poor laws. Many policies devised at a local level during this period attempted to contain escalating poor relief expenditures experienced from the 1790s onwards. All of these policies, however, fell short of becoming 'general' or legally binding policies. Yet, the making of some of these policies have attracted attention from historians, not least those policies that the architects of the Amendment Act found to be 'resented' the most.[58] This includes Speenhamland-style allowance systems, which were apparently the 'master evil' of the old poor laws.[59] The policy was thought to cause 'indolence' and 'parish dependency', and even the cause of an increase in the population.[60] As Poynter stresses, this represents a 'preoccupation with a phenomenon which was never more than one among the many expedients practised under the old Poor Law'.[61] Although historians have revealed that the actual adoption of Speenhamland-style scales was not as widespread as was first thought, the origins of this type of allowance system has received much attention.[62] Like the 'original' Speenhamland system, most 'allowance' or 'bread' 'scales' or 'systems' were devised and sanctioned by the Bench. Poynter, therefore, believed that such policies were developed out of sheer frustration by the magistracy. Their responsibilities, to both the landowning and labouring classes, meant that they developed a policy of compromise, one that would support the poor but would not increase the cost of wages. It is little surprise then that Hobsbawm and Rudé, in their study of the Swing Riots of 1830, viewed the policy as an 'emergency measure, introduced at a time of famine, designed to hold off mass unrest'.[63] Griffin, however, provides a more cautionary perspective by stating that pre-existing schemes, such as those in Dorset in 1792, were not formulated during years of particular adversity.[64] Nevertheless, the allowance system had symbolised the continued interest and innovation of the magistracy in poor law policy during the late nineteenth century.[65]

Besides allowance systems, other policies were devised at the local level. From the allowance system came the 'Roundsman', 'billet', 'yardland' or 'stem' systems, whereby parish officers offered the labour of men to farmers at a reduced cost, much below their usual wage. There was a great number of variations of the scheme, including pauper auctions, whereby parishioners would bid for the labour of unemployed labourers, and the fixing of labour rates, whereby a rate was levied against each ratepayer who either paid the rate to employ pauper labour or paid the rate to the parish without acquiring any labour. Labour rates became commonly used in the south of England in the 1820s, especially after the purported successes of the parish of Oundle (Northamptonshire), which had devised the 'Oundle plan'. Griffin argues that such schemes, in comparison to allowances that were promoted by magistrates, were '[v]estry generated ... with no basis in statute law'.[66]

The top-down policy-making process associated with the Poor Law Amendment Act has been thoroughly researched.[67] Early interpretations of the derivation and purpose of the legislation focused on the importance of Benthamite ideas, and then contributions began to emphasise the importance of 'incrementalism' and 'empiricism' as guiding principles.[68] Brundage contended that scholars had overemphasised the role of the Benthamites in the origin of the New Poor Law and ignored the fact that large landowners supported the law for their own ends.[69] Other examinations have focused on the role that political economists played in making the New Law.[70] Political economic doctrines proved persuasive to many politicians, both Whig and Tory, and led to something of a shift towards the framing of reforms in terms of the free market rather than the older languages of morals and paternalism.[71] Since the 1970s, historians have demonstrated that the passage of the Act was an evolutionary, rather than revolutionary, step. Peter Dunkley argued that the Amendment Act, when placed in the context of political debates rather than abstract ideas, reveals that there was a 'spur to and reflection of a general transformation in social attitudes during the early nineteenth century'.[72]

Brundage states that it is difficult to know what exactly caused the increased governmental intervention more generally at this time.[73] Indeed, whilst political economic and Benthamite thought impacted on the creation of the Amendment Act, there was a 'rapidly growing religious movement' that was also influential. From the mid eighteenth century, Evangelicalism was being embraced by the upper and middle classes.[74] Those following this religious movement tended to support charity and individual moral reform over and above poor relief. Some even advocated the abolition of the poor laws altogether. The movement wanted to find a way of using the power of the state to create a solution that limited the extent of the state's responsibilities.[75]

Important steps have also been made in clarifying the origins of pre-Amendment Act statutory policy. Thomas Gilbert's Act of 1782 was a private – as opposed to a government-pursued – piece of legislation passed in what historians claim was a supportive moral and parliamentary context. The Act empowered parishes to group together or act alone to provide a workhouse for vulnerable members of the parish. According to Marshall, Gilbert's aim was to provide the vulnerable with separate or renewed accommodation different from the 'dens of horror', i.e. the regular parish workhouse, marking 'a new wave of humanitarian feeling' in England.[76] The origins of other significant pieces of enabling legislation have also received attention, notably the Sturges Bourne Acts of 1818 and 1819 that allowed the formation of a select vestry and appointment of an assistant overseer to take control of parochial relief provision. According to Brundage, it was the 'economic and social crises of the immediate post-war period' that 'put poor law reform back on the list of urgent matters for the country's political leaders'.[77] The Select Committees, convened in 1817 and 1818 to address the issue of poor relief, favoured, as Wells suggests, the reinforcement of local elites' control over the traditional vestries rather than a radical reform of the relief system.[78]

By mobilising the understandings of two groups identified in social science literature, 'stakeholders' and 'key actors', we can also better understand key moments in the policy process. Stakeholders can be defined as 'decision makers, officers, service users and agencies engaged in related work', those who act in groups and often have politically informed viewpoints. Key actors, on the other hand, are a much more limited group of individuals of stakeholders who, according to Spicker, have an important role in the policy-making process on their own terms.[79] The presence of stakeholders at local and national government meetings denotes a more participatory nature of policy-making today and illustrates the move away from top-down policy-making to policy-making through networks of 'reciprocity and interdependence ... negotiation and diplomacy'.[80] We can identify the role of these groups in the past without being anachronistic, and also locate them throughout the top, bottom and indeed middle tiers of policy negotiation. There is a wealth of literature detailing the influence of local landowners, ratepayers and the magistracy in policy-making at the local level. For instance, Dunkley examined how the intervention of magistrates varied from place to place, but they were especially active 'in those districts where the pressure of poverty and the burden of the rates were greatest'.[81] His work also suggests that ratepayers and parish officers can be conceptualised as a single stakeholder group in rural England because they had largely the same aim: 'to minimise all demands on their capital assets'.[82] This book does not especially focus on magistrates, ratepayers or landowners, but it does acknowledge their influence on the policy process, and how – at certain moments – these groups took an unlikely stance on pauper policies. Yet this book contends that there were other individuals who were also influential – including land stewards, parish vestrymen, reverends, overseers, and workhouse committees. After 1834 this did not necessarily change, but the centralisation of the welfare administration allowed new groups to influence the shape of policies, including Assistant Commissioners working under the direction of the Commission, and groups of workers that the new system depended on, such as medics. Innes has outlined several direct ways in which civil society interacted with the parliamentary system, other than voting, including petitioning the government and obtaining an interview on a Select Committee.[83] These dynamics during the early years of the New Poor Law have received little attention.

Although we have developed comprehensive knowledge of how policies were made, we have little knowledge about how policy ideas were diffused. A strand of research has evolved in the social sciences, especially in political and international studies, which 'uses, discusses and analyzes the processes involved in lesson-drawing, policy convergence, policy diffusion and policy transfer' between political systems, organisations or different countries.[84] Much of the research about the development of the United Kingdom's social policies over the last 30 years has focused on the influence of US policies, notably the welfare-to-work schemes.[85] Policy transfer, which affects *all* stages of the policy process, has not received the attention of poor law historians. At a time when the centralised welfare authorities had little power over welfare provision, the parish vestry, overseen by magistrates, was the governing body for welfare. How would these individuals engage in 'policy transfer'? From the late eighteenth century onwards, there 'a huge crop of pamphlets ... mostly written by farmers, ratepayers, and clergymen closely concerned with administration, and eager to have their proposals adopted nationally', proliferated.[86] This is illustrative of the desire of many local officials to exchange their knowledge on how 'best' to provide poor relief. Moreover, we do not know whether, when the Poor Law Commission was established, the exchange of knowledge lapsed. As Bochel and Bochel suggest, policy transfer relies on the 'dissatisfaction with existing programmes or policies and a consequent demand to do something new'.[87] We need to ask, therefore, what sorts of information were being sought and for what reasons?

*Policy implementation*

The second stage of the policy process I would like to examine and then assess in the poor law literature is policy implementation. According to Hill, policy studies of the 1970s viewed policy implementation as the 'missing link' between policy-making and its outcomes. After Pressman and Widavsky's seminal work, *Implementation*, a plethora of studies emerged examining implementation as a discrete stage in the policy process.[88] As Hill writes, though, '[t]here has been a tendency to treat policies as clear-cut, uncontroversial entities, whose implementation can be quite separately studied', arguing that 'it is wrong to take it for granted that this process will be smooth and straight-forward'.[89] Indeed, the policy process should be seen as a series of interlinked stages that influence one another, rather than a series of discrete stages. Van Meter and Van Horn view implementation as 'actions by public or private individuals (or groups) that are directed at the achievement of objectives set forth in prior policy decisions'.[90] In this respect, policy implementation stage is an extension of policy-making.

Akin to the policy-making stage, policy implementation can be viewed from 'top-down' or 'bottom-up' perspectives. According to Sabatier, as with policy-making, policy implementation starts 'with a policy decision by governmental (often central government) officials'.[91] Hogwood and Gunn, amongst others, have set out to define what they believe are 'ten preconditions necessary to achieve the perfect implementation', according to Hill.[92] These preconditions emphasise the need for various factors to ensure optimum policy implementation, such as a single and independent implementing agency with unlimited supply of the necessary resources and a complete understanding of agreed objectives. This assumes, as do further similar studies, that policies are the property of policy-makers at the top and their desires are to 'minimise implementation deficit'.[93] In order to see policy implementation in this way, policies are viewed as rigid, and successful policy outcomes can be 'measured' against a series of 'outcomes' or 'goals'.[94] For some social scientists this view of policy implementation is flawed. The decisions and actions of those who implemented policies, rather than the boards that dictated implementation, should also receive attention. This perspective gained momentum in the 1980s, especially after Elmore's work, which, in a US context, perceived that 'implementation actors [are] … forced to make choices between programmes which conflict or interact with each other'.[95] As Hill suggests, this perspective understands Gunn and Hogwood's preconditions but allows for the fact that these rarely exist in reality. As a consequence, the everyday decisions and actions involved in implementation should be researched.

Out of all the social policies implemented during the last years of the old poor laws, it is the implementation of allowances that we know most about. By the early 1800s, 11 per cent of the population of England and Wales was in receipt of some form of relief. Particular regions exceeded this average, such as in the south-east and south-west where 14.2 per cent and 13.7 per cent of the population was in receipt of relief respectively.[96] 'Relief in aid of wages', as the Webbs put it, had its origins in the Elizabethan Acts, and was further legitimised in the late eighteenth century by Sir William Young's Act of 1796 (36 Geo. III c.23). The Webbs wrote that the strategy had become 'devastatingly common throughout the countryside of southern England and some parts of the north and midlands, though not in the populous urban centres'.[97] Using the answers of those parishes that had completed and returned the 1832 Queries, Hobsbawm and Rudé demonstrated how prolific the allowance system was: in 14 counties, located in the south and the Midlands, 50 per cent or more of the parishes used allowance systems.[98] This picture was in reality much more complicated, though. Langton, upon examining the policy from parliamentary as well as parish records in Oxfordshire, illustrates that although the mechanism of the scale was adopted, the exact remittances would sometimes be set by the parish rather than the magistrates. This means that 'although bread scales were common, the actual scales used varied widely from place to place'.[99] The value of allowances changed temporally as well as spatially. Snell argues that 'the scale was heavily curtailed over time, to become only two-thirds to a half of its 1795 value by the 1820s'.[100] Regardless of how prolific the allowance system was, both the Webbs and Blaug have argued that 'hardly any of the dire effects ascribed to the Old Poor Law stand up in the light of available empirical knowledge'.[101] Since the 1980s we have come to the understanding that 'historians, economists, and demographers … emphasize that relief under the old poor law was essentially a *response* to population growth, under-employment, and low wages, rather than their *cause*'.[102] Williams, after an analysis of two communities in Bedfordshire, also argued that allowances had not induced early marriages and larger families but was rather a policy brought in to deal with the deteriorating condition of the labouring class.[103] This brings into focus another aspect of policy adoption and implementation during the late eighteenth and early nineteenth centuries. Parishes adopted and rejected allowances, as well as other locally derived policies, at different times. The myriad options available to the parish meant that parish relief was customised for each individual claimant.[104]

Historians have also examined the adoption and implementation of Local Acts under the old poor laws. 'Local Acts' were pieces of legislation passed at the governmental level but which only applied to the relief provision of a specific parish or group of parishes. The Acts consisted of rules as to different types of relief to be given to different types of people, and in what institutional setting relief was to occur. The first 'Corporation of the Poor' was formed in Bristol in 1696, and from this point onwards the idea spread. By 1711, incorporations were established in 15 different cities.[105] Incorporations in rural locales were also permitted, but were much less common. The Webbs' assessment of the incorporations came to the conclusion that the 'long-drawn-out experiments in the establishment of incorporated bodies for Poor Law administration … make up a confused medley which it is difficult to analyse or to classify'.[106] Nevertheless, the workhouse was central to the relief policies issued by incorporations. Several studies of incorporations have been undertaken, including Hitchcock's case studies of the Bristol, Exeter, London and Norwich incorporations and Tomkins' examinations of several urban workhouses in the Midlands and north of England.[107] Some studies have even examined the negotiations that took place between the Commission and the Guardians in control of relief under Local Acts, such as Clark's study of the Southampton Incorporation.[108] Digby found that four out of the seven incorporations of Norfolk persisted into the New Poor Law, confirming her overall belief that the desires of local landowners continued to be met after centralisation.[109] In addition, Driver has created a national picture of 'non-conformity' by mapping the 45 Local Act unions and parishes that remained in place in 1856. In the south of England, these Local Acts remained in place mainly in large market towns and cities.[110]

As noted, much ink has been devoted to the implementation of the Amendment Act. A significant body of research has accumulated on the conditions experienced within New Poor Law Union workhouses.[111] Notwithstanding the 'newness' of the legislation, though, most academics have sought to show how both relief practices and welfare officials' relief administration practices had remained the same after 1834. The bulk of this research has formed into what has been called the 'continuity thesis'. For instance, Rose illustrated that the allowance system for the able-bodied continued well beyond 1834 because the Commission was unable to prohibit outdoor relief to the able-bodied.[112] Rose highlighted the Commissioners' lack of power to actually overcome middle- and working-class resistance, especially within the north of England.[113] Digby found that local relief officials would remain 'stubbornly independent' of central authority. Even when formed into Boards of Guardians, landowners and farmers continued to assert their influence in the administration of poor relief.[114] According to this research, the Commission had reinforced rather than undermined the powers of local elites.[115] This consensus position has been challenged, most notably by Williams. The Commission wanted, according to Williams, to reduce the numbers of able-bodied men in receipt of outdoor relief. There was no intention to reduce the number of women, elderly or young in receipt of relief.[116] When drawing this distinction it is possible to demonstrate that the Commission reduced the overall number of able-bodied men receiving outdoor relief.[117] In view of this evidence, the Commission had been successful in bringing about change to relief provision and administration.

Further literature has offered a more complex picture of how the Amendment Act was implemented, most notably through focusing on the roles of other key actors in the 'welfare process' after 1834. Harling demonstrates that many of the employees appointed by Boards of Guardians, including masters, matrons, porters and nurses, had experience of working in workhouses. In consequence, there was a gradual transition in providing relief according to the new stipulations.[118] Even parish officers continued to provide relief well beyond the passage of the Amendment Act. As Snell demonstrates, overseers had to provide relief in kind and accommodation in urgent situations and could also admit individuals into union workhouses. They also continued to chase relatives for maintenance payments and take settlement cases to the magistrates.[119] Nevertheless, Harling argues that the new roles of Assistant Commissioners meant that local relief practices 'would never again go entirely unquestioned'.[120] Dunkley made the same point after an examination of the Commission's intervention in poor relief provision during the 'hungry forties'.[121]

The overwhelming focus on the implementation of the 1834 Amendment Act has obscured significant features of the preceding legislation, especially the implementation of enabling or 'noncompulsory' policies created in the final decades of the old poor laws. Enabling legislation, Digby explained, was 'grafted on to the Elizabethan bases of the Old Poor Law', modifications that each parish vestry could choose to implement or not.[122] One of these pieces of legislation was, as noted, Gilbert's Act of 1782, which allowed parishes to form unions and is widely thought to have inspired the compulsory union formations stipulated by the 1834 Amendment Act.[123] Gilbert's Act is often mentioned in passing, but such references are only tacit acknowledgements of its impact on the lives of the poor.[124] Digby's study of Norfolk is the only work that has thus far actually examined the adoption of Gilbert's Act. She found that the legislation slowed down the establishment of Local Act workhouses in the county, because it was less expensive, although new research suggests this pattern does not hold throughout England.[125] Digby's research, though, was focused on assessing the impact of the 1834 Amendment Act on the operation of the poor laws in the county rather than analysing the implementation of Gilbert's Act per se.[126] Consequently, our understandings of the Act are not effectively grounded in observed histories. As mentioned, Marshall claimed that

Gilbert's Act marked the start of 'a new wave of humanitarian feeling' in England.[127] Others have argued that this period is characterised by the opposite feeling, supposedly due to the hostile attitudes of the landed elite towards the poor and the 'greediness' of farmers.[128] Such contradictory statements graphically demonstrate the need for an analysis of why and how Gilbert's Act was adopted and implemented.

Sturges Bourne's Acts (1818 and 1819) have also been neglected. Passed in the context of the unprecedented increase in poor rates, the intention was to give more powers to local vestrymen to clamp down on too generous relief provisions to the poor through the employment of a salaried overseer (an 'assistant overseer') and the formation of a select vestry. The impacts of this legislation remain poorly understood. The Poor Law Report acknowledged that 'the Acts under which the ratepayers are empowered to elect a committee for the management of their parochial concerns have proved highly beneficial'. Yet, they also argued that select vestries were not popular, that meetings were sparsely attended and, when the vestry did sit, they had 'no power', made 'injurious' relief decisions and were infrequently recorded.[129] This perspective on Sturges Bourne's reforms has been left largely unquestioned, although the examination of two select vestries in Sussex by Wells and the insights of Neuman (Berkshire) and Digby (Lancashire and Yorkshire) show that the legislation may have achieved its purpose in reducing relief costs.[130] A more detailed assessment of the implementation of enabling legislation is needed, of both Gilbert's Act and Sturges Bourne's Acts, in order to understand the impact these had upon the welfare process prior to 1834.

The examination of the implementation of these laws has in part been hindered by their 'enabling' status. This 'opt in' nature makes this legislation seemingly of low importance. This is especially the case for key enabling Acts passed in the final years of the old poor laws, including Gilbert's Act and the Sturges Bourne's Acts. As Wells wrote, 'the adoption of Sturges Bourne has not been systematically studied, merely commented upon'.[131] Two-thirds of ratepayers during an ordinary, or 'open', vestry had to agree to adopt the provisions of Gilbert's Act, although it also had to secure the approval of a magistrate.[132] Select vestries under Sturges Bourne's legislation were also established by a majority vote from the ratepayers, and such an agreement stood in place until 14 days after the next Annual Appointment of Overseers (usually on Lady Day). Thereafter, it would be renewed at another open vestry. Similarly to Gilbert's Act, the formation of a select vestry also required the seal of a magistrate. Assistant overseers were elected and confirmed in a similar way, requiring the support of two magistrates.[133] It must not be forgotten that the Poor Law Amendment Act was also 'adopted' by parishes in a similar fashion, although under immense pressure from the Commission. The Commission had no powers to change or remodel Gilbert's Parishes, Unions and Local Incorporations without the consent of the Guardians. Indeed, many parishes resisted adopting the legislation for years and, in some cases, even decades.[134]

It is worth mentioning here that the uptake of enabling Acts may have preceded implementation, i.e. a parish vestry may have formally agreed to adopt the legislation before implementing it. There was, therefore, an intermediate stage between policy-making and implementation in the policy process, namely policy *adoption*. Social scientists should be forgiven for their oversight of this, not least because the British state was a much weaker legislative body prior to the late twentieth century. But in order for the policy process model to work in earlier contexts, this needs to be acknowledged, especially when utilising statistics published in British Parliamentary Papers, as will be discussed in Chapters 2 and 3. Whether policy adoption should gain a place on the policy process wheel is, though, questionable. Indeed, adoptions of enabling Acts by parish vestries at this time did not necessarily lead to an implementation of the Acts. Plus, the implementation of the Acts, and the implementation of practices encouraged and legitimised by the Acts, was not necessarily formalised with an agreement to adopt the legislation.

*Policy development and change*

The stages of the policy process may have blurred edges, but there is also a 'succession of feedback loops between them'.[135] For instance, when a policy is proving difficult to implement, the governing body sometimes receives this information and is able to change the policy through amendment or the passage of a new policy. As Bochel and Bochel contend, '[i]f policies are seen as originating from particular decisions that are aimed at achieving particular goals, it would seem natural and appropriate that those who make those decisions, at central or local government level, would wish to determine the effects of their decisions or actions'.[136] This is what they term a 'rational' model of decision-making that, unlike other more fragmented models, views the process of making policies as a 'means–end' process.[137] Two aspects of policy can be evaluated: the outcomes of policy and the individuals implementing policies.[138] Although evaluation comes after the implementation stage, it also comes after a degree of monitoring and, therefore, the gathering of information.[139] The collection and evaluation of information produced through monitoring is not devoid of bias, though. As Parsons explains, 'the evaluation of the actual impact of policy on problems is something which is essentially a matter of *values* rather than *facts*: numbers mean whatever policy-makers want them to mean'. And he goes further, arguing that the analysis of policies moulds the 'context and agenda within which problems are being defined and constructed … [which] takes us back to the start of the policy cycle – problem definition and agenda setting'.[140] Clearly, the political contexts within which policies are reviewed and then (re)made cannot be ignored.

In terms of recent UK social policies, Bochel and Bochel notice that 'much of the assessment of policy success or failure in social policy has been impressionistic and anecdotal', with much research being undertaken by academics and pressure groups rather than by policymakers themselves.[141] The question is, therefore, how much attention have historians paid to the attempts made *at the time* to evaluate and change policies? At this stage of the policy process, poor law literature is strong in one area alone: the Royal Commission's evaluation of the old poor laws. Brundage, for instance, outlines how Nassau Senior, in writing the first half of the Poor Law Report, relied upon 'a good deal of anecdotes of corruption and abuse', details that were represented 'in such a way that readers could only conclude that the existing system was grievously flawed and in need of drastic reform'.[142] As King notes, the Royal Commission used the responses of the Rural and Town Queries to present 'a ramshackle system of local welfare initiatives that bore only a limited resemblance to what the state thought was happening. Generous allowances encouraged idleness and immorality, undermining the desirable self-help ethic which should have lain at the heart of welfare. The result was spiralling relief bills and a vicious circle of poverty'.[143]

The bias of the Poor Law Report and how it constructed a 'problem' and promoted change is widely acknowledged. But how was the Amendment Act itself scrutinised? The Amendment Act was a controversial piece of legislation. The anti-New Poor Law movement quickly sought to expose flaws in the operation of the new relief system. Their zealous activities and the new central accountability for poor relief meant that local problems in the administration of relief became of national concern. The print media played an important role, reporting claims of neglect and abuse towards relief claimants. Roberts has discovered that between 1837 and 1842 *The Times* reported 16 wife and husband separations, 32 accounts of punishments, 14 cases of overcrowding, 24 cases of inadequate diets, 10 cases of diseased conditions and 7 workhouse-based murders. Outside of the workhouse, there were 42 reported cases of inadequate outdoor relief to the aged and infirm, and 33 instances where emergency relief was refused.[144]

Whilst all of these cases garnered public attention, few escalated into welfare scandals. As Butler and Drakeford contend, scandals are produced through 'the process whereby everyday tragedies are transformed into something extraordinary; the process whereby events that are local and personal become national and public; the process whereby the specific comes to stand for the general'.[145] Thus, whilst all scandals had initially developed from 'everyday tragedies', not all everyday tragedies escalated into scandals. Still, everyday tragedies and scandals during the early years of the New Poor Laws *have* caught the attention of poor law historians, but no distinction has been made between the two categories.

Neglect and abuse cases under the New Poor Law have been viewed and therefore used in poor law research as a representation of people's feelings about the new system. Roberts argues that *The Times* reports demonstrate the lengths to which the anti-New Poor Law movement went to garner publicity over cases of maladministration. On the other hand, Henriques believed that such cases reflected 'a climate of opinion in which abuses were more likely to occur', a climate that was of the Commission's own making.[146] More recent research has moved beyond these interpretations. Using the correspondence between the Commission and a Board of Guardians regarding the death of Henry Williams in Llantrisant, Stewart and King demonstrated the complexities faced at both local and national levels when implementing the Amendment Act.[147] Others, including McCord and Wells, have also examined local–centre relations through the correspondence created during similar periods of turmoil.[148] A further study by Peter Dunkley took a different approach, suggesting that cases of abuse clearly occurred before 1834, but that because the New Poor Law was organised on a central basis, local problems now assumed national importance.[149]

Regardless of the number of welfare *scandals* that occurred under the first period of centralised welfare provision, the only scandal universally acknowledged in studies of the New Poor Law is the Andover Union Scandal of the 1840s.[150] Here, malnourished paupers gnawed on the bones they were supposed to crush for the Guardians to sell as fertiliser.[151] Memory of this scandal has endured for two key reasons. First, it has been utilised as a graphic example of maladministration, evoking a clearly 'grim symbolic feature' of life behind the workhouse doors.[152] Second, the Andover Scandal is also believed to have put the final nail in the coffin of the Commission, the Commission being left to expire without renewal by Parliament in 1847.[153]

Rather than examine the scandal alone, historians need to trace how such scandals infiltrated into policy-making, development and change during the early years of the New Poor Law. Indeed, within policies there are what Spicker calls 'meta-rules', rules that 'determine how decisions are made, how they are changed, how they are decided on and enforced'.[154] The use of these rules facilitate the implementation of policies and result in the development of further policies. The meta-rules of the Amendment Act have been heralded as one of the 'the most important clauses' of that legislation because they defined the powers of the Commission. Indeed, their use resulted in the production of legally binding stipulations, each agreed upon by the Secretary of State.[155] The implementation of these policies had to be checked by the Poor Law Commission. Section 16 of the Amendment Act provided the Commissioners with the power to release General Orders that could contain instructions applying to all, or a large proportion, of the unions under their charge.[156]

Significant numbers of Orders were released by the Commission and some of these have been studied, although the interpretations are somewhat incomplete.[157] For instance, Rose has focused on the Outdoor Relief Prohibitory Order (1844) and Hodgkinson examined the General Medical Order (1842).[158] Rose contends that it had always been the mission of the Commission to stop all outdoor relief to the able-bodied poor, so when the Order was sent to the localities it had come as no surprise to many Boards of Guardians. In addition, the Commission had sent union-specific Orders to the Guardians to stop outdoor relief payments after the establishment of union workhouses.[159] Hodgkinson attributes the Medical Order to the pressures of the British Medical Association.[160] As such, the genesis of Orders has always been attributed to external pressures or the determination of the Commission. How local events, such as scandals, infiltrated into the development of the Commission's policies has therefore been somewhat overlooked.

This chapter has argued for a 'policy process' perspective of understanding of the poor laws. It is a perspective that separates out the stages of pauper policies, rather than group them together under the imprecise label of 'administration'. By applying this perspective to our current knowledge of the poor laws over a crucial period of transition, 1780 to 1850, a series of gaps in our current knowledge come to light. This book now addresses four important overlooked avenues of enquiry with a series of thematic chapters, all of which were outlined in detail at the end of the Introduction. To recap, Chapters 2 and 3 analyse the adoption and implementation of two sets of enabling Acts, Gilbert's Act and Sturges Bourne's Acts respectively. Chapter 4 is concerned with policy transfer under both the old and New Poor Laws, whilst Chapter 5 traces the impact of welfare scandals upon the development of policies by the Commission. This research has relied on a large variety of sources from an expansive geographical location. The final section of this chapter therefore outlines the sources consulted and how they were read for the purpose of providing insight into the policy process.

### Sources and the policy process

Any account of the policy process under the poor laws has to be (re)constituted from records created by those in positions of authority: parish officers, such as vestrymen, and workhouse Guardians, magistrates, Poor Law Commissioners and their secretaries and assistants. I have consulted a broad range of local administrative documents (including workhouse minute books, vestry minute books and overseers' accounts), post-1834 administrative documents (Board of Guardians' minute books, correspondence between the Guardians and the Commission, correspondence between Assistant Commissioners

and the Commission) and a range of poor law-related publications.
I use publications that were written to disseminate ideas about poor
relief practices prior to 1834, mainly a sub-section of those pamphlets
that leapt off the printing press during the last decades of the old poor
laws, and the various official publications issued by the Poor Law
Commission to issue rules and guidance.

Sampling these records did not follow the straightforward pattern
as I initially hoped. To start with I selected 12 New Poor Law Unions
from across the south of England, analysing both their old and New
Poor Law records over a hundred-year period, from 1750 to 1850.
However, information about policies adopted and implemented
under the old poor laws was not forthcoming – not least due to the
lack of document survival and damage. Indeed, old poor law administrative records were kept in the parish chests of parish churches
before being transferred to county or city record offices, which made
the documents vulnerable to damage. During the research for this
book I came across stories of church fires, both accidental and arson,
which consumed parish chests, and the case of a child who perhaps
thought no harm would be caused by pouring water into one. These
events either impaired or devastated documents. As such, I had to
adopt a strategic approach by using catalogue descriptions to pinpoint
documents created specifically during the implementation of both
Gilbert's and Sturges Bourne's Acts, including select vestry minute
books and workhouse minute books. Some clues for those parishes
that adopted this legislation came from Parliamentary Returns and
newspaper adverts, but by no means not all. Whilst a variety of parish
records have been used in both Chapters 2 and 3, the former does
rely particularly on collections of documents created in the administration of the Alverstoke (Hampshire) Gilbert's Parish, and of Lord
Egremont's Gilbert's Unions of Sutton and Easebourne. These papers
withstood much deterioration and are richly detailed, especially the
latter collection, which, alongside workhouse committee minute
books, contained receipts, contracts, treasurers' books and details of
relief claims and relief provision.

Similar detective work was involved in linking together and finding
the variety of documents used in Chapters 4 and 5, though on this occasion to link together a wide variety of documents including publications,
minutes and correspondence. One pamphlet often led me to another,
some of which were accessible through various online collections or in

the British Library, and others in county record offices. Official publications, including those written by the Poor Law Commission, such as their Annual Reports and Official Circulars, were consulted in an assortment of archives and the British Library, whilst Hansard's *Parliamentary Debates* was accessed on paper and online. Although I started most of my Parliamentary Paper research from microfilm collections, I moved to using the House of Commons Parliamentary Papers Online. The evidence gathered by Select Committees, especially the 'Minutes of Evidence', or interviews with those who administered and claimed poor relief, informs significant amount of the analysis of New Poor Law scandals. These interviews were likely to have been intimidating, for both welfare administrator and claimant, and we need to carefully consider the pressure on the interviewees to give particular answers under such circumstances, especially due to the probability that that Commission would ask leading questions.[161] Since the interviewees' words were shaped and then documented by the relatively powerful, they are, to use Steedman's term, 'enforced narratives' and need to be recognised as such.[162]

This book deploys an *interpretative* rather than *literal* reading of documents, not only because the production of documents impacts on its contents, but also because piecing together policy processes requires understandings beyond 'facts'.[163] All administrative documents were necessarily created with underlying motives and within uneven power structures, and necessarily have to be read and interpreted through the eyes of their creators. We can elucidate, rather than just be aware of, the predetermined views of the author by revealing how the author 'performs' their identity, and authority, within the record.[164] The policy process approach is somewhat similar to the aims of the interpretative readings of documents, as it promotes the understanding of 'the exercise of power and influence as well as the development of policies'.[165] As such, this book is interested not only in the contents of records produced in the administration of the poor laws, but also the processes that generated these records and the data within them. This approach has informed the history written in this book.

## Notes

1    L.H. Lees, *Solidarities of Strangers: The English Poor Laws and the People, 1700–1948* (Cambridge, 1998), p. 33.

2  S. Hindle, *On the Parish? The Micro-Politics of Poor Relief in Rural England c.1550–1750* (Oxford, 2004), p. 363.

3  O.H. Hufton, *The Poor of Eighteenth-Century France 1750–1789* (Oxford, 1974); A. Tomkins and S. King, 'Introduction', in S. King and A. Tomkins (eds.), *The Poor in England, 1700–1850: An Economy of Makeshifts* (Manchester, 2001), p. 1.

4  T. Hitchcock, P. King and P. Sharpe, *Chronicling Poverty: The Voices and Strategies of the English Poor, 1640–1840* (Basingstoke, 1996).

5  T. Hitchcock, P. King and P. Sharpe, 'Introduction: chronicling poverty – the voices and strategies of the English poor, 1640–1840', in Hitchcock *et al.* (eds.), *Chronicling Poverty*, p. 1.

6  A. Levene, 'The origins of the children of the London Foundling Hospital, 1741–1760: a reconsideration', *Continuity and Change*, 18 (2003), 201–35; A. Levene, 'The mortality penalty of illegitimate children: foundlings and poor children in eighteenth-century England', in A. Levene, T. Nutt and S. Williams (eds.), *Illegitimacy in Britain, 1700–1920* (Basingstoke, 2005), pp. 34–49; T. Evans, '"A good character of virtue, sobriety, and honesty": unmarried mothers' petitions to the London Foundling Hospital and the rhetoric of need in the early nineteenth century', in Levene *et al.* (eds.), *Illegitimacy in Britain*, pp. 86–101; T. Evans, *Lone Mothers in Eighteenth-Century London* (Basingstoke, 2005); P. Jones, 'Clothing the poor in early-nineteenth-century England', *Textile History*, 37 (2006), 17–37; A. Levene (ed.), *Narratives of the Poor in Eighteenth-Century Britain*, 5 volumes (London, 2006).

7  For example, A. Tomkins, 'Pawnbroking and the survival strategies of the urban poor in 1770s York', in King and Tomkins (eds.), *The Poor in England*, pp. 166–98.

8  King and Tomkins, *The Poor in England*; T. Hitchcock, *Down and Out in Eighteenth Century London* (London, 2004).

9  A. Tomkins, *The Experience of Urban Poverty: Parish, Charity and Credit, 1723–82* (Manchester, 2006).

10  S. Williams, 'Earnings, poor relief and the economy of makeshifts: Bedfordshire in the early years of the New Poor Law', *Rural History*, 16 (2005), 21–52.

11  Williams, 'Earnings, poor relief', p. 39.

12  S.A. Shave, 'The dependent poor? (Re)constructing the lives of individuals "on the parish" in rural Dorset, 1800–1832', *Rural History*, 20 (2009), 67–97; B. Stapleton, 'Inherited poverty and life-cycle poverty: Odiham, Hampshire, 1650–1850', *Social History*, 18 (1993), 339–55; S. King, 'Reconstructing lives: the poor, the Poor Law and welfare in Calverley, 1650–1820', *Social History*, 22 (1997), 318–38; S. King,

*Poverty and Welfare in England 1700–1850: A Regional Perspective* (Manchester, 2000), pp. 127–34; S. Williams, *Poverty, Gender and Life-Cycle under the English Poor Law, 1760–1834* (Woodbridge, 2011); H. French, 'An irrevocable shift: detailing the dynamics of rural poverty in southern England, 1762–1834 – a case study', *Economic History Review*, 68 (2014), 769–805.

13  K.D.M. Snell, *Annals of the Labouring Poor: Social Change and Agrarian England 1660–1900* (Cambridge, 1985), p. 358.

14  Shave, 'The dependent poor'.

15  T. Hitchcock, '"Unlawfully begotten on her body": illegitimacy and the parish poor in St Luke's Chelsea', in Hitchcock *et al.* (eds.), *Chronicling Poverty*, pp. 70–86.

16  J. Harley, 'Material lives of the poor and their strategic use of the workhouse during the final decades of the English Old Poor Law', *Continuity and Change*, 30 (2015), 71–103.

17  Levene, *Narratives of the Poor*.

18  A. Tomkins, 'Self presentation in pauper letters and the case of Ellen Parker, 1818–1827', *Women's History Notebooks*, 6 (1999), 2–7.

19  T. Sokoll (ed.), *Essex Pauper Letters, 1731–1837* (Oxford, 2001).

20  J.S. Taylor, 'Voices in the crowd: the Kirkby Lonsdale Township letters, 1809–36', in Hitchcock *et al.* (eds.), *Chronicling Poverty*, pp. 109–26.

21  S. King, '"Stop this overwhelming torment of destiny": Negotiating financial aid at times of sickness under the English Old Poor Law, 1800–1840', *Bulletin of the History of Medicine*, 79 (2005); S. King, '"It is impossible for our vestry to judge his case into perfection from here": managing the distance dimensions of poor relief under the old poor law', *Rural History*, 16 (2005), 161–89; S. King, 'Regional patterns in the experiences and treatment of the sick poor, 1800–40: rights, obligations and duties in the rhetoric of paupers', *Family and Community History*, 10 (2007), 61–75.

22  P. Jones, '"I cannot keep my place without being deascent": pauper letters, parish clothing and pragmatism in the South of England, 1750–1830', *Rural History*, 20 (2009), 31–49; S. King, '"I fear you will think me too presumptuous in my demands but necessity has no law": clothing in English pauper letters, 1800–1834', *International Review of Social History*, 54 (2009), 207–36.

23  King, '"I fear you will think me too presumptuous"', p. 207.

24  Emphasis in the original; K.D.M. Snell, 'Belonging and community: understandings of "home" and "friends" among the English poor, 1750–1850', *Economic History Review*, 65 (2012), 2.

25  A. Gestrich, E. Hurren and S. King (eds.), *Poverty and Sickness in Modern Europe: Narratives of the Sick Poor 1780–1938* (London, 2012).

26   D. Green, 'Pauper protests: power and resistance in early nineteenth-century London workhouses', *Social History*, 31 (2006), 159. Also see D. Green, *Pauper Capital: London and the Poor Law, 1790–1870* (Farnham, 2010), pp. 157–87.

27   A. Clark, 'Wild workhouse girls and the liberal imperial state in mid-nineteenth century Ireland', *Journal of Social History*, 39 (2005), 389–409; V. Crossman, 'The New Ross Workhouse riot of 1887: nationalism, class and the Irish poor laws', *Past and Present*, 179 (2003), 135–58.

28   Hitchcock *et al.*, 'Introduction: chronicling poverty', p. 2.

29   T. Hitchcock, 'A new history from below', *History Workshop Journal*, 57 (2004), 296; Hitchcock, *Down and Out*, p. 239.

30   Jones, '"I cannot keep my place without being deascent"', p. 31.

31   *Oxford English Dictionary*.

32   A. Gestrich, E. Hurren and S. King, 'Introduction', in Gestrich *et al.* (eds.), *Poverty and Sickness in Modern Europe*, p. 2.

33   J. Mason, *Qualitative Researching*, second edition (London, 2002), p. 115.

34   C. Steedman, 'Enforced narratives: stories of another self', in T. Cosslett, C. Lury and P. Summerfield (eds.), *Feminism and Autobiography: Texts, Theories, Methods* (London, 2000), pp. 25–39.

35   Hitchcock, *Down and Out*, p. 132.

36   Green, 'Pauper protests', p. 159.

37   T. Hitchcock and R. Shoemaker, *London Lives: Poverty, Crime and the Making of a Modern City, 1690–1800* (Cambridge, 2015), p. 4.

38   W. Parsons, *Public Policy: An Introduction to the Theory and Practice of Policy Analysis* (Cheltenham, 1995), p. 14.

39   P. Spicker, *Policy Analysis for Practice: Applying Social Policy* (Bristol, 2006), p. 15.

40   For example, see C. Bochel and H. Bochel, *The UK Social Policy Process* (Basingstoke, 2004), pp. 10–11; C. Alcock, G. Daly and E. Griggs (eds.), *Introducing Social Policy*, second edition (London, 2008); H. Bochel, C. Bochel, R. Page and R. Sykes (eds.), *Social Policy: Issues and Developments*, second edition (London, 2008).

41   J. Baldock, N. Manning and S. Vickerstaff, 'Social policy, social welfare, and the welfare state', in J. Baldock, N. Manning and S. Vickerstaff (eds.), *Social Policy*, second edition (Oxford, 2003), p. 27.

42   L. Charlesworth, *Welfare's Forgotten Past: A Socio-Legal History of the Poor Law* (Abingdon, 2010), p. 4.

43   R. Hodgkinson, *The Origins of the National Health Service: The Medical Services of the New Poor Law, 1834–1871* (London, 1967).

44   D. Marshall, *The English Poor in the Eighteenth Century: A Study in Social and Administrative History* (London, 1926), p. 128.

45  J. Innes, *Inferior Politics: Social Problems and Social Policies in Eighteenth-Century Britain* (Oxford, 2009), p. 47.
46  Spicker, *Policy Analysis for Practice*, p. 29.
47  Bochel and Bochel, *The UK Social Policy Process*, p. 10. This is their interpretation of Hogwood and Gunn's tenth identification of the use of the term policy.
48  P. Bridgman and G. Davis, *Australian Policy Handbook* (Sydney, 1998), cited in Spicker, *Policy Analysis for Practice*, p. 30.
49  Spicker, *Policy Analysis for Practice*, p. 30.
50  Bochel and Bochel, *The UK Social Policy Process*, p. 16.
51  Parsons, *Public Policy*, p. xvii; for further discussion of the problems, see M. Hill, *The Public Policy Process*, sixth edition (Abingdon, 2013), pp. 153–60.
52  M. Hill, *The Policy Process in the Modern State*, third edition (Hemel Hempstead, 1997), p. 1.
53  Spicker, *Policy Analysis for Practice*, p. 35.
54  Spicker, *Policy Analysis for Practice*, p. 26.
55  Spicker, *Policy Analysis for Practice*, p. 27.
56  A. Brundage, *The English Poor Laws, 1700–1930* (Basingstoke, 2002), p. 52.
57  D. Marshall, 'The Nottinghamshire reformers and their contribution to the New Poor Law', *Economic History Review*, 13 (1961), 396.
58  S. Webb and B. Webb, *English Poor Law History, Part 1: The Old Poor Law* (1927, London, 1963), p. 182.
59  BPP 1834 (44) Report from His Majesty's Commissioners for Inquiring into the Administration and Practical Operation of the Poor Laws, p. 279, cited in M. Rose, 'The allowance system under the New Poor Law', *Economic History Review*, 19 (1966), 607.
60  Snell, *Annals of the Labouring Poor*, p. 120.
61  J.R. Poynter, *Society and Pauperism: English Ideas on Poor Relief 1795–1834* (London, 1969), p. xxiv.
62  J.L. Hammond and B. Hammond, *The Village Labourer* (1911, London, 1978), pp. 107–11; Webb and Webb, *English Poor Law History, Part 1*, p. 178; M. Neuman, *The Speenhamland County: Poverty and the Poor Laws in Berkshire, 1782–1834* (New York, 1982); M. Neuman, 'A suggestion regarding the origin of the Speenhamland Plan', *English Historical Review*, 84 (1969), 317–92; C.J. Griffin, *Protest, Politics and Work in Rural England, 1700–1850* (Basingstoke, 2014), pp. 29–34.
63  E. Hobsbawm and G. Rudé, *Captain Swing* (London, 1969), p. 48.
64  C.J. Griffin, '"Employing the poor": the experience of unemployment in post-Napoleonic rural England' (unpublished paper), p. 4.
65  Poynter, *Society and Pauperism*, pp. 79–80.

66   C.J. Griffin, *The Rural War: Captain Swing and the Politics of Protest* (Manchester, 2012), p. 35.

67   In Scottish and Irish contexts as well, see R. Mitchison, 'The making of the old Scottish poor law', *Past & Present*, 63 (1974), 58–93; R.A. Cage, *The Scottish Poor Law 1745–1845* (Edinburgh, 1981); P. Gray, *The Making of the Irish Poor Law, 1815–1843* (Manchester, 2009).

68   W. Lubenow, *The Politics of Government Growth: Early Victorian Attitudes Toward State Intervention 1835–1838* (Newton Abbot, 1971), cited in P. Dunkley, 'Whigs and paupers: the reform of the English poor laws, 1830–1834', *Journal of British Studies*, 20 (1981), 125.

69   A. Brundage, 'The landed interest and the New Poor Law: a reappraisal of the revolution in government', *English Historical Review*, 87 (1972), 27–48; A. Brundage, *The Making of the New Poor Law: The Politics of Inquiry, Enactment, and Implementation, 1832–1839* (London, 1978).

70   R. Cowherd, *Political Economists and the English Poor Laws: A Historical Study of the Influence of Classical Economics and the Formation of Social Welfare Policy* (Ohio, 1977).

71   Brundage, *The English Poor Laws*, pp. 59–62. This is explored in more detail in P. Mandler, 'Tories and paupers: Christian political economy and the making of the New Poor Law', *Historical Journal*, 33 (1990), 81–103.

72   Dunkley, 'Whigs and paupers', p. 125. Also see Eastwood's work, which contends that although it was a 'contest between different strategies for reform', Benthamite thought was integral to the creation of the Amendment Act; D. Eastwood, 'Rethinking the debates on the poor law in early nineteenth-century England', *Utilitas*, 6 (1994), 115.

73   Brundage, *The Making of the New Poor Law*, p. 181.

74   Brundage, *The English Poor Laws*, p. 37.

75   For more about the views and actions of nineteenth-century Evangelicals in social policy, see B. Hilton, *The Age of Atonement: The Influence of Evangelicalism on Social and Economic Thought, 1795–1865* (Oxford, 1988), pp. 75–114.

76   Marshall, *The English Poor*, p. 159; A.W. Coats, 'Economic thought and poor law policy in the eighteenth century', *Economic History Review*, 13 (1960), 39–51.

77   Brundage, *The English Poor Laws*, p. 48.

78   R. Wells, 'Poor-law reform in the rural south-east: the impact of the "Sturges Bourne Acts" during the agricultural depression, 1815–1835', *Southern History*, 23 (2001), 56.

79   Spicker, *Policy Analysis for Practice*, pp. 70–2.

80   Spicker, *Policy Analysis for Practice*, p. 22. Spicker cites the work of Rhodes on this matter, a foreword about the complexities and general trends

noticed in the formation of contemporary policy through these routes; R. Rhodes, 'Foreword: Governance and networks', in G. Stoker (ed.), *The New Management of British Local Governance* (Basingstoke, 1999), pp. xii–xxvi.

81   P. Dunkley, 'Paternalism, the magistracy and poor relief in England, 1795–1834', *International Review of Social History*, 24 (1979), 381.

82   Dunkley, 'Paternalism, the magistracy and poor relief', p. 392.

83   J. Innes, 'Legislation and public participation 1760–1830', in D. Lemmings (ed.), *The British and Their Laws in the Eighteenth Century* (Woodbridge, 2005), pp. 102–32.

84   D.P. Dolowitz and D. Marsh, 'Learning from abroad: the role of policy transfer in contemporary policy-making', *Governance: An International Journal of Policy and Administration*, 13 (2000), 5.

85   Dolowitz and Marsh, 'Learning from abroad', p. 15. Also in other areas, such as crime policy, as demonstrated in T. Jones and T. Newburn, *Policy Transfer and Criminal Justice: Exploring US Influence over British Crime Control Policy* (Maidenhead, 2007).

86   Snell, *Annals of the Labouring Poor*, p. 110.

87   Bochel and Bochel, *The UK Social Policy Process*, p. 195.

88   J. Pressman and A. Wildavsky, *Implementation* (Berkeley, 1973).

89   Hill, *The Policy Process*, pp. 128–9.

90   D. Van Meter and C.E. Van Horn, 'The policy implementation process: a conceptual framework', *Administration and Society*, 6 (1975), 445, cited in Hill, *The Policy Process*, p. 129.

91   P.A. Sabatier, 'Top-down and bottom-up approaches to implementation research', in M. Hill (ed.), *The Policy Process: A Reader* (Hemel Hempstead, 1993), p. 267.

92   Hill, *The Policy Process*, p. 130. Hill refers to two of their works: L. Gunn, 'Why is implementation so difficult?', *Management Services in Government*, 33 (1978), 169–76; B.W. Hogwood and L. Gunn, *Policy Analysis for the Real World* (London, 1984).

93   Hill, *The Policy Process*, p. 131. Hill refers to P. Sabatier and D. Mazmanian, 'The conditions of effective implementation: a guide to accomplishing policy objectives', *Policy Analysis*, 5 (1979), 481–501.

94   Hill, *The Policy Process*, pp. 138, 140.

95   Hill, *The Policy Process*, p. 138. This is Hill's reading of Elmore; see R. Elmore 'Backward mapping: implementation research and policy decisions', *Political Science Quarterly*, 94 (1980), 185–228.

96   P. Jones, 'Swing, Speenhamland and rural social relations: the "moral economy" of the English crowd in the nineteenth century', *Social History*, 32 (2007), 278; J.P. Huzel, 'The labourer and the poor law, 1750–1850', in G. Mingay (ed.), *The Agrarian History of England and Wales, Volume 6: 1750–1850* (Cambridge, 1989), p. 770.

97  Webb and Webb, *English Poor Law History, Part 1*, p. 151.

98  Sussex, Hampshire, Suffolk, Berkshire, Wiltshire, Oxfordshire, Buckinghamshire, Devon, Northamptonshire, Essex, Huntingdonshire, Cambridgeshire, Kent and Norfolk; Hobsbawm and Rudé, *Captain Swing*, p. 47.

99  J. Langton, 'The geography of poor relief in rural Oxfordshire 1775–1834', *School of Geography Research Papers, University of Oxford*, 56 (2000), 44.

100 Snell, *Annals of the Labouring Poor*, p. 109.

101 M. Blaug, 'The myth of the Old Poor Law and the making of the New', *Journal of Economic History*, 23 (1963), 176; see also Webb and Webb, *English Poor Law History, Part 1*, p. 127.

102 A. Digby, *The Poor Law in Nineteenth-Century England and Wales* (London, 1982), p. 13. Boyer makes a counter argument in G. Boyer, 'Malthus was right after all: poor relief and the birth rate in south-eastern England', *Journal of Political Economy*, 97 (1989), 93–114.

103 S. Williams, 'Malthus, marriage and poor law allowances revisited: a Bedfordshire case study, 1770–1834', *Agricultural History Review*, 52 (2004), 82.

104 Shave, 'The dependent poor'.

105 T. Hitchcock, 'Paupers and preachers: the SPCK and the parochial workhouse movement', in I. Davison, T. Hitchcock, T. Keirn and R.B. Shoemaker (eds.), *Stilling the Grumbling Hive: The Response to Social and Economic Problems in England, 1689–1750* (London, 1992), p. 145.

106 Webb and Webb, *English Poor Law History, Part 1*, p. 144.

107 T. Hitchcock, '*The English workhouse: a study in institutional poor relief in selected counties, 1696–1750*' (unpublished PhD thesis, University of Oxford, 1985). In chapter 3, pp. 46–91, Hitchcock provides an overview of the different incorporations that were all established in different years: Bristol was under a Local Act from 1696, Exeter from 1698, Norwich from 1711 and London's Incorporation was established on the authority of the 1662 Settlement Act and therefore, according to Hitchcock, could not assert as much power over poor relief matters as those established under Local Acts. Tomkins examined the Oxford workhouse (which obtained a Local Act in 1771), the Shrewsbury workhouse (which did not have a Local Act until 1784) and York (which did not have a Local Act); Tomkins, *The Experience of Urban Poverty*.

108 A. Clark, '*The administration of poor relief in Southampton 1830–1850*' (unpublished BA dissertation, University of Southampton, 1960).

109 A. Digby, *Pauper Palaces* (London, 1978), map on p. 33 shows Local Act Incorporations of Mitford and Launditch, Norwich, Forehoe, Tunstead and Happing, Loddon and Clavering, Buxton and the East and West

Flegg. After the implementation of the Amendment Act, Norwich, Forehoe, Tunstead and Happing and the East Incorporations remained in place; p. 58.

110 F. Driver, *Power and Pauperism: The Workhouse System 1834–1884* (Cambridge, 1993), p. 45. One notable exception was the rural parish of Stoke Damerell (Devon).

111 Monographs include M.A. Crowther, *The Workhouse System 1834–1929* (Athens, GA, 1981); N. Longmate, *The Workhouse: A Social History* (1974, London, 2003); S. Fowler, *Workhouse: The People, the Places, the Life behind Doors* (Kew, 2007); Driver, *Power and Pauperism*.

112 Rose, 'The allowance system'.

113 Rose, 'The allowance system'; N. Edsall, *The Anti-Poor Law Movement, 1834–44* (Manchester, 1971); J. Knott, *Popular Opposition to the 1834 Poor Law* (London, 1986); Driver, *Power and Pauperism*, pp. 112–30; D. Ashforth, 'The urban poor law', in D. Fraser (ed.), *The New Poor Law in the Nineteenth-Century* (London, 1976), pp. 128–46. For a summary of the anti-New Poor Law riots in England, see Griffin, *Politics, Protest and Work*, pp. 34–41.

114 Digby, *Pauper Palaces*, p. 229. Digby's point that the social policies dealing with the unemployment adopted at the parish level continued during the New Poor Law is also expressed in A. Digby, 'The labour market and the continuity of social policy after 1834: the case of the eastern counties', *Economic History Review*, 28 (1975), 69–83.

115 Brundage, *The Making of the New Poor Law*. See also B.K. Song, 'Continuity and change in English rural society: the formation of poor law unions in Oxfordshire', *English Historical Review*, 114 (1999), 314–89; K.D.M. Snell, *Parish and Belonging: Community, Identity and Welfare in England and Wales 1750–1950* (Cambridge, 2006), especially pp. 207–338 where Snell demonstrates that the continuation of outdoor relief was linked to 'common sense, morality, financial prudence and the enduring sense of parochial feeling'; p. 329.

116 K. Williams, *From Pauperism to Poverty* (London, 1981), p. 57.

117 Williams, *From Pauperism to Poverty*, Statistical Appendix, section D 'Relief to men without work', pp. 179–95.

118 P. Harling, 'The power of persuasion: central authority, local bureaucracy and the New Poor Law', *English Historical Review*, 107 (1992), 30–53.

119 Snell, *Parish and Belonging*, pp. 345–50.

120 Harling, 'The power of persuasion', p. 53.

121 P. Dunkley, 'The "Hungry Forties" and the New Poor Law: a case study', *Historical Journal*, 17 (1974), 329–46.

122 Digby, *Pauper Palaces*, p. 32.

123 For instance, see Innes, *Inferior Politics*, p. 99.

124 Examples include Webb and Webb, *English Poor Law History, Part 1*, pp. 149–313; Marshall, *The English Poor*, pp. 87–160; P. Slack, *The English Poor Law, 1531–1782* (1990, Cambridge, 1995); M. Rose, *The English Poor Law 1780–1930* (Newton Abbott, 1971), pp. 25–6; King, *Poverty and Welfare*, pp. 24–6; Brundage, *The English Poor Laws*, pp. 10–15, 21–2, 50–1; D. Fraser, *The Evolution of the British Welfare State*, third edition (Basingstoke, 2003), pp. 37–8; Longmate, *The Workhouse*, pp. 24–33; A. Levene, *The Childhood of the Poor: Welfare in Eighteenth-Century London* (Basingstoke, 2012) pp. 9, 27, 133.

125 S.J. Thompson, 'Population growth and corporations of the poor, 1660–1841', in C. Briggs, P.M. Kitson and S.J. Thompson (eds.), *Population, Welfare and Economic Change in Britain 1290–1834* (Woodbridge, 2014), p. 200.

126 Digby, *Pauper Palaces*.

127 Marshall, *The English Poor*, p. 159.

128 P. Mandler, 'The making of the New Poor Law redivivus', *Past and Present*, 117 (1987), 134.

129 S.G. Checkland and E.O.A. Checkland (eds.), *The Poor Law Report of 1834* (1834, Harmondsworth, 1974), p. 199.

130 Wells, 'Poor-law reform in the rural south-east', pp. 52–115; Neuman, *The Speenhamland County*, pp. 176–83; A. Digby, *The Poor Law in Nineteenth-Century England and Wales* (London, 1982), p. 7.

131 Wells, 'Poor-law reform in the rural south-east', p. 59.

132 22 Geo. III c.83, I and III.

133 59 Geo. III c.12, I and VII.

134 As stipulated in the Amendment Act, 4 & 5 Wm. IV c.76, XXXII, cited in M. Rose, 'The anti-Poor Law movement in the north of England', *Northern History*, 1 (1966), 89.

135 Hill, *The Policy Process*, p. 24.

136 Bochel and Bochel, *The UK Social Policy Process*, p. 178.

137 Bochel and Bochel, *The UK Social Policy Process*, p. 31.

138 Parsons, *Public Policy*, p. 543.

139 Hogwood and Gunn, *Policy Analysis for the Real World*.

140 Parsons, *Public Policy*, p. 602; my emphasis.

141 Bochel and Bochel, *The UK Social Policy Process*, p. 178.

142 Brundage, *The English Poor Laws*, p. 65.

143 King, *Poverty and Welfare in England*, p. 227.

144 D. Roberts, 'How cruel was the Victorian Poor Law?', *Historical Journal*, 6 (1963), 98–9.

145 I. Butler and M. Drakeford, *Scandal, Social Policy and Social Welfare*, revised second edition (Bristol, 2005), p. 1.

146 Reading of Henriques by Bernard Harris, *The Origins of the British Welfare State: Social Welfare in England and Wales, 1800–1945* (Basingstoke, 2004), p. 50; U. Henriques, 'How cruel was the Victorian Poor Law?' *Historical Journal*, 11 (1968), 365–71.
147 J. Stewart and S. King, 'Death in Llantrisant: Henry Williams and the New Poor Law in Wales', *Rural History*, 15 (2004), 69–87.
148 N. McCord, 'The implementation of the 1834 Poor Law Amendment Act on Tyneside', *International Review of Social History*, 14 (1969), 104–7; R. Wells, 'Andover antecedents? Hampshire New Poor-Law scandals, 1834–1842', *Southern History*, 24 (2002), 91–217.
149 Dunkley, 'The "Hungry Forties"'.
150 For instance, Brundage, *The English Poor Laws*, pp. 87–8; P. Wood, *Poverty and the Workhouse in Victorian Britain* (Stroud, 1991), p. 100; D. Roberts, *The Victorian Origins of the Welfare State* (New Haven, 1960), pp. 120, 128.
151 I. Anstruther, *The Scandal of the Andover Workhouse*, second edition (Gloucester, 1984).
152 Wells, 'Andover antecedents?', p. 91.
153 Brundage, *The English Poor Laws*, p. 88.
154 Spicker, *Policy Analysis for Practice*, p. 24.
155 Rose, *The English Poor Law*, p. 95.
156 5 & 6 Vict. c.57, XVI.
157 W.C. Glen, *The Consolidated and Other Orders of the Poor Law Commissioners and of the Poor Law Board* (London, 1855).
158 Hodgkinson, *The Origins of the National Health Service*; Rose, 'The allowance system'.
159 Rose, 'The allowance system', p. 609.
160 Also see A. Digby, *Making a Medical Living: Doctors and Patients in the English Market for Medicine, 1720–1911* (Cambridge, 1994), p. 244.
161 Wells, 'Andover antecedents?', p. 156.
162 Steedman, 'Enforced narratives', pp. 25–39.
163 L. Prior, *Using Documents in Social Research* (London, 2003), p. 26.
164 A. Baker, J. Hamshere and J. Langton, *Geographical Interpretations of Historical Sources* (Newton Abbot, 1970), p. 104.
165 Bochel and Bochel, *The UK Social Policy Process*, p. 6.

# 2

# Gilbert's Act: workhouses for the vulnerable

Who shall separate us
Goodwill towards men[1]

The inscriptions from the two Sussex workhouse seals above clearly illustrate the central purpose of Gilbert's Act – to allow a group of parishes to band together to create a kinder, more humanitarian workhouse compared to their forerunners. The creation and passage of the Act, however, was not a clear-cut exercise and the results were not as far-reaching as Gilbert himself might have wanted. Thomas Gilbert was first elected as a Member of Parliament for Newcastle-under-Lyme in 1763 and subsequently represented Lichfield until his retirement in 1794.[2] Through his work as chief land agent to Lord Gower, Gilbert had developed an immense political, legal, commercial and industrial knowledge that enabled the Gower estate to become one of the most prosperous in England. The source of Gilbert's interest in poor law reform is unclear. It may have stemmed from his role as agent, which had allowed him to see the administration of the poor laws, from his position as a paymaster for a charity of naval officers' widows, or from his brother's work administrating poor relief. Personal anecdotes about poor relief administration are noticeably absent from his pamphlets, suggesting that he had little practical experience, and he was not an active justice of the peace, a role that would have brought him into contact with both the poor and the poor relief administrators.[3] Within a few months of arriving in Westminster, though, he was appointed to a committee that sought to 'resolve' the debt of the Gloucester workhouse, a topic that gave rise to heated debates on the benefits of indoor relief schemes.[4] Perhaps it was from these discussions that he developed his first bill, for the 'Employment and better relief of the poor', which proposed that Commissioners be appointed to draw up relief districts for which local-level committees would be elected and charged with establishing workhouses for the reception of their poor, a prototype of the 1834 Poor Law Amendment Act.[5] The bill was debated in 1765 and passed the House of Commons but failed to gain enough support in the House of Lords by just seven votes.[6]

In the early 1770s basic returns on the workhouses and – a close relative – houses of correction were already being made and were completed in 1771, and Gilbert revised his plans in a publication four years later.[7] Although several of his resolutions were accepted by the Commons for reform, a bill on workhouses was not created.[8] There was then an evolution in Gilbert's ideas about the purpose of the work-house, although it is unclear what the cause was. The relevant House of Commons Committee records were destroyed in the 1834 fire, and even if they had survived they may not have shed much light on the topic.[9] In his 1775 pamphlet Gilbert wrote that workhouses 'should contain as many poor, as can conveniently be managed under the care of one set of officers', making no distinction between the types of poor who should be accommodated.[10] Gilbert then seems to have withdrawn from debating pauper policies for several years – perhaps due either to the opposition to his ideas, as played out in writings by other pamphleteers, or to the discouragement of schemes involving local taxation and borrowing during the American War – once again it is not clear.[11]

Gilbert's next pamphlet, published in 1781, presented a fresh view: that the 'vulnerable' poor – the aged, infirm and young – should be accommodated in the workhouse and the able-bodied given employment and outdoor relief. This policy idea may have developed from the information he had gleaned from the recent Parliamentary Returns on Houses of Industry, or from other pamphlets purporting to have found some scheme or other to reduce relief. Gilbert noted that whilst some workhouses had 'succeeded very well, in Places where they have been duly attended by Gentlemen respectable in their Neighbourhood', others were much 'less beneficial'. Their overall success was 'precarious'.[12] Gilbert thought that such old parish work-houses, including those founded after Knatchbull's Act of 1723, 'were generally inhabited by all Sorts of Persons … Hence arise Confusion, Disorder, and Distresses'.[13] As Marshall noted, to Gilbert old parish workhouses were 'dens of horror'.[14] They were too uncomfortable for those who were in poverty through no fault of their own and places where the young were susceptible to 'Habits of Virtue and Vice' learnt from 'bad characters'. For the sake of both the poor and the rates, Gilbert thought that workhouses should be reformed to house the vulnerable and promote industrious behaviour.[15] These ideas culminated in a new bill and Gilbert's Act of 1782.[16]

It is possible to decipher the aims of Gilbert's reforms from his plan and the legislation itself. The Act enabled parishes to provide a workhouse solely for the accommodation of the vulnerable.[17] Although such residents were, as Gilbert put it, 'not able to maintain themselves by their Labour' outside of the workhouse, they were still to 'be employed in doing as much Work as they can' within the workhouse.[18] This perhaps reflected a commonly held view in poor law reform debates at the time: that the vulnerable could work for their own moral benefit, to produce something in return for their poor relief.[19] The able-bodied were to be found employment and outdoor relief, with indoor relief only provided on a temporary basis.[20] Those who refused work (the 'idle') were to endure 'hard Labour in the Houses of Correction'.[21] The Act also allowed parishes to unite together to provide a workhouse. According to King, Gilbert's Act was the first real breach of the old poor law principle of 'local problem – local treatment', not least because it permitted poor relief administration to transcend parish boundaries.[22] Yet not only were there already many incorporation workhouses that had been established under Local Acts and were owned by sets of parishes in operation by 1782, as introduced in the Introduction and Chapter 1, it was also the case that under Gilbert's Act any single 'Parish, Town, or Township' was permitted to implement Gilbert's Act alone.[23] This led Driver to explicitly acknowledge singular Gilbert's Act *Parishes* as well as Unions.[24]

Workhouses established under Gilbert's Act were to be managed in a different way compared to the older parish workhouses. Gilbert believed that the poor laws had been 'unhappily' executed 'through the misconduct of overseers'.[25] Such officers tended to 'gratify themselves and their Favourites, and neglect the more deserving Objects', a dim view that was shared by other commentators on the old poor laws of the time.[26] In correction, Gilbert's Act proposed two positions that essentially bypassed the overseers' role in issuing relief: a Visitor and several Guardians, roles that were frequently appointed in work-houses established under Local Acts. In Gilbert's Act each Union or Gilbert's Parish was to appoint one Visitor whose role, similar to that of a chairman under the New Poor Law, was to bring strategies to the board table, make policy decisions and give direction to the Guardians, parish vestries and workhouse staff.[27] One Guardian was to be elected for every parish in a union. The Visitor and Guardians met once a month to organise and administer relief. Within these meetings they could establish year-long contracts with third parties 'for the Diet or Cloathing of such poor Persons ... and for the Work and Labour of such poor Persons'.[28] Magistrates were also given further powers concerning the establishment and management of workhouses under Gilbert's Act. They had to authorise the adoption of Gilbert's Act and the building of new workhouses and annually review their progress in the form of returns made to the local Quarter Sessions.[29] Overseers, and assistant overseers, continued to collect the poor rates and issue outdoor relief and employment schemes.[30]

Historians have been remarkably quiet about what Gilbert thought about his legislation; Joanna Innes is a notable exception. Innes uses his legislation as a case study in the trend for eighteenth-century government to pass 'permissive' or 'enabling' legislation, allowing the localities to choose their own policy solutions. 'Gilbert himself', she writes, 'saw the act which bears his name as an unsatisfactory com-promise' on a number of fronts.[31] He wanted the Act to be compul-sory but, as she explains, in his 1765 pamphlet it is clear that, after talking with others, he decided to make only 'gradual advances'. He also wanted those who had enough property to qualify as a Guardian to petition the Quarter Sessions to create a union, which was far more top-down than the legislation that allowed unions to form with the support of two-thirds of all ratepayers from each interested parish. An Act, which was introduced during a period of national fiscal con-straint, therefore had to be implemented by financially wary small ratepayers.[32] Interestingly, just five years after the passage of the Act, Gilbert himself acknowledged the difficulties in creating unions 'in the mode and terms' legislated.[33] As such, Gilbert realised the Act could only be a short-term solution during the crisis in poor relief. Although Innes believes Gilbert's initial ideas – for a compulsory district-based system – served as inspiration for the 1834 Amendment

Act, her emphasis suggests that what was actually passed in 1782 was weak and had little permanence in the pauper policy landscape. This adds further fuel to the dominant perspective on the Act introduced in Chapter 1. Perhaps historians, as well as Gilbert, though, have been too quick to judge the reform before exploring the impact it had on the ground, especially in regions with high levels of poverty such as the south of England.

## Gilbert's Act in the south of England

There are several estimates as to the number of parishes that adopted Gilbert's Act in England and Wales. According to the Select Committee on Poor Relief of 1844, there were apparently 68 Gilbert's Unions and 3 Gilbert's Parishes (a total of 1,000 parishes), although a separate return of Gilbert's Unions (1844) lists 76 adoptions (1,075 parishes).[34] The Webbs, though, acknowledged 67 unions, totalling 924 parishes, whilst ignoring the fact that single parishes could, and did, adopt the Act unilaterally.[35] The overall impact of the Act was, according to the Webbs, 'relatively trifling'.[36] This statement goes a long way in helping us to understand our lack of knowledge about Gilbert's Act. As the Webbs created the sub-discipline of poor law studies, and subsequently influenced many later social histories of social welfare, their interpretations of the Act's importance went unchallenged for many years. Indeed the same figure is repeated by poor law historians Poynter and, more recently, King.[37] Felix Driver states that only 'one thousand parishes containing half a million people' had welfare administered according to the Act, a finding replicated and referenced by Innes, whilst Norman Longmate claims that about '1 in 16' parishes implemented the Act.[38] Further interpretative problems have arisen from these estimates, most notably concerning the geography of adoption. The Webbs argued that unions were 'practically all rural in character; the great majority in south-eastern England, East Anglia and the Midlands, with a few in Westmoreland and Yorkshire; none at all in Wales, in the west or south-west of England, or north of the Tees'.[39] Conversely, Peter Mandler stated that the Act 'was taken up almost exclusively in urban and industrial areas, apart from a unique cluster in East Anglia'.[40] Whilst the geography of the adoption has been interpreted in diverse ways, vast patches of England were, according to these interpretations, untouched by the Act.

The returns completed for the Rural and Town Queries reveal a little more information about Gilbert's Act adoptions within the local contexts prior to the passage of the Amendment Act, but these also suffer from the same shortcomings. To start with, the Rural Queries asked the parishes whether they had a workhouse. This reveals a distinctive pattern of institutional relief provision within the region of focus (see Table 2.1). Approximately half of all parishes in West Sussex and Hampshire provided relief within a workhouse. The proportion of parishes that provided relief in a workhouse declines the further west we travel, with 36 per cent and 30 per cent of the parishes in Wiltshire and Somerset respectively providing a workhouse for their parishioners. Dorset, however, was the lowest with just 13.3 per cent of parishes providing relief in a workhouse. The majority of towns and cities that answered the Town Queries had a workhouse in operation on the eve of the New Poor Law (19 out of 22).[41] This, of course, may be a reflection of the types of parish that answered the survey (i.e. those that ran an institution) rather than a reflection of indoor relief provision in urban localities per se. The three places that returned a questionnaire and had not managed a workhouse included the very small market towns of Cerne Abbas (Dorset) and Dulverton (Somerset) and the larger cloth-producing town of Trowbridge (Wiltshire).

The Town Queries included the question 'Have you a Local Act for the Management for the Poor?' This provoked positive responses about the uptake of Gilbert's Act as well as the creation of Local Acts. Respondents for Newport (Hampshire) explained it was under a Local Act created for the Isle of Wight, and those for Southampton explained that six parishes had been united in a Local Act (13 Geo. III).[42] Bristol's respondent proudly announced that their status as an 'incorporation' had been established since the reign of William and Mary, but explained another Act was granted on 22 May 1822 to strengthen the powers of the union, and a further Act in 1831 altered and amended their original Act. Three urban parishes of Salisbury were united under a Local Act in 1770.[43] Other places, such as Bradford-on-Avon (Wiltshire), stated that the officers were indeed acting under a Local Act (24 Geo. III) that permitted them to appoint an assistant overseer.[44] The question did not specifically address whether the parishes adopted enabling legislation, although three parishes, namely Poole (St James), Alverstoke and Lymington, voluntarily disclosed this information, explicitly stating

**Table 2.1:** Parishes providing relief within a workhouse in 1832, according to the Rural Queries (question 22)[187]

| County | Number of parishes answering in county | Number of parishes | | | Percentage of parishes | | |
|---|---|---|---|---|---|---|---|
| | | Providing relief in a workhouse or poorhouse (not including rent-free cottages) | Without a workhouse or poorhouse | No answer | Providing relief in a workhouse or poorhouse (not including rent-free cottages) | Without a workhouse or poorhouse | No answer |
| Dorset | 15 | 2 | 4 | 9 | 13.3 | 26.7 | 60 |
| Hampshire | 57 | 27 | 20 | 10 | 47.4 | 35.1 | 17.5 |
| Somerset | 20 | 6 | 11 | 3 | 30.0 | 55.0 | 15.0 |
| West Sussex | 32 | 16 | 5 | 11 | 50.0 | 15.6 | 34.4 |
| Wiltshire | 25 | 9 | 12 | 4 | 36.0 | 48.0 | 16.0 |
| Total | 149 | 44 | 47 | 26 | 36.7 | 40.2 | 22.2 |

Source: BPP 1834 (44) XXXI, Report from His Majesty's Commissioners for Inquiring into the Administration and Practical Operation of the Poor Laws. Appendix B.1. Answers to the Rural Queries in Five Parts. Part 2. Question 22.

that they were operating under Gilbert's stipulations. The Rural Queries, unfortunately, did not ask a similar question. When detailing whether they had provided relief within a workhouse (question 22), six parishes responded that they shared a workhouse with one or more parishes. The respondent for Chale explained that the parish was consolidated under the Isle of Wight's Local Act of 1771. According to further archival research, which I will detail below, the rest of the parishes were administering relief through Gilbert's Act, although only one of the respondents for one of the parishes explicitly mentioned the Act itself.[45]

The information contained in the Queries presents only a partial account of the adoption of Gilbert's Act. Indeed, they include some information about which parishes had adopted which acts to establish workhouses, yet not all of the parishes explicitly noted the legislation they had adopted and not all parishes that may have adopted Gilbert's Act completed a return. However, we can obtain a much fuller picture of the scale of Gilbert's Act adoptions by combining this data with the information obtained from the local administrative records, such as vestry minutes, and the correspondence of the Assistant Poor Law Commissioners.[46] Indeed, four parishes that claimed to be sharing a workhouse with other parishes in response to question 22 of the Rural Queries could be confirmed as parishes within Gilbert's Unions using these other sources. Whilst this chapter does not attempt to provide a definitive list of Gilbert's Act adoptions in Wessex and West Sussex, a significant number of adoptions have come to light, illustrating that many parishes of the south of England adopted Gilbert's Act.

Table 2.2 shows the number of identified 'adoptions' of Gilbert's Act in Wessex and West Sussex, 'adoptions' being either Gilbert's Parishes or Gilbert's Unions. Nine adoptions have been found for West Sussex, seventeen in Hampshire, two on the Hampshire–Surrey border, two in Wiltshire and two in Dorset. No adoptions were found in Somerset. The fact that more adoptions have been identified in some counties compared to others is not surprising considering that, as discussed above, the management of a workhouse was a more popular parish strategy to provide relief to the poor in the east of the region compared to the west. The adoptions of Gilbert's Act in Surrey (eight) and Gloucestershire (two) have also been included here due to the availability of this information.

**Table 2.2:** Identified Gilbert's Act Parishes and Unions

| County | Name of Gilbert's Parish or Union | Parish or Union | Initial number of parishes (on first formation) | Eventual number of parishes | Date established |
|---|---|---|---|---|---|
| Dorset | Cranborne | P | 1 | 1 | ? |
| | Poole | P | 1 | 1 | 1813 |
| Gloucestershire | Cheltenham | P | 1 | 1 | 1811 |
| | Westbury-on-Trym | P | 1 | 1 | 1802 |
| Hampshire | Alverstoke | P | 1 | 1 | 1799 |
| | Bishopstoke | P | 1 | 1 | ? |
| | Boldre | P | 1 | 1 | ? |
| | Farnborough | U | 2 | 4 | 1794 |
| | Froyle | P | 1 | 1 | ? |
| | Headley | U | 3 | 3 | 1795 |
| | Hordle | P | 1 | 1 | ? |
| | Hursley | P | 1 | 1 | 1829 |
| | Lymington | P | 1 | 1 | 1809 |
| | Medstead | P | 1 | 1 | ? |
| | Micheldever and East Stratton | U | 2 | 2 | 1826 |
| | Milford [on Sea] | P | 1 | 1 | 1816 |
| | [New] Milton | P | 1 | 1 | ? |
| | Otterbourne | P | 1 | 1 | ? |
| | Selbourne | P | 1 | 1 | ? |
| | South Stoneham | P | 1 | 1 | Approx. 1792 |
| | Winchester | U | 2 | 2 | ? |

| Region | Parish | P to U | 1 | 2 | Year |
|---|---|---|---|---|---|
| Hampshire and Surrey borders | Aldershot and Bentley | | 1 | 2 | Approx. 1818, Aldershot joined in 1824 |
| | Ash | U | 4 | 5 | 1806 |
| Surrey* | Cranleigh | P | 1 | 1 | 1793 |
| | Ewhurst | P | 1 | 1 | 1799 |
| | Farnham | P | 1 | 1 | Approx. 1790 |
| | Frensham | P | 1 | 1 | 1795 |
| | Frimley | P | 1 | 1 | ? |
| | Godalming | P | 1 | 1 | 1786 |
| | Hambledon | U | 4 | 9 | 1786 |
| | Reigate | U | 5 | 5 | 1795 |
| West Sussex | Arundel | P | 1 | 1 | ? |
| | Easebourne | U | 16 in 1799 | 16 | 1792 |
| | East Preston | U | 5 | 19 | 1791 |
| | Petworth | P | 1 | 1 | ? |
| | Sidelsham | U | ? | 5 | ? |
| | Sutton | U | 8 | 17 | 1791 |
| | Thakeham | U | ? | 6 | 1789 |
| | Westhampnett | U | ? | 11 | ? |
| | Yapton | U | ? | 3 | ? |
| Wiltshire | Devizes | U | 2 | 2 | 1796 |
| | Mere | P | 1 | 1 | 1814 |

Source: See Appendix part (a) for the earliest evidence for this table and part (b) for a list of parishes that formed the Gilbert's Act Unions.

* Judith Hill identified only five Gilbert's adoptions in Surrey, namely Ash, Hambledon, Reigate, Cranleigh and Farnham; J. Hill, 'Poverty, unrest and the response in Surrey, 1815–1834' (unpublished PhD thesis, University of Roehampton, 2006), p. 178.

There were significant clusters of Gilbert's Unions and Parishes, as illustrated in Figure 2.1. The largest cluster was in West Sussex, where at least 80 parishes were providing relief under Gilbert's Act at different times over the course of the period as a whole. Most of these can be mainly attributed to the substantial landowner Lord Egremont, who resided at Petworth House. Egremont had particular control over the Gilbert's Parish of Petworth and the Unions of Easebourne and Sutton and engaged in philanthropic activity towards the poor throughout his life.[47] Another notable cluster can be found on the Hampshire and Surrey borders.[48] In addition, a long line of coastal parishes from Milford on Sea to Gosport implemented the Act, as well as a sporadic scattering of inland parishes. Some parishes along this expanse of southern England were growing urban parishes, including South Stoneham, Lymington and Gosport.

The adoption of Gilbert's Act varied temporally as well as spatially. As illustrated in Table 2.2, the exact dates of the adoption of Gilbert's Act by 23 Gilbert's Parishes and Unions have been retrieved as well as the approximate dates for three Gilbert's Parishes and Unions. Although this is a small number, it can confirm some of the observations made about the adoption of the Act. Of these, only three had adopted the legislation before the end of the 1780s. This confirms the views of Sir William Young and Sir Frederick Morton Eden, who, writing 14 and 15 years respectively after the passage of the Act, both noted that 'few' unions had formed.[49] Yet by the end of the 1790s, we find 13 more adoptions of the Act. Thus, the decade in which Young made his observations was the most popular decade for new adoptions of Gilbert's Act in the south of England. As Driver notes, 'there was [also] a slow and steady increase in the number of Gilbert's Unions formed during the early nineteenth century'.[50] This is true within the study region. Between 1800 and 1820 there were eight more adoptions of Gilbert's Act. Wells stated that many areas adopted the Act in the late 1820s.[51] The union formed from the parishes of Micheldever and East Stratton (1826) and the adoption of the Act in Hursley (1829), all in the county of Hampshire, provides evidence for his claim.

## Why was Gilbert's Act adopted?

Finding an answer to why Gilbert's Act was adopted is hindered by a lack of explicit documentary evidence. Indeed, vestry minute books

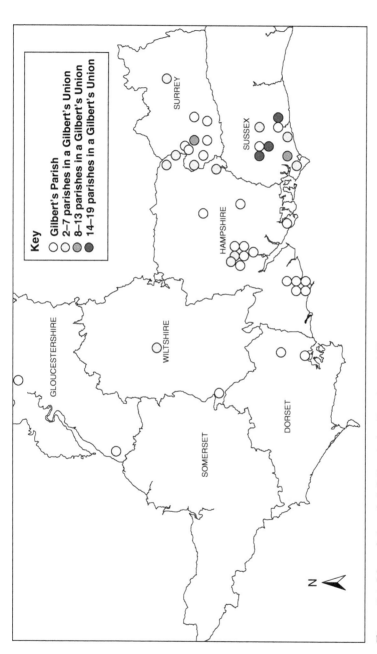

**Figure 2.1** Map of identified Gilbert's Act Parishes and Unions

were used to place memos of the topics of future meetings and the policy adoptions that resulted from these meetings, rather than the stage in between: the 'decision-making' process. Enough evidence exists to make some tentative suggestions, however. Gilbert's Act itself provided two potential advantages for parishes: the establishment of well-maintained accommodation for vulnerable groups of the poor and, through uniting with other parishes, the provision of a joint workhouse and, therefore, the opportunity to economise relief provision. Both of these aspects of Gilbert's Act were attractive. Just outside the region in focus, a Gilbert's Union that never came to fruition in East Sussex has left a proposal for the formation of a union of more than ten parishes.[52] The reasons discussed for uniting were very clearly related to these benefits, as well as Gilbert's ideals. The first point mentioned was that by combining small sums of money from multiple parishes (between £100 and £150 each) a large and good quality institution could be built. All the parishes could also jointly employ a 'respectable' governor, a man who would be capable of superintending a manufactory. Obviously a manufactory was intended to work the inmates as much as possible, as suggested by the mention that it would 'employ aged Persons & young Children'. The document also suggests the intention to house and employ the able-bodied poor as well. For instance, it states that the house should be the location to 'employ the Poor and the Idle'.[53]

There were strong economic reasons for adopting Gilbert's Act, as the above proposal indicates. We can assume that Lord Egremont made his decision to adopt the Act based on a similar rationale. By uniting the parishes he had influence over, it was possible for him to offer a well-maintained workhouse and, over time, hopefully make savings in poor relief expenditure in the process. He would have also avoided creating specific Local Acts, which, as Digby explains, was more expensive compared to adopting enabling legislation.[54] Sir Thomas Baring, who owned East Stratton, had always paid 'great interest in the management of its poor', and consented to a union with Micheldever.[55] This may not explain why the gentry engineered the adoption of Gilbert's Act in singular parishes, such as Egremont's Gilbert's Parish of Petworth. This may have been due to the desire to keep the local governance of his home parish private and solely under his oligarchic control. Nevertheless, Gilbert's Parishes were also established on the assumption that they would also reduce the cost of maintaining the poor. The clergy and parish officers of Boldre (Hampshire), which had adopted Gilbert's Act as a solitary parish in the 1790s, were keen to promote both the beneficial effects to the poor of their new workhouse and the considerable savings made. In a pamphlet describing their adoption of the Act, they claimed they had saved £157 1s 6d in the poor rates in 1796 compared to the previous year.[56]

The economic benefits of adopting the Act could overshadow the benefits of the Act for the vulnerable poor, especially after the end of the Napoleonic Wars. As shall be explored in detail below, committees established under the Act soon after it had passed changed the ways in which they implemented the Act over time. The most important change was to make an agreement with a contractor for the management of the workhouse. The contractor would be paid a fixed price per head per week or a lump sum to maintain the poor. The poor would then work in the workhouse or a separate manufactory, and any profit could be kept by the contractor. Contracts often lasted 6–12 months. There were many potential complications, though: for instance, the contractors could stipulate that they must be paid to maintain a minimum number of people per week, which guaranteed the contractor a minimum income. In addition, the parish(es) would have subsidised the contractor for the cost of supplying the house with wheat when it went above a certain price per bushel at the local markets. Obtaining a profit from this business would also have depended on other rules stipulated within the contracts, such as the percentage of profit that should be expended on the poor as a reward for their labour.[57] The contracting system provided two main economic advantages.[58] Not only did it add an element of competition in the cost of managing the workhouse, but by setting minimum numbers of inmates to be accommodated in the workhouse the Board could offer more of their parishioners indoor relief without incurring an extra fee. Of course, it could also tie the Board into an expensive contract if the cost of provisions lowered during the course of the agreement.

The timing of the adoption of Gilbert's Act also gives us an indication of the rationales behind its adoption. Those which adopted the Act in periods of economic depression in the late eighteenth and early nineteenth centuries may have placed poor rate savings at the forefront of their reasoning to embrace the legislation. As Figure 2.2 illustrates, the most popular decade for adopting Gilbert's Act in the

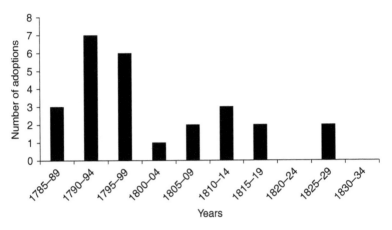

**Figure 2.2** Adoption of Gilbert's Act according to year

south of England was the 1790s. The economic motives for adopting
Gilbert's Act can also be found in minute books. In 1814, the year
after the Act's adoption, the vestrymen of Poole St James praised the
work of the Visitor and Guardians that had made a 'considerable saving' for the parish.[59] In 1821 the vestrymen of Botley (Hampshire)
arranged a meeting to consider adopting Gilbert's Act.[60] Five years
later, after they received a letter from magistrates and gentlemen, they
considered again the merits of adopting the Act. The authors of the
letter attended a vestry meeting held in the South Stoneham poor-
house, and asked the Botley gentlemen to consider joining with other
parishes, including South Stoneham, under Gilbert's Act, a plan 'likely
to prove beneficial to all who are assessed to the Rates'.[61] Although
Botley vestrymen made further enquiries about the proposed plan,
they did not follow it through. The parishes that adopted the Act after
the Napoleonic Wars may have been keen for similar savings. Gilbert's
Act, therefore, could have been adopted in the early nineteenth century due to the concern amongst magistrates and the gentry over the
rising cost of poor relief in their localities. Only through the perusal
of more detailed administrative records in other regions of England,
though, can this statement be made with more certainty.

Economic reasons may have also accounted for the expansion of
Gilbert's Unions and the unofficial agreements to accommodate the
poor of neighbouring parishes within Gilbert's workhouses. Table 2.2

shows that at least five Gilbert's Unions permitted more parishes to join their regime over the course of their lifetime. When examining maps of Gilbert's Unions in the early 1830s throughout the country, the Poor Law Commissioner George Lewis sarcastically noted that the East Preston Union was 'more compact than most of the others'.[62] This observation was not incorrect because some of the other West Sussex Gilbert's Unions contained parishes that were not contiguous with the bulk of the united parishes.[63] Lewis thought it was the 'voluntary' nature of policy adoption that caused 'the extremely irregular combination of the parishes', which had, he claimed, 'very doubtful legality'.[64] The Sutton Union had also expanded. After the original union of the eight parishes, by 1804 several clusters of parishes were added as well as a single parish. In 1807 another five parishes wanted to join the union, which would have made the union 20 parishes large. The Sutton Board soon understood, however, that their long-standing and reliable contractor, Daniel Bryan, would only continue on the terms of the contract if the union remained as it was.[65] As this example demonstrates, such supposedly haphazard formations were the result of strategic negotiation and decision-making.

The unofficial arrangements between Boards of Gilbert's Act Parishes and Unions and the parish officers of other parishes also had an economic rationale. In West Sussex, a parish officer of North Stoke placed one family, the only paupers of the parish, into the nearby Sutton Union workhouse for a small fee.[66] Similar agreements were made in Surrey and Hampshire. The Gilbert's Parish of Cranleigh built a workhouse that could accommodate 150 people, which was far too large for their needs. Subsequently, the parish decided to receive the paupers of neighbouring Wonersh into the workhouse for a negotiated sum.[67] The contractor of the Alverstoke workhouse was permitted to receive paupers from 'other parishes' and in 1834 received six parishioners from nearby Hayling Island, for whom the contractor received three shillings per head per week.[68] There may well have been further instances of this, but when such agreements were made on the hoof, for instance when accommodation was needed urgently, it is likely such negotiations were not recorded within minute books.

Evidence of the reasons why parishes did *not* adopt Gilbert's Act is scarce in the archive. It is clear, however, that some vestrymen simply did not want to change the relief regime they already had in operation. The first time the Botley vestrymen considered adopting Gilbert's Act was on 14 March 1821. The vestry decided to adjourn the meeting until half past six o'clock in the evening at the Dolphin Inn. Only one overseer attended. The lack of interest meant that nothing would be agreed upon.[69] A similar instance occurred at Titchfield in 1806. A committee was appointed in April to examine poor relief, both the rates and expenditure, and in May it was decided they should meet to consider whether Gilbert's Act should be adopted for the parish.[70] The committee made a strong case for the adoption of the legislation – administrators would have 'duties clear and distinct', a Visitor 'would be able to relieve the distress more judiciously and prevent imposition' and accounts could be settled every month rather than every year.[71] The supposed benefits of Gilbert's Act did not provoke an immediate uptake of the Act. The decision was deferred, although an examination of the subsequent vestry minutes suggests that the topic was not reconsidered.[72] The lack of interest in adopting Gilbert's Act could have stemmed from concerns that implementing the Act would be difficult and onerous. The Millbrook (Hampshire) vestrymen, in 1817, made enquiries into a union with at least four nearby parishes under Gilbert's Act, only to decide that the 'association would not [at] present be practable [sic]'.[73]

### Relief provision under Gilbert's Act

The expansion of unions and informal boarding-out agreements may have been influenced by the pursuit of economy, but it also meant that Gilbert's Act impacted on the welfare of many more of the poor than previously thought. As a consequence, it is important to understand how Gilbert's Act was implemented. This section examines the relief provided in the parishes that had adopted Gilbert's Act in Wessex and West Sussex. First, it provides an overview of the populations of Gilbert's Act workhouses. Second, it examines the relief provision to easily identifiable 'vulnerable' groups, children and the aged, infirm and ill. Third, it details the employment and tasks undertaken within the workhouse and, lastly, examines the evidence we have of whether the able-bodied were accommodated in the workhouse, a practice that went against the ethos of Gilbert's initial ideas.

*The workhouse population*

Indoor relief provision was of central importance to the operation of Gilbert's Act. Although the composition of a workhouse population was the result of policy decisions, which I will come to, the overall numbers within a workhouse depended upon socio-economic conditions, which created demand for relief provision, but also, more fundamentally, workhouse infrastructure. Starting with the latter point, bricks and mortar dictated the maximum capacities of institutions. There was a wide range of workhouses in operation under Gilbert's Act and in Wessex and West Sussex there appear to have been two main types. First, those workhouses that were adapted from parish-owned cottages or other buildings purchased by the parish. The extent of these adaptations varied greatly from place to place. The Hursley workhouse was originally a cluster of 'Parish lodging-houses', but alterations, funded by the local large landowner Sir William Heathcote, enabled the accommodation of 49 people with the establishment of two courtyards and the division of the inhabitants into two groups, male and female.[74] The Hordle workhouse was also formed of cottages. As a plan sketched by the Assistant Poor Law Commissioner Colonel Charles Ashe A'Court shows, by 1834 the building still largely resembled cottages and could only accommodate 20 people.[75] The Boldre workhouse was adapted from an old farmhouse, and the parish also rented 50-acres of land. Whilst the land was worked upon by the able-bodied men, according to a parish employment scheme, the farmhouse and garden accommodated 70 inmates.[76] Second, there were purpose-built workhouses constructed after the adoption of the Act, many of which can be found amongst the larger unions. Presumably the combined resources of multiple parishes enabled the building of large workhouses that were intended to serve multiple parishes from the outset. The single Gilbert's Parish of Alverstoke built a workhouse to accommodate 300 individuals. A'Court's detailed sketch shows that it consisted of an early panopticon design, had separate yards, workrooms and infirmaries for men and women and cost £12,000 to erect.[77]

The capacities of workhouses varied from place to place. Yet, their 'maximum' capacities could be stretched at times of need. The Hordle workhouse, which, as noted above, was meant to accommodate 20 people, once housed 23.[78] This did not necessarily cause any disruption to the management of the workhouse. The Alverstoke

Guardians, however, once allowed the population of their workhouse to reach 537 and the 'factory' building was converted into a dormitory.[79] Contractual agreements also influenced the number of people accommodated within a workhouse, as did agreements between parishes. The Aldershot and Bentley parishes united under Gilbert's Act used the workhouse located in, and owned by, the parish of Aldershot that could accommodate 40 individuals. The Bentley parish gave the Aldershot parish £20 per year for its use. This flat rate may have incentivised the parish officers of Bentley to send as many of their relief claimants as possible into the house to reduce their own parish's expenditure on outdoor relief.[80]

Although there are many one-off counts of Gilbert's Act workhouse populations, for instance within Assistant Commissioner's correspondence, there are few workhouses that left population information over time. One exception was the Headley workhouse, which served the parishes of Headley, Kingsley and Bramshot in Hampshire. The main workhouse accommodation was situated opposite a courtyard, sheds and pigsties. Outside this complex was a workhouse garden of approximately two acres. The capacity of the workhouse was 75–80 people and by 1835 it was managed by a contractor at 2s 10d per head per week. The contractor paid for a minimum of 36 inmates in the house, and the parishes agreed that at least 14 should come from Headley, 6 from Kingsley and 16 from Bramshot.[81] Inmate population figures are available for this union from 1795 to 1820, but relate only to those sent from the parish of Headley. According to Figure 2.3, there was a fairly steady number of poor in the workhouse from Headley throughout this period, although there was a notable increase in 1800 and 1801 and another, though smaller, peak in 1805. Evidently, more people were accommodated in the workhouse during years of particular hardship. There is, however, evidence that a contractor was in residence during this period, and they may have secured a 'minimum' number agreement with the parish before 1834. In this context, more people may have been given indoor rather than outdoor relief to save the parish money, and the relationship between need and numbers of inmates is further complicated.[82]

The population of another, albeit larger, Gilbert's Act workhouse also varied year on year. The management of the Easebourne Union left a very comprehensive record of the workhouse population. The workhouse was purpose-built with an imposing entrance and a square

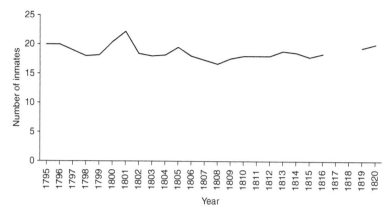

**Figure 2.3** Average annual number of inmates from Headley parish in the Headley Union workhouse, 1795–1820[185]

formation enclosing a courtyard (see Figure 2.4). There were several different rooms for working in, including a 'Booth for Old People to pick Wool in', a brew house, two dining rooms, stabling, two prison cells and a room to place the deceased. The union catered for 16 parishes during the course of this period and was run by a contractor. Treasurer William Bridger kept workhouse population counts from 1797 to 1827, in copies of returns sent to the Michaelmas Quarter Sessions, held in September or October each year.[83] According to Gilbert's Act, the account had to be made a fortnight prior to the Session, for the perusal of local magistrates, and include 'the Number of poor Persons distinguishing their Age and Sex … at the Time of making such Account'.[84] So typically the counts were made during harvests and as such may underestimate the number of people who entered the workhouse throughout the year. But before I examine these, Bridger also returned average figures for these years except in 1799 and 1800, illustrated in Figure 2.5, which we have to assume were created somehow from counts gathered over the 12 months prior to each Michaelmas Quarter Session. According to these counts we see more evidence that Gilbert's Act workhouses housed more people during years of hardship, particularly in 1800–02, 1805–07, 1811–14 and 1816–21. These fluctuations reflect the periods of distress in the south of England identified by Roger Wells.[85] However, from 1822 we see a marked decline in the number of poor living in the workhouse.

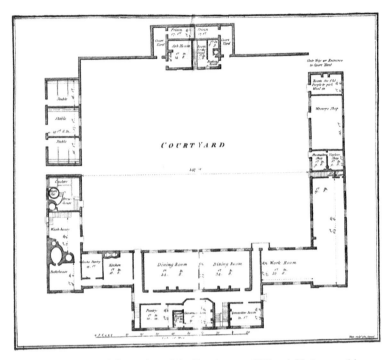

**Figure 2.4** Ground-floor plan of the Easebourne Gilbert's Union workhouse

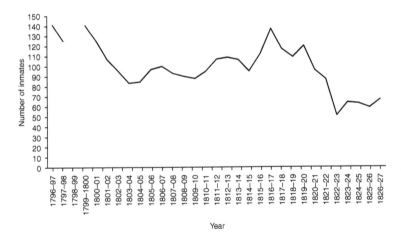

**Figure 2.5** Average annual number of inmates in the Easebourne Union workhouse, 1796–1827

So although socio-economic conditions worsened, fewer individuals were in the workhouse after 1822 compared to before. Examining the sex and ages of the inmates adds further detail to this pattern.

The Easebourne workhouse mainly accommodated male inmates, with an average of 55 per cent of inmates being male and 45 per cent female. The proportion of males being accommodated here was high compared to New Poor Law workhouses, which predominately housed women.[86] This is also high compared to other rural old poor law workhouses, such as Beaminster (Dorset), where two female inmates were accommodated for every one male inmate, as well as metropolitan workhouses, such as St Martin-in-the-Fields, where approximately 68 per cent of admissions were female.[87] Figure 2.6, which shows the numbers of females and males in the workhouse in September or October 1797 to 1827, illustrates a more complex pattern, however. From these numbers we can observe that there were more female than male inmates prior to 1800, and after the four-year gap for which there are no age-specific data, there was always a greater number of male inmates in the workhouse compared to female inmates except in the year 1813. Whilst the number of female inmates in the Easebourne workhouse reached over 50 on just two occasions during this period,

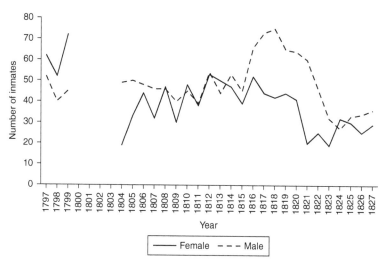

**Figure 2.6** Average annual number of female and male inmates in the Easebourne Union workhouse, 1797–1827

1812 and 1816, the number of male inmates reached over 50 in eight years, 1812, 1814 and 1816–21. The dramatic rise in the number of males entering the workhouse between 1815 and 1821 correlates with the demobilisation of soldiers at the end of the Napoleonic Wars and the post-war economic depression.[88] Notably, the predominance of a male workhouse population may have occurred earlier in other work-houses in rural England, such as in Terling in Essex where males out-numbered females in the 1790s. As Susannah Ottaway explains, this coincided with a move by parish officials to house older parishioners in the workhouse, and men admitted had an average age of 70.1 years.[89] Figure 2.6 conceals the varying proportions of different age groups within the patterns at Easebourne.

The age-specific data provided by the Easebourne accounts can help answer the question of the extent to which Gilbert's Act workhouses were primarily concerned with the accommodation of the vulnera-ble. Children and the elderly were necessarily vulnerable according to Gilbert's definition, whilst those of middle age could be vulner-able through their health, such as illness or a disability, or through their situation, such as being a single parent, pregnant or widowed. Admission and discharge registers would have provided information as to the reasons for admittance, but these had either not been used or had not survived for this region. Nevertheless, the Easebourne treas-urer returned the number of inmates in the workhouse according to three categories: those aged 14 and under, those aged 60 and over and those of middle age, 15–59-year-olds. The majority of inmates in the workhouse between 1797 and 1827 were aged 14 and under (42 per cent). The elderly, those aged 60 and over, comprised 29 per cent of the workhouse population. The middle group, consisting of 15–59-year-olds, accounted for the same proportion.

This age-specific data can be analysed in more detail if it is dis-played according to sex. Figure 2.7 shows that girls under 15 years of age were the largest group of female residents in the workhouse until 1815, when the numbers of young females aged under 15 in the workhouse declined and the numbers of females aged between 15 and 59 increased. The number of females aged between 15 and 59 was exceeded by the females below 15 years of age for a brief period of two years, 1819 and 1820, but then remained the largest group of women within the house until the record stops in 1827. Elderly female residents, those aged 60 years and over, were the smallest female

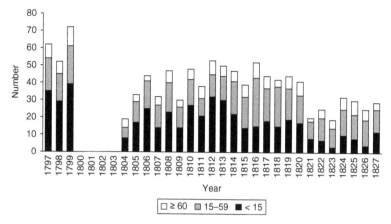

**Figure 2.7** Female inmates in the Easebourne Union workhouse according to age, 1797–1827

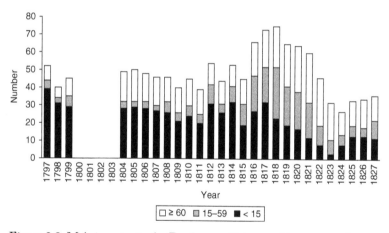

**Figure 2.8** Male inmates in the Easebourne Union workhouse according to age, 1797–1827

population within the workhouse, except for several years in the 1820s when the numbers of those aged between 15 and 59 declined.

Figure 2.8 illustrates that males aged less than 15 years were the largest group of male residents in the workhouse until 1818, when they matched the number of male residents aged 60 years and older. The number of boys in the workhouse then declined until 1824 when the numbers increased again into the mid-1820s. The males aged between 15 and 59 were the smallest group within the workhouse until 1816. This age group only returned to being the smallest age group of males within the workhouse in 1824. Between 12 and 19 elderly men, those aged 60 years and over, were accommodated in the workhouse between 1804 and 1816. Thereafter the numbers had gradually increased to 28 in 1821. From that year their number had generally declined, although from 1819 to 1827 elderly men remained the largest male age group within the workhouse.

There are significant patterns amongst the easily recognisable vulnerable groups, the young and the elderly. After 1804, boys outnumber girls and elderly men consistently outnumber elderly women. Overall, more vulnerable-aged males seem to have been placed in the workhouse than vulnerable-aged females. The numbers of elderly females and males, however, generally appear to have been stable throughout the period, especially compared to the other age groups. This is a different pattern from that found in Terling where the workhouse increasingly accommodated older residents towards the end of the eighteenth century. A quarter of the workhouse population were aged 60 or over up to 1790, rising to 82 per cent by 1798, reducing the space available for residents from other age groups, including the young.[90] In Easebourne, the decrease in young residents appears much later, in the 1820s, which may have been the result of concerted efforts amongst the Easebourne Union officials to apprentice children.

Although many people worked before the age of 15 and after the age of 59, the category of inmates used for the returns of 'between 15 and 59' can be used to examine the number of people of working age within the workhouse.[91] According to Figure 2.7, the number of female inmates from this category was relatively stable, although there were increased numbers in particular years such as 1816. Figure 2.8 shows low numbers of men aged 15–59 years in the workhouse until 1816 when the number dramatically rises into the early 1820s. The demobilisation of soldiers after the Napoleonic Wars, in addition to poor harvests, meant that many individuals who would have normally been able to work during the year could not obtain work. Only the most able-bodied from the community were employed and, therefore, those individuals who had not previously asked for relief now did so. As Wells observed, 1821–23 were detrimental years for the labouring classes and 1825 was a particularly wet year, so for the number of 15–59-year-old males within the house to then decline year on year from 1822 to 1826 suggests another policy was at work.[92] The implementation of a select vestry or appointment of an assistant over-seer in the constituent parishes may have reduced the numbers of people receiving relief, as the next chapter will show. The establish-ment of employment or allotment schemes could have also have had an impact.[93] In addition, the use of alternative accommodation, such as parish cottages, could have also reduced their number. Although Lord Egremont's 'Petworth Emigration Scheme', for parishioners of Petworth and surrounding parishes, was not established until 1832, both families and single people were encouraged to leave the area throughout the 1820s.[94]

There were fluctuating, yet consistently significant, proportions of people in the Easebourne workhouse in the middle-aged category. Yet, without more specific information about each pauper it is impos-sible to identify those within this group who were actually 'vulnera-ble'. Registers not only would have provided such information, but they would have also given us an indication of how long particular individuals stayed within the workhouse at a time. Indeed, it may be the case that able-bodied men also spent time in the workhouse during the cold seasons when the demand for agricultural workers was at its lowest. Some comparative analysis, with other Gilbert's Act workhouse populations or rural old poor law institutions during the same period, would be illuminating. Figures recently recovered on the Beaminster (Dorset) workhouse population between 1810 and 1834, for instance, show a spike in the number of inmates from 1816 that remained high for a decade, with the highest number of overall pop-ulation as well as able-bodied men in the workhouse in 1822.[95] This provides some evidence that even though the Easebourne workhouse was operating under Gilbert's Act, it may have been accommodating individuals left vulnerable by the economic circumstances. The lack of seasonal figures, though, and indeed further research from compara-ble places and time periods, prevents similar comparisons.[96]

*Relief provision to the vulnerable*

Before I examine relief provided within the workhouse, to children, the elderly and infirm, it is important to outline the fact that individ-uals for whom the Gilbert's Act workhouse was designed were not always admitted to the workhouse. Analysis of the Sutton Case Papers, which contain the relief decisions of the union Guardians at committee meetings, reveals that many other forms of relief were offered to the vulnerable poor.[97] Table 2.3 displays the relief provision to easily identifiable vulnerable groups whom Gilbert intended to enter a Gilbert's Act workhouse. From these 33 cases, just five resulted in an order to go into the workhouse and only two stipulated that individuals' children should enter the workhouse. Other forms of relief provided to the claimants were outdoor relief in money and/or in kind (usually flour), employment (although some were told to find their own), and the care of a relative. It seems this Board was economising by using other strategies to relieve the poor, some of which cost the parishes nothing. Outdoor relief was by far the most popular form of relief provision, and reports by Assistant Commissioners illustrate a similar pattern. For instance, in the parish of Headley the A'Court noticed that a total of six poor in receipt of regular outdoor relief were 'all either old or young'.[98] Evidently, in parishes that adopted Gilbert's Act, we cannot assume indoor relief was always given to groups assumed to be vulnerable according to age.

The ill and infirm were another vulnerable group that a Gilbert's Act workhouse was supposed to accommodate. But again, many other forms of relief were provided to them instead of admittance to the workhouse. Table 2.4 details 13 cases of illness and infirmity extracted from the Sutton Case Papers, where the relief decision is mentioned. Here the overwhelming majority of relief was provided in money and in kind. In two of the cases, medical relief was offered within the individuals' own homes. In one instance, it was directed that a friend look after the individual until she herself could make a claim for relief in person at the next Board meeting. This decision appears strategic on the part of the Guardians, not least as this individual may have recovered and therefore be able to earn her own living by the time of the next Board meeting. As the table shows, at times the board refused assistance to unwell individuals in a more straightforward manner: when they had no apparent settlement rights to any parish in the union.

Clearly some of the vulnerable whom Gilbert wanted to be occupants of the workhouse were given alternative forms of assistance. Indeed, only three individuals from the Sutton Case Papers were

**Table 2.3:** Relief provision to typically 'vulnerable' groups of people in the Sutton Union

| Provision / Claimant | Workhouse | | Outdoor relief | | | Employment | | | Relative | | Other | |
|---|---|---|---|---|---|---|---|---|---|---|---|---|
| | Workhouse | Child in workhouse | Money | Kind | Money and kind | To search for work | See employer about wages | Employ found by Guardian | Husband/father to provide money | Relative to maintain person at the moment | Cannot interfere/nothing more provided | Unknown provision |
| Elderly | ✓ (1) | | ✓ (2) | ✓ (1) | ✓ (1) | | ✓ (2) | | | | ✓ (1) | ✓ (3) |
| Young | ✓ (1) | | | | | ✓ (1) | | | | | | |
| Widows, widowers and deserted women | ✓ (1) | ✓ (1) | ✓ (2)* | ✓ (1) | | | | ✓ (2)* | ✓ (1) | | ✓ (1) | ✓ (3) |
| Single women | ✓ (1) | ✓ (1, parent refuses) | ✓ (3) | ✓ (2) | | | | | | ✓ (1) | ✓ (2) | ✓ (1) |

* One of the relief claimants in both of these categories was provided with money and the Guardian was to also find them employment.

**Table 2.4** Cases of illness and infirmity where outcome is noted from the Sutton Case Papers

| Case details | Outcome |
| --- | --- |
| Ill man | No relief on account of settlement |
| Ill daughter (typhus fever) | Medical relief at home |
| Ill man (aged 40) | Outdoor relief in money |
| Ill daughter | Outdoor relief in money |
| Ill husband going into an infirmary | Family receive outdoor relief in money and kind |
| Ill children (aged 2) | Outdoor relief in money, medical relief at home and relief in kind as medical man suggests |
| Ill wife | Outdoor relief in kind |
| Ill man (aged 25) who had been in hospital | Admitted to the workhouse and found work |
| Ill husband (aged 79) | Husband and wife admitted to the workhouse |
| Friend's daughter ill | To be looked after by friend and woman to attend the next meeting |
| Ill man (accident) | Outdoor relief in kind |
| Ill man (accident) (aged 17) | Admitted to the workhouse |
| Widow with two children, one unable to work | Guardian to appoint widow (work for the parish) |

Source: Sutton Union, Sutton Case Papers, 1837–49, WSRO WG3/4.

admitted to the workhouse. Two of these cases were of young men who either had had an accident or were previously in hospital, whilst the other case was of an infirm man aged 79 who was admitted to the workhouse with his wife. These cases, therefore, represent longer-term illnesses for which, in the case of the two men, the individuals needed long-term care, and it made economic sense to provide their board and lodging.

Children
Nearly half of the total population within the Easebourne Gilbert's Union workhouse were children aged 14 years or under. Similarly when the Boldre workhouse was first opened, of the approximately 40 people admitted, between 20 and 30 were children.[99] An important question to ask is how children reached the workhouse in the

first instance. Section 30 of Gilbert's Act states that children who become chargeable to the parish 'from Accident or Misfortune' were to be placed into the workhouse.[100] 'Accident and Misfortune' could be interpreted in several different ways, but overall it advocated the placement of any young vulnerable parishioner in the workhouse. As a consequence, some children would have entered with their parent(s). For instance, the Sutton Case Papers contain details about the claim of Mrs Barttlet, aged between 50 and 60, 'whose husband deserted her' and her family. One of her children (male, aged 7–8 years old) earned 1s a week 'hurding Cows' and the mother gained one gallon of flour a week from the parish. This was not enough, and the Guardian of Burton was told to 'give the Woman & her Boys an Order to be admitted into the Poorhouse'.[101] Sometimes just part of a family entered the workhouse, even when both mother and father were alive and living together but their combined salary was insufficient to maintain them. George Fletcher earned 12s a week, paid no rent and had a wife and five children. The Board of Guardians recommended that the Burton Guardian consider sending 'apart of the Family into the Poorhouse' unless they thought it was more 'proper to allow them some outdoor relief'.[102]

The Guardians of the Sutton Union frequently admitted children into the workhouse without their parents. For instance, in 1837 a widow by the name of Bauchman from Bury, with two teenage girls, requested money and clothes. The Guardians ordered that the youngest child should enter the workhouse and that no outdoor relief should be allowed.[103] According to Gilbert's Act, the Guardians had to secure the permission of the parent(s) of any child under seven years of age whom they wanted to put in the workhouse.[104] In the same year, widow Phoebe Ladler, who had three children including a girl aged six, applied for relief. The Board instructed the Guardian of Bury to 'give her an Order to send the Girl into the Poor House', but Ladler refused.[105] It is evident that the Guardians had to comply and accept her refusal. Even when both parents and their child(ren) entered the house, there was still a risk that the families would live, for the majority of the time, apart. In the Alverstoke workhouse, children slept in a room under the care of two or three women. These women were selected 'for the children to mix with instead of their own mothers at all times'. The children could have been a 'disturbance to her [the mothers'] work and the workers in the same place'.[106]

Gilbert, in his plan, argued that the 'future Diminution of the Poor's Rates' depended on developing children's morals, 'Habits of Virtue and Vice' and industriousness.[107] Guardians concurred and directed their attention to 'the reformation in the morals of the young in particular'.[108] There is little surprise then that when children entered the workhouse their lives were, as with their elders', inextricably linked to employment and education. For instance, in 1837 the Poor Law Commission told the East Preston Gilbert's Union Board to make clear classifications and separation of their paupers in the house to bring it into line with the organisation within New Poor Law Union workhouses. The response of the Guardians was to highlight the divisions they had long implemented, including a separate area where just 'children male and female are daily employed in Sack making under the personal superintendence of the Governor'.[109] Gilbert's Act itself does not detail how children should be employed in the workhouse, so Boards often made their own policies. For instance, the Alverstoke Board made the children knit stockings, make mops and pick oakum.[110] Children in South Stoneham knitted stockings in 1822. Two years later they received the decision of group of local magistrates, which stated that 'all Labourers [should] be found work even Boys at the Age of 10 Years and Girls at the Age of 12 Years are recommended to be kept in employment which direction the Guardian has acted up to, by receiving such Boys and Girls (for whom employment cannot otherwise be found) into the House'.[111] It is clear that the magistrates, as well as the Visitor and Guardians, were keen to get the children into employment. And the lack of it outside the workhouse could be a reason for them to enter it.

Whilst such employments may have fostered habits of industry amongst the children, the Guardians treated their labour as a source of income. When the Alverstoke Guardians assessed the employment of the children in 1806 they noted that oakum-picking in particular was making a 'profit'.[112] Under Gilbert's Act it was legal to place, 'let' or 'farm' children out to work in manufactories away from the workhouse. Although this practice was undertaken in some general parish workhouses, such as Wimborne Minster (Dorset), which sent children to a watch chain manufactory, it was not a popular strategy amongst Gilbert's adoptees.[113] Instead contracts were often forged with those who could superintend the children within the workhouse. In 1804 the Alverstoke Guardians decided to enter into an agreement with Mr John White of Gosport, who had 'proposed to employ a certain number of the Children in the House to work for him in the Manufactory and to allow a certain Sum per Week for the labour of each Child'. This policy idea was renewed nine years later.[114]

Although the education of children was not stipulated in Gilbert's Act, some boards provided schooling. Education within the workhouse appears to have been organised informally, especially compared to employment. Indeed, it was probably due to the amount of work the children were undertaking that their education in some institutions was restricted to the Sabbath Day. The Guardians of the Sutton Union started educating the children in the house by paying a lady named Mary Bacon 'One Shilling for Sunday, and a Sundays Dinner' for her efforts in 'teaching all the Children of the House, to read, and to say their prayers every Sunday throughout the year'.[115] A similar practice was in place at the Easebourne Union, where a Sunday School was established in 1800, organised and part-funded by a local vicar.[116] There were 'two weekly schools' in the Otterbourne and Boyatt Union.[117] Many committees decided to pay the teacher a fixed sum per week, such as the Schoolmistress at Lymington.[118] Often, though, Guardians had secured the help of volunteers to teach the children. The clerk to the Reverend Morgan Reynolds, for instance, provided the children catechetical instruction free of charge.[119] A large proportion of their education was undoubtedly religious. In one year the Sutton Guardians bought 24 prayerbooks and 24 'testaments' alongside 48 spelling books and 72 'spelling cards'.[120]

Some Boards decided to send the children to schools within the immediate vicinity of the workhouse. There was apparently no space for a schoolroom in the Hursley workhouse, so the children went to the village school at the cost of 3s each per week, paid by the parish. The children returned to the workhouse for meals and lodgings.[121] In Alverstoke, a school was established according to the 'National system', the monitorial system of education used in Church of England National Schools. Here children were taught reading and writing and practised sewing and serving, which the Guardians believed would be useful experience for their future employment.[122] This highly structured educational programme differs greatly from the occasional, mainly religious, education provided in the places mentioned above. Also, the amount of education provided to children varied over time as well as from place to place. For instance, in 1796 the children of

Boldre workhouse attended a Sunday School, but by 1834 A'Court was staggered to find that '[t]here is in fact no school whatever'.[123]

Children, unlike their elderly and infirm fellow inmates, were expected to leave the workhouse. Gilbert's Act stipulates that the Visitor and Guardians should only be kept 'until such Child or Children shall be of sufficient Age to be put into Service, or bound Apprentice to Husbandry, or some Trade or occupation'.[124] This policy was adhered to. The Visitor and Guardians of the Sutton Union thought that children should be removed from the workhouse as soon as possible, and in 1792 they agreed that they should be employed in agricultural service as soon as they were capable.[125] In 1821 the Alverstoke Board reminded themselves that they needed to apprentice the boys and send the girls into service.[126] Some older children were even ordered into the house until work could be found for them. In 1839, 16-year-old Ellen from Duncton had 'no means of living' and was residing with her mother since her father had died. The Guardians recommended that she enter the workhouse so that the matron, Mrs Bryan, could 'do what she can for her & endeavour to get her a place [in service]'.[127]

Aged, ill and infirm
As shown in Tables 2.3 and 2.4, the elderly, ill and infirm in the Sutton Union were not automatically admitted to the workhouse. Only 1 of the 11 relief claimants aged 60 years and older resulted in admission to the workhouse and only a few of those suffering long-term ailments were accommodated. The workhouse could be used to intimidate vulnerable individuals and sometimes admission depended on them adhering to certain terms, as these cases testify. An 81-year-old man from Barlavington named Moody claimed relief for himself, his second wife and their two daughters. He received poor relief of 3s per week with three gallons of flour and was managing to pay his own house rent. On application for further relief, the Guardians stated they 'are [of the] Opinion that no furt[her] Relief be allowed him, but their be he told unless he sets rid of his two ... [daughters] his Relief will be taken off, and will be sent into the House'.[128] At Lymington the elderly were told to 'give up the Pension' they received and enter into the workhouse.[129] In one such case the vestry threatened to discharge an elderly man named John Alyes 'unless he Assigns his Pension to this Parish'.[130]

There is little information about relief provision for the elderly, ill and infirm once *within* the workhouse, perhaps because other groups that had more chance to make a living, such as the young and able-bodied, absorbed the Guardians' time and concern. Nevertheless, we can develop a sense of how these groups were treated on an every-day basis through an examination of the spaces provided for the elderly, ill and infirm. Many workhouses had a separate room for the elderly, and separate rooms for the ill and infirm. The Bishopstoke and Lymington workhouses, for instance, had sick wards, and the latter also had two special rooms for lying-in women and two for the 'sick and refractory'.[131] This was not always the case, though. A'Court, when visiting the Hursley workhouse, was shocked by the disorganisation caused by the lack of division between 'the old – the idle and profligate'. Yet, from A'Court's sketch of Hursley, it is clear it had a 'cage' for the placement of disorderly inmates.[132] The provision of separate spaces for the inmates, therefore, varied from place to place and was often restricted by architecture and cost. When designing their workhouse, the Alverstoke Guardians planned to build a separate ward for the aged and infirm as well as a detached hospital ward.[133] Later they claimed their 'aged and infirm [were] comfortably lodged'.[134] A'Court's sketch of this workhouse showed separate infirmaries for female and male residents at opposite sides of the workhouse and a separate 'infirm room' located at the centre of the workhouse.[135] The Guardians were worried that the purpose of these rooms would change after a contractor took over the maintenance of the workhouse. As a consequence, article 17 of the contract clearly stated that the contractor must 'reserve as many other rooms as the Visitor and Guardians may consider necessary for the comfort of the aged and infirm'.[136]

Special treatment in the Alverstoke workhouse extended beyond considerations of bricks and mortar. During the harsh winter of 1808, described in the minute book as 'severe and long', the Alverstoke Guardians decided 'that the old people were obliged to have fires in their rooms'. This had reportedly 'caused a greater expenditure of Coals than usual' because the extra fuel was purchased in a small amount during the cold season rather than in bulk prior to the peak season.[137] Older people were provided with warmth, regardless of the expense to the parish, plus extra food. Special food provision to the vulnerable was especially advocated by Gilbert, though. In

a pamphlet published prior to the passage of the law, he explained
that it was very unjust that the able-bodied would 'generally con-
sume the best provisions'.[138] The supply of tea to all men and women
in the house was common, but the elderly and infirm were allowed
extra tea and also some sugar.[139] Not surprisingly, these provisions
were constantly being monitored due to their cost. In Alverstoke,
the special workhouse committee examined the possibility of reducing these extras, but decided that 'the indulgence of Tea & Sugar to
all such infirm & old Persons' would remain at the discretion of the
Visitor and Guardian. In addition, the Medical Officer of the workhouse was to inform the committee of 'such Cases as in his Opinion
may require the indulgence medicinally'.[140] Boulton and Schwarz
detail similar special treatment of elderly inmates of Westminster's
St Martin-in-the-Fields workhouse during the eighteenth and early
nineteenth centuries, suggesting that it was common to see elderly
residents as worthy of extra care, and expense, compared to their
fellow inmates.[141]

There is little indication that the elderly, ill and infirm undertook
a strict employment regime within the Gilbert's workhouse. Some
Boards, such as the Alverstoke Visitor and Guardians, recognised
that many of the inmates were 'past labour'.[142] Nevertheless, in workhouses such as Easebourne there were separate workrooms for the
'Old People to pick Wool in'. When these vulnerable groups did
undertake work, however, there is evidence to suggest that men and
women usually had different tasks. Elderly and infirm female inmates
undertook general domestic tasks. In Boldre their main tasks were
'cooking, mending, and washing'.[143] At Lymington A'Court noted
that the old and infirm and young females were also engaged in
household work and mending clothing.[144] Male elderly and infirm
were designated specific tasks. The governors at Easebourne, and
subsequently the workhouse contractors, instructed the 'old men' to
make brooms and use spun yarn to create mops, and at Boldre they
tended the workhouse garden.[145] In Lymington A'Court noted how
they 'feed the pigs – look after the parish Cow and Horse – occasionally assist in the Garden & take out daily a given quantity of vegetables into the Town for sale on the Parish account'.[146] These jobs were
not as strenuous as farm labouring. It appears that the Guardians,
master and matron had considered the abilities of inmates before
allocating them work.

*Employing the 'vulnerable'*

Gilbert strongly believed in promoting 'industry' amongst paupers and thought this could be achieved by 'compelling every poor Person to labour who is able to work; to take proper Care of those who are not'.[147] Gilbert's aim has, at times, been misinterpreted. George Nicholls, Poor Law Commissioner until 1847, wrote in his *History of the English Poor Law* that the Gilbert's workhouse was 'strictly ... a poorhouse ... to designate it a workhouse seems a misnomer'.[148] He was comparing Gilbert's workhouses with what came later, the New Poor Law Union workhouses where work was used to deter individuals from entering the institution (see Chapter 5). However, simply because Gilbert's workhouses were supposed to accommodate 'none but the Aged, Infirm, and Impotent, who are not able to maintain themselves by their Labour', this did not mean that some form of work was not undertaken. As Gilbert stressed in his plan, the inmates were 'to be *employed in doing as much Work as they can*'.[149] Gilbert Act adoptees explicitly embraced this principle. The Board at Mere (Wiltshire), for instance, noted that they were 'employing the Poor in the house *capable* of Work'.[150] Similarly, at Boldre the 'inhabitants are all employed in that business they are most fit for'.[151]

Many inmates were engaged in work that contributed to the economy of the workhouse. As the analysis of tasks undertaken by the elderly suggests, this work was gender-specific. Female inmates were predominantly engaged in domestic tasks whilst men were predominantly working outside. At Lymington, women would sit and work in the kitchen whilst the men were outside, apart from when they were allowed in a separate 'sitting room' where they were engaged in less strenuous tasks.[152] The gendered division of labour is reflected in the spaces of workhouses, especially those that had been adapted or built after the adoption of Gilbert's Act. For instance, in the Hursley workhouse the women's day room was situated next to the kitchen. Opposite these rooms were the bake- and wash-houses. The Alverstoke workhouse placed the women's yard and rooms on the matron's side of the building, which included a kitchen, scullery and wash-house. The men's yard and rooms were situated on the master's side of the building, where there was space for a manufactory and workshop. As this plan suggests, some Gilbert's Boards employed the inmates within manufactories alongside domestic tasks. These appear to have been predominantly clothing manufactories. In the Easebourne Union, women prepared and span 'coarse wool for collar clothes and the refuse for mops, flax for coarse linen fabrick for sheets and shirting' as well as blankets.[153] In Alverstoke, many paupers were placed 'under the Instruction of Women, who learn'd them to knit Stockings ... and several employd in a Manufactory' producing 'Blankets, Coverlids, flannel, Spinning Mop yarn &c.'. Many of these items were actually sold to the house itself, with the rest taken to local markets.[154] At Boldre inmates were employed in spinning, and the master had even developed a 'spinning-wheel tune' that, when sung by the inmates, possessed a rhythm 'well adapted to the motion of the wheel'.[155]

Unsurprisingly, employing the poor in this way was not always a profitable venture. To start with, the establishment of Board-managed manufactories was slow and the resulting financial advantages took a long time to emerge. As the Alverstoke Guardians commented over five years into their adoption of Gilbert's Act: 'the Manufactory has ... not come up to what the Committee originally expected, [but] it is nevertheless in a progressive state of improvement'.[156] A similar situation was felt by the Easebourne Guardians. When summing up the state of employment for the sessions in 1797, William Bridger wrote:

> [t]he remarks in former years' accounts to the sessions, respecting the mode of Employing the Paupers, still continue to apply. The profits of the manufacture are barely, if at all, sufficient to answer the Expences of a superintendent &c; without computing the Interest of the Capital; wear & Tear of Tackle &c.[157]

In the following year this had continued and after the goods were sold, the takings at market were similar to the cost of the raw materials. The point of making the vulnerable work as much as they could was to provide some income for their maintenance. But by 1798 it was not just uneconomical modes of work being blamed, but 'their unskilfullness or want of attention has, tis conceived, wasted more [money] than their Earnings'.[158]

Obtaining profits by working the vulnerable was difficult, and many larger institutions resorted to obtaining a workhouse contractor. The Easebourne Union established agreements with third parties to maintain the poor, as permitted under Section 2 of Gilbert's Act. These contracts allowed the 'governor' to become (or be replaced by) a contractor.[159] The Sutton Union was the first of Egremont's unions to contract out their workhouse in 1793, just two years after the formation of the union. The impact on the employment of those in the workhouse was immediate. The chosen contractor was Mr Northwood, who had worked in Hereford for five years and had been 'brought up' in sacking manufactory.[160] As a result, by the next August a sacking manufactory was considered for the employment of the poor and not long after it was established and sacks were sold.[161] The Easebourne Union was soon to follow. After 'more than 4 years Trial, under three Several Governors', they decided to find a contractor. On 1 May 1798, Easebourne contracted out their poor at 2s and 8d per head per week. This rate varied from year to year. From therein, the workhouse inmates worked in a coarse woollen manufactory until at least 1827. Wool and hemp were transported to the house, and the poor made blankets and sheets as well as horse cloths and hempen sacks.[162]

Not all inmates experienced dramatic employment changes when a contractor took charge. When the Alverstoke Board decided to contract for the maintenance of their poor, it is clear that no new form of employment was found in the manufactory. Domestic employment also had to continue as before. The Alverstoke Guardians directed, under Article 4, that the contractor had to 'employ as many paupers or other persons as may be necessary for cooking and serving up the victuals ... for washing, cleansing and keeping an order the Poor House'.[163] In addition, the workhouse gardens were also consistently worked.[164] Farnham had *already* established a blanket manufactory when they needed a contractor in 1794. It was expected that this enterprise would continue into the future, not least as it was detailed upon the advertisement alongside the number of poor the contractor had to maintain and the size of the workhouse garden.[165]

It was a common practice that the poor were provided with a nominal sum of money for their efforts. These payments took various forms and became known as an 'allowance', a 'gratuity' and, in Easebourne, 'encouragement money'. Workhouses at Alton (Hampshire), Winton (Winchester) and the Gilbert's Parish of Farnham also gave out 'gratuities'.[166] This allowance came out of the profits of all types of labour – both within and out of the workhouse – including women's 'household' tasks such as 'needle work in making Paupers Clothes &c' and 'Knitting worsted and yarn for stockings'. At Easebourne it was set at a rate of two pence from every shilling.[167] Such payments were subject to change throughout the lifetime of the institution. The committee appointed by the Alverstoke Guardians to examine the management of the workhouse in 1822 believed that the '[g]ratuities and rewards given to the paupers and others in the poor house ... have very considerably increased during the last three years'. Alongside other suggestions to reduce the cost of administering relief, the committee advised the Board that these sums 'ought to be discontinued'.[168] For some Gilbert's Unions and Parishes, encouraging the poor to adopt certain modes of behaviour, to be moral and industrious, conflicted with cost.

### A space solely for the vulnerable?

The stipulations in Gilbert's Act should have created what Digby called an 'asylum for the impotent poor'.[169] It was important to Gilbert that the able-bodied were provided relief outside of the workhouse because the 'Clamorous and Disorderly always make confusion; they disturb the Peace and Quiet of the Old and Infirm'.[170] Allowing the able-bodied into the workhouse would have been a violation of the law and go against the spirit of the Act. As already illustrated, in some Gilbert's Parishes and Unions there were a significant number of people of 'working age' in the workhouse. Whether these were unwell or infirm inmates or whether they were capable of labouring is rarely clear. From workhouse population figures organised according to month, however, it may be possible to gain some insight into the stability of the population over the year. The proposition is, if Gilbert's Act workhouses contained just the elderly, infirm and children, then we would expect a stable population within the house over the entire year. If there were able-bodied inmates within the workhouse, we might expect them to leave during the time of year when employment was plentiful – May to September – and re-enter the workhouse when it was not.[171] Two sources lend themselves to this analysis: the numbers of parishioners from the Headley parish entering the Headley Gilbert's Act workhouse and the returns kept by the treasurer of the Easebourne workhouse. According to the Headley archive, there was actually little significant difference in the number of inmates belonging to the Headley workhouse over the course of the year, between 18.22 people and 19.22 each month of the year between 1795 and 1820. This could be a reflection of the capacity of the workhouse and the informal and formal agreements

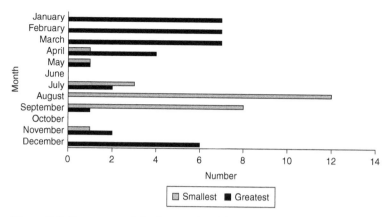

**Figure 2.9** Frequency of the 'greatest' and 'smallest' population months in the Easebourne Union workhouse, 1797–1827[186]

between the parishes and the contractors. Nevertheless, the highest number within the workhouse is in January and the lowest is in September. The Easebourne workhouse population returns show a similar pattern (Figure 2.9), with the highest number of inmates in the house from November to April and the lowest from July through to September.

There is a notable link between the time of the year and the population of the workhouse. Yet this information may obscure as much as it reveals. For instance, if the workhouse population declines when work is plentiful, then those not usually 'able to maintain themselves by their Labour', as Gilbert puts it, may have been leaving the workhouse rather than the able-bodied per se.[172] The seasonality of workhouse numbers may have reflected two other issues. First, it costs more to live in the winter, increasing the pressure on elderly people, in particular, to seek poor relief. Second, research on the number of sick episodes and sick days shows that sickness rates increase from October to December and peak in January to March.[173] As such, the increasing population in the winter could be caused by the growing needs of vulnerable groups and sick parishioners, rather than simply an increased number of able-bodied poor. In addition, the able-bodied may have resided in the house whilst working in the workhouse manufactory, workshops and garden, a phenomenon that neither of these sources can expose. They also may have stayed in the workhouse for a relatively short period of time. The Guardians and claimants, in this scenario, were therefore using the workhouse as a temporary measure.

Qualitative sources provide a more nuanced picture of the adherence and non-adherence to Gilbert's ideals. In the Sutton Case Papers we see that William Peachey of Slindon, aged 22, explained that he had been out of work for five weeks and did not save any money during the harvest. The Guardians suggested that 'Mr Cooper would continue to employ him'.[174] In some instances, obtaining assistance was not a smooth process. On many occasions it appears that the Visitor of the Sutton Union had to remind the Guardians of their responsibility to provide relief or employment for their able-bodied parishioners. For example, Thomas Rout claimed that his family, a wife and seven children, were 'totally destitute' because not only was he unable to obtain employment for his children, his usual income from working in the woods (up to 12s per week) would not commence again until the middle of winter. He had approached the Guardian and the farmers of Slindon on a previous date, but he claimed 'they have no work'. Reverend Thomas Sockett, the Visitor, was very forthright in making the parish recognise their responsibility for providing relief. Writing to Mr William Lane, the Guardian of Slindon, he states it is the role of 'a guardian to take care that the man & his family do not suffer from a want of necessary food – I need not remind you that you alone are responsible to the law in this and all similar cases'. There was, Sockett thought, no need to send Rout to the Board when the parish should be able to order relief to him on their own accord. Sockett was angry with the manner in which Slindon parish was allocating 'employment and support' to the paupers.[175] Lane responded to Sockett, with a list of excuses for their ill-treatment of Rout, but partially redeemed himself by informing him that he was now out on the roads and when he was 'not employed we have made it up in provisions'.[176] The Visitor even had to arrange for groups of paupers to be treated according to the law. Abraham Carver and Thomas Harwood from Sutton, both married with children to support, turned up at the Board together in July 1840. Both work and wages were drying up. With the Guardian of Sutton parish not being present, the Visitor Sockett wrote to him stating that these labourers 'must be found employ at fair wages, or in some way provided with food for their families – The Guardian is personally responsible to do this'.[177] A year before this, Sockett's patience, reminding the Guardians of their responsibilities towards able-bodied men, was clearly already waning. At the end of a note in the summer of 1839 that started with a complaint about how '[t]his man Lucas is constantly coming to me from Bury', he penned 'I am sick of these Union Parishes'.[178]

It is clear that the Sutton Union and other Gilbert's Act adoptees also put able-bodied men in Gilbert's Act workhouses. For instance, in March 1840 three labourers in their twenties entered the Board room together from the parish of Bury, stating they had hardly worked during the winter, but usually had enough to do during the hay and harvest season. The solution was for the parish overseers 'to find these some Employment by Task work – or to given them an Order to go in into the House an[d] to give them some children Relief … to keep them from starvg'.[179] Whether this was a temporary measure or not is difficult to decipher. Nevertheless, evidence from other Gilbert's Unions and Parishes suggests that the placement of the able-bodied within the workhouse was a long-held policy. The Easebourne workhouse had a woollen manufactory, but it was common practice that '[m]en and boys, who are able, are let to work at Husbandry to the neighbouring Farmers'. According to the treasurer, placing the able out to work in such a manner was the 'only employment that Yields any Profit to the undertaking'.[180] This strategy did not change when a contractor was appointed. As Bridger states, 'the strongest Paupers he still continues to hire out for Husbandry work', and their earnings from 1 May 1798 to Lady Day 1799 were £19 12s 6d.[181] A'Court noted that other parishes were following a similar scheme, such as the Hursley and Bishopstoke Boards, which allowed their able-bodied men to work for 'private' individuals and the wages thus earned were put into the parish purse.[182] Lymington Board followed a slightly different scheme. Here men who worked outside the workhouse received their own wages and paid a small amount towards their board and lodgings each week.[183]

### Conclusion

In Chapter 1 I argue that a part of the policy process under the old poor laws was the adoption and implementation of enabling Acts, and how examining them is key to our understanding of how the old poor law operated and affected relief recipients' lives. Most accounts of Gilbert's Act to date have been negative or slight, and were often skewed by the Royal Commission's own lack of interest in the Acts prior to the passage of the Amendment Act. I show here that Gilbert's Act, proposed with clear intentions, appealed to many parish vestries and local landowners. The adoption of Gilbert's Act was widespread across the south, and whilst both Gilbert's Parishes and Unions were founded through negotiation, the sizes and styles of their workhouses varied from planned institutions to adapted cottages with gardens and small-scale farms. Adopting the Act permitted the parishes to pay special attention to those who were in poverty through no fault of their own, thereby safeguarding their entitlement to relief, whilst permitting economising practices such as employing the poor and contracting out. These two very different, although not incompatible, benefits of adopting Gilbert's Act had filtered into the rationales of adoptees. Yet, in practice, perhaps one rationale became more important than the other. Indeed, there were many adoptees in the 1790s and several adoptions of the Act into the 1820s, suggesting that economy rather than the care of the vulnerable was a prime motivation for adopting Gilbert's Act. This suggests that enabling legislation could be adopted, and therefore used, in a manner akin to a strategy, to enable a parish to change their policies during a time of added pressure on poor relief provision.

Ultimately, did Gilbert's Parishes and Unions care for the vulnerable – as was Thomas Gilbert's intention – or did they further harm their vulnerable charges? The answer is not clear-cut due to the multiple ways in which the Act was implemented on the ground. Not only did the application of Gilbert's Act vary from place to place, but it also varied over time. Whilst one place adopted one strategy of caring for the vulnerable, it did not mean all of the areas adopted this strategy. Educating children, for instance, was not stipulated in Gilbert's Act but even within one region provision varied from ad hoc and limited to organised, and therefore more advantageous to the inmates. The comforts provided to the elderly and infirm in one place were reduced in another. Whilst Headley might not have admitted the able-bodied into the Gilbert's Act workhouse, many other Gilbert's Parish and Union workhouses did. Enabling legislation could, therefore, also be adapted to suit the challenges faced in particular local contexts.

The placing of some of the able-bodied into a Gilbert's Act workhouse may have been the most economical way of maintaining the poor, but it violated the rules of Gilbert's Act and went against the founding ethos of the legislation. These findings reflect those that resulted from the research undertaken by the Poor Law Commission on the operations of Gilbert's workhouses in other parts of the country in the 1830s. The Commission reported that in Wallingford (Oxfordshire) the Board let in both the vulnerable and the able-bodied, whom, to the Commission's surprise, they had not even endeavoured to separate. In addition, the Thurgarton Gilbert's workhouse (Nottinghamshire) had turned into a 'deterrent' institution during the last ten years of the old poor laws by enforcing a 'workhouse test'. To the Webbs this meant that the Gilbert's workhouse was really 'nothing better than a General Mixed Workhouse of the old type'.[184] Although population rates seem comparable to non-Gilbert's Act workhouses, estimating how widespread this practice was amongst Gilbert's Parishes and Unions is very difficult. The qualitative research here shows that it was not always the case that the Guardians offered able-bodied working age people entry to the workhouse, let alone those unwell and ill individuals who perhaps should have gained easy entry. There were also varying levels of ability amongst the 'able-bodied' and 'vulnerable' too, which made individuals' labour desirable at some times of the year and less so at others. In this case, therefore, perhaps so many people were left vulnerable during years of economic crisis that Boards, with one eye on the parish purse, thought that the policies under Gilbert's Act that they initially agreed to had to be shifted.

## Notes

1  Mottos from the seals of the Easebourne and Sutton Unions respectively with date of formation 1792, examples of which can be found on contracts; PHA/6514 and 15.

2  R.S. Thompson, 'Gilbert, Thomas (*bap.* 1720, *d.* 1798)', *Oxford Dictionary of National Biography* (Oxford, 2004; online edition, September 2013). Online: www.oxforddnb.com/view/article/10703 (last accessed 18 January 2016).

3  J. Innes, 'Gilbert, Thomas (*c.* 1720–98)', in D. Rutherford (ed.), *The Biographical Dictionary of British Economists*, Volume 1 (Bristol, 2004), pp. 246–9.

4  A.W. Coats, 'Economic thought and poor law policy in the eighteenth century', *Economic History Review*, 13 (1960), 46.

5  T. Gilbert, *A Scheme for the Better Relief and Employment of the Poor* (London, 1764).

6   S. Webb and B. Webb, *English Poor Law History, Part 1: The Old Poor Law* (1927, London, 1963), p. 170.

7   Coats, 'Economic thought and poor law policy', p. 47.

8   T. Gilbert, *Observations upon the Orders and Resolutions of the House of Commons, With Respect to the Poor, Vagrants, and Houses of Correction* (London, 1775).

9   Coats, 'Economic thought and poor law policy', p. 47, fn 7.

10  Gilbert, *Observations*, p. 28.

11  Innes, 'Gilbert, Thomas'.

12  T. Gilbert, *Plan for the Better Relief and Employment of the Poor; for Enforcing and Amending the Laws Respecting Houses of Correction, and Vagrants; and for Improving the Police of This Country. Together with Bills Intended to Be Offered to Parliament for Those Purposes* (London, 1781), p. 3.

13  Gilbert, *Plan for the Better Relief*, p. 6.

14  D. Marshall, *The English Poor in the Eighteenth Century: A Study in Social and Administrative History* (London, 1926), p. 160.

15  Gilbert, *Plan for the Better Relief*, p. 11.

16  Repealed in 1871 in the Statute Law Revision Act; Webb and Webb, *English Poor Law History, Part 1*, p. 171.

17  22 Geo. III c.83, XXIX.

18  Gilbert, *Plan for the Better Relief*, p. 7.

19  J. Innes, 'The state and the poor: eighteenth century England in European perspective', in J. Brewer and E. Hellmuth (eds.), *Rethinking Leviathan: The Eighteenth-Century State in Britain and Germany* (1999, Oxford, 2004), p. 251.

20  22 Geo. III c.83, XXXII.

21  Gilbert, *Plan for the Better Relief*, p. 7; also see 22 Geo. III c.83, XXXII.

22  S. King, *Poverty and Welfare in England 1700–1850: A Regional Perspective* (Manchester, 2000), p. 25.

23  22 Geo. III c.83, I; for figures on incorporations, see recent revisionist work by S.J. Thompson, 'Population growth and corporations of the poor, 1660–1841', in C. Briggs, P.M. Kitson and S.J. Thompson (eds.), *Population, Welfare and Economic Change in Britain 1290–1834* (Woodbridge, 2014), pp. 189–225.

24  F. Driver, *Power and Pauperism: The Workhouse System 1834–1884* (Cambridge, 1993), p. 45.

25  Gilbert, *Observations*, p. 3.

26  Gilbert, *Plan for the Better Relief*, p. 9. For instance, Richard Burn's *The History of the Poor Laws* condemned parish officers for being too harsh towards the poor and fraudulent with the poor rates; R. Burn, *The History of the Poor Laws: With Observations* (London, 1764).

27  22 Geo. III c.83, II, VIII and X.
28  22 Geo. III c.83, II and VII.
29  22 Geo. III c.83, XII.
30  22 Geo. III c.83, VIII.
31  J. Innes, *Inferior Politics: Social Problems and Social Policies in Eighteenth-Century Britain* (Oxford, 2009), p. 99.
32  Innes, 'Gilbert, Thomas'.
33  Innes, *Inferior Politics*, p. 105, fn 56.
34  Driver, *Power and Pauperism*, p. 44, fn 45; 1844 (543) Report from the Select Committee on Poor Relief (Gilbert Unions); together with the minutes of evidence, appendix and index [hereafter BPP 1844 (543) Report from the Select Committee on Gilbert's Act].
35  Webb and Webb, *English Poor Law History, Part 1*, pp. 173, 275. From *Ninth Annual Report of the Poor Law Commissioners*, app. A.2 (London, 1843).
36  Webb and Webb, *English Poor Law History, Part 1*, p. 276.
37  J.R. Poynter, *Society and Pauperism: English Ideas on Poor Relief, 1795–1834* (London, 1969), p. 12; King, *Poverty and Welfare*, p. 25.
38  Driver, *Power and Pauperism*, p. 44; Innes, *Inferior Politics*, p. 99; Innes, 'Gilbert, Thomas'; N. Longmate, *The Workhouse: A Social History* (1974, London, 2003), p. 30.
39  Webb and Webb, *English Poor Law History, Part 1*, p. 275. The Webbs also suggest that the list of unions formed under the Act provided in the *Ninth Annual Report of the Poor Law Commissioners* is 'incomplete', and '[n]o general description of the working of these is known to us', apart from in some incidental descriptions in the Annual Poor Law Reports by the requisite commissioners; see p. 273, fn 1.
40  P. Mandler, 'The making of the New Poor Law redivivus', *Past and Present*, 117 (1987), 133.
41  BPP 1834 (44) XXXV, Report from His Majesty's Commissioners for Inquiring into the Administration and Practical Operation of the Poor Laws. Appendix B.2. Answers to the Town Queries in Five Parts. Part 2. Question 15.
42  As examined in A. Clark, 'The administration of poor relief in Southampton 1830–1850' (unpublished BA dissertation, University of Southampton, 1960).
43  Although another Act was passed in 1830 stipulating that the poor rates for cottages under £10 in value were to be paid by the landlords.
44  This is also mentioned in a pamphlet: T. Bush, J. Jones, Jr, T. Tugwell and W. Barker, 'Parochial regulations relative to the management of the poor of Bradford, Wilts; with notes, tendering to promote economy and comfort in the work-house' (Bristol, 1801), p. 14. In addition, the parish

of Ellingham (next to Ringwood and the New Forest) was under a Local
Act; A'Court's correspondence, 'Notes on the several Parishes in the division of Ringwood', 'Ellingham', 27 November 1834, TNA MH32/1.

45   See Appendix 1b, Bentley and Long Sutton (Hampshire) and Clapham,
Singleton and Tillington (West Sussex). Just Long Sutton mentioned
being united under Gilbert's Act.

46   Wells states, '[t]here is probably more data on the evidentially-obscure
post-1782 Gilbert Unions among these papers than anywhere else'; R.
Wells, 'Review of P. Carter (ed.), Bradford Poor Law Union: Papers and
Correspondence with the Poor Law Commission 1834 to January 1839
(Woodbridge, 2004)', *English Historical Review*, 490 (2006), 233.

47   C. Rowell, 'Wyndham, George O'Brien, third earl of Egremont (1751–
1837)', *Oxford Dictionary of National Biography* (Oxford, 2004; online
edition, 2006). Online: www.oxforddnb.com/view/article/30141 (last
accessed 18 January 2016).

48   This cluster was of particular concern to the Commission under the
New Poor Law; Poor Law Commission, *Fourth Annual Report of the
Poor Law Commissioners* (London, 1838), p. 5.

49   W. Young, *Considerations on the Subject of Poorhouses* (London, 1796),
p. 29, cited in Webb and Webb, *English Poor Law History, Part 1*, p. 275;
F.M. Eden, *State of the Poor*, Volume 1 (1797, Bristol, 2001), p. 366.

50   Driver, *Power and Pauperism*, p. 44.

51   Wells, 'Review of P. Carter (ed.), *Bradford Poor Law Union*', p. 237. For
instance: Micheldever and East Stratton (Gilbert's Union, Hampshire,
1826) and Hursley (Gilbert's Parish, Hampshire, 1829).

52   Proposal for the formation of [a Gilbert's Union] based on the parish
of Fletching to build a Workhouse at Piltdown or Chelwood Common,
n.d., ESRO AMS4899/1. Parishes in the proposed union were: Newick, Isfield, Little Horsted, Ringmer, Uckfield, Framfield, Bruxted,
Maresfield, Fletching, Chailey, Lindfield and Horsted Keynes, but the
document does suggest that if Chemwood Common was used for the
location of the workhouse, then the parishes of East Grinstead, West
Hoadly, Worth and Ardingly could be added.

53   An antiquarian, writing in 1929, believed the proposal was 'in keeping
with the spirit of Gilbert's Act'; H.D. Gilbert (Uckfield, Sussex) to Mr
Bridges, 26 July 1929, found in ESRO AMS4899/1.

54   Digby suggests that Gilbert's Act had 'slowed the incorporating movement in Norfolk' because Gilbert's Act was 'much cheaper to set up'
compared to 'incorporation under an expensive local act of Parliament';
A. Digby, *Pauper Palaces* (London, 1978), p. 46.

55   A'Court's correspondence, 'Notes on every Parish in the Winchester
Division', 'East Stratton', November 1834, TNA MH32/1. Baring was

resistant to the Poor Law Amendment Act interfering with this arrangement; A'Court (Bishopstoke) to PLC, 1 June 1835, TNA MH32/1.

56  J. Walter, T. Robbins and W. Gilpin, *An Account of a New Poor-House
    Erected in the Parish of Boldre: In New Forest near Lymington* (London,
    1796), p. 11.

57  Between 40 and 60 people per week was stipulated in the contracts at
    Sutton Union; Contracts of Mary Bryan and Daniel Bryan of Petworth
    [to 1803] or Daniel Bryan [1804 on], and the Visitor and Guardians
    of Sutton United Parishes for the Governorship of the Workhouse, and
    the care, feeding, clothing etc. of the poor; with bonds, 1802–36, PHA/
    6514-48. Thomas Green entered into a contract with Donhead St Mary
    for one year in April 1825, which stipulated that he was to receive 4s per
    head per week, and to have at least 25 individuals within the workhouse.
    If fewer than 25 individuals were in the house, he would be paid for at
    least that number. Later in the year, however, the vestry decided not to
    fix a minimum number in the future. Donhead St Mary Vestry with
    Charlton St John Minute Book, 14 April and 31 August 1825, WSA
    PR/Donhead St Mary Vestry with Charlton St John/980/22.

58  There were many types of contracting. This has been examined in Webb
    and Webb, *English Poor Law History, Part 1*, pp. 280–313.

59  Poole, Churchwardens' Account Book (with Vestry Minutes), 12 April
    1814, DHC PE/PL CW1/1/4.

60  Botley, Vestry Minute Book, 14 March 1821, HRO 40M75/PV1.

61  Botley, Select Vestry Minute Book, 21 December 1826, HRO 40M75/
    PV2.

62  BPP 1844 (543) Report from the Select Committee on Gilbert's Act,
    interview of G. Cornewall Lewis, p. 16.

63  R. Wells, 'The poor law 1700–1900', in K.C. Leslie and B. Short (eds.),
    *A Historical Atlas of Sussex: An Atlas of the History of the Counties of East
    and West Sussex* (Chichester, 1999), p. 71.

64  BPP 1844 (543) Report from the Select Committee on Gilbert's Act,
    interview of G. Cornewall Lewis, p. 16. Lewis claimed that those par-
    ishes that joined after the initial establishment of the union were now
    under the rules of the Poor Law Commission. Whether this practice
    was in fact legal or not is not of direct concern here, but this indicates
    the nature of how some unions expanded.

65  Daniel Bryan and Mary Bryan managed the workhouse from October 1802
    to 1804 and then Daniel Bryan managed the workhouse alone after her
    death to at least October 1836; Sutton Union Contracts, contract of 4 Octo-
    ber 1802, WSRO PHA/6514; contract of 2 November 1835, PHA/6547.

66  BPP 1844 (543) Report from the Select Committee on Gilbert's Act,
    interview of T. Sockett, pp. 196–7.

67   Cranleigh, Vestry Minute Book, 12 December 1821 and 1 January 1822, SHC P58/1/1; Original agreement under which Cranleigh adopted Gilbert's Act, Copy agreement, 8 June 1793, SHC QS2/6/1793/Mid/31.

68   A'Court's correspondence, 'Notes on the parishes in the division of Fareham including Portsmouth', 'Alverstoke and Gosport', 21 December 1834, TNA MH32/1.

69   Botley, Vestry Minute Book, 14 March 1821, HRO 40M75/PV1.

70   Titchfield, Vestry Minute Book, 8 April and 15 May 1806, HRO 37M73/PV1.

71   Titchfield, Vestry Minute Book, Report of the Committee, 3 June 1816, HRO 37M73/PV1.

72   Titchfield, Vestry Minute Book, committee meeting, 27 May 1806, HRO 37M73/PV1.

73   Parishes included Eling, Nursling, Minstead and Dibden; Millbrook, Vestry Minute Book, 17 and 30 January 1817, SCRO PR10/8/1. In the following year it was decided to raise the topic again, although this time it considered whether they should place the parish under the Act alone. It was succinctly noted that the legislation was 'not desirable for in this Parish to adopt'; Millbrook, Vestry Minute Book, 27 July 1818, SCRO PR10/8/1.

74   A'Court's correspondence, 'Notes on every Parish in the Winchester Division', 'Hursley', 1 March 1834, TNA MH32/1.

75   A'Court's correspondence, 'Notes on the Parishes in the Lymington Division', 'Hordle', 3 December 1834, TNA MH32/1.

76   A'Court's correspondence, 'Notes on the Parishes in the Lymington Division', 'Boldre', 3 December 1834, TNA MH32/1.

77   A'Court's correspondence, 'Notes on the parishes in the division of Fareham including Portsmouth', 'Alverstoke and Gosport', 21 December 1834, TNA MH32/1.

78   A'Court's correspondence, 'Notes on the Parishes in the Lymington Division', 'Hordle', 3 December 1834, TNA MH32/1.

79   A'Court's correspondence, 'Notes on the parishes in the division of Fareham including Portsmouth', 'Alverstoke and Gosport', 21 December 1834, TNA MH32/1. This appears to have been in 1821; Alverstoke, Guardians' Minute Book, Annual report 1821, HRO PL2/1/1.

80   A'Court's correspondence, 'Notes on the magisterial division of Alton', 'Bentley', 23 February 1835, TNA MH32/1.

81   A'Court's correspondence, 'Notes on the magisterial division of Alton', 'Headley', 2 February 1835, TNA MH32/1.

82   Payments per head per week varying from 2s 6d to 3s 10d throughout the period; Headley, Workhouse Account Book, 1795–1829, HRO 57M75/PO16.

83  Easebourne Union, Copies of the yearly accounts of William Bridger, Treasurer of the Easebourne United Parishes, 1797–1827, PHA/7869.

84  22 Geo. III c.83, XII.

85  R. Wells, 'Social protest, class, conflict and consciousness in the English countryside 1700–1880', in M. Reed and R. Wells (eds.), *Class, Conflict and Protest in the English Countryside, 1700–1880* (London, 1990), pp. 121–214.

86  A. Hinde and F. Turnbull, 'The populations of two Hampshire workhouses 1851–1861', *Local Population Studies*, 61 (1998), 38–52; D.G. Jackson, 'Kent workhouse populations in 1881: a study based on the census enumerators' books', *Local Population Studies*, 69 (2002), 51–66; D.G. Jackson, 'The Medway Union workhouse, 1876–1881: a study based on the admission and discharge registers and the census enumerators' books', *Local Population Studies*, 75 (2005), 11–32; N. Goose, 'Workhouse populations in the mid-nineteenth century: the case of Hertfordshire', *Local Population Studies*, 62 (1999), 52–69.

87  J. Harley, 'Material lives of the poor and their strategic use of the workhouse during the final decades of the English Old Poor Law', *Continuity and Change*, 30 (2015), 71–103; J. Boulton and J. Black, 'Paupers and their experience of a London workhouse: St-Martin-in-the-Fields, 1725–1824', in J. Hamlett, L. Hoskins and R. Preston (eds.), *Residential Institutions in Britain, 1725–1970: Inmates and Environments* (London, 2013), p. 85. These were admissions between 1725 and 1817.

88  See Wells, 'Social protest'; E.L. Jones, *Seasons and Prices: The Roles of the Weather in English Agricultural History* (London, 1964), pp. 153–65.

89  S.R. Ottaway, *The Decline of Life: Old Age in Eighteenth-Century England* (Cambridge, 2004), p. 250.

90  Ottaway, *The Decline of Life*, pp. 250–1.

91  For instance, Humphries found that children born between 1627 and 1790 started working, on average, aged 12 and those born between 1791 and 1820 at the age of 10; see J. Humphries, *Childhood and Child Labour in the British Industrial Revolution* (Cambridge, 2010), p. 176.

92  Wells, 'Social protest', p. 129.

93  There were not many allotment schemes before 1830, but there were some 'potato grounds'; see J. Burchardt, *The Allotment Movement in England: 1793–1873* (Woodbridge, 2002).

94  S. Haines and L. Lawson, *Poor Cottages & Proud Palaces: The Life and Work of Reverend Thomas Sockett of Petworth 1777–1859* (Hastings, 2007), pp. 155–8; also see W. Cameron and M. McDougall Maude, *Assisting Emigration to Upper Canada: The Petworth Project 1832–1837* (Montreal, 2000).

95  Harley, 'Material lives of the poor'.

96  The majority of poor law specialists examine the populations of early large urban institutions or New Poor Law Unions, for which figures are more readily available in the archive.

97  Sutton Union, Applications for relief and miscellaneous correspondence (herein called the Sutton Case Papers), 1837–49, WSRO WG3/4.

98  A'Court's correspondence, 'Notes on the magisterial division of Alton', 'Headley', 23 February 1835, TNA MH32/1.

99  Walter *et al.*, *An Account of a New Poor-House*, p. 5.

100  22 Geo. III c.83, XXX.

101  Sutton Union, Sutton Case Papers, 9 July 1838, WSRO WG3/4.

102  Sutton Union, Sutton Case Papers, 5 March 1840, WSRO WG3/4.

103  Sutton Union, Sutton Case Papers, [no day or month] 1837, WSRO WG3/4.

104  22 Geo. III c.83, XXX.

105  Sutton Union, Sutton Case Papers, 15 May 1837, WSRO WG3/4.

106  Alverstoke, Guardians' Minute Book, Annual report 1820, HRO PL2/1/1.

107  Gilbert, *Plan for the Better Relief*, p. 11.

108  Alverstoke, Guardians' Minute Book, 24 February 1800, HRO PL2/1/1.

109  Copy of Memorial signed by the Visitor and Guardians of East Preston [Gilbert's] Union to PLC, WSRO WG2/7.

110  Alverstoke, Guardians' Minute Book, 1 April 1806, HRO PL2/1/1.

111  South Stoneham, Vestry Minute Book, 4 June 1822 and 5 January 1824, SCRO PR9/14/2.

112  Alverstoke, Guardians' Minute Book, 1 April 1806, HRO PL2/1/1. Furthermore, the South Stoneham Board had noted the 'fair progress' the stocking manufactory was making; South Stoneham, Vestry Minute Book, 4 June 1822, SCRO PR9/14/2.

113  Wimborne Minster Insurance Policy, 1815, DHC PE/WM OV8/2; minutes in Wimborne Minster, Vestry Minute Book, 1745–1808, DHC PE/WM VE1/1; minutes in Wimborne Minster, Select Vestry Order book, 1818–22, DHC PE/WM VE2/1; Wimborne Minster, Overseers' Correspondence, Henry Jenkins, Contractor (Christchurch) to Overseers (Wimborne Minster), 1 March 1819, DHC PE/WM OV13/4; Wimborne Minster Overseers' Correspondence, Henry Jenkins, Contractor (Christchurch) to Mr John Drew, Vestry Clerk (Wimborne Minster), 13 March 1821, DHC PE/WM OV13/6.

114  Alverstoke, Guardians' Minute Book, 3 August 1804 and 20 April 1813, HRO PL2/1/1.

115  Sutton Union, Guardians' Minute Book, 4 February 1793, WSRO WG3/1/1.

116  Easebourne Union, Letters concerning the establishment of a Sunday school, letter from E.M. Poznty(?) to Mr Tyler (Petworth), 26

November 1800 and R. Lloyd (Midhurst) to Mr Tyler (Petworth), 14
November [no year], PHA/10940.

117 A'Court's correspondence, 'Notes on every Parish in the Winchester
Division', 'Otterbourne & Boyatt', November 1834, TNA MH32/1.

118 A'Court's correspondence, 'Notes on the Parishes in the Lymington
Division', 'Hordle', 3 December 1834, TNA MH32/1.

119 Sutton Union, Guardians' Minute Book, 2 October 1809, WSRO
WG3/1/6.

120 Sutton Union, Guardians' Minute Book, 6 May 1816, WSRO WG3/
1/8. In 1821 they bought six testaments and six small common prayer
books for the use of the children; Sutton Union, Guardians' Minute
Book, 1 January 1821, WSRO WG3/1/9.

121 A'Court's correspondence, 'Notes on every Parish in the Winchester
Division', 'Hursley', 1 March 1834, TNA MH32/1.

122 Alverstoke, Guardians' Minute Book, Annual report 1820, HRO PL2/
1/1. Apparently 64 boys and 58 girls attended, but it is unclear whether
these children all came from the house or from the parish as a whole.

123 Walter *et al.*, *An Account of a New Poor-House*, p. 20 (apparently the
elderly went with the children); A'Court's correspondence, 'Notes on
the Parishes in the Lymington Division', 'Boldre', 3 December 1834,
TNA MH32/1.

124 22 Geo III c.83, XXX.

125 Sutton Union, Guardians' Minute Book, 1 October 1792, WSRO
WG3/1/1.

126 Alverstoke, Guardians' Minute Book, Annual report 1821, HRO
PL2/1/1.

127 Sutton Union, Sutton Case Papers, 7 February 1839, WSRO WG3/4.

128 Sutton Union, Sutton Case Papers, 2 October 1837, WSRO WG3/4.

129 Lymington, Vestry Minute Book, 16 August 1821 and 22 February
1827, HRO 42M75/PV2.

130 Lymington, Vestry Minute Book, 6 September 1827, HRO 42M75/
PV3. These individuals are likely to have been registered as Chelsea
Out-pensioners, not least because – as other minutes in Lymington
illustrate – there are other Chelsea Out-pensioners in this parish.

131 A'Court's correspondence, 'Notes on every Parish in the Winchester
Division', 'Bishop Stoke', November 1834, TNA MH32/1; A'Court's
correspondence, 'Notes on the Parishes in the Lymington Division',
'Hordle', 3 December 1834, TNA MH32/1.

132 A'Court's correspondence, 'Notes on every Parish in the Winchester
Division', 'Hursley', 1 March 1834, TNA MH32/1.

133 Alverstoke, Guardians' Minute Book, 24 February 1800, HRO PL2/1/1.

134 Alverstoke, Guardians' Minute Book, 5 May 1800, HRO PL2/1/1.

135 A'Court correspondence, 'Notes on the parishes in the division of Fareham including Portsmouth', 'Alverstoke and Gosport', 21 December 1834, TNA MH32/1.

136 Alverstoke, Guardians' Minute Book, 18 December 1822, HRO PL2/1/1.

137 Alverstoke, Guardians' Minute Book, 19 April 1808, HRO PL2/1/1.

138 Gilbert, *Plan for the Better Relief*, p. 7.

139 Alverstoke, Guardians' Minute Book, 6 August 1818, HRO PL2/1/1.

140 Alverstoke, Guardians' Minute Book, 15 January 1819, HRO PL2/1/1.

141 J. Boulton and L. Schwarz, '"The comforts of a private fireside"? The workhouse, the elderly and the poor law in Georgian Westminster: St Martin-in-the-Fields, 1725–1824', in J. McEwan and P. Sharpe (eds.), *Accommodating Poverty: The Housing and Living Arrangements of the English Poor, c. 1600–1850* (Basingstoke, 2013), pp. 221–45.

142 Alverstoke, Guardians' Minute Book, 20 April 1813, HRO PL2/1/1.

143 Walter *et al.*, *An Account of a New Poor-House*, p. 6.

144 A'Court's correspondence, 'Notes on the Parishes in the Lymington Division', 'Lymington', 3 December 1834, TNA MH32/1.

145 For brooms, see summary 1797–98 and 1798–99, and for woollen mops, see summary 1809–10, in Easebourne Union, Copies of the yearly accounts of William Bridger, Treasurer of the Easebourne United Parishes, 1797–1827, PHA/7869; Walter *et al.*, *An Account of a New Poor-House*, p. 6.

146 A'Court's correspondence, 'Notes on the Parishes in the Lymington Division', 'Lymington', 3 December 1834, TNA MH32/1.

147 Gilbert, *Plan for the Better Relief*, pp. 1–2.

148 G. Nicholls, *History of the English Poor Law, Volume 2: 1714–1853* (London, 1898), p. 89.

149 Gilbert, *Plan for the Better Relief*, p. 7; my emphasis.

150 Mere, Vestry Minute Book, 11 April 1822, WSA 2944/78.

151 Walter *et al.*, *An Account of a New Poor-House*, p. 6.

152 A'Court's correspondence, 'Notes on the Parishes in the Lymington Division', 'Lymington', 3 December 1834, TNA MH32/1.

153 Easebourne Union, Copies of the yearly accounts of William Bridger, Treasurer of the Easebourne United Parishes, 1797–98 summary, PHA/7869.

154 Alverstoke, Guardians' Minutes Book, Annual report 1804, HRO PL2/1/1.

155 Walter *et al.*, *An Account of a New Poor-House*, p. 19.

156 Alverstoke, Guardians' Minute Book, 8 April 1806, HRO PL2/1/1.

157 Easebourne Union, Copies of the yearly accounts of William Bridger, Treasurer of the Easebourne United Parishes, 1796–97 summary, PHA/7869.

158 Easebourne Union, Copies of the yearly accounts of William Bridger, Treasurer of the Easebourne United Parishes, 1798–99 summary, PHA/7869.

159 22 Geo. III c.83, II.

160 Sutton Union, Correspondence and proposals for farming the poor, 21 July 1793, PHA/6570. It is clear that he took the position of contractor later that year; Sutton Union, Minute Book, 2 December 1793, WSRO WG3/1/1.

161 Sutton Union, Guardians' Minute Books, 4 August 1794, WSRO WG3/1/2.

162 The manufactory is mentioned throughout the summaries from the summary of 1798–99 to 1826–27. For detail about the horse cloths and hempen sacks, see summary 1804–05, for brooms see summary 1797–98 and 1798–99, and for woollen mops see summary 1809–10, in Easebourne Union, Copies of the yearly accounts of William Bridger, Treasurer of the Easebourne United Parishes, PHA/7869.

163 Alverstoke, Guardians' Minute Book, 18 December 1822, HRO PL2/1/1.

164 BPP 1844 (543) Report from the Select Committee on Gilbert's Act, interview of Joseph Cave, p. 152; Alverstoke, Guardians' Minute Book, 8 February 1821, HRO PL2/1/1.

165 *Hampshire Chronicle*, 12 May 1794.

166 Alverstoke, Guardians' Minute Book, 26 November 1799, HRO PL2/1/1.

167 Although the way in which it was distributed is unknown, i.e. it could have been provided at the governors' or Guardians' discretion, in proportion to the number of days or hours worked or simply to all those who did work. Easebourne Union, Copies of the yearly accounts of William Bridger, Treasurer of the Easebourne United Parishes, 1796–97 and 1797–98 summaries, PHA/7869.

168 Alverstoke, Guardians' Minute Book, 28 August 1822, HRO PL2/1/1.

169 Digby, *Pauper Palaces*, p. 32.

170 Gilbert, *Plan for the Better Relief*, p. 6.

171 The pasture harvest was approximately from late May through to August and the arable harvest from mid to late July through to September.

172 Gilbert, *Plan for the Better Relief*, p. 7.

173 B. Harris, M. Gorsky, A.M. Guntupalli and A. Hinde, 'Long-term changes in sickness and health: further evidence from the Hampshire Friendly Society', *Economic History Review*, 2 (2012), 719–45.

174 Sutton Union, Sutton Case Papers, 10 October 1839, WSRO WG3/4.

175 Sutton Union, Sutton Case Papers, 23 July 1840 and letter from Thomas Sockett (Petworth) to William Lane, 23 July 1840 (Slindon), WSRO WG3/4.

176  Sutton Union, Sutton Case Papers, William Lane (Slindon) to Thomas Sockett (Petworth), 26 July 1840, WSRO WG3/4.

177  Sutton Union, Sutton Case Papers, 27 July 1840, WSRO WG3/4.

178  Sutton Union, Sutton Case Papers, 26 August 1839, WSRO WG3/4.

179  Sutton Union, Sutton Case Papers, 5 March 1840, WSRO WG3/4.

180  Easebourne Union, Copies of the yearly accounts of William Bridger, Treasurer of the Easebourne United Parishes, 1797–98 summary, PHA/ 7869.

181  Easebourne Union, Copies of the yearly accounts of William Bridger, Treasurer of the Easebourne United Parishes, 1798–99 summary, PHA/ 7869.

182  A'Court's correspondence, 'Notes on every Parish in the Winchester Division', 'Bishop Stoke' and 'Hursley', 1 March 1834, TNA MH32/1.

183  Lymington, Vestry Order Book, 1807–17, HRO 42M75/PV10, see especially order on 9 May 1808.

184  Webb and Webb, *English Poor Law History, Part 1*, p. 275.

185  Figures based on calculating the average number of inmates within the workhouse per year from monthly counts.

186  In some years the treasurer noted two or three months with the greatest or smallest populations. These have been included in the figure as separate entries.

187  The following Rural Queries were not included because either the answers covered an area larger than a parish (e.g. magistrate's divisions) and/or they represented duplicate answers, or they had answered the 'Town Queries'; Dorset: 'Blandford (Division)', 'Cerne Abbas'; Hampshire: 'Bishopstoke and other Parishes around', 'Isle of Wight'; Somerset: 'Hundreds of Bruton, Catash, Horethorne, and Norton-Ferris', 'Chilton Canteloe Parish and Yeovil District', '(Vale of Taunton), Bagborough, Bishop's Lydeard, Combe-Florey, Cothelstone, Kingston', 'Dulverton', 'Yeovil'; West Sussex: 'The Lower Division of Chichester Rape (consisting of the parishes of Harting, Rogate, Terwick, Trotton, Chithurst, Iping, Stedham, Lynch, Woolbeding, Easebourne, Farnhurst, Linchmere, Lodsworth, Selham, Graffham, Heyshott, Cocking, Bepton, Didling, Trey)'; Wiltshire: 'District of Hungerford & Ramsbury', 'Pitton and Farley United Parishes', 'Warminster', 'West Grimstead, Pitton, & Farley'.

# 3

# Restricting relief: the impact of Sturges Bourne's reforms

The end of the Napoleonic Wars in 1815 effected a severe agricultural and manufacturing depression, as discussed in the Introduction. As David Eastwood contends, 'the post-war depression generated the most acute crisis in the entire period' between 1780 and 1840, with national poor relief expenditure rocketing from 1816 onwards.[1] In 1817, following the collection of national statistics on poor relief expenditure, a House of Commons Select Committee was appointed to investigate the operation of the poor laws.[2] The Select Committee comprised 40 gentlemen, including Thomas Frankland Lewis, later a Commissioner of the New Poor Law, and chairman William Sturges Bourne, chair of the Hampshire Quarter Sessions from 1817 to 1822 and later a member of the Royal Commission on the Poor Laws, 1832–34.[3] The aim of Sturges Bourne and the Select Committee was not, however, to abolish the old poor laws – as many commentators had called for – but to develop legislation that permitted reform of the existing parish administrative structure.[4] The result was a series of parliamentary bills, two of which became known as the 'Sturges Bourne Acts' of 1818 and 1819. The 1818 Act allowed voting rights in open vestries to be weighted according to a vestryman's property rating, whilst the Act of 1819 permitted parishes to appoint select vestries and assistant overseers, two measures designed to allow parishes to restrict relief.

Notwithstanding that, as Steven King has suggested, the Acts had 'fundamental consequences for the experience of being poor', their adoption and impact on the provision of poor relief has been little researched and as such remains poorly understood.[5] This lack of systematic attention is perhaps understandable for two reasons.

First, the Royal Commission's Poor Law Report of 1834 stated that, whilst the reforms were potentially 'highly beneficial', in practice they were unpopular. Those select vestries that were appointed were sparsely attended and prone to making 'injurious' and poorly documented relief decisions.[6] Second, analysis of the implementation of the reforms has been hindered by their 'enabling' status, the 'opt-in' nature making the legislation of seemingly low importance. The reforms have thus been left in the shadow of that which followed – the Poor Law Amendment Act 1834. This condescension of posterity is perhaps best summed up by the Webbs. To them the measures were an 'example of the inability of this generation to grapple effectively with its problems'.[7]

This perspective on Sturges Bourne's reforms has been left largely unquestioned. In the words of Wells, 'the adoption of Sturges Bourne has not been systematically studied, merely commented upon'.[8] Standard texts on poor law history therefore tend to detail the reforms as part of wider 'legislative context' chapters, but then pass over the uptake and effects of the reforms.[9] A two-parish analysis by Wells (of Sussex), and short surveys of the adoption of Sturges Bourne's reforms by Mark Neuman for Berkshire, Anne Digby for Lancashire and Yorkshire, and most recently David Green for London, are notable exceptions to this rule. Yet, apart from the last study, which argues that the measures were ineffective in the metropolis because London already possessed many similar relief-granting bodies, these studies all demonstrate that the legislation appears to have achieved its stated objective of reducing relief costs.[10] Neuman, for instance, found that the new regime led to a 33 per cent reduction in relief expenditure in the Berkshire parish of White Waltham in the first year of adopting a select vestry, whilst the 'heavily pauperised' parish of Bray reduced its poor relief expenditure by 37 per cent.[11] Clearly the reforms could make a considerable impact on the nature of relief and poor relief claimants of the early nineteenth century.

After detailing the specific facets of Sturges Bourne's reforms, this chapter considers first the nature and pattern of adoption – focusing specifically upon its two main provisions: select vestries and assistant overseers – before going on to consider the impact of the reforms on the poor. After establishing overall trends in England as a whole, the analysis offers a more detailed understanding of the uptake in several counties in southern England. Focusing on the parish-level administration of Sturges Bourne's reforms allows me to show how the complex 'micro-politics' operated when innovations in the delivery of relief were applied on the ground, an approach influenced by Lyn Hollen Lees' and Steve Hindle's work on the 'welfare process'.[12] As outlined in Chapter 1, Lees and Hindle have used this term to encapsulate the complex web of interactions within the 'micropolitics', the negotiations involved in claiming and providing poor relief.[13] In order to get at these dynamics during the implementation of Sturges Bourne's reforms, especially how administrators judged and treated relief claimants, this chapter draws on select and open vestry minutes, overseers' accounts and other administrative documents from parishes throughout the region of focus. The approach of this chapter, similar to that in the preceding chapter on Gilbert's Act, allows us to move beyond the more socially abstract economic and political dynamics of the reforms and to offer instead an evaluation of their everyday human effects.

## Sturges Bourne's Acts of 1818 and 1819

Before examining the impact of Sturges Bourne's reforms, it is important to first outline the several clauses of the two Acts. The first Sturges Bourne's Act permitted parishes to reset the weighting of vestry votes on the basis of one vote for the first £50 worth of property with a sliding scale thereafter up to a maximum of six votes for £150 or more. Those without property were also barred from attending vestry meetings. Whilst this was controversial, and attracted opposition for making the vestry an exclusive group, the Committee believed that the major ratepayers would better control the expenditure of the poor rates and reduce corruption. As Bryan Keith-Lucas puts it, the measure was intended to take the administration of poor relief 'out of the hands of the poor themselves'.[14]

The 1819 Act was specifically concerned with the mechanisms of relief provision, and permitted any parish to 'establish a Select Vestry for the concerns of the Poor' of between five and 20 'Substantial Householders or Occupiers'.[15] The select vestry had to be voted for by the majority of members of the open vestry and renewed annually therein, the official written agreement requiring the signature of one magistrate.[16] The majority of the members of the select vestry elected a chairman who had a casting vote on unresolved decisions.

The select vestry was required to meet at least once every 14 days, and its role was:

> to examine into the State and Condition of the Poor of the Parish, and to inquire into and determine upon the proper Objects of Relief, and the Nature and Amount of the Relief to be given; and in each case take into Consideration the Character and Conduct of the poor Person to be relieved, and shall be at liberty to distinguish, in the Relief to be granted between the deserving, and the idle extravagant or profligate.[17]

Once such inquiries were made, the overseer was bound to abide by the decisions of the select vestry and administer relief accordingly, except in cases of 'sudden Emergency or urgent Necessity'.[18]

The select vestry was not just a relief issuing body, though, for the 1819 Act also permitted loans to be made to the poor that would then be repaid in weekly instalments.[19] Scholars of local government, most notably Eastwood, have suggested, however, that the idea of a committee composed exclusively for the administration of relief was not itself a new practice. Separate committees were formed prior to the 1819 Act with the specific task of managing the welfare of the poor. Dorchester, for instance, had a system akin to a select vestry from 1794, before deciding in 1821 to place the pre-existing committee under the regulations of Sturges Bourne.[20] Committees were also frequently formed to undertake a specific task on behalf of the wider vestry. In the spring of 1798, for instance, the Wincanton (Somerset) vestry established a committee of nine men 'to examine into the Managemt. and expenditure of the Workhouse'.[21]

Sturges Bourne's 1819 Act also permitted the appointment of assistant overseers, to be sanctioned annually by two magistrates after checking the applicant's financial indemnity agreement. In return for undertaking 'all such of the Duties of the Office of Overseer of the Poor', and any specified in the contract of his appointment, the assistant would receive a salary set by members of the vestry.[22] According to Eastwood, this section of the Act encouraged 'a few would-be bureaucrats to devote themselves to parish administration', thereby promoting a growing 'professionalism', akin to a 'poor law civil service'.[23] Indeed, assistant overseers were paid a salary from the parish purse and were reappointed on an annual basis. But just as select vestries were not an entirely new idea before the passage of the 1819 Act, neither were assistant overseers. Variously called 'perpetual', 'deputy', 'acting', 'standing' and 'rating' overseers, such pre-Sturges Bourne appointees were often to be found collecting the rates, distributing poor relief, managing poorhouses and even playing the church organ.[24] Some rural parishes in Wessex and Sussex employed assistant overseers many years before the Sturges Bourne reforms, the large, sparsely populated parish of Chew Magna (Somerset) making such an appointment as early as 1769.[25] Chew Magna, according to George Nicholls, was archetypal: the appointment of assistant overseers was particularly desirable in large rural parishes where collecting the rates and distributing poor relief was particularly onerous.[26] These early 'assistant overseers' were usually salaried, but not always exclusively supported from the parish funds. In 1811 the Bruton (Somerset) vestry appointed Thomas Bord as a 'rating overseer' to collect the rates. His salary was £20 a year, but only half came from the poor rates. Each ordinary overseer was also to contribute £5 from their own pocket, as it was a task that, by law, they were supposed to undertake themselves.[27]

The 1819 Act also contained a series of other optional directives. One such clause allowed parishes to procure 20 acres of land on which to work the poor.[28] Another clause allowed parish vestries to both build and expand parish workhouses for the accommodation of the poor.[29] Furthermore, parishes were also permitted to enter into arrangements with adjoining parishes for the hire or purchase of workhouses, thus imitating the provisions of Gilbert's Act.[30] According to Wells, appointing a select vestry whilst also providing relief according to Gilbert's Act was forbidden in Sturges Bourne's 1819 Act.[31] Indeed, several parish officials at the time thought this to be the case, with three parishes in Hampshire informing the Poor Law Commission in the Rural Queries that they could not adopt Sturges Bourne's Act because they had adopted Gilbert's Act.[32] An examination of the Act shows, however, that it was *not* strictly forbidden: a penultimate section of the 1819 Act contained a proviso merely expressing that the Act does not intend to alter the 'Powers, Directions, Provisions or Regulations' of Gilbert's Act and those stipulations contained in Local Acts 'for the Maintenance, Relief or Regulation of the Poor'. All magistrates and parish officials were, therefore, able to decide for themselves whether also to adopt the provisions of Sturges Bourne's Act.[33]

Magistrates retained their importance in parishes adopting the implementation of the poor laws under Sturges Bourne's Acts. One magistrate alone could issue relief in cases of emergency to a claimant from a parish operating a select vestry, as they could for a claimant from a parish with an open vestry. Yet the Sturges Bourne Acts endeavoured to make it harder for parish relief decisions to be overturned. After hearing a complaint from an individual, just one magistrate was required to direct an open vestry to alter their decision. A claimant from a parish operating a select vestry, however, needed the support of two magistrates.[34] According to Dunkley, the role of magistrates to act as a referee on relief decisions meant that minimum standards of relief were often met.[35] King concurs.[36] Wells, on the other hand, demonstrates how magistrates united with their own class, the propertied, to use poor relief as a way to control the community.[37] By analysing the notebooks of Samuel Whitbread, Peter King found a benevolent magistrate who had overturned two-thirds of the cases he heard. But such decisions were not necessarily replicated by others.[38] Depending on the disposition of each magistrate, therefore, the need for an additional magistrate to support a complaint regarding a select vestry decision may have put an additional barrier between the claimant and their poor relief, as Sturges Bourne had intended. Before a vestry could act according to Sturges Bourne's measures, though, magistrates also had to ratify the appointments. Only one signature was needed for a select vestry appointment and two were needed for an assistant overseer's appointment. This may have been because of the financial risks involved in the appointment of a suitable, and reliable, paid official. Although the magistrates' approval was a standard part of the process in the official adoption of enabling legislation, it could often serve as a barrier to its implementation, as will be discussed in the next section.

### The adoption of Sturges Bourne's poor law reforms

Parishes could adopt both of the main enabling aspects of the Sturges Bourne Acts or just one, i.e. just a select vestry or an assistant overseer. As the Webbs claimed, answers to question 32 of the Rural Queries of the 1834 Poor Law Report suggest that, for the sample counties, the appointment of an assistant overseer was far more popular than the appointment of a select vestry (see Table 3.1).[39] There are, however, methodological problems to consider with this source. Some parishes that did not explicitly state that they had a select vestry in their

**Table 3.1** Parishes with select vestries and assistant overseers in 1832, according to the Rural Queries

| County | Number of parishes answering in county | Number of parishes | | | | | Percentage of parishes | | | | |
|---|---|---|---|---|---|---|---|---|---|---|---|
| | | Select vestry only | Assistant overseer only | Both | Neither | No answer | Select vestry only | Assistant overseer only | Both | Neither | No answer |
| Dorset | 14 | 0 | 0 | 0 | 6 | 8 | 0.0 | 0.0 | 0.0 | 42.9 | 57.1 |
| Hampshire | 57 | 2 | 14 | 8 | 24 | 9 | 3.5 | 24.6 | 14.0 | 42.1 | 15.8 |
| Somerset | 20 | 1 | 6 | 5 | 5 | 3 | 5.0 | 30.0 | 25.0 | 25.0 | 15.0 |
| West Sussex | 32 | 0 | 7 | 1 | 13 | 11 | 0.0 | 21.9 | 3.1 | 40.6 | 34.4 |
| Wiltshire | 25 | 0 | 5 | 6 | 10 | 4 | 0.0 | 20.0 | 24.0 | 40.0 | 16.0 |
| Total | 148 | 3 | 32 | 20 | 58 | 35 | 2.0 | 21.6 | 13.5 | 39.2 | 23.6 |

Source: BPP 1834 (44). Part 2. Question 32. Several answers to the Rural Queries were not included because the answers related to an area larger than a parish (such as magistrate's divisions) and/or they represented duplicate answers, or a response was completed about the parish in the Town Queries. For a list see Chapter 2, Table 2.1 and note 187 in Chapter 2.

reports alluded to the existence of a select vestry, whilst some parishes also stated that they had 'Perpetual' or 'Acting' overseers as opposed to assistant overseers.[40] In both instances, I have included such respondents in the select vestry and an assistant overseer tallies respectively. Notwithstanding such issues, 56 responses to the Rural Queries from Wessex and West Sussex explicitly stated that their parish adopted at least one of the two main provisions of Sturges Bourne's 1819 Act, whilst 58 respondents had neither provision in place. Thus, when taking into account the number of parishes that failed to respond to the question, 37.1 per cent of parishes answering the Rural Queries from this region positively stated they had adopted one or more of the two main provisions of Sturges Bourne's 1819 Act. We can also deduce that those parishes which engaged with the legislation were more likely just to appoint an assistant overseer, or to appoint an assistant overseer alongside a select vestry, than just to adopt a select vestry.

The main limitation of figures of adoption as derived from the Rural Queries is that they only formally record the number of parishes that had either a select vestry or an assistant overseer, or both, at the time the returns were taken. Many more parishes had previously appointed a select vestry and an assistant overseer and subsequently abandoned them. The Rural Queries provide some hints as to this complexity where especially detailed responses provided a potted history of their relationship with the Act. For instance, the respondent from Pulborough in West Sussex wrote: '[t]here has been a Select Vestry, but it is now discontinued, not being deemed beneficial'.[41] At North Curry (Somerset) there was no select vestry, and the assistant overseer had been appointed only nine months prior to the return.[42]

The adoption (and possible abandonment) of these policies can be traced over time through the use of Parliamentary Returns produced by the Select Committee on Poor Rate Returns, which, from 1819 to 1834, collated the number of parishes with select vestries and assistant overseers in England and Wales. Figure 3.1 shows the percentage of parishes in England as a whole and in the selected counties that appointed a select vestry between 1819 and 1834. As shown, select vestries were initially more popular in the sample counties than in England as a whole; however, the number of select vestries in other areas of the country rose much more rapidly in the early 1820s, so that by 1825 the percentage of parishes with select vestries in the selected southern counties was slightly lower than the

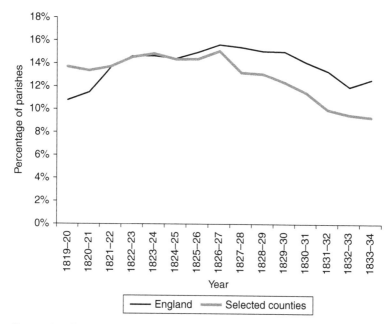

**Figure 3.1** Percentage of parishes in England and selected southern counties of England with a select vestry, 1819–34

national average. Thereafter, the number of select vestries throughout the country and – in greater proportion – the southern sample counties fell. By 1833–34, less than 10 per cent of parishes in the study counties had a select vestry in operation.

There was a very different pattern in assistant overseer appointments compared to select vestry appointments (Figure 3.2). The proportion of parishes with assistant overseers in both England and the study counties increased over time, albeit unevenly. Between 1825 and 1827 there was a significant increase in the proportions of parishes with assistants, and, again, a steady increase during the early 1830s. Notably the policy was always more popular in Wessex and West Sussex than in England as a whole. These figures, however, conceal the numbers of parishes that adopted the policies for only short periods of time and those parishes that continued to use select vestries and assistant overseers over extended periods of time. This is because the annual returns did not provide the names of parishes adopting each policy, only the number of parishes with a select vestry

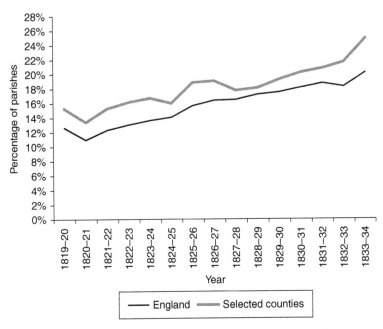

**Figure 3.2** Percentage of parishes in England and selected southern counties of England with an assistant overseer, 1819–34

and the number of parishes with an assistant overseer in each county. Although we cannot tell from the returns exactly *which* parishes had adopted, and continued to operate under, the enabling Act and at what times, it can be deduced that more parishes adopted Sturges Bourne's provisions at some time than the crude figures suggest.

The main reason why open vestries adopted the provisions of Sturges Bourne's 1819 Act was to reduce poor relief expenditure. This is further illustrated by the data presented above, which shows that both schemes markedly increased in popularity during years of economic strain. Moreover, many of the parishes that responded to the Rural Queries in the south explicitly noted that a saving had been made in the poor rates after implementation of the Act.[43] This reflects Neuman's findings in Berkshire, noted above. A larger number still also noted, albeit vaguely, that the Act was 'advantageous' or produced 'a good effect in the parish'.[44] All was not entirely positive in Wessex, though. Five parishes noted that the Act had very little effect, including Tillington (West Sussex) where it was observed that '[t]he effect has not been beneficial'.[45]

The appointment of assistant overseers and select vestries was influenced, as well as restricted, by a number of other factors. As noted, assistant overseers were particularly useful in rural parishes with widely dispersed populations. At Burghclere (Hampshire) it was reported that '[a]n Assistant Overseer is necessary in this parish, the cottages being scattered'.[46] Here, it was likely that the parish asked the assistant overseer both to collect the poor rates and to distribute poor relief payments. Assistant overseers working in larger parishes tended to have a higher salary, reflecting the labour required to supply relief to the poor in all corners. William Finder, for instance, was paid £50 by the vestry of Kings Somborne (Hampshire), a parish that covered 8,000 acres. Eling (Hampshire), at 10,960 acres, some of which was on the New Forest fringe, paid their assistant overseer £60 per annum.[47] Select vestries, on the other hand, could only be introduced in parishes that had a sufficient number of large landowners to create the select vestry in the first place, the Act stipulating that at least five individuals were needed for a select vestry. Many rural parishes in the south of England were, however, dominated by a small number of large landowners. At Old Shoreham (west Sussex), for instance, it was reported that the reforms were not adopted because 'there … [was] no resident Farmer in the Parish but myself'.[48] It is possible that such parishes, and many urban parishes, could have already had an exclusive relief-granting body in place, such as those parishes acting under Gilbert's Act and Local Acts to provide workhouses. As outlined earlier, though, this did not necessarily deter the individual parishes within unions from acquiring a select vestry. Indeed, it is striking that the same factors that limited the adoption of select vestries in rural southern England were also replicated in the capital. Parishes such as Southwark and the City of London, as Green relates, were too small to operate a select vestry, whilst many other London parishes 'operated, however poorly, under private local acts'.[49]

There were two stages to the formal adoption of Sturges Bourne's provisions: a vote from ratepayers in favour of the provision, and the approval of magistrates. At both of these stages, plans to adopt the legislation could be scuppered. By far the more controversial of the two key policies was the select vestry, not least because it placed relief administration in the hands of the few. Besides, many parishes had a long tradition of appointing assistants for their overseers, thereby rendering the new legislation instantly familiar. Open vestries that had already adopted restricted and weighted votes under the 1818 Act also introduced select vestries with apparent ease. Other open vestries had more unpredictable decision-making processes. In Hinton Charterhouse, near Bath, the 'principal paymasters' voted in favour of a select vestry whilst the small ratepayers opposed the move, therefore a select vestry could not be appointed. It was reported that one man who had lived in the parish for 40 years but had never sat on the vestry decided to attend that particular meeting and vote against the measure, reinforcing social historians' long-held assumptions that smaller ratepayers sided with the poor rather than with the bigger farmers.[50]

Not only did these local dynamics impact on the initial votes for a select vestry, but they also generated complex administrative histories. As Wells related, the 'Westbourne select vestry was soundly defeated on one occasion, while Ticehurst's retreated several times'.[51] Yet the reappointment of select vestries also depended on their effectiveness. Indeed, if a select vestry had not actively undertaken measures to reduce relief expenditure it was unlikely that it would be appointed again. Amport, for instance, had once had a select vestry but reported that 'it is now given up, in consequence of non-attendance of the members'.[52] Only four or five farmers attended the fortnightly meeting of the select vestry at Mottisfont (Hampshire), so relief was left to the discretion of the assistant overseer.[53] Some parishes even levied fines on those who failed to turn up, to ensure that a sufficient number of people were present to make decisions.[54] It appears that the Royal Commission's claim that select vestries were poorly attended, as noted above, was broadly accurate.

The role of magistrates was also potentially problematic. According to Wells, the magistrates at the Battle Petty Sessions supported, and even promoted, the policies developed and decisions made by the select vestries. Indeed, the majority of relief refusals brought to the sessions by individuals remonstrating against the decisions were rejected, especially those based on moral grounds. This reinforced the views and decisions made by the select vestries and assistant overseers, which, in turn, buttressed the legitimacy of adopting the measures. This, to Wells, was strong evidence that magistrates in the south-east generally 'supported the central tenets of Sturges Bourne'.[55] Such a harmonious working relationship did not hold throughout southern England. Evidence from Parliamentary Papers suggests a much more complex relationship. It was reported by many parish officers that select vestries brought beneficial effects, including a reduction in the poor rates, and magistrates supported their endeavours, yet it was also noted that parishes encountered difficulties with their magistrates.[56] In Shepton Mallet (Somerset) a select vestry was voted in by the ratepayers in 1822, but the magistrates refused to ratify it.[57] As Snell notes, this was because Sturges Bourne's Acts were a 'move against the power of the magistracy' in that, although open vestry decisions could be overturned by one magistrate, select vestry decisions had to be overturned by two.[58] The independence that appointing a select vestry would bring parish authorities was certainly understood by the parish officials. As one Hampshire vestry stated: 'that no effectual measures can be adopted for the employment of the Poor till the Parish shall be made less dependent upon the Magistrates, by placing itself under the operation of the Act for the establishment & regulation of Select Vestries'.[59]

Even in places where select vestry appointments had been ratified by magistrates, magistrates could undermine the efforts of select vestries by overturning their decisions. At Holcombe (Somerset) the magistrates paid 'little or no courtesy … to the orders of the select vestry'. According to the parish officers, the poor would constantly 'fly to a magistrate' for an appeal of the vestry's decision, thereby giving relief claimants 'the upper hand of the parish'. Select vestries needed, the Holcombe respondents contended, 'stronger and more efficient powers … independent of magistrates'. In the following year, the select vestry effected no savings and the poor rates increased. By 1825, the select vestry had been abandoned, the blame for its demise placed on the 'determined opposition shown to all its measures, by the magistrates'.[60] This strikes at the more general tension between parish officials and magistrates in the administration of relief under the old poor laws. The vestry clerk of Chiddingly (East Sussex) believed the business of the select vestry would be 'done much better' without the 'interference' of magistrates.[61] It is important to note, though, that many other parish officials believed that magistrates were not a nuisance, but rather provided a useful mechanism by which claimants could be heard, thus keeping the parish in check.[62] Either way, magistrates could make or break a select vestry.

## Relief provision under Sturges Bourne's reforms

The next four sub-sections of this chapter assess the impact of Sturges Bourne's poor law reforms on relief provision. As already detailed, the measures reflected, and thus legitimised, the actions of pre-existing forms of select vestries and proto-assistant overseers. These subsections therefore draw upon not only the policies and practices of select vestries but also those of open vestries and other relief-granting bodies, such as workhouse committees, where relevant. Whilst this offers further elucidation, it also demonstrates how the ethos of Sturges Bourne's reforms filtered into the practices of other economising parishes, affecting many more people's lives in the early nineteenth century than previously thought.

*Inspecting the poor*

Upon appointment, a select vestry usually reviewed the relief provided to those in regular receipt of support, and then reviewed those who claimed relief irregularly. Assistant overseers signed an agreement, requiring the sanction of two magistrates, which stipulated their task, alongside setting rates, of collecting rates, keeping the accounts, issuing relief and investigating the circumstances of relief claimants. At Droxford (Hampshire), assistant overseer John Dollar was instructed to 'make enquiry as to the Character and Circumstances of the Person or Persons applying for such relief'.[63] At Bishop's Waltham (Hampshire), James Perrin was told to 'enquire into the character circumstances & condition of all Persons applying for relief of his her & their family & to report thereon to the rest of the Parish officers'.[64] Other parishes' instructions were similar, closely following the language and ethos of Sturges Bourne's legislation.

Once at the parish pay-table, the select vestry wanted to *see* the poor and question them as to their situation. Particular members of families were asked to attend the vestry. In 1822, the Botley (Hampshire) select vestry ordered that Joseph Thomas and all of his family should attend the next meeting, the select vestrymen wanting to obtain more detailed information about their circumstances.[65] Occasionally, specific groups of the poor were asked to attend. For instance, the Fareham (Hampshire) select vestry asked all those receiving relief for bastard children to present themselves.[66] There were serious repercussions for those not adhering to the select vestries' stipulations. In 1833, the Winsford (Somerset) select vestry asked Ann Crockfield to bring her eldest daughter, aged ten, to attend the next vestry. When she failed to attend, her regular allowance was stopped. At a subsequent meeting, Ann did present her daughter to the select vestry, claiming that her daughter had been unable to attend the previous meeting because she had a lame foot. The excuse did not wash with the select vestry: Ann's pay was reduced to five shillings a month on the basis that her eldest daughter was 'fit' to be bound as an apprentice.[67] Occasionally acquaintances would be sent to the vestry on the claimant's behalf, invariably with little effect. In April 1824, William Fidow required assistance from Corsham (Wiltshire) parish, sending a third party to make his claim to the select vestry. The vestrymen were not satisfied with the representation and stipulated that William must attend 'himself' or he would not be relieved.[68]

Once in the vestry, it was expected that the poor would detail their circumstances, including their occupations, earnings and living arrangements, and relief was refused if such information was not divulged. At Botley, William Whitlock was not allowed any further relief because he failed to give an account of his earnings over the last fortnight.[69] A similar stance was also taken by some open vestries during the 1820s. William Evans and James Cole attended a Wimborne Minster (Dorset) vestry in 1829, but on failing to give an account of their earnings, the parish refused to pay their house rents. In his family's worsening situation, William's wife claimed poor relief. As well as being frowned upon for being 'without her husband', she had also failed to give an account of her husband's earnings. When this information was finally provided by the family, it was looked upon with suspicion. The following month, William attended the vestry and detailed his weekly earnings (12s 10d) and rent (1s 6d). This was, according to the vestry, a very unsatisfactory account of his earnings.[70] It is little wonder then that select vestries therefore resorted to asking employers directly for a list of employees and weekly wages.[71] In some instances even the employer's wages were placed under scrutiny. Mr Watts, of Fareham, was accused by the select vestry of not paying sufficient wages to a male labourer called Edwards. Edwards, and his family, were offered the workhouse, rather than an increase in outdoor relief, possibly in the hope that Watts would increase his wages.[72]

Through their investigations, select vestries also knew about alternative forms of welfare available to parishioners, with those questioned about their circumstances having to reveal details not only about their family circumstances and living arrangements, but also about their membership of local friendly societies ('clubs'). On hearing that clubs would not pay out for a claim, the select vestry would often take the issue further to prevent their having to relieve the individual from parish funds. When an unwell Nathaniel Hayward turned up to the Corsham select vestry, stating that his club refused him 'pay', the gentlemen decided that their assistant overseer should take the matter to a magistrate.[73] Select vestries were well aware that individuals subscribing to a friendly society would reduce the parish's liabilities if the person later needed assistance. As such, 'topping up' club payments to afford a claimant proper relief might appear to have contravened the spirit of Sturges Bourne's 1819 Act, but it would still be far cheaper than having fully to relieve the individual. For instance, Elizabeth Clothier, a parishioner of Chew Magna, received just 18 pence per week from the club, probably on account of illness. The select vestry agreed that this payment was too low and she was given five shillings per month from the parish purse.[74] Parishes also *used* the poor's membership of such clubs to reduce their own expenses. For instance, when in 1830 the parish of Wimborne Minster decided that Thomas Scutt should go into the poorhouse, it was ordered that the overseers should receive his 'Club money'.[75] Due to the benefits these clubs brought to the parish finances, it is unsurprising that the select vestrymen also encouraged the poor to retain their memberships. One man was given three shillings a week 'as long as he remain on the Club'.[76]

Even if the poor did not attend the pay-table, parishes with assistant overseers could still find out about claimants' circumstances, the assistant overseer being ordered to survey the poor and relay any information back to guide the relief decision. Indeed, the assistant overseer – who was also the workhouse master – of Wimborne Minster was authorised by the parish vestrymen to 'hire a Horse at the expense of the parish to inspect the state of the poor in the outskirts of the parish'.[77] On many such occasions, vestries and select vestries ordered assistants to visit particular individual claimants and assess whether or not they actually needed relief. For instance, one assistant overseer was asked to visit a man who had asked for money to pay for his rent and 'enquire into his Case'.[78] Surveillance extended beyond salaried assistant overseers' actions: evidence from minute books suggests that the everyday lives of the poor were also under scrutiny from the wider rate-paying community. For instance, one Winsford man applied for 'assistance' during his wife's illness, but because a Mr Paul had seen her 'fetching water' that morning, her illness was deemed fictitious and the claim rejected.[79] Individuals who claimed for relief from their settled parish but were resident elsewhere were arguably the most vulnerable to economising practices, since the claims made in their 'pauper letters' were relatively easy to reject. For instance, Corsham parish on one occasion rejected all the letters they had received from Manchester, Leeds and Brentford asking for relief.[80] Another select vestry recorded the letters they had received, frequently noting alongside: 'not to be answer'd'.[81] Occasionally an assistant overseer would be asked by the vestry to attend the non-resident poor, in order to obtain first-hand information as to the claimant's circumstances. In 1835, the vestrymen of Clutton (Somerset) even went so far as to send their assistant overseer to Monmouthshire to enquire into the case of William Parker, who had requested regular non-resident relief payments.[82]

*'Character and conduct'*

From the very foundation of the Elizabethan poor laws, Hindle tells us, 'it fell to overseers (and to the ratepayers and vestrymen who elected them) to construct the calculus of eligibility according to which the entitlements of the poor were computed'.[83] Whilst the Settlement Acts of the late seventeenth and early eighteenth centuries constrained the number of individuals eligible to claim relief in each parish, in order to determine each parishioner's eligibility, parish administrators divided parishioners into two crass categories: the 'deserving' and the 'undeserving'. Although historians, such as José Harris, suggest this distinction was not universally put into practice, Sturges Bourne's 1819 Act explicitly promoted it through the assessment of claimants' 'Character and conduct'.[84] Consequently, in adopting parishes, the morals of the poor came under greater scrutiny. Receiving welfare provision meant that, as Steve Hindle has put it, 'the range of personal choice that paupers might make about their personal conduct and ethical behaviour' was reduced. In seventeenth-century England the distinction between deserving and undeserving was manifested through a series of expectations: church attendance, industriousness, sobriety and deference.[85] This sub-section shows how Sturges Bourne's second Act allowed parish officers to reinforce these same expectations with vigour.

Those in regular receipt of outdoor relief and those living in workhouses were expected to attend church. The select vestry of Whiteparish (Wiltshire) noted that if the workhouse residents did 'not attend some place of worship on Sundays their Days allowance for the Day be stop'.[86] The Botley select vestry issued similar directions, specifically targeting 'every man who is on the Parish'.[87] These policies had not only resulted from select vestry discussions, but some open vestries also issued similar directives.[88] Unlike open vestries, however, select vestries frequently remonstrated with individuals thought able to have prevented their own poverty, especially those whose unemployment was believed to be their own fault. In Fareham, Richard Couzens and William Hawkins were refused relief on the grounds that 'they had left their work and from their general Character they were therefore considered as idle & profligate'.[89] Henry Noble's claim for 'work' was rejected by a select vestry in Whiteparish, which also requested that he bring a letter 'stating the reason he was Discharged from Esq. Boltons employ'.[90] The vestry obviously had its suspicions that Henry had been dismissed due to his own misdemeanours, and as such, this errand had no other purpose than to reprimand Henry. It was not just leaving or being dismissed from work that put individuals' entitlement to assistance in jeopardy. At Botley, John Dowling was not employed by the parish because 'he has neglected to apply for work which he knew of'.[91] Women's work was also placed under the spotlight, with one Wincanton man's regular family allowance stopped on account that 'his wife refuses to work'.[92]

Select vestries also insisted that claimants be sober and publicly grateful for their relief. Not only was drunkenness disruptive, but it was also evidence of profligacy. The Chew Magna vestry, for instance, decided to 'discontinue all relief to persons who are found spending their time or money in a public house'.[93] Likewise, Henry Cannon was refused work by the Wincanton select vestry because he was a 'habitual drunkard'.[94] By 1833, the parish of Botley no longer operated a select vestry, but its punitive legacy lived on when the open vestry penalised Joseph Terry for 'repeated drunkenness' by refusing to find him employment.[95] At Fareham, more drastic action was taken. Not only was relief to be stopped to those 'found Tippling in a Publick House', but it was decided that a 'list of persons receiving parochial relief be given to the Landlords of all the Publick Houses'.[96] The select vestry at Wimborne Minster even tried to stop the 'problem' at source: the magistrates were asked to reprimand one landlord who not only sold alcohol during Divine Service but also allowed two paupers to drink so much one Sunday that they were 'unable to return home till Monday morning'.[97]

Behaviour that did not reflect the expected deference from claimants had repercussions. Regular relief was often reduced for behaviour referred to as 'bad conduct' or for 'misdemeanours'. The Wincanton select vestry gave Robert Day three shillings temporary relief, rather than his regular allowance, for bad conduct.[98] James Burin would have received a new pair of shoes had he not 'abused some of the members of the Select Vestry' in Winsford; instead they gave him four shillings towards the cost of a pair.[99] Relief was also curtailed for less dramatic acts of disrespect towards the vestry. Two men were turned away by the select vestry in Whiteparish because they had not attended at the 'proper time'.[100] Whilst bad conduct was condemned, it appears that good conduct was rewarded, albeit very rarely. James Phillips received two pounds for his '[g]eneral good conduct' in Botley.[101]

Select vestries also restricted relief to those claimants who had the potential to poach – doubly unacceptable as both an illegal practice and evidence that they could supplement their living – by refusing relief to claimants with dogs.[102] At Botley, those with dogs would not be 'exonerated from paying the poors rate'.[103] It is worth noting that this policy was also occasionally applied by ordinary vestries,[104] whilst other types of exclusive relief-permitting bodies also adopted the policy. For instance, the 'Court of Guardians' in Southampton, the town operating under a Local Act, in 1824 ruled that one woman's weekly pay should be stopped on account of her keeping a dog. It was reported in the local press that, soon after the decision, the woman presented a dead dog at the pay-table, thus dramatically proving to the authorities she was now without her dog.[105]

Vestrymen had generally assumed that if someone could maintain an animal, they could maintain themselves. Animals should be sold before relief was sought. This may have also been a factor in their dislike of dog ownership, although other animals were also perceived as a source of income. Relief claimants with pigs were told to sell them before they were granted relief. For instance, Robert Martin of

Broomfield (Somerset) was refused a shirt for his boy on account of 'haveing sow & pig'.[106] Larger animals that assisted labourers to undertake heavy tasks were also used as a reason to refuse relief. James Norris was instructed by the Corsham select vestry to get rid of an ass before he tried to claim for relief again.[107] The Chew Magna select vestry thought that Joshua Emery 'ought' to sell his two donkeys 'to support his family'.[108] Neuman found a parish in Berkshire that created a general policy to prevent claims for relief from those with a horse *and* cart.[109] Select vestries sometimes refused loans to those labourers who wanted to buy animals to assist them in their work. Isaac Bauchamp's request for a loan to enable him to buy a donkey had been rejected by the Whiteparish select vestry regardless of the fact he would have used it to draw heath from the common to be sold as fuel. Such an occupation may have supplemented or replaced his regular parish relief.[110]

Although relief was overwhelmingly tailored to each individual's behaviour, there were occasions when select vestries issued general policies in relation to the 'conduct' of their parishioners. The Millbrook (Hampshire) select vestry set a special small rate of relief for those individuals 'whose Conduct shall appear not to deserve any more allowance'.[111] We also know that individuals and families were given less relief according to their stage in the life-course, or whether they were a widow(er) or single woman with a bastard child or children, as examined above.[112] The Millbrook select vestry, however, had moved one step beyond this to produce blanket policies based on character.

### *The attack on outdoor relief*

Select vestries paid particular attention to the amount of outdoor relief being given to individuals and their families through magistrate-set 'Speenhamland-style' scales. As introduced in Chapter 1, such scales were in widespread use throughout rural southern England and were intensely disliked by the Royal Commission of 1832. In Hampshire, where 74 per cent of parishes that answered the Rural Queries allocated relief according to a scale, select vestries were particularly attuned to such issues.[113] In 1822 at Nether Wallop, it was decided that 'married paupers applying for Relief be allowed so much as will make up their wages the amount of a Gallon Loaf and sixpence Pr Head for their respective families'.[114] Many select vestries, not surprisingly, attempted to alter scales with a view to saving money. At East Woodhay, also in 1822, the very nadir of the post-war agricultural depression, it was agreed that all monthly allowances would be reduced in proportion to the reduction in the price of provisions.[115] In other Hampshire parishes a seasonal reduction in monthly allowances was implemented. At Hambledon in 1824 it was stipulated that all persons who received monthly pay and 'who leave the Parish for work during the Harvest month' shall receive no allowance during that month, and that half of all claimants' monthly pay during harvest 'shall be taken off'. The following year, the policy became more stringent: all monthly pay was stopped during the harvest month.[116]

All regular outdoor relief maintenance payments, whether allocated according to a Speenhamland-style scale or not, came under closer scrutiny in parishes that had adopted the provisions of Sturges Bourne's Act. Many select vestries had made lists of those receiving outdoor relief. The select vestry of Broomfield, near Bridgwater, for example, decided to start a brand new book to detail the 'Allowances of the poor' in the year of their election (1821). On the left-hand side of each page, the claimants' names were recorded, alongside the sum of their weekly allowance and details of their family. Along the top of the page were column headings 'Character', 'Wages', 'Employers', 'Complaints of the Poor', what they were 'allow'd' and 'Why allow'd or disallow'd'. These relief tables allowed the parish to review the relief allocated to the poor, both regular and extra amounts, in relation to the broader household economy. Confirming the purpose of these charts, the select vestry agreed several times throughout 1821 that payments were 'Sufficient for the support of the Paupers'.[117] Other parishes had similar ideas, with some creating lists to allow for systematic checks upon specific groups of relief claimants.[118] Wimborne Minster parish officers, for instance, made lists of people with bastard children and those receiving house rents.[119] The open vestry at Fareham directed the parish surgeon to provide the select vestry with a list of all persons 'Ill and unable to work on Wednesday morning in every week' prior to the meeting of the select vestry.[120] The select vestry was to allocate relief with this information in mind and catch those 'faking' ailments.

The 1819 Act, as noted, permitted select vestries to issue loans rather than provide relief, with magistrates empowered to chase individuals for repayments. Loans were often allocated for purchasing one-off items rather than for maintenance; for example, money was

loaned to William Strongmell to purchase a saw by the select vestry of Fareham.[121] Whilst parish loans enabled individuals to obtain
expensive items that would help them procure work, in the past many
parishes would have either bought these items for the individual, or
at least paid for part of them. Some select vestries decided to permit smaller loans to certain relief claimants. At Botley, for example, it
was directed that no mechanic or handicraft person be allowed money
when out of work except in the form of a loan.[122] Clearly, this policy
was meant to deter individuals from claiming relief unless absolutely
essential. Larger sums of money were, on occasion, offered to individuals without the stipulation that the sum of money be paid back to
the parish purse. Such sums were again expended on items to enable
individuals to work. The select vestry at Hambledon gave John Merritt
£6 so that he could purchase a horse and cart and thus, at least in theory, earn a living for himself and his family. The members of the select
vestry noted that he had 'been Lame a long time and a great expence
to the parish'. The same select vestry also gave £5 to George Kiln on
condition that he not apply for parish relief for at least two years.[123]

Occasional payments – sometimes called 'Extras' – were also curtailed under the direction of select vestries. House rents and poor
rates were commonly paid by parishes in the rural south, but this
practice was increasingly challenged.[124] In 1825, the select vestry at
East Woodhay (Hampshire) resolved that the practice be stopped,
and at Corsham the select vestry told the overseers to 'call on the
Landlords' to reduce rents.[125] Other one-off payments were curtailed,
including clothing and textiles; some select vestries even decided to set
aside dedicated days for the receipt of clothing and textile requests.[126]
Again, these were attempts to control the volume of claims and dis-
tributions. Numerous other strategies were also developed. First,
limits were set on the clothing provided to parish apprentices. The
select vestry of Angmering set a maximum cost of 30 shillings for
each female taken into service.[127] Second, clothing was given, but the
cost was to be repaid as a loan. William Savage's relief illustrates this
point. He was provided with a shirt by the Whiteparish select vestry
whilst a patient in the local infirmary, but rather than being given the
shirt, he was asked to reimburse the parish 'in the Harvest'.[128] Third,
items were issued to the poor in the hope that they returned the article. Bruton started to loan blankets to the poor – prior to the passage
of the Acts – in 1815.[129]

Taking a very different approach, in 1832, the Wincanton select vestry established a clothing 'society' with the purpose of *assisting* poor parishioners in procuring clothing. Similar to the rules of charity-based penny clothing clubs, every person was allowed to contribute one penny a week to a clothing fund that had its own dedicated secretary and treasurer.[130] At the end of the financial year, the parish would then add half of the amount saved during the year from the poor rates. If the scheme worked, the select vestry had thereby managed to get the poor to fund the cost of two-thirds of their own clothing. Also in the early 1830s, the select vestry of Wimborne Minster directed that a subscription be raised for the purpose of procuring clothing, fuel and other necessities for the use of the poor.[131] As such, the parish tried to alleviate their financial burdens through the promotion of charity. Giving relief in fuel, such as wood and coal, was also curtailed under select vestries. Claims for services that enabled the poor to heat their homes had also been restricted, such as in west Somerset where peat-turf digging services were refused to some parishioners.[132]

*Renewed interest in workhouse policy*

Although Sturges Bourne's 1819 Act was not a 'workhouse act' per se, several of its clauses encouraged the use of workhouses as part of newly restricted regimes. Drawing on the example of the Ticehurst select vestry, Wells notes that on claimants' first appearance at the pay-table, many able-bodied relief recipients and the children of relief-receiving families were asked to enter the workhouse.[133] Similarly, the Fareham select vestry directed that 'all Persons having relief whose Friends or Children cannot support them are to be taken into the House'.[134] Similar forms of 'workhouse test' were also ordered in Berkshire, with one parish offering claimants only indoor relief and supplying them only with coarse bread.[135] Whilst some select vestries filled their workhouses in an attempt to reduce relief costs, others specified that workhouses were exclusively for certain social groups. The Chew Magna select vestry collated a '[l]ist of people to leave the poorhouse or to be taken before the justices and prosecuted according to law', whilst Whiteparish decided that 'families occupying apartments in the poor houses ... be given notice by the overseers to quit and give up possession at the end of one month from the date of notice'. In other parishes, then, families were forced to find their own accommodation.[136] The motivation behind all such policies was inevitably economy. This was clearly demonstrated by attempts to charge rents to poorhouse residents – as at Shipley (west Sussex) and Fareham – and to put poorhouse residents to work.[137]

Workhouse management regimes were also targeted by select vestries. Indeed, there was a particular enthusiasm amongst select vestries to start 'farming' their indoor poor to save the parish money and to revise workhouse regulations accordingly.[138] The Corsham select vestry decided to farm out its poor to Mr Isaac Roberts, who was then responsible for the maintenance and employment of the indoor poor.[139] In other parishes, such as Bishop's Waltham, it was the open vestry that directed the select vestry to obtain a 'farming' contract.[140] Nevertheless, in previous years, the select vestry at Bishop's Waltham considered 'farming' the poor of the parish independently of the open vestry.[141] From the 'articles of agreement' between Mr Isaac Roberts and the Corsham select vestry, the select vestry clearly still wanted to retain some control over the management of the workhouse. The articles allowed members of the select vestry to visit the poorhouse and settle disputes between Roberts and the residents.[142] This was also the practice at Fareham where the contractor was 'subject to the inspection of the select vestry'.[143]

The administration of pauper work was central to many select vestries, not least in managing parish employment schemes for their under- and unemployed outdoor poor. Such schemes are too complex to detail in full here and have been discussed elsewhere.[144] Parish make-work schemes had been in operation since the Elizabethan poor laws and were common throughout southern England by the 1800s. It is unsurprising that select vestries also organised similar schemes. The Wincanton select vestry, for instance, directed unemployed labourers to dig parts of the parish land ('Ball Common' and the 'Brick yard') and to build and maintain parish roads.[145] In 1832, it decided to set a separate 'labour' rate and duly allocated labourers to work for ratepayers in what was a more elaborate employment system holding ratepayers accountable for the wages of labourers.[146] Such schemes gained in popularity in the rural south and south-east of England in the 1820s. This may have been the result of the publicity surrounding the apparently successful adoption of a similar scheme at Oundle, Northamptonshire, in 1822.[147] Throughout the south, parishes such as Eversley adopted the labour rate system directly as a result of hearing or reading about the 'Oundle plan', though others, such as Wincanton, only adopted the practice after it had been formally legitimised in the 1832 Labour Employment Act.[148] Similarly, the select vestry of Bruton set up a scheme 'according to the provisions of the said Act'. Within this scheme, able-bodied men with families would receive between seven and eight shillings per week and 'Lads and aged Persons' would receive between four and six shillings.[149]

When parish work was made available to the poor, it was important that the wages could sustain labouring families. At the same time, regulating labour costs ensured parish work was not more desirable than ordinary work, and by setting minimum wages the ratepayers could ensure that they were not being undercut by one another. After enquiring into the wages given to 'independent' labourers, one select vestry paid their labourers no 'more [than] one shilling per week less than the wages given by the occupiers for labour of equal value'.[150] Clearly, many select vestries also followed the directions of magistrates when setting minimum wages. At New Alresford (Hampshire), single men were given sixpence per day for their labour by the 'recommendation' of the magistrates.[151] Select vestries not only set the wages of those working on and off the parish, but also made enquiries for those searching for work. In 1823, the Broughton (Hampshire) select vestry heard how William Gale was unable to gain sufficient custom as a collar-maker. The select vestry offered to 'find him such work as the Officers shall direct at the regular pay of the Parish'.[152] Other select vestries were more opportunistic. In 1819 Mr Billis, the Fareham assistant overseer, was directed to take the 'names of all single men applying for relief with a view of sending them to Work at the Arundel Canal'.[153]

As stated, Sturges Bourne's 1819 Act also permitted parishes to acquire up to 20 acres of land for the employment of the poor. According to Jeremy Burchardt, this policy was 'rarely acted on'.[154] Evidence suggests that select vestries did, however, work the poor on newly acquired land, such as in Horsted Keynes (west Sussex) where relief recipients tended potato crops on rented fields.[155] Select vestries used other land-based schemes in their plan to reduce poor relief. The ratepayers directed to employ labourers in Wimborne Minster were ordered to allot each of their workers with a quarter to half an acre of arable land to be cultivated 'in their leisure hours' and by 'parts of their families not otherwise employed'. No rent would be charged until the end of the first year, and if it could not be paid by a labourer the overseers were obliged to pay instead. To encourage the labourers to cultivate their land well, the select vestry planned to reward those who had 'managed their land best' and had 'received the least aid' from the parish.[156] Whilst this promoted industrious habits and 'independence' from parochial relief amongst the labouring poor, it would also reduce poor rates. More conventionally, select vestries rented land and allotted portions to individuals. In 1831, the Wimborne Minster parish, building on its earlier policies, considered renting an entire farm before settling on renting a portion of land for spade husbandry.[157] The stipulations linked to allotment provision could be particularly stringent. In 1833, the select vestry at New Alresford decided to hire ten acres of land to be let to male labourers 'on condition that such poor persons shall discharge themselves from all liberty for the parish to find him work & relief after the expiration of six months from the time of such taking'. William Butler was the first candidate for the scheme and was given one-and-a-half acres with the select vestry paying for the ploughing and sowing of Butler's patch with wheat and barley by way of 'encouragement'.[158]

## Conclusion

Sturges Bourne's policies facilitated parishes to adopt a more rigorous approach to relief administration. Select vestries paid close attention to relief scales and other regular maintenance costs, extra payments, employment – on the parish or otherwise – and indoor relief. Blanket policies reduced the relief provided to defined groups of claimants. Loans were made and repayments vigorously pursued, and, at the same time, employment stipulations were developed to promote self-sufficiency and reward industriousness. Indeed, possibly one of the most absurd and counterproductive attempts to reduce relief costs was made by the select vestry of Shipley, which, in the 1820s, decided to stop providing tools to those employed by the parish, except 'Bars, Malls, and Pikes for Stone digging'.[159] These were all measures introduced with the intention of saving the parish money. In particular, the inspection of the poor and attempts to gauge individuals' character and conduct were illustrative of a more residualist relief system at work. This enabling legislation tended to reinforce the distinction, first developed in the Elizabethan era, between the 'deserving' and 'undeserving' poor. Furthermore, Sturges Bourne's provisions permitted a select group of individuals to enquire into the lives of relief claimants, whose living arrangements, work, illegal pursuits, ailments, possessions and leisure activities were all closely scrutinised. Knowledge of these aspects of claimants' lives allowed officials to restrict individuals' opportunities to obtain statutory relief. So whilst open vestries could undertake such inquiries, Sturges Bourne's legislation *supported* and *encouraged* these actions.

The details of how parish policy developed in relation to assistant overseers and under the auspices of the select vestry are necessarily complex, but, it is important to note, they were not always derived from the parish itself. Magistrates exerted some influence over their decisions, which suggests that there was some cooperation between magistrates and the parish authorities in some localities. Select vestries also took on board the policies developed by other parishes. As noted above, the Oundle plan found its way to Eversley and was subsequently implemented in 1822. This raises interesting questions about the nature of social policy development under the old poor law, especially regarding the role and importance of 'policy transfer' from place to place. Further research is needed to better understand how select vestries developed policies that mirrored those being promoted by organisations outside the statutory relief system. Indeed, the provision of allotments from 1830 onwards was linked to the efforts of the Labourer's Friend Society, 'whose effective campaign' had 'promote[d] allotments as the most plausible remedy for the social problems of the countryside'.[160] Again, it appears that not all policies implemented by local poor law authorities had originated from local governance, but rather inspiration was often derived from other poor law authorities and organisations beyond the parish and even parliament.

Although the establishment of select vestries was more controversial amongst some small ratepayers and magistrates than the appointment of assistant overseers, the examples used above demonstrate that some relief-restricting practices were implemented without officially appointing either a select vestry or an assistant overseer. This does not demonstrate the lack of importance of the official legislation; rather, on the contrary, such evidence is suggestive that the ethos of Sturges Bourne's Acts was pervasive. Perhaps such parishes were avoiding the structures and labels 'select vestry' and 'assistant overseer' because of how controversial they were amongst both ratepayers and rural workers alike. For instance, assistant overseers received mental and physical maltreatment in the Swing Riots. Labourers at Brede (East Sussex) attempted to 'remove' their assistant overseer by placing him in a cart, which had been especially constructed to enable the men to work on the roads, and dumping him over the parish boundary. This was a practice repeated throughout the Weald.[161] Select vestries were also targeted by protesters. Three men, aged 30, 22 and 17, were sent to the House of Correction for three months in November 1822 for rioting in a select vestry meeting in Northiam in East Sussex.[162] In the same county, vestries and select vestries frequently offered rewards to catch those sending threatening letters; the letter pinned to the Mayfield vestry door and addressed to the overseer was particularly direct in its denunciation of reformed regimes: 'Wee do Intend Washing Our Hands inn Your Blood'.[163] Whilst the thoughts and feelings of relief claimants on the appointment and operation of Sturges Bourne's reforms await systematic analysis, it is apparent that reactions were hostile. To Swing activists, and the labouring class before 1830, the select vestry was the site within which a more restrictive and punitive relief scheme came into existence, and the assistant overseers were the 'face' of the dreaded new system.

## Notes

1  R. Wells, 'Poor-law reform in the rural south-east: the impact of the "Sturges Bourne Acts" during the agricultural depression, 1815–1835', *Southern History*, 23 (2001), 53; D. Eastwood, *Governing Rural England: Tradition and Transformation in Local Government 1780–1840* (Oxford, 1994), p. 128.

2  Eastwood, *Governing Rural England*, p. 128.

3  A. Brundage, *The English Poor Laws, 1700–1930* (Basingstoke, 2002), p. 48; D. Eastwood, 'Bourne, William Sturges (1769–1845)', *Oxford Dictionary of National Biography* (Oxford, 2004). Online: www.oxforddnb.com/view/article/3012 (last accessed 18 January 2016).

4  J.R. Poynter, *Society and Pauperism: English Ideas on Poor Relief 1795–1834* (London, 1964), pp. 223–48.

5  S. King, *Poverty and Welfare in England 1700–1850: A Regional Perspective* (Manchester, 2000), p. 26. See Wells' study of their adoption in two Sussex parishes: 'Poor-law reform in the rural south-east', p. 59.

6  S.G. Checkland and E.O.A. Checkland (eds.), *The Poor Law Report of 1834* (1834, Harmondsworth, 1974), p. 199.

7  S. Webb and B. Webb, *English Poor Law History, Part 2: The Last Hundred Years* (1929, London, 1963). p. 43.

8 Wells, 'Poor-law reform in the rural south-east', p. 59.
9 Examples include: L.H. Lees, *Solidarities of Strangers: The English Poor Laws and the People, 1700–1948* (Cambridge, 1998), p. 41; S. Williams, *Poverty, Gender and Life-Cycle under the English Poor Law* (Woodbridge, 2011), pp. 78, 95.
10 Wells, 'Poor-law reform in the rural south-east', pp. 52–115; M. Neuman, *The Speenhamland County: Poverty and the Poor Law in Berkshire, 1782–1834* (New York, 1982), pp. 180–3; A. Digby, *The Poor Law in Nineteenth-Century England and Wales* (London, 1982), p. 7; D.R. Green, *Pauper Capital: London and the Poor Law, 1790–1870* (London, 2009), pp. 88–91.
11 Neuman, *The Speenhamland County*, p. 183, cited in Brundage, *The English Poor Laws*, p. 51.
12 For an introduction to the politics of the parish, see K. Wrightson, 'The politics of the parish in early modern England', in P. Griffiths, A. Fox and S. Hindle (eds.), *The Experience of Authority in Early Modern England* (Basingstoke, 1996), pp. 10–46. Research with a focus on the micro-politics of poor relief includes: D. Eastwood, 'The republic in the village: the parish and poor at Bampton, 1780–1834', *Journal of Regional and Local Studies*, 12 (1992), 18–28; S. Hindle, 'Power, poor relief, and social relations in Holland Fen, c. 1600–1800', *Historical Journal*, 41 (1998), 67–96; S. Hindle, *On the Parish? The Micro-Politics of Poor Relief in Rural England c.1550–1750* (Oxford, 2004); J. Healey, 'The development of poor relief in Lancashire, c. 1598–1680', *Historical Journal*, 53 (2010), 551–72.
13 Hindle, *On the Parish?*; Lees, *Solidarities of Strangers*.
14 58 Geo. III c.69; B. Keith-Lucas, *The Unreformed Local Government System* (London, 1980), pp. 98–9.
15 59 Geo. III c.12, I.
16 59 Geo. III c.12, I. The select vestry could operate from any time, but it would expire 14 days after the annual appointment of overseers.
17 59 Geo. III c.12, I.
18 59 Geo. III c.12, I.
19 59 Geo. III c.12, XXIX. Magistrates could have also made an Order for the repayment of a loan, and non-payments could result in imprisonment in a Common Gaol or House of Correction.
20 Eastwood, *Governing Rural England*, pp. 129, 176.
21 Wincanton, vestry minutes of 2 May and 25 May 1798, SHC D\PC\winc/1/3/1.
22 59 Geo. III c.12, VII. An assistant overseer could continue working until he resigns, dies or the parish revokes his appointment.
23 Eastwood, *Governing Rural England*, p. 177; Brundage, *The English Poor Laws*, p. 52.

24   The assistant overseer was from Bampton; Eastwood, *Governing Rural England*, pp. 177–8.
25   Chew Magna, vestry minutes of 23 January 1769, SHC D\P\che.m/9/1/1.
26   G. Nicholls, *History of the English Poor Law, Volume 2: 1714–1853* (London, 1898), p. 187.
27   Bruton, vestry minutes of 15 April 1811, SHC D\P\brut/9/1/2.
28   Also mentioned in C.J. Griffin, 'Parish farms and the poor law: a response to unemployment in rural southern England, c.1815–35', *Agricultural History Review*, 59 (2011), 184.
29   59 Geo. III c.12, XII, XIII and XIV, and VIII. Section X also gave parishes permission to sell workhouses. This was not necessarily contradictory because this measure would have assisted parishes to purchase or build larger premises to house parishioners.
30   59 Geo. III c.12, XI. Two magistrates had to ratify the arrangement, whilst the workhouse could not be located more than three miles from the parish.
31   Wells, 'Poor-law reform in the rural south-east', p. 88. Note that Wells does not cite Sturges Bourne's Act itself.
32   Parishes of Boldre, Millford and Milton (Hampshire); BPP 1834. Part 2. Question 22.
33   59 Geo. III c.12, XXXVI. One section of Sturges Bourne's 1819 Act referred to the stipulations of Gilbert's Act about the sale, purchase and renting of land and buildings for the use of the poor; 59 Geo. III c.12, XVIII.
34   59 Geo. III c.12, II.
35   P. Dunkley, 'Paternalism, the magistracy and poor relief in England, 1795–1834', *International Review of Social History*, 24 (1979), 371–97.
36   King, *Poverty and Welfare*, p. 32.
37   R. Wells, 'Social protest, class, conflict and consciousness in the English countryside, 1700–1880', in M. Reed and R. Wells (eds.), *Class, Conflict and Protest in the English Countryside 1700–1880* (London, 1990), pp. 145–7.
38   P. King, 'The rights of the poor and the pole of the law: The impact of pauper appeals to the summary court 1750–1834', in S. King, ed., *Poverty and Relief in England 1500–1800* (forthcoming); also see Williams, *Poverty, Gender and Life-Cycle*, p. 93.
39   S. Webb and B. Webb, *The Parish and the County* (1906, London, 1963), p. 166; BPP 1834 (44) XXXII Report from His Majesty's Commissioners for Inquiring into the Administration and Practical Operation of the Poor Laws. Appendix B.1. Answers to the Rural Queries in Five Parts. Part 3. Question 32 [hereafter BPP 1834].

40  Select vestry: BPP 1834. Part 3. Question 32. Bramshaw (Hampshire); Alternative wording of assistant overseer: BPP 1834. Part 3. Question 32. Pitton and Farley, and Norton Bavant (Wiltshire).

41  BPP 1834. Part 3. Question 32. Pulborough (West Sussex).

42  BPP 1834. Part 3. Question 32. North Curry (Somerset).

43  BPP 1834. Part 2. Question 32. Eling and Romsey Extra (Hampshire); Arundel (West Sussex); Box, Chippenham, Fisherton Anger and Ramsbury (Wiltshire).

44  BPP 1834. Part 2. Question 32. Amport, East Woodhay, Minstead, Nether Wallop, Odiham, Sherfield English, Weyhill and Widley (Hampshire); Batcombe, Brompton Regis, Crowcombe, Nether Stowey, Stogumber and Stoke St Gregory (Somerset); Rogate (West Sussex); Corsham (Wiltshire).

45  BPP 1834. Part 2. Question 32. Bentley Liberty, Whitchurch (Hampshire); Bishop's Hull, Curry Rivell (Somerset); Tillington (West Sussex).

46  BPP 1834. Part 2. Question 32. Burghclere (Hampshire).

47  Colonel Charles Ashe A'Court, 'Notes on every parish in the Winchester Division'; 'Notes on the several parishes in the division of Romsey', November 1834, The National Archives TNA MH32/1.

48  In Old Shoreham (West Sussex) there were only three farmers: BPP 1834. Part 3. Questions 28 and 32. Old Shoreham. In 1870, Wilson classified 65 per cent of parishes in Sussex (using a sample of 300 parishes) as either 'one estate', 'not much divided' or 'in few hands'. J.M. Wilson, *The Imperial Gazetteer of England and Wales*, 6 volumes (Edinburgh, 1870), cited in B. Short, 'Landownership in Victorian Sussex', in K.C. Leslie and B. Short (eds.), *An Historical Atlas of Sussex: An Atlas of the History of the Counties of East and West Sussex* (Chichester, 1999), pp. 98–9.

49  Green, *Pauper Capital*, p. 89.

50  BPP 1823 (570) Report from the Select Committee on Poor Rate Returns, Appendix E, 'Somerset', 'Charterhouse Hinton', p. 18. It is well known that small farmers and crafts producers supported the plight of the labouring class during the Swing Riots, not least because of their own economic insecurity. See E.J. Hobsbawm and G. Rudé, *Captain Swing* (London, 1969); C.J. Griffin, *The Rural War: Captain Swing and the Politics of Protest* (Manchester, 2012).

51  Wells, 'Poor-law reform in the rural south-east', p. 96.

52  BPP 1834. Part 2. Question 32. Amport (Hampshire).

53  Colonel Charles Ashe A'Court, 'Notes on the several parishes in the Division of Romsey', November 1834, TNA MH32/1.

54  A fine of 2s and 6d was levied in Nether Wallop, 1s in Shipley and 6d in Hartley Wintney; Nether Wallop, select vestry minute of 11 April

1825, HRO 93M83/PV1; Shipley, select vestry minute of 16 April 1829, WSRO Par162/12/1; Hartley Wintney, vestry minute of 25 March 1830, HRO 85M76/PV2.

55  Wells, 'Poor-law reform in the rural south-east', pp. 82, 88.

56  BPP 1823 (570) Report from the Select Committee on Poor Rate Returns, Appendix E, 'Somerset', 'Lydeard St. Lawrence', p. 18; 1824 (420) Report from the Select Committee on Poor Rate Returns, Appendix F.1., 'Somerset', 'Banwell', p. 21.

57  BPP 1823 (570) Report from the Select Committee on Poor Rate Returns, Appendix E, 'Somerset', 'Shepton Mallet', p. 18. There is no evidence to suggest that the vote was not legitimate and no reason for the magistrates' refusal to ratify the measure is given in this report.

58  K.D.M. Snell, *Annals of the Labouring Poor: Social Change and Agrarian England 1660–1900* (Cambridge, 1985), p. 117.

59  Millbrook, vestry minute of 9 November 1820, SCRO PR10/8/1.

60  BPP 1826 (330) Report from the Select Committee on Poor Rate Returns, Appendix F, 'Somerset', 'Holcombe', pp. 18, 20–1.

61  BPP 1834. Part 4. Question 44. Chiddingly (East Sussex).

62  BPP 1834. Part 4. Question 44. My review of the answers given to Question 44 of the Rural Queries, 'What do you think would be the effect, immediate and ultimate, of making the decision of the Vestry or Select Vestry in matters of Relief final?' for the counties of Dorset, Hampshire, Somerset, Wiltshire and West Sussex. For instance, in Downton (Wiltshire), Samuel Payne (assistant overseer) expressed that the decisions made by the vestry should not be final because it '[w]ould not be beneficial. Magistrates in this neighbourhood rarely supersede the decisions of Select Vestries of character. In small parishes where no Gentry reside great oppression from the Farmers would follow this plan. Magistrates seldom or never order relief, if the Overseer offers to take the Pauper into the Poorhouse.' The Castle Coombe (Wiltshire) parish answered that the removal of the magistrate from the welfare process would cause 'an immediate rural rebellion throughout the country'.

63  Droxford, vestry minute of 11 November 1819, HRO 66M76/PV3.

64  Bishop's Waltham, vestry minute of 9 July 1819, HRO 30M77/PV1.

65  Botley, select vestry minute of 22 May 1822, HRO 40M75/PV2.

66  Fareham, select vestry minute of 22 May 1819, Portsmouth City Record Office CHU43/2C/1.

67  Winsford, select vestry minute of 15 and 29 April, 13 May 1833, SHC D\P\wins/9/1/1.

68  Corsham, select vestry minute of 4 April 1824, W&SA PR/Corsham: St Bartholomew/1812/9.

69  Botley, select vestry minute of 6 September 1825, HRO 40M75/PV2.

70  Wimborne Minster, select vestry minutes of 6 October, 3 November and 1 December 1829, DHC PE/WM VE2/3.
71  Whiteparish, select vestry minute of 22 September 1832, W&SA PR/Whiteparish: All Saints/830/32.
72  Fareham, select vestry minute of 23 June 1819, PCRO CHU43/2C/1.
73  Corsham, select vestry minute of 18 August 1826, W&SA PR/Corsham: St Bartholomew/1812/9.
74  Chew Magna, vestry minute of 3 December 1824, SHC D\P\che.m/9/1/1.
75  Wimborne Minster, select vestry minute of 22 July 1831, DHC PE/WM VE2/3. There is evidence that the vestries of Wimborne Minster had been held in the 'Club Room' since 1809 and select vestries had been meeting there into the 1830s, indicating a close relationship between the two; Wimborne Minster, vestry minutes, 1809–49, DHC PE/WM VE1/2.
76  Chew Magna, vestry minute of 3 December 1824, SHC D\P\che.m/9/1/1.
77  Wimborne Minster, vestry minute of 26 March 1833, DHC PE/WM VE1/2.
78  Corsham, select vestry minute of 29 September 1826, W&SA PR/Corsham: St Bartholomew/1812/9.
79  Winsford, select vestry minute, 31 March 1834, SHC D\P\wins/9/1/1.
80  Corsham, select vestry minute of 14 October 1825, W&SA PR/Corsham: St Bartholomew/1812/9.
81  Wimborne Minster, select vestry minute of 9 March 1830, DHC PE/WM VE2/3.
82  Clutton, vestry minute of 14 August 1835, SHC D\P\clut/9/1/1.
83  Hindle, *On the Parish?*, p. 257.
84  Harris suggests that commentators believed a distinction had not been maintained in the late nineteenth century under the New Poor Law; J. Harris, 'From poor law to welfare state? A European perspective', in D. Winch and P.K. O'Brien (eds.), *The Political Economy of British Historical Experience, 1688–1914* (Oxford, 2002), pp. 431–2. Alannah Tomkins starts her book with an example of relief given in 1739 to a man, Francis Wheeler, who would have normally been viewed as 'undeserving' at the time; A. Tomkins, *The Experience of Urban Poverty: Parish, Charity and Credit, 1723–82* (Manchester, 2006), pp. 1–3.
85  S. Hindle, 'Civility, honesty and the identification of the deserving poor in seventeenth-century England', in H. French and J. Barry (eds.), *Identity and Agency in England, 1500–1800* (Basingstoke, 2004), p. 38.
86  Whiteparish, vestry minute, 5 December 1834, W&SA PR/Whiteparish: All Saints/830/32.

87 Botley, select vestry minute, 17 July 1822, HRO 40M75/PV2.
88 For instance, in Bury it was 'Agreed that all Pauper's attend church'; Bury, vestry minute of 29 May 1828, WSRO Par33/12/1.
89 Fareham, select vestry minute, 22 May 1819, PCRO CHU43/2C/1.
90 Whiteparish, select vestry minute of 6 July 1832, W&SA PR/Whiteparish: All Saints/830/32.
91 Botley, select vestry minute of 19 May 1823, HRO 40M75/PV1.
92 Wincanton, select vestry minute of 29 December 1831, SHC D\PC\winc/1/3/2.
93 Chew Magna, select vestry minute of 1 October 1819, SHC D\P\che.m/9/1/3.
94 Wincanton, select vestry minute of 20 December 1831, SHC D\PC\winc/1/3/2.
95 Botley, vestry minute of 6 January 1833, HRO 40M75/PV1.
96 Fareham, select vestry minute of 10 November 1819, PCRO CHU43/2C/1.
97 Wimborne Minster, select vestry minute of 19 June 1821, DHC PE/WM VE2/1.
98 Wincanton, select vestry minute of 20 December 1831, SHC D\PC\winc/1/3/2.
99 Winsford, select vestry minute of 9 December 1833, SHC D\P\wins/9/1/1.
100 Whiteparish, select vestry minute of 11 October 1834, W&SA PR/Whiteparish: All Saints/830/32.
101 Botley, select vestry minute of 17 July 1822, HRO 40M75/PV2.
102 For the use of dogs to poach, see D. Hay, 'Poaching and the game laws on Cannock Chase', in D. Hay, P. Linebaugh and E.P. Thompson (eds.), *Albion's Fatal Tree: Crime and Society in Eighteenth-Century England* (London, 1975), pp. 189–253.
103 Botley, vestry minute of 27 April 1834, HRO 40M75/PV1; Neuman found the same order had been created in the select vestry of Thatcham (Berkshire), Neuman, *The Speenhamland County*, p. 182.
104 For an early example, see: Whitechurch Canonicorum, vestry minute of 2 August 1796, DHC PE/WCC VE1/3.
105 *Southampton Herald*, 31 May 1824.
106 Broomfield, Allowances of the poor, select vestry minute of 16 May 1821, SHC D\P\broo/13/2/2. Pigs, unlike all other animals, caused a noticeable odour as well, leading to complaints from fellow parishioners; Winsford, Vestry Minute Book, select vestry minute of 15 September 1834, SHC D\P\wins/9/1/1.
107 Corsham, select vestry minute of 7 May 1824, W&SA PR/Cosham: St Bartholomew/1812/9.

108 Chew Magna, select vestry minute of 31 October 1834, SHC D/P/ che.m/9/1/3.
109 Neuman, *The Speenhamland County*, p. 182.
110 Whiteparish, select vestry minute of 22 September 1834, W&SA PR/ Whiteparish: All Saints/830/32.
111 Millbrook, vestry minute of 25 June 1821, SCRO PR10/8/1.
112 See also S.A. Shave, 'The dependent poor? (Re)constructing the lives of individuals "on the parish" in rural Dorset, 1800–1832', *Rural History*, 20 (2009), 67–97.
113 Hobsbawm and Rudé, *Captain Swing*, p. 47.
114 Nether Wallop, select vestry minute of 21 June 1822, HRO 93M83/PV1.
115 East Woodhay, select vestry minute of 23 April 1822, HRO 27M77/PV1.
116 Hambledon, select vestry minutes of 7 August 1824 and 23 July 1825, HRO 46M69/PV1.
117 For instance, Broomfield, Allowances to the poor, select vestry minutes of 16 May, 13 June and 27 June 1821, SHC D\P\broo/13/2/2.
118 From 1820 Beaminster kept a book containing similar tables, containing the names of individuals and families, plus their ages and respective earnings; Beaminster, Lists of families with earnings, 1820–36, DHC PE/BE OV9/1. Large printed forms were used in the parish of Lindfield to record similar demographic detail, in addition to a range of relief headings: 'Flour', 'Potatoes', 'Work', 'Or Other Relief' and 'Money'; Lindfield, September and November 1820, WSRO Par416/13/2 and 3.
119 Wimborne Minster, select vestry minute of 11 August 1829, DHC PE/ WM VE2/3.
120 Fareham, select vestry minute of 21 July 1819, PCRO CHU43/2C/1.
121 Fareham, select vestry minute of 16 June 1819, PCRO CHU43/2C/1.
122 Botley, select vestry minute of 29 April 1823, HRO 40M75/PV2
123 Hambledon, select vestry minutes of 21 January 1826 and 20 November 1830, HRO 46M69/PV1.
124 BPP 1834. Part 2. Question 21 ('Are Cottages frequently exempted from Rates? and is their Rent often paid by the Parish?'). From the returns received from parishes of Dorset, Hampshire, Somerset, Wiltshire and West Sussex that answered this question, 93.9 per cent frequently or occasionally exempted or paid poor rates on behalf of labouring families and poor parishioners and 71.4 per cent frequently, occasionally or paid in part rents from the poor rates. The latter figure includes parishes that mentioned they rented cottages and other accommodation on behalf of parishioners. For more information about the provision of parish housing under the old poor law, see J. Broad, 'Housing the rural poor in southern England, 1650–1850', *Agricultural History Review*, 48 (2000), 151–70; on what happened to parish property after the Poor

Law Amendment Act, see R. Wells, 'The Poor Law Commission and publically-owned housing in the English countryside, 1834–47', *Agricultural History Review*, 55 (2007), 181–204.

125 East Woodhay, Vestry Minute Book, select vestry minute of 3 May 1825, HRO 27M77/PV1; Corsham, select vestry minute of 9 December 1825, W&SA PR/Cosham: St. Bartholomew/1812/9.

126 For instance, the Broomfield select vestry decided in 1821 to have two days in the year on which clothing would be allowed, a policy extended to four days in 1825: select vestry minutes, 18 September 1821 and 29 April 1825, SHC D\P\broo/13/2/2. Also see the separate 'Clothing accounts', 1810–36, SHC D\P\can 13/2/10.

127 Angmering, vestry minute, 27 May 1829, WSRO Par6/12/1.

128 Whiteparish, select vestry minute of 12 April 1833, W&SA PR/Whiteparish: All Saints/830/32.

129 Bruton, select vestry minute of 31 December 1815, SHC D\P\brut/9/1/2.

130 For literature on the use of clothing clubs and societies, see P. Jones, 'Clothing the poor in early-nineteenth-century England', *Textile History*, 37 (2006), 17–37; V. Richmond, '"Indiscriminate liberality subverts the morals and depraves the habits of the poor": a contribution to the debate on the poor, parish clothing relief and clothing societies in early-nineteenth century England', *Textile History*, 40 (2009), 51–69; V. Richmond, *Clothing the Poor in Nineteenth-Century England* (Cambridge, 2013), pp. 186–211.

131 Rules to join the society were clarified in a meeting on 27 January 1832: Wincanton, select vestry minutes of 12 and 27 January 1832, SHC D\PC\winc/1/3/2; Wimborne Minster, select vestry minute of 18 November 1831, DHC PE/WM VE2/3.

132 Whilst some people still had their turf cut by someone employed by the parish, some individuals' claims were refused, such as Grace Grunter who had previously benefited from the service; Winsford, Vestry Minute Book, select vestry minutes of 23 June 1834 and 20 July 1835, SHC D\P\wins/9/1/1.

133 Wells, 'Poor-law reform in the rural south-east', p. 65.

134 Fareham, select vestry minute of 7 July 1819, PCRO CHU43/2C/1.

135 Neuman, *The Speenhamland County*, p. 182.

136 Chew Magna, vestry minute of 15 February 1833, SHC D\P\che.m/9/1/1; Whiteparish, select vestry minute of 15 September 1834, W&SA PR/Whiteparish: All Saints/830/32.

137 Fareham, select vestry minutes of 9 June 1819 and 14 June 1823 PCRO CHU43/2C/1; Horsted Keynes, select vestry minute of 26 March 1832, WSRO Par384/12/2. Shipley had a price scale fixed in 1829 (under

12 years of age, 4d per day; between 12 and 15, 6d; over 15, 9d; and 'Old Men', 12d) and regulated the hours of parish work; Shipley, select vestry minutes of 16 and 30 April 1829, WSRO Par162/12/1.

138 For instance, Shipley, where the general vestry was asked by the select vestry to obtain a contractor and the select vestry subsequently revised the workhouse regulations; Select Vestry Minute Book, select vestry minute of 29 April 1830, WSRO Par162/12/1.

139 Corsham, Select Vestry Order Book, 22 April 1825 (adverts) and 20 May 1825 (appointment and terms of agreement, articles 6, 7 and 21), W&SA PR/Corsham: St. Bartholomew/1812/9.

140 Bishop's Waltham, Vestry Minute Book, vestry minute of 17 March 1828, HRO 30M77/PV1.

141 Bishop's Waltham, Vestry Minute Book, select vestry minute of 28 April 1828, HRO 30M77/PV2.

142 Corsham, Select Vestry Order Book, select vestry minutes of 22 April and 20 May 1825, W&SA PR/Corsham: St. Bartholomew/1812/9.

143 Fareham, Select Vestry Minute Book, vestry minute of 1 March 1826, PCRO CHU/43/2B/3.

144 Griffin, 'Parish farms and the poor law'; M. Blaug, 'The myth of the Old Poor Law and the making of the New', *Journal of Economic History*, 23 (1963), 151–84; M. Blaug, 'The Poor Law Report re-examined', *Journal of Economic History*, 24 (1964), 229–45; G. Boyer, *An Economic History of the English Poor Law, 1750–1850* (Cambridge, 1990), pp. 15–21. For an analysis of when relief recipients were employed by the parish during their life-course, see Shave, 'The dependent poor?'.

145 Wincanton, Vestry Minute Book, vestry minutes of 9 March 1832 and 24 October 1833, SHC D\PC\winc/1/3/2.

146 Wincanton, Vestry Minute Book, vestry minutes of 3 November 1832, 14 December 1832 and 12 December 1833, SHC D\PC\winc/1/3/2. The labour rate system is where a parish agrees 'a rate, levied against the poor rate assessment, which either had to be paid or the rate-payer had to "discharge"' the rate by employing 'surplus' labour (defined as the number of labourers left over after an allocation of labourers based on either the rates, rental or acreage) at a set wage; C.J. Griffin, '"Employing the poor": the experience and unemployment in post-Napoleonic rural England' (unpublished paper), p. 29; also see references in note 143.

147 Griffin, '"Employing the poor"', p. 29; R. Wells, 'Social protest, class, conflict and consciousness in the English countryside 1700–1880', in M. Reed and R. Wells (eds.), *Class, Conflict and Protest in the English Countryside, 1700–1880* (London, 1990), p. 142; M. Rose, *The English Poor Law 1780–1930* (Newton Abbott, 1971), pp. 57–8.

148  Eversley, select vestry minute of 17 November 1822, HRO 6M77/PV1;
     Wells, 'Social protest, class, conflict and consciousness', p. 142. The Act
     was passed on 9 August 1832 and was officially entitled 'An Act for
     the better Employment of Labourers in Agricultural Parishes until the
     Twenty-fifth Day of March One thousand eight hundred and thirty-
     four' (2 & 3 Geo. IV c.96).
149  The scheme was repeated in 9 October 1834; Bruton, vestry minutes of
     11 October 1833, SHC D\P\brut/13/1/3.
150  Whiteparish, select vestry minutes of 22 September 1832 and 23
     November 1832, W&SA PR/Whiteparish: All Saints/830/32.
151  New Alresford, Vestry Minute Book, select vestry minute of 2 Novem-
     ber 1832, HRO 45M83/PV1.
152  Broughton, select vestry minute of 8 May 1823, HRO 137M71/PV1.
153  Fareham, select vestry minute of 29 May 1819, PCRO CHU43/2C/1.
154  J. Burchardt, *The Allotment Movement in England: 1793–1873* (Wood-
     bridge, 2002), p. 34.
155  Horsted Keynes, select vestry minute of 26 March 1832, WSRO
     Par384/12/2.
156  If any rent after the first year was irrecoverable, the overseers were
     obliged to pay for it from the parish rates; Wimborne Minster, select
     vestry minute of 27 November 1829, DHC PE/WM VE2/3.
157  Wimborne Minster, select vestry minute of 27 November 1829, DHC
     PE/WM VE2/3. Plans mentioned, but no evidence the policy was
     undertaken; Wimborne Minster, select vestry minute of 26 November
     1831, DHC PE/WM VE2/3. The piece of land desired was offered by
     the landowner (Mr Machell) at £50 per year, an offer that was rejected
     by the board; Wimborne Minster, select vestry minute of 28 November
     1831, DHC PE/WM VE2/3.
158  New Alresford, select vestry minute of 29 November 1833, HRO
     45M83/PV1. As Burchardt notes, deciphering the precise motiva-
     tions behind the creation of allotments is difficult. Either way, Sturges
     Bourne's Act of 1819 facilitated parishes to act as the regulators of such
     schemes; Burchardt, *The Allotment Movement*, p. 34.
159  Shipley, select vestry minute of 16 April 1829, WSRO Par162/12/1.
160  J. Burchardt, 'Rural social relations, 1830–50: opposition to allot-
     ments for labourers', *Agricultural History Review*, 45 (1997), 166.
     For research on the work of the Labourer's Friend Society and other
     societies during this period, also see R. Wells, 'Historical trajecto-
     ries: English social welfare systems, rural riots, popular politics,
     agrarian trade unions, and allotment provision, 1793–1896', *South-
     ern History*, 25 (2003), 100–5; Burchardt, *The Allotment Movement*,
     pp. 70–97.

161 C.J. Griffin, 'The violent Captain Swing?', *Past and Present*, 209 (2010), 167, 173–4; Griffin, *Rural War*, pp. 134, 183–4.
162 Griffin, *Rural War*, p. 54; Sussex Winter Assizes, 12 November 1822, TNA Assi94/1896.
163 Griffin, *Rural War*, p. 55; *Sussex Advertiser*, 10 January 1825.

# 4

# Policies from knowledge networks

Before the creation of the Poor Law Commission after the passage of the Poor Law Amendment Act of 1834, there was no central welfare authority to suggest the ways in which parishes should administer poor relief. The basic nature of the stipulations of various statutory poor laws, as discussed in preceding chapters, meant that parish officials were inclined to adhere to the generic stipulations of the old poor laws and then adopt enabling Acts, or create Local Acts, as and when the vestry desired. Vestries implemented policies to suit their own ideas and needs, as well as the local context of the parish. This chapter explores the ways in which officials exchanged information on the practice of relief provision, often creating networks of information exchange. Information was often presented and promoted as 'best practice'. Even though this term has developed in a more contemporary setting, I will demonstrate how it can be read in the presentation and exchange of various pauper policies – there was advice about how 'best' to establish new workhouses, how 'best' to furnish the poor with food and clothing and even how 'best' to deliver first aid.[1] The chapter then explores how parish officials sought to exchange ideas of 'best' practice through conversations and correspondence with individuals including contractors and local gentry. The second half of the chapter considers how local knowledge and information about pauper policies were transferred from place to place after the passage of the Amendment Act. The local networks still exchanged ideas, ideas that were occasionally promoted through publications produced by the Poor Law Commission. Whilst they may initially have known very little about the places within which they were implementing the Amendment Act, Assistant Commissioners were also able to assist in this process of knowledge exchange, and even promote the 'best' practices derived from the localities so that they were applied throughout New Poor Law Unions. Overall, this chapter attempts to show that pauper policy knowledge was not constrained by parish boundaries before 1834, and was not strictly 'top-down' thereafter.

## Under the old poor laws, c.1780–1834

*Correspondence*

Parish officials commonly corresponded with other officials to exchange information. Within a month of adopting Gilbert's Act in 1799 the committee at Alverstoke in Hampshire had received 'information' from a number of other institutions across the county. Alton, which had a new workhouse just seven years prior to the message, provided details on 'the manner of employing the poor there – the sort of manufactory carried on – the mode of feeding the Paupers – the Cost of building the House of Industry – the earnings of the people and other information'.[2] The united parishes at Winchester and Farnham had furnished the Alverstoke committee with a similar account, although the latter had also informed them of 'the Cost of the Buildings ground and Workshops with the dimensions these'.[3] Arguably, the Farnham workhouse had the greatest impact on the establishment of the Alverstoke workhouse. Farnham had rebuilt their workhouse in 1791 and it soon gained a reputation as a model workhouse. Eden noted how the house was built 'on a good plan, and stands in an excellent situation' and since its usage the mortality rates amongst the poor had 'much decreased'.[4] In the very first meeting of the Alverstoke committee, the men asked Mr Wilmot to evaluate the old workhouse and 'plan and Estimate' for 'a House of Industry to be erected on Ever Common agreeably to the plan of Farnham'.[5] They subsequently introduced 'a plan formed on the principles of the Farnham Workhouse together with such improvements as may be thought advantageous'. The Alverstoke committee did not simply want to build an exact copy of the Farnham workhouse; they wanted to adapt it according to their own requirements. Accordingly, Mr Wilmot 'laid before the Committee a ground plan of Farnham Workhouse but on a scale proportioned to the magnitude of this parish together with some suggestions of his for improvement'.

Officials also became curious as to how other workhouses were being managed. The Alverstoke committee first examined the provisions given to inmates in other workhouses. In Farnham, 2s 10d was expended on each pauper per week, whilst the Winton (Winchester) workhouse spent a penny less. These costs were then compared with those incurred by the Alverstoke Guardians whilst running their old workhouse. Mr Wooldridge, the Alverstoke workhouse master who also kept accounts, reported that, on average, 3s 9¾d was expended on their residents. This dissimilarity was, according to the Alverstoke committee, not due to any difference in the cost of provisions. Rather, these other workhouses had fed their poor differently, had grown their own vegetables and reared their own pigs. The Alverstoke committee noted that about one-third of the residents within these workhouses contributed towards the cost of their own maintenance. The Alton inmates earned the largest sum, at 3s 4d, and the Farnham and Winton inmates raised 2s 4d and 2s respectively. These details about feeding and working the poor had enabled the Alverstoke men to make some predictions as to their own savings. The establishment of a workhouse farm and a change of the workhouse diet would save the ratepayers £340. In addition, they thought that the new workhouse would keep 'away the Lazy', or those 'idle and disorderly', creating an estimated saving of £114. In total, the Alverstoke committee believed that the new system would immediately save the ratepayers of Alverstoke approximately £924.[6]

Information was requested by officials as and when it was needed. In 1820s Alverstoke, this information led to a change in the management of the poor. Several of the men attended the poorhouse of a neighbouring parish to ascertain 'whether the Poor were well fed and clothed' after the parish decided to farm their poor. The subcommittee had also contacted 'the several parishes of Fareham, Brighton, South Stoneham, Newington, Portsmouth, and Maidstone' about farming-out policies.[7] Their survey stretched, on this occasion, along the south coast and into the south-east. Portsmouth was the only one of these coastal parishes to have been surveyed by Eden, who described its workhouse as 'neither well contrived, nor well managed'.[8] Evidence gathered by the Alverstoke sub-committee in 1822 suggested that large financial savings could be made through farming out the poor. After the 'most diligent Enquiries and mature Deliberation', the sub-committee recommended the Alverstoke workhouse should follow suit.[9] They decided to follow, more precisely, the scheme at Maidstone, which, although not a Gilbert's Act workhouse, had a long history of operating a workhouse economically.[10] The rationale of the Alverstoke men appears clear: 'because it appears to your committee that by such conditions the necessary comforts of the Poor are amply and liberally provided for', plus 'the duties of the contractor as well as of the Parochial offices are accurately and effectual precautions are adopted for the prevention of errors and abuses in carrying the system into execution'.[11] At the end of August, the committee reported that 'the Parish generally had experienced great Benefit by adopting the System of Farming the Poor'.[12] Evidently, such enquiries exerted an important influence over both the establishment and management of southern workhouses.

*Visits*

Visits to well-managed workhouses in neighbouring districts were also important sources of information. There are many fragments of evidence to suggest that parish officers visited neighbouring parishes with institutions. Parish officials from Bradford-on-Avon (Wiltshire) knew about the 'plan adopted in the work-house of the neighbouring parish of Westbury' for clothing their poor. They could specify the sources of the materials used at Westbury to make clothing, aprons and petticoats, as well as its costs and manufacture.[13] The amount of such detailed information indicates parish officers were conferring with one another. The information exchanged could also be formal in nature. For instance, the select vestry at Millbrook (Hampshire) considered adopting the 'Bye Laws and Regulations' for the management of the poor used in Eling, a neighbouring parish.[14] There is even stronger evidence that officials visited one another's workhouses. Nearly four years after they adopted Gilbert's Act, the Alverstoke Guardians crossed the Solent to visit the workhouse on the Isle of Wight, situated in Newport. The Alverstoke chairman, Robert Forbes, later announced that the Visitors and Guardians had 'been to the House of Industry in the Isle of Wight, enquired into the Economy of that House, and had adopted into this; some of its regulations'.[15] The workhouse visited was part of the welfare regime in one of the two rural incorporations in the south of England. Indeed, the island's parishes were incorporated under a

Local Act of 1771 that permitted a group of Guardians to provide for the poor who could not maintain themselves by admitting them to a purpose-built workhouse in Newport and letting them procure employment outside during the harvest season.[16] After mentioning the visit, the chairman Robert Forbes went into immense detail about food provision. The Newport inmates were 'served at one Table, each person having its allowance in a Tin pan, three times each day always Hot'. The paupers were given meat five times a week, in addition to potatoes, other vegetables and beer, and 'yet', as Forbes stated, 'the Sustenance of each person does not cost above 2s 7½d per Week'. His notes had embraced the discourse of economy. It was this evidence, gathered on their visit, that placed a '[s]trong conviction' that they 'had adopted the best and most Economical plans'.[17]

The Isle of Wight Incorporation continued to be a source of inspiration for the Alverstoke committee. Some 15 years after their first recorded visit, a sub-committee of three men from Alverstoke set out to explore the Isle of Wight's workhouse for the second time. They reported that they had 'examined every part of that Institution accompanied by the Governor and Matrons and can bear testimony to the excellent system maintained there', concluding that 'there are various regulations in that establishment which it may be desirable to adopt'. It was the provision of food, and the way in which it was provided, that again caught the sub-committee's attention. The men recommended making the workhouse dietary more liberal than that provided on the Isle of Wight. They also suggested baking and boiling potatoes, 'avoiding the expensive plan of mashing'. In addition, each table would have a set proportion to be distributed equally between the diners. Each table would accommodate inmates of a similar age, although the sexes would be divided: the boys' tables would be under the superintendence of the '[i]ndividuals who now instruct them in reading and writing', and the elderly would also be separated from the other inmates. As a consequence, more equipment for the distribution of food would be acquired ('Buckets, Trenchers and Wooden Cans') as well as furniture for the elaborate seating arrangements ('Tables and Benches'). The three Alverstoke men reported that whilst the workhouse had informed their suggestions, 'your Sub Committee are not prepared to recommend that in every particular Instance the Example of the House of Industry at Newport should govern that of Alverstoke'.[18] This indicates that they had paid particular attention to how they could *adapt* the practices for their own smaller workhouse on the mainland.

Field trips made by individuals to institutions of interest were important in the dissemination of information. Conversely, individuals with experience of reforming workhouses would visit those *seeking* the advice. John Rutter was a printer and solicitor from Shaftesbury (Dorset). In the early nineteenth century he had attended vestry meetings in Shaftesbury, during which 'his attention was aroused and his feelings excited by various cases of misery'. Regardless of high expenditure on the poor rates in the town, he argued that these funds had not prevented 'want, or even ... nakedness'.[19] Reform, he concluded, was necessary. Rutter, in his pamphlet of 1819, wrote how he sought information 'from the Governors of ... establishments at Boldre near Lymington, at Sturminster [Newton, Dorset], at [St] Martin's in the Fields London, and from several others'. Whilst Rutter only mentioned the names of these parishes, it was the scheme in Fordingbridge (Hampshire) that caught his attention. Here the poor rates were high, the outdoor poor were 'indolent and miserable', the indoor poor were 'anything but industrious and comfortable' and the workhouse was 'a disgrace and burden'. That was before June 1808, when a new 'plan of management' was established.[20]

One individual, Jesse Upjohn, was pivotal to the reforms in Fordingbridge. Upjohn set out to improve the workhouse through his superintendence, with the support of 'a Committee of the respectable inhabitants' of the town, as well as magistrates and 'neighbouring Gentlemen' who had also 'afforded very material support to the new system, and greatly contributed to its success'. He believed his direction and superintendence had produced good results: children were taught 'industrious and sober habits' and 'immorality and profligacy' became rare. Women who were 'little above the dregs of debauchery' on entering the workhouse now left the workhouse with 'considerable competition' arising over them for employment as servants. After the initial outlay of expenses to commence this process, the rates had been reduced to six shillings in the pound. Whilst this was a typical ruins-to-reform story of workhouse improvement, the connection between the two men, Upjohn and Rutter, is intriguing. Rutter called Upjohn 'one of our Townsmen'. Whilst Rutter explicitly expresses how he had examined Upjohn's 'documents', in likelihood the two men had met to exchange their ideas in person.[21] Clearly these networks of individuals, who visited each other's institutions, were pivotal in developing workhouse policies and applying these ideas in workhouses prior to 1834.

*Contractors, the wealthy and the land steward*

Pamphlets, correspondence and visits predominantly occurred between the welfare authorities. Parish officials sought, and were influenced by, those who had made their living working within the welfare system. Of increasing importance in the late-eighteenth- and early-nineteenth-century workhouse was the contractor. The contractor was required to manage the workhouse in return for a fixed payment and the profits (if there were any) of the inmates' labour. This position was of importance to rural workhouses operating under Gilbert's Act, as detailed in Chapter 2, but also other workhouses not founded on any particular Act, such as the workhouse in St Bartholomew's of Corsham (Wiltshire).[22] Consequently, finding the right contractor for their particular needs was an important task for parish officials managing rural southern workhouses.

Contractors competed within a national job market, and so acquiring their interest required advertisements to be placed in national and local newspapers. After the Sutton Union of west Sussex advertised in a national newspaper for contractors in 1793 they received offers from individuals close to home – from Chichester and Hastings – as well as offers from Hereford, Oxford, Norwich, Winchcomb (Gloucestershire) and Tamworth (Staffordshire).[23] After its neighbour, the Easebourne Union, submitted a similar advert in 1818 they received offers from Easebourne itself, Burwash (East Sussex), Ropley Stoke (Hampshire), Birdcage Walk (London) and Watford (Hertfordshire).[24] After advertising the position in 1821, offers came from Steyning (West Sussex) and Colchester, Epping and South Ockendon in Essex.[25] The authors of these proposals outlined the terms upon which they could accept the contract. In 1825, prospective contractors Charles Mott and N.L. Drouet wrote to Alverstoke, stating that 'our wish is to meet the Visitor and Guardians upon the lowest possible terms' whilst being 'remunerated fairly for the very irksome and disagreeable duties attendant upon the undertaking'. This was the same Charles Mott who 'made a large fortune' from managing several workhouses in Newington (Surrey) and Lambeth, experience that led to his appointment as the Assistant Commissioner for London in 1834.[26]

Their letter demonstrates that contractors, just like parish officials, were familiar with the prices of each other's business. Whilst detailing the prices for which they would maintain the poor, Mott and

Drouet made reference to the very agreeable price for maintaining the poor offered to the contractor Mr Pilbrow in Maidstone.[27] Such knowledge may have helped to secure the committee's agreement.

'Farming' the poor was criticised at the time, not least due to the potential for corruption and the abuse of the poor.[28] Although cheaper offers were more likely to be accepted, the officials were also interested in the contractors' aptitude and ideas. Contractors caught the attention of the officials for their sound management skills and the ability to implement structured work, which they thought would produce industrious paupers as well as savings. The committee embraced new employment ideas for the workhouse with particular enthusiasm. The Sutton Union committee accepted an offer from Mr Northwood who had worked in Hereford for five years previously and had a great knowledge of the manufacture of sacks, an employment that, he suggested, would be manageable and profitable.[29] By the following August, a sacking manufactory was considered for the employment of the poor, and not long after a manufactory was established and sacks were soon sold.[30] Other types of employment were only briefly mentioned thereafter, and in 1795 they sold their spinning wheels to the neighbouring Easebourne Gilbert's Union.[31] Into the 1830s, the committees of Gilbert's Unions in West Sussex continued to express their particular desire to work with contractors who had previously been involved in sacking manufactory.[32]

Parish officials also drew on the experience of those involved in local charities. Parish blanket-loaning schemes are a case in point.[33] Often founded and funded by wealthy individuals, the charities were intertwined with statutory welfare provision. In 1800 a local reverend wrote to Mr Tyler, Lord Egremont's steward, to express great happiness that 'the Guardians of the Easebourne Poor House approve of my proposal for a Sunday School' in the workhouse. Although they had the correct books, they required a schoolmaster or mistress with wages of about £3 per annum. He explained that 'Lady Montague Mr Pagnty and myself will contribute'.[34] Mrs Pagnty was keen on funding their religious education, not least because she thought the children were 'in a state of perfect ignorance'.[35] Parish work and training schemes were established in a similar way. For instance, in 1797 the Hampshire parish of Bentley established a 'School for employing Girls by knitting Gloves' by public subscription. Within the first year, the girls in the school had made 2,197 pairs of yarn gloves, 60 pairs of worsted gloves and their parents had made (within their own homes) 971 pairs of gloves. This 'school' was not dissimilar to a workhouse manufactory combined with a warehouse, holding materials and finished garments to sustain a cottage industry. The Bentley vestrymen gave this away, however, by saying that it was a beneficial scheme for the poor as there was no other possible way of employing female children (and their mothers) for the best part of the year. As such, in 1798, the poor rates were expended on the school and a mistress (of not more than £10 a year) akin to those established within workhouses.[36] Although little remains in the archive about how such schemes originated, it is clear that they were funded, and therefore supported, by those not directly employed by the parish.

Contractors and individuals from the wider community transmitted new ideas into the *parish* workhouse system. For those welfare authorities under the oligarchic control of a large landowner, the transfer of information was to be somewhat different. As mentioned above, the full-time clerk and steward to Lord Egremont was William Tyler, who also oversaw the agents on Egremont's other estates in Somerset, Yorkshire and Ireland. He was appointed clerk to the committees of parishes operating under Gilbert's Act as soon as the welfare authorities were established.[37] Regardless of the fact that he was Egremont's employee, Tyler also received a generous wage from the authorities he served and was subject to the same rules as the voluntary members of the committees, even receiving penalties for non-attendance at meetings.[38] Being a clerk to several of the welfare authorities under Egremont's control meant that he was able to transfer information between them. In 1818, for instance, the Easebourne Union committee received offers from contractors to manage the workhouse. He noted that the expiring contract with Mr Mills was set at 3s 6d per head per week, but his new offer was 3d more. Mr Mills' price and those of other offers that came in the post were compared, then Tyler compared these offers against the rate contracted for the 'Petworth Poor' and the 'Sutton Poor'.[39] It is likely that other aspects of workhouse management were compared in a similar manner, if not noted down. This fragment of evidence demonstrates the much broader role of Egremont's steward. Tyler was pivotal in introducing not only welfare reforms to West Sussex, but also agricultural improvements, including experimenting with new crop varieties from London and promoting new animal breeds, most notably

Southdown sheep. New agricultural machinery, such as ploughs and threshing machines, was also dispersed between Egremont's estates.[40] This reflects the purpose of a steward more broadly, 'as "mediator" between rural and urban communities, and between aristocrats and rural labourers', thereby obtaining information in one place and acting upon it within another.[41]

*Publications*

Parish officials, contractors and the benevolent wrote and spoke to one another, whilst stewards went about their daily duties making contracts and suggestions. Through these discussions, tried-and-tested practices and new ideas penetrated parish boundaries, entering into the realms of statutory welfare. There was one further way in which information about welfare practices could move: through publications. This was always the case under the poor laws, *The Compleat Parish-Officer* being an early example. A popular handbook for parish officials, this publication ran to nine editions throughout the eighteenth century.[42] During the late eighteenth and early nineteenth centuries, however, these publications contributed to a national debate about the causes of poverty, the condition of the poor and poor law reform. Arthur Young's *Annals of Agriculture and Other Useful Arts*, a periodical published between 1784 and 1815, also played a part in this national debate, bringing both the discussions of the legislature and local reforms to wider attention.[43] Importantly these journals also serialised the work of early social investigators including Fredrick Morton Eden's three-volume history, *The State of the Poor*, which included a history of poor relief, commentary on legislature, descriptions of the condition and lives of the poorest and a survey of how the poor law operated in 31 counties across England and Wales. His work put 'the views of a moderate and well-informed man' on the stage of national welfare debate, alongside the likes of Thomas Malthus and Jeremy Bentham.[44] Indeed, Eden was cynical about the ability of the parliamentary acts to relieve the condition of labourers – his 'natural law remedy for the disease was the substitution of voluntary charity and self-help for the Poor Laws'.[45] As Poynter acknowledges, the pages contained 'fact and comment, rather than a treatise'.[46] Eden reported the living conditions and welfare provision from selected parishes and townships over the whole of England. This social investigation was widely read, not only by national policy-makers, but by parish officials. This meant his work was of local as well as national significance. Indeed parish officials undertook their own investigations in the style of Eden, taking on the objective recording of facts and figures such as parish populations and poor relief costs – even the parish relief investigations by the Assistant Commissioner Colonel Charles Ashe A'Court for the Royal Commission mimics this style. But as well as informing the methods with which to examine poor relief, it was Eden's findings that were often referred to. A group of men from Bradford-on-Avon, writing about their endeavours in their workhouse, footnoted the changes made in food provision in the Norwich workhouse, stating: '[s]ee a very curious and useful account of this work-house in Sir Fredric Eden's second Vol. p. 477'. So useful were such publications that the Wiltshire men asked, 'would it not be advantageous to the kingdom at large, to have in every workhouse of magnitude, a small library of those books, which refer to the management of the poor, or which treat of domestic economy?'[47] Evidently, there was an appetite for 'fact and comment' at the parish level.

Whilst national surveys had been published for all to see, the endeavours of other individuals about local reforms were also published, usually in the form of a pamphlet, and available locally. This meant that studies of the conditions of the poor and their welfare provision, in places outside Eden's circuits, made it onto people's bookshelves. There were two sorts of 'local' publication. The first were publications purporting to have successfully reformed their workhouses, containing the ruin-to-reform narrative mentioned above. Examples include the aforementioned pamphlet produced in 1801 by four parish officials in Bradford-on-Avon and a pamphlet written in 1797 about the workhouse on the edge of the New Forest at Boldre. It was authored by the famous naturalist William Gilpin, Reverend of Boldre, alongside John Walter and Thomas Robbins.[48] Whilst these individuals' intentions may have been to inspire reforms akin to their own, such publications acted to advertise their own personal successes as well as those of the parish. The second type of publication was written primarily to rally support from individuals for a new scheme of welfare provision. For instance, Rutter's pamphlet was written to raise people's awareness of 'the existing distresses in the Town of Shaftesbury, and the proposed remedy'.[49] As suggested above, pre-existing practices had served as an inspiration to these remedies. There were, therefore, direct links between the first and second types of publication.

The first type of publication contained a description of how a bad workhouse could be successfully reformed and contained instructions and guidance. A multi-authored pamphlet about the Bradford-on-Avon workhouse was written to be used as a handbook. Their seven-point plan at the start of the publication contains instructions on how to allocate relief. Outdoor relief, it stated, should be allocated for a limited period, an additional overseer should be appointed to inspect the poor, 'unworthy' persons should be removed from allowance lists with no appeal and testimonies should be procured for those remaining on allowance lists. Other points stressed the need to prevent people from becoming a future burden on the poor rates: the most industrious poor should be given relief in distress to prevent them from selling their goods and entering the workhouse and medical aid should be given to everyone without delay as immediate attention would prevent relapses.[50] Their final piece of advice was to have a well-managed workhouse. To this end, four sets of rules applied: 'Regulations Relative to the Committee for Superintending the Work-house', 'Regulations Relative to the Internal Management of the Work-house', 'Rules To be observed by the Poor in the Work-house' and 'General Regulations Relative to the Work-house, and Out-Poor'.[51] Subsequently, the workhouse dietary was described and several recipes were detailed at length, including those for four 'cheap Soups'.[52] The last sections of the pamphlet contained advice about medical treatment, including practical guidance on 'the Recovery of the Apparently Dead', how to treat 'the dying', and how to prevent and suppress epidemic fevers and chills. This guidance was assembled from a range of sources, from the Royal Humane Society to a Bristol physician.[53]

Conversely, the pamphlet produced by Gilpin was a more descriptive account of the reforms introduced by the parish officers, and was less prescriptive. The reformers wrote that the old parish workhouse was such a 'wretched place' that in 1792 the parish officers and rate-payers decided 'to build a new one on a better site'. They obtained a 'respectable master and mistress' to have management of the house and 'a monthly Committee of the gentlemen and farmers of the parish' was organised to oversee it.[54] The reformed workhouse was a success, according to pamphleteers, who wrote that the poor cost the parish 'less than half the expence they cost the parish before'.[55] This was teamed with moral reform. The wild landscape of the forest had supposedly encouraged the parishioners' own wild characteristics, appearances and morals; 'a forest', they stated, 'is not the best nursery of virtue'.[56] The authors noted the case of Young, a female pauper whose mother was 'a noisy, bawling woman' and whose father had been sentenced for deer-stealing. Young, as well as suffering from a disease in her hands, was 'agitated'. Once in the workhouse, though, she became penitent and calmer than the rest of her family, and soon became the superintendent of several working children. The authors proudly wrote that she was now part of the 'workhouse family'.[57] The pamphlet contained several other vignettes with similar supposedly happy endings.

The information in these pamphlets did not just arise from the meetings held between parish officers. Footnotes in the Bradford-on-Avon pamphlet reveal references not only to Eden's *State of the Poor* but to other publications. Thomas Ruggles' *History of the Poor* (1793), also serialised in *Annals of Agriculture*, was referred to in the pamphlet on several occasions.[58] Ruggles, an acting magistrate in Essex and Suffolk, established a woollen manufactory in a workhouse school in 1787. The Bradford-on-Avon men thought that this was 'an interesting experiment' and Ruggles' accounts, illustrating that a small profit could be gained from the industry, were quoted in the Bradford-on-Avon pamphlet in their entirety.[59] Ruggles' informa-tion was also used to support the policy that articles should be made, or bought directly from a manufacturer, rather than purchased from a local shopkeeper.[60] When the Bradford-on-Avon men described the workhouse dietary, they quoted Count Rumford's opinion that the use of barley meal in soup was 'at least three or four times as nutritious' as wheat flour, and noted how 'Count Rumford's boil-ers' might be advantageous for the cooking of potatoes.[61] Rumford (Sir Benjamin Thompson) was an American scientist, designer and explorer who moved to Bavaria in the 1780s to take the position of Bavarian Army Minister. It was here he witnessed immense poverty, and developed a new calling: 'to apply the discoveries of science to the everyday life of the poor'.[62] He established workhouses in Munich, became famous for his workhouse dish 'Rumford's Soup', established potato crops in Bavaria and wrote widely about his efforts and the subsequent reduction in poverty. His published work was one of the strongest 'foreign influences' on British social policy at the time.[63]

Reports of reforms closer to home had also been a source of inspiration to other parishes. For instance, the Bradford-on-Avon gentlemen referred to Reverend Thomas Gisborne's plan for supplying milk 'at a cheap rate', which featured in the reports of the Society for Bettering the Condition and Increasing the Comforts of the Poor (SBCP).[64] The Society was established in 1796 by 'a group of evangelical churchmen, friends of William Wilberforce'. The founding member, Sir Thomas Bernard, was a retired conveyancer, former governor of Massachusetts and avid philanthropist. The SBCP's aims were to promote 'the science' of welfare, to promote Christian values and to examine, in their words, 'everything that concerns the happiness of the poor'. Its patron was King George III and many members were well-known bishops, Members of Parliament, lay peers and the landed gentry – an 'illustrious committee', as Poynter put it, including 'philanthropists such as William Morton Pitt, Patrick Colquhoun and the Earl of Winchilsea'.[65] After a request from the Bishop of Durham, a co-founder of the SBCP, Gisborne documented how, in Barton-under-Needwood (Staffordshire), a 'respectable tradesman' decided to use 19 acres of land to keep dairy cattle.[66] The milk was then carried to the centre of the village and sold at a reduced price and in amounts 'regulated by the number of children in the family, and by other similar circumstances'. The plan was of benefit to the poor who, at a time of concerns over food quality, could observe the carriage of milk from the field to the village, therefore seeing it was fresh and not adulterated in any way.[67]

Endeavours at Shrewsbury also received extensive coverage by pamphleteers who thought the workhouse 'admirably directed'.[68] The six parishes of Shrewsbury established a workhouse under the management of a Board of Directors after the passage of a Local Act in 1784.[69] In the 1790s, a pamphlet was published about its management and thereafter Eden also described the establishment.[70] Such exposure meant that the Shrewsbury workhouse gained a reputation, just as the Farnham workhouse had, as a well-managed institution.[71] For instance, the Bradford-on-Avon gentlemen mentioned the ventilation system at Shrewsbury, developed by Sir Jerome Fitzpatrick, and several other matters relating to its domestic economy.[72]

Overall, these pamphlets' footnotes reveal that a variety of other publications had served as sources of information for their welfare practices. And whilst local pamphlets were also quoting nationally important ideas and surveys, the same happened the other way around. Plus, although the printed guidance was often referred to in order to reinforce preconceived ideas, they could also inspire and stimulate reform. The Boldre-based pamphlet appears to have been widely read by parish officials in the south of England, not least because extracts from the pamphlet were placed in the SBCP's own publications.[73] The extracts were selected by the Bishop of Durham, who apparently knew William Gilpin 'well'.[74] The reforms administered by Gilpin *et al.* then reached far and wide. As noted above, Rutter referred to Boldre in his pamphlet about the need for a joint workhouse for the parishes of Shaftesbury, but relied heavily upon the details of the Fordingbridge workhouse. Fordingbridge also grabbed the attention of the parish of Fletching near Uckfield (East Sussex), almost a hundred miles from Fordingbridge. Fletching was under the watchful eye of Lord Sheffield, John Baker Holroyd, an intermittent MP and militiaman who had bought Sheffield Park in 1769.[75] He invested significant amounts of money in the 'improvement of his estate', including for the relief of the poor.[76] He was, more generally, concerned with the poor rates in the northern district of Pevensey and was keen to implement reforms that bettered the 'condition' of the labouring poor, including being prepared to pay for the building of a new workhouse; the parish was only charged for interest on the outlay.[77]

Fletching, as noted above, was involved in plans to form a Gilbert's Union with 11 other parishes, but these ideas fell by the wayside for unknown reasons.[78] The parish officers then produced a poster, presumably under Sheffield's instruction, outlining that 'the establishment of a workhouse in so large a parish as FLETCHING, should no longer be delayed'. When constructed, a handbill was drafted informing local residents of the near-completion of their new workhouse. It was also sent to nearby large landowners, including Lord Egremont. The parish officers of Fletching found Boldre's policies a source of inspiration for their own reforms. They believed that:

> the parish of Boldre was nearly the same as that of the parish of Fletching: the workhouse was in ruins, a considerable sum of money was borrowed, a substantial, convenient and airy workhouse was built on a better site; at the head of which a respectable governor and matron were placed, and the minister and parish officers met monthly

to superintend the establishment, and notwithstanding the mode of subsisting the poor was not as parsimonious as it might have been, yet the expence was reduced to less than half what it had been before.

Thereafter they quoted the exact accounts contained in Gilpin *et al.*'s pamphlet, illustrating that miraculous savings could be accrued after changes to their welfare system. Whilst the vestrymen at Fletching wanted to build a new workhouse, they were not willing to adopt Boldre's policies wholesale. Whilst the workhouse would not exclude the able-bodied and work was thought to be essential to the success of the house, rather than enter into an agreement with contractor or instruct the master or matron to superintend the work, Fletching designed an alternative arrangement. People were employed to instruct the poor, keeping a third of the produce made, whilst a master and matron managed all other aspects of the workhouse. The matron of the house would oversee the girls' domestic work and ensured that girls were fit for service when they left the house.[79] By the end of July 1811, a new workhouse had been built and was ready to receive inmates.[80] Despite the direct inspiration the East Sussex gentlemen owed to Boldre's reforms, Fletching had the confidence to tweak them to form their own plans.

## Under the New Poor Law, *c.*1834–47

Despite of the presence of a central welfare authority, evidence can still be found after the 1834 Amendment Act of welfare officials conferring with one another in the form of correspondence and visits. The first part of this section, therefore, examines the knowledge networks between Boards of Guardians. The next two sub-sections examine the role of the Poor Law Commission in the transfer of locally derived knowledge. The lens is firstly drawn to the role of the Assistant Poor Law Commissioners and then finally to the role of the Commission based at Somerset House.

*Boards of Guardians*

Despite the creation of the central authority, the lines of communication established between welfare officials under the old poor laws did not collapse. Boards of Guardians worked together to administer relief according to the stipulations of the Amendment Act. In the 1830s and 1840s unions in the south of England communicated in order to place their poor in workhouses when their own parish housing was not sufficient, or when they were still in the process of building a central workhouse. The Kingsclere Guardians (Hampshire) placed their poor in the Newbury Union (Berkshire), and the Fareham Guardians (Hampshire), with a workhouse too large for their needs, approached the neighbouring union of Droxford (Hampshire) to offer spaces in their workhouse.[81] The Dulverton Union (Somerset), which consisted of 11 parishes on edge of Exmoor, remained without a workhouse until 1854, possibly due to its small population.[82] In 1839 the Guardians contacted the Tiverton Guardians (Devon), asking them to take some people into their workhouse.[83] The terms offered by the Tiverton Guardians were, however, declined by the Dulverton Board and they decided to approach the Williton Union (Somerset) about a similar arrangement.[84] Negotiations did not commence until 1844 after an Assistant Commissioner had intervened.[85] The Dulverton and Williton Unions entered into dialogue and terms were then agreed.[86] After being informed of the scheme by the Dulverton Guardians, the Commission believed the arrangement was illegal – regardless of their Assistant's ideas.[87] This may have been in reaction to the scandal (1836–37) concerning three boys accommodated in the Fareham Union from the neighbouring Droxford Union who had been severely punished by the workhouse master and schoolmistress.[88]

Other unions discussed the possibility of merging permanently. Indeed, the Droxford Union had initially hoped to unite with the Fareham Union.[89] In June 1836 the Cranborne Union (Dorset) decided to approach the Wimborne Union (Dorset) about merging into one union. The Cranborne Board believed such intentions would lead to 'additional means of classification for the paupers'; that is, the possibility of having more workhouse accommodation in which inmates could be divided, 'saving a considerable expenditure'.[90] After a meeting of two committees formed from both Boards of Guardians, and the approval of the Commission, the merger was complete.[91] These communications illustrate how Guardians from neighbouring unions worked together to provide relief under the new workhouse system. Nevertheless, the majority of correspondence between unions about the administration of the Amendment Act involved more mundane, everyday matters.

In the early years of the New Poor Law, unions had to procure items and the services of individuals to effectively run a workhouse-based welfare system. Boards of Guardians shared information about what items and employees they should find, and copied each other's methods of acquiring them. In 1836 the Warminster Union Guardians (Wiltshire), for instance, decided to advertise for a medical officer by placing advertisements in several county newspapers. Their direction to the union clerk was to make the advertisement 'similar to the one issued by the Guardians of the Devizes Union' (Wiltshire).[92] Furnishing the workhouse economically, with inexpensive and yet long-lasting furniture and equipment, was a major priority. The Guardians preferred to buy tried-and-tested goods. In 1835 the Mere Union Guardians (consisting of parishes from Wiltshire, Dorset and Somerset) asked bedstead-makers in Bristol whether they could provide a sample of single and double frames that they had made for the Bradford-on-Avon Union (Wiltshire).[93] Similarly, the Clutton (Somerset) Guardians purchased a piece of drying apparatus that was based on one fitted in the nearby Axbridge Union (Somerset) workhouse.[94] How the Guardians knew of others' purchases is not specified in the records, although suppliers may have used their past sales record to persuade other Boards of Guardians to purchase their goods. Indeed, the Guardians at the Shaftesbury Union (Dorset) contacted the neighbouring Wincanton Union (Somerset and Dorset) to ascertain the respectability of people offering tenders for the workhouse.[95]

There is evidence, though, that Boards of Guardians were proactive in seeking information about goods. The Clutton clerk noted that the Guardians had correspondence with Barnstaple Union (Devon) about their 'Steam Cooking Apparatus'. The Clutton Union then invited tenders from companies to supply the same equipment.[96] The clerk had also been directed to write to the Guardians of the Keynsham and Bridgwater Unions (Somerset) 'to know how the Cocoa nut fibre answers for bedding'. The Keynsham Union Guardians were willing to report that they bought this bedding fibre and found it satisfactory.[97] Guidance on clothing and medical supplies was also sought by Guardians in a similar manner. For instance, Wincanton Union needed to acquire new clothing and wanted to inspect the clothing provided in nearby Sherborne (Dorset).[98] The Bridgwater Guardians desired to know how Yeovil (Somerset) obtained trusses for the poor.[99] Sometimes, however, Guardians requested products produced by a union rather than the Guardian's opinions. For instance, Kingsclere Union (Hampshire) Guardians asked the Cuckfield Union (West Sussex) Guardians about the terms on which they would supply them with shoes.[100] This request was likely to have been provoked by an advertisement or a handbill.

Communication between Boards of Guardians went further than obtaining advice on the best articles to purchase for the workhouse and its inmates. Once the Shaftesbury Union contacted the unions of Blandford (Dorset), Sturminster Newton (Dorset), Tisbury (Wiltshire) and Wincanton 'to ascertain whether any and what kind of relief is extended to able-bodied Labourers in their respective Unions being in employ on the ground of having large families'.[101] More frequently, though, Boards of Guardians were seeking guidance about the new administrative methods through which the New Poor Law Union workhouses should be run. The Guardians of the Cranborne and Wimborne Union (Dorset) wrote to the master of Abingdon Union requesting a copy of the forms he used to keep 'account of the Clothing taken from Paupers on their admission into the Workhouse'. In the following month the Guardians wrote to the master of the Poole Union (Dorset) 'for a Print of the Stamp used by him in marking the Bedding and Clothes used in the House'.[102]

Forms and stamps had little direct impact upon the relief of the poor, but Guardians shared other information that directly impacted upon relief practices, not least regarding dietary schemes. Although a circular letter containing six 'model' dietary tables had been sent to Boards of Guardians by the Commission in 1836, it was left to the Guardians to 'select ... one which appears to be the best adapted for each particular Union'.[103] As Charles Mott, the Assistant Poor Law Commissioner, suggested, '[u]niformity of diet as to quality can hardly be attained, nor indeed is it absolutely necessary'. The dietary tables adopted by each union were subject to constant revision throughout the nineteenth century, according to both the costs of different foodstuffs and what Mott called 'provincial habits'.[104] Realising the flexibility of the dietary system, Boards of Guardians compared their dietary tables. In 1838, the Clutton Union requested a copy of Shepton Mallet's (Somerset) dietary table and the 'opinion' of the Guardians on it. Within a week the Clutton Board had obtained both the dietaries used in the Shepton Mallet and Keynsham Unions and planned, alongside the medical officers, to consider the 'best' dietary table to be adopted in the workhouse.[105] Such comparisons continued into the late 1840s.[106]

Guardian minute books also leave traces of the conversations between Guardians held in person. The tradition of Guardians and officials visiting workhouses to understand pauper policies and practices continued after the implementation of the New Poor Law. The Bridport (Dorset) Guardians wanted to observe several meetings of the Guardians in the neighbouring union of Beaminster (Dorset) in 1837.[107] In July 1836 the Reverend Junior Kitson of Marksbury parish requested permission for two Keynsham Guardians to sit in on a Board meeting of the Guardians in the neighbouring Clutton Union and inspect their plans for the new workhouse. Permission was granted and the Keynsham Guardians reciprocated the favour by allowing the Clutton Guardians to attend one of their meetings.[108] New workhouses were planned with some consideration of the benefits of workhouses already standing, as had been the case before the Amendment Act. Many examples can be drawn upon from the region to illustrate this point. The Kingsclere Guardians, for instance, had come to a final decision on what building to construct after consulting 'the Plans already adopted in other Unions'.[109]

Some unions, which were advanced in the process of establishing the new workhouse system, became something akin to schools for the staff of other unions. Guardians often arranging for their employees to receive training within other unions before taking up their duties. The Mere Guardians asked the neighbouring Wincanton Union if it would be possible for their newly appointed workhouse schoolmistress to 'pass a short time in the work house school ... to learn the system'.[110] This request demonstrates that the Guardians did not just want the staff to know what to do, information that would eventually flow from the Commission, they wanted their staff to receive some practical knowledge of how to do it before undertaking their positions.

Guardians further demonstrated their conscientious nature by looking to their neighbours for advice on staff wages. The activities of the Droxford Board in 1844 provide a case in point. Inmates were permitted to practise their religion within the workhouse grounds and could be visited by 'any licensed minister of the[ir] religious persuasion'.[111] Some Boards allowed inmates to visit local places of worship, usually under the supervision of workhouse staff, whilst other Boards, such as Droxford, decided that ministers would visit the workhouse on a regular basis. Uncertain of the rate to pay a chaplain for such visits, the clerk asked eight nearby unions for details of their chaplains' tasks and salaries. After seven replies, the Board decided that although their chaplain had more onerous duties than the neighbouring unions, his salary should be reduced to £40.[112] There was an additional incentive to set the wages of other, more mobile, groups of union staff in this way. A master and matron resigned from the Clutton Union to work for the Stroud Union (Gloucestershire) on the 'inducement' of higher wages. When the schoolmaster and schoolmistress wanted to follow, the Clutton Guardians commented bitterly that such actions would generate 'extravagant rivalry between Boards of Guardians'.[113] Boards would compare wages not only for reasons of economy but also to retain their employees. The Fareham Union, for instance, desired the details of the wages and allowances (e.g. food and lodgings) given to the master and matrons of seven unions 'from the County of Hants'.[114] One Guardian of the Bridgwater Union asked the Commission for advice on the wages to be given to their medical officers, and in the same letter mentioned the wages set in the Sherborne and Dorchester Unions.[115] Such comparisons did not always mean the Guardians could overcome demands for higher wages, as Chapter 5 will show.

*The 'eyes and ears of Somerset House'[116]*

As demonstrated, information about how to supply a workhouse with goods and services passed between unions, in the form of correspondence and visits. The Commission had also been pivotal in the spread of locally derived knowledge and practices. In 1834 the Commission appointed nine Assistants, their number increasing to 21 by 1836. The Assistants were first sent to the southern counties of England 'which were most heavily pauperised'. When they arrived in their districts, usually formed of several counties, they had 'to secure the general assent of the parochial officials and the local Justices to an immediate grouping of parishes into Unions'.[117] After this, they oversaw the appointment of Guardians and encouraged the establishment of a workhouse. The Assistants had much to endure. As well as the exhaustion (letters to the Commission frequently refer to how worn out they, and their horses, had become), they experienced resistance to the Act particularly in the north of England, and encountered the heavily entrenched local interests in poor relief across much of the country.[118] Assistant Commissioners could at times be naive, cultivating resistance in the south amongst purportedly more paternalist landowners. Indeed, Thomas Sockett, a reverend appointed on Lord Egremont's estate, noted that Assistant Henry Pilkington 'had a map with him and stuck a pair of compasses into it, and swung them round; he formed unions with a pair of compasses; he knew nothing whatever of the localities of the neighbourhood; he never asked for information'. Pilkington was applying the Commission's ideal – that there should be a market town at the centre of every union, and the surrounding parishes should join, thus creating a circle. When Lord Egremont found out that a parish that 'belonged to him' was put into the Westhampnett Union, which was mainly formed of parishes controlled by the Duke of Richmond, he did not want to hear about the New Poor Law ever again.[119]

Although resistance to the new legislation was apparent in most parts of England, by the end of the 1830s, 587 unions had been formed across England and Wales, containing approximately 80 per cent of parishes in England and Wales.[120] So it is worth highlighting a more optimistic picture of the Assistants put forward by historians such as Harling, who argued that they 'were able to secure a modicum of bureaucratic efficiency against the odds' so that locally established powers 'would never again go entirely unquestioned'.[121]

After the establishment of unions, it was the duty of Assistants to offer directions on how to manage the new workhouse-based relief system. Assistants visited Boards of Guardians, but such visits were infrequent because of the number of unions they had to oversee. As such, it was much more common for Assistants to offer directions through correspondence. It is worth examining an example of this process in detail here, in order to understand both the influence of Assistant Commissioners, how they asserted their influence and the impact it had on the practices of relief provision in New Poor Law Unions.

Many Boards of Guardians in the south of England turned to the Assistants for advice when implementing work programmes in their workhouses, as encouraged in the legislation of the Amendment Act. The main form of employment advocated by Assistants A'Court and Edward Carleton Tufnell was bone-crushing. A'Court, who was appointed during the Royal Commission to investigate parish relief under the old poor laws and worked for the Poor Law Commission from the outset, initially formed unions within a district containing Dorset, Hampshire and Wiltshire. The first unions to be formed, and therefore the first to have adopted bone-crushing, belonged to Hampshire (Alton and Fordingbridge) and Wiltshire (Alderbury, Tisbury and Warminster).[122] The Hartley Wintney Union (Hampshire) was soon to follow. In October 1838 they installed a bone mill 'at the recommendation and the knowledge of the Assistant Commissioner'.[123] In 1838, the Fareham Union enquired into the benefits of having a mill. After receiving a letter from A'Court, they decided to defer their decision until he had visited them personally, when they would receive 'the benefit of his personal advice and assistance' on the matter.[124] In the summer of 1835, Tufnell travelled with A'Court to form various unions across these three counties. A'Court said it was 'delightful to act with such a colleague' and in a region where he was so well known.[125] Thereafter, Tufnell started forming his own unions, in Dorset, Somerset and Kent.[126] It appears that Tufnell was influenced by A'Court's decisions, and would often refer to adopting A'Court's strategies when writing about his own progress to the Commission, including the setting of poor rates.[127] Unsurprisingly, therefore, Tufnell was also a keen advocate of bone-crushing. By the end of 1840, the able-bodied were crushing bones in 15 unions in Hampshire, 7 in Wiltshire, 5 in Dorset and 3 in Somerset.[128] In April 1842 Tufnell started superintending the Gloucestershire unions, where he suggested that they should also adopt bone-crushing employment for the able-bodied. The Stroud Guardians, for instance, stated that 'the crushing of bones was first introduced into our workhouse not only under the sanction of Mr. Tufnell ... but by the recommendation of that gentleman'.[129]

It is clear that the Assistants thought this form of employment was the best possible form of employment. The Cranbook Guardians (Kent) requested Tufnell 'to suggest the *best mode* of employing the able-bodied inmates of the workhouse' and 'in answer to this letter ... Mr. Tufnell recommended the crushing of bones'.[130] This process, whereby the Assistants offered a form of 'best practice', was replicated on numerous further occasions.[131] To further persuade some Guardians, the Assistants had even drawn upon the successes of certain unions when proposing that other unions should adopt a similar practice. When the Warminster Guardians informed the Commission that they had hired out labourers and received their wages in return, the Commissioners were shocked. A'Court was also concerned, claiming that he had no knowledge that the 'ruinous system' had been underway and informed the Commissioners that he had written to the clerk immediately suggesting they bought crushing equipment 'as used in the Alderbury Union'.[132] Alderbury was likely to have been the very first New Poor Law Union to have adopted bone-crushing. Rather than answering the questions of the Wimborne Union Guardians, A'Court directed them to ask Mr Whitworth, the clerk of the Alderbury Union, for a sketch of the equipment used by the inmates in the workhouse, the price of the equipment, the price they received per bushel of crushed bones and whether there was any 'inconvenience' found from the 'offensiveness of the Bones'.[133] Even when unions had commenced employing inmates on bone-crushing, they continued to contact each other for similar information. The Bridport Guardians, who had adopted the employment in 1840, wrote to the Winchester and Andover Guardians two years later to ascertain the weight of bones they gave to each able-bodied man to crush per day.[134] Evidently, Boards that established bone-crushing employment in their workhouses were sources of both inspiration and information to their fellow Boards of Guardians.

The diffusion of advice from Assistants resulted in uneven patterns of practices. The Webbs noted that bone-crushing 'had been widely adopted in the new workhouses after 1835'.[135] This was in part true, in that bone-crushing, similar to other employments such as stone-breaking and oakum-picking, was practised throughout England and Wales. According to returns made in 1844, a total of 104 unions in England and two in Wales were employing workhouse inmates in bone-crushing.[136] It is important to note that this snapshot type of survey did not record the many unions that had implemented and subsequently ceased bone-crushing prior to 1844, the Clutton Union in north Somerset being one such example.[137] Nevertheless, the returns do show a high concentration of unions with bone-crushing work in Wessex (53 unions), other counties in the south-west (15 unions) and the south-east (18 unions) (see Table 4.1). This was as the Poor Law Commissioner George Nicholls detailed when he wrote that the employment was predominantly practised in the 'western and southern counties'.[138] As all workhouses had to employ their poor, and bone-crushing did not require expensive equipment, all unions could have *potentially* adopted the scheme.

**Table 4.1:** Bone-crushing in New Poor Law Unions according to region, 1844

| Region | Counties | | Number of unions with bone–crushing work |
|---|---|---|---|
| Wessex | Dorset | | 10 |
| | Somerset | | 12 |
| | Hampshire | | 19 |
| | Wiltshire | | 12 |
| | | Total | 53 |
| South-west | Cornwall | | 3 |
| | Devon | | 7 |
| | Gloucestershire | | 5 |
| | | Total | 15 |
| South-east | Kent | | 2 |
| | Surrey | | 3 |
| | Sussex | | 13 |
| | | Total | 18 |
| Home counties | Bedfordshire | | 2 |
| | Berkshire | | 2 |
| | Hertfordshire | | 2 |
| | | Total | 6 |
| East Anglia | Cambridge | | 1 |
| | Lincoln | | 1 |
| | Norfolk | | 2 |
| | | Total | 4 |
| Midlands | Derbyshire | | 2 |
| | Oxfordshire | | 4 |
| | Salop [Shropshire] | | 1 |
| | Staffordshire | | 1 |
| | | Total | 8 |
| Country | Union | | |
| Wales | Bridgend and Cowbridge | | 1 |
| | Newtown and Llanidloes | | 1 |
| | | Total | 2 |

Source: BPP 1845 (41) Return.

It does not appear to be the case that bone-crushing occurred in the areas where bone dust may have been in higher demand as fertiliser, such as the arable-intensive south-east. This suggests that the efforts of A'Court and Tufnell resulted in a distinctly regional pattern.

## The Commission's correspondence and publications

After the passage of the Amendment Act, information about local practices was not only circulated between Guardians, and the Assistant Commissioners in conjunction with Boards of Guardians. The Commission itself had acted as a catalyst for the spread of local knowledge and practices. This happened in two main ways: through correspondence from the central Commission, and the subsequent selection, publication and circulation of this correspondence and other similar articles of information.

In the years 1836 to 1845 the Commission received an average of 29,954 letters per annum. After the initial establishment of New Poor Law Unions, it was reported that the majority of this correspondence related 'to the appointment of Union paid Officers, the regulation of their salaries, the alteration of their districts, the consideration and examination of complaints preferred against them, & their dismissal when these complaints are substantiated'.[139] In these letters, the Commission did not simply offer guidance, or reiterate the contents of the Amendment Act, they also referred to practices within other unions. For instance, in 1835 the Commissioner, John George Shaw Lefevre, told the chairman of the South Stoneham Union in Hampshire that they would like to issue an Order to prohibit the provision of outdoor relief to all able-bodied poor. Lefevre wrote that the Order had already been issued to the Hursley Union, which was located just north of South Stoneham.[140] The South Stoneham Board of Guardians were informed, therefore, that their neighbours were more advanced in administering welfare under the New Poor Law. This would have at least reinforced the message that the Commission thought it was desirable for South Stoneham to follow suit.

A great many of the letters that passed between the Boards of Guardians of individual unions and the Poor Law Commission were published in the Commission's 'Official Circular'.[141] These contained information 'directed by the Poor Law Commissioners to be printed, chiefly for the use of the members and permanent officers of

Boards of Guardians, under the Poor Law Amendment Act'. A clue to their purpose comes from their starting sentence, usually along the lines of: '[t]he Poor Law Commissioners, on a review of their minutes, directed that the minutes and correspondence on the following subjects should be printed and circulated for the information of Guardians and officers of the several Unions'.[142] Accordingly, the circulars contained information on a wide range of topics and not just in the format of correspondence. One issue of the 'Official Circular' in 1845 contained information on the potato crop, the auditing of accounts, legislation relating to lunatics, medical attendance to the poor, using the press to locate deserters and copies of a recent General Order.[143] There were, therefore, two tiers of information provided in circulars: general advice about how to administer relief according to the Amendment Act, and the legally binding General Orders. The latter will be discussed in more detail in the following chapter. Of more importance here is the selection and publication of correspondence containing local practices – and the Commission's views on such practices.

Between 1840 and 1846, the practices or queries of at least 428 different unions were referred to by name within the Official Circulars. Many union names were redacted. However, using this figure and the number of unions established by 1840, over 73 per cent of unions had their queries or reports of their practices printed for a national audience. And this did not cease when the Poor Law Board took over, with 407 different unions referred to in Official Circulars between 1847 and 1851. The Official Circulars contained a precis of the letter sent to the Commission and the full Commission's response. Each piece of correspondence selected and published was slightly different from those previously published, indicating that each piece had been something akin to a precedent on that particular topic. First, the query of the corresponding union was outlined and then the Commission's response. This response often contained information relating to how other unions resolved their own dilemmas. A particularly detailed response of this nature was published in an Official Circular of July 1842. Bicester Union (Oxfordshire) wrote to the Commission to enquire as to the 'best plan to adopt in erecting a mill to employ the able-bodied men'. The Commission offered some general advice about the types of flour mills available to buy, mills consisting of steel were common but those containing stones resulted in smoother flour.

They then referred to the Frome Union's steel mill (Somerset), which was expensive to run and had since discontinued, and the Hungerford and Reading Union (Berkshire) mills, which contained a much-favoured burr stone. The Commission then offered the details of the suppliers of the mills, their costs and the numbers of able-bodied men who could work on each mill at once. The Commission then took into account the local contexts of Bicester, which was apparently less 'pauperized' than Hungerford, and 'recommended to the notice of the Board, a mill similar to that at Reading'.[144] The Commission believed this information may have been of use to other Guardians making similar decisions.

It is clear that Boards of Guardians took notice of the contents of the Official Circulars. As detailed above, the Commission offered little advice on how to employ the indoor poor. Most of their effort was expended on how to employ the outdoor poor and dispelling myths that workhouse employments were lowering the market price of manufactured goods such as clothing. Nicholls, there was 'no order or direction by the Commissioners on the subject [of bone-crushing], the mode of employment being left to the discretion of the guardians'.[145] Whilst no formal directions can be detected in the correspondence I examined between the Commission and the unions selected for this book, the Commission had advocated this form of employment in southern England on at least one occasion. In 1842 the Honiton Guardians wrote to the Commission, saying that they were unable to find suitable employment for their able-bodied men. The Commission responded by informing the Guardians that stone-breaking, hand corn-milling and oakum-picking were suitable employments, as well as bone-crushing. This letter was then selected and published as a circular in February 1843.[146] This caused a steep rise in the adoption of bone-crushing in the south-west, as shown in Figure 4.1. In 1843 and 1844 workhouses in Devon (6) and in neighbouring counties, such as Somerset (5), started bone-crushing work. The publication of their advice in the Official Circular thus impacted on the practices being adopted by unions in England and Wales.

The Official Circulars were not just published for the perusal of Boards of Guardians. The Commission itself used them for reference. For instance, the Beaminster Union was in correspondence with the Commission about the allowances of tea and sugar for the infirm poor.

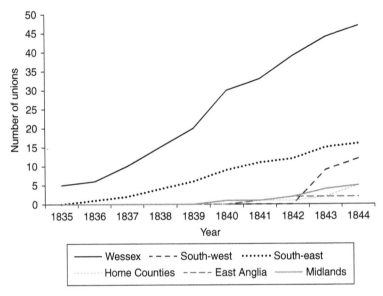

**Figure 4.1** The adoption of bone-crushing in New Poor Law Union workhouses in England, 1835–44

The Commission advised them to refer to number 20 of the Official Circular on the subject.[147] This contained a report from the Assistant Commissioner Henry Parker regarding the allowance of 'extras'.[148] The Guardians often discussed the Commission's directions with union staff, and further evidence suggests that circulars were shown to the inmates themselves. The Warminster Guardians decided that copies of an 1844 circular, about detaining vagrant inmates in the workhouse until midday after their evening's stay, would be pinned up in the workhouse.[149]

Unlike general advice, rules issued by the Commission in the form of General Orders were legally binding. Boards of Guardians did not, however, fear challenging the Commission over the contents of General Orders. The modification of the workhouse rules provides a straightforward example of this point. In 1835 the Commission released 'Orders and Regulations' that stipulated how workhouses should be managed.[150] In 1842 the Commission decided to update the rules because many minute issues had arisen through the 'practice' of implementing the law over the previous seven years.[151] For example, rather than holding religious services at workhouses, many Guardians allowed the inmates to attend local churches and chapels. The Order contained two new rules: that 'a member of the established church' and 'a dissenter from the established church' may attend public worship, except able-bodied female paupers with illegitimate children.[152] The South Stoneham Guardians directly challenged this policy, and in the following year the Commission made a U-turn. A new Order was released, for workhouses in 81 areas including South Stoneham, to allow such women to worship 'in like manner as the other inmates'.[153] As the next chapter will demonstrate, though, Guardians could not always persuade the Commission to alter their rules.

Another publication that was important in the dissemination of local knowledge was the Annual Poor Law Report. The production of Annual Reports was compulsory. Similar to the process by which a report had to be completed by Gilbert's Act committees and submitted to magistrates every year, the Commissioners had to submit a 'general Report of our Proceedings' for perusal by the principal Secretaries of State. The Report was also to be presented before both Houses of Parliament.[154] The Reports contained several key components: a copy of the report submitted to the Secretary of State from the three Commissioners, and a series of appendixes. These usually contained reports from the Assistant Commissioners on their progress in implementing the new system in their districts, documents issued by the Commission, correspondence received by the Commission and returns on the numbers of people receiving relief in each union. Copies of the report were sent to the clerk and chairman of every Board of Guardians and union auditors. Some Assistants asked for more copies and sent these to local landowners and other individuals interested in the new welfare system.[155] On several occasions during 1836 and 1837, A'Court asked for a few copies of the Second Annual Report to be sent to him in Southampton and on the Isle of Wight.[156] In 1838 he met a magistrate in Dorchester who supported the Amendment Act and wished to obtain back copies of the Annual Reports.[157] 'Influential proponents' were also sent copies on request, and of course the reports could also be purchased.[158] Evidently, the Annual Reports had reached a wide audience, from those implementing the Amendment Act to those individuals whose confidence the Commission wished to gain.

Material published within the Reports had been selected very carefully, so there is little surprise that they have been tagged as the 'official publicity channel' of the Commissioners.[159] The coverage given to Sussex proves this point. One union that had adopted the principles of the Amendment Act in an exemplary manner was Westhampnett. The Webbs called it a '"model Union" of the time'.[160] Brundage thought it 'a model of strict poor relief from the outset'.[161] Due to the influence of the large landowner, the fifth Duke of Richmond, parishes smoothly transferred from administering relief under Gilbert's Act to the Amendment Act. This may not be surprising, not least because in preceding years the Duke had run the Westhampnett parish workhouse – which was used as the union workhouse – with a deterrent ethos. The Duke was also a cabinet minister well-disposed to the principles of the Amendment Act, and the chairman of the Board of Guardians until his death. The 'elected' Westhampnett Guardians comprised Richmond's tenant farmers, and the union clerk was his land agent and solicitor.[162] In the First Annual Report, Assistant Commissioner Pilkington referred to the idleness of able-bodied men: in Yapton and Felpham men were in gravel pits doing 'nothing'. Within a year they had 'a better system of discipline': inmates had new work on a corn mill. However, as Pilkington announced, there was not enough labour within the house 'to keep the mill going'.[163] A transcription of the clerk's letter featured within Pilkington's report, full of encouraging statements such as '[w]e have but few applications for relief' and '[w]e have no complaints from the inmates'. This may have been of some relief to the Commission because, on Pilkington's first visit, frequent disturbances 'prevailed amongst the labourers' in the area. Pilkington attributed these disturbances to people 'with no honest plea for asking relief', and told them 'the new law was their friend, rather than their enemy'.[164] These labourers were anti-New Poor Law protesters, clearly angry about the introduction of the New Poor Law. The Second Annual Report contained statements from officials from all over Sussex claiming to have witnessed similar savings and a reduction in 'surplus labour'.[165] Sussex was, however, a county of contrasts. The Reports said little about the reluctance of another landowner, Lord Egremont, to allow his Gilbert's Union to dissolve or abide by the new relief system.[166] This difference was publicly known, and was even the subject of mockery in the local press.[167] In addition, the city of Chichester continued to administer relief under their Local Act of 1753.[168]

Regardless of their inherent bias, it is worth sketching out how the Annual Reports were used to implement the Amendment Act. The publication had been used by the Commission in a similar way to their Official Circulars: to inform Boards of Guardians of the Commission's viewpoints and policies. For instance, in the early months of 1838 the two unions of Warminster (Wiltshire) and Cricklade and Wootton Bassett (Wiltshire) wanted to provide relief to several able-bodied men in the harsh winter weather.[169] The Commission replied to both unions in the same way. They stated that the Act permitted outdoor relief in cases of sudden and urgent emergency, that they had to be notified of every case and that they should look at pages 41 and 42 in the Third Annual Report (1837) for the Commission's views, views expressed when Guardians in Kent, Berkshire and Oxfordshire asked the same question.[170] These pages suggested that Boards of Guardians should offer a place in the workhouse, to try to receive labour in return for any relief and people should only claim outdoor relief as a last resort.[171] Such a response was common practice when policies had already been noted in the pages of a published report.

References to the Annual Reports extended beyond matters of indoor and outdoor relief. In 1845 the Mere Guardians informed the Commission that they wanted to provide a 'deserted' woman and her five children with £20 to move to Canada, to live with their husband/father who had left three years previously.[172] Rather than receive the approval that they had been expecting, the Guardians were told to read a couple of pages in the Eighth Annual Report (1842) where the Commission discouraged the use of the poor rates for emigration for families where a father absconded.[173] On another occasion, an enquiry from a vicar and churchwarden, emigration was sanctioned but again the Commissioners referred to their Annual Reports.[174] The same pages of the Eighth Report were noted alongside a reiteration in the Eleventh Report (1845). The latter suggested that victuals, utensils and clothing for the emigrants' voyage should be provided from the poor rates.[175] Not only do these examples illustrate some development in the Commissioners' policy-making, but they also indicate that the Commission intended that both Guardians and parish officials, who created and implemented a range of policies including emigration schemes, would read their Reports.

**Conclusion**

The multiple ways in which parish officials drew upon networks in order to obtain information about how to 'best' administer the poor laws meant that local practices were not confined within parish and union boundaries. Under the old poor laws, parish officers communicated and visited one another's parishes with great enthusiasm. This custom continued after 1834 between Boards of Guardians. In the latter case, this illustrates that the implementation of the New Poor Law was not simply a top-down process. It was one where Guardians sought advice from each other and trained each other's staff. It also demonstrates that although welfare practices and experiences were diverse under the old poor law, there may have been more similarities than hitherto considered. These are not similarities based on the generosity of poor relief, as King has argued.[176] Rather, there were administrative similarities, based on policy and practices. These are not similarities that can be easily clustered into large geographical units, such as counties and regions, as King has claimed. Rather, similarities existed between neighbouring parishes – and parishes 100 miles apart. The spoken and, critically, written word allowed for the exchange of information between parish officials and Boards of Guardians over distance. This illustrates that each parish official and, later, each Board of Guardians was part of a broader network comprising their fellow welfare administrators. It was a network in which administrators could engage in an informal dialogue, and therefore disseminate information horizontally, outside a rigid top-down model.

Welfare administrators had an acute awareness of the progress made in establishing and managing welfare systems both nearby, in their county as a whole and to some extent even in the country as a whole. Under the old poor laws, this knowledge had in part been produced through the experiences of contractors and the publication of local experiments. The national circulation of contractors and publications enabled information to travel significant distances. And the publication of such local practices by the SBCP boosted their presence amongst the information-hungry welfare administrators. Sir Thomas Bernard declared on behalf of the SBCP:

> Let us therefore make the inquiry into all that concerns the POOR, and the promotion of their happiness, a SCIENCE; let us investigate *practically*, and upon *system*, the nature and consequences, and let us

unite in the extension and improvement, of those things which experience hath ascertained to be beneficial to the poor.[177]

With such an introduction as this, how could the extracts of local
experiments presented in the SBCP's publications be perceived by a
reader as anything other than recommendations about how best to
provide relief to the poor? Their tactics – and subsequent impacts –
are clearly comparable with that of another religious society, the
Society for Promoting Christian Knowledge (SPCK), during an earlier period in the history of English social policy.[178] The interest of
these organisations in workhouse reforms meant that knowledge of
the reforms even travelled beyond England to America. After being
printed in the SBCP's volumes, Gilpin's writing on the Boldre's
reforms were reprinted and read in the parishes of Philadelphia.[179]

Stewards would also collect and share information from different places. Whether under the direction of Lord Egremont or not,
William Tyler was able to compare the prices of contractors. In all
likelihood, he was also able to standardise the rules and nature of
relief provision, and therefore the welfare experience, of a large number of relief recipients living within parishes owned by, or in contact
with, Lord Egremont. Equally, the presence of the steward at committee meetings could have stifled parish officials' desires to communicate, and therefore innovate, beyond his lordship's realms.

Although the Commissioners were often unaware of the extent
of conferring between the Boards of Guardians, they were certainly familiar with how they had been providing relief. Assistant
Commissioners played a pivotal role in overseeing the implementation of the Amendment Act and all subsequent New Poor Law
legislation. How Assistant Commissioners had offered advice, and
how Boards of Guardians sought it in the first instance, had a direct
impact on the ways in which welfare was provided. Reflecting on
the labour enforced in workhouses, Nicholls wrote: '[t]he Kind of
labour on which the inmates of the several workhouses should be
employed, rested entirely with the boards of guardians, who best
knew the circumstances of their several districts'.[180] Nicholls' impres-
sion was inaccurate. The kind of labour on which the inmates of the
several workhouses were employed had actually been influenced by
the Assistant Commissioners, regardless of their local contexts. Both
A'Court and Tufnell had the same answer for all unions enquiring

what sort of work they should implement in their workhouse. They disseminated a particular localised practice, and promoted it as a form of best practice, as the best possible way in which labour could be obtained from the able-bodied male inmates. This calls into question the nature of Boards of Guardians. The very fact that Boards of Guardians were susceptible to ideas of best practice from the Assistant Commissioners weakens the notion, at least within the south, that the locality had retained its independence after 1834. The willingness of local authorities to accept the advice of the Assistant Commissioners could be perceived as a vindication of the view that many local elites had sympathy for poor law reform.[181]

The second half of this chapter illustrated how the Commissioners at Somerset House interacted with and actively spread local practices. Advice was not formed and had not been disseminated in a simple way. Their Annual Reports were undoubtedly, as Brundage puts it, a 'means of influencing public opinion' in favour of the New Poor Law.[182] How the publications of the Commission were used to disseminate best practice should now also receive serious consideration. The Annual Reports and Official Circulars impacted on welfare provision in a similar way to how publications, produced prior to passage of the Amendment Act, impacted on welfare provision. Of course, the choices as to how to provide relief under the old poor laws were wide-ranging and there were fewer stipulations over what types of relief could be offered to different 'classes' of poor, as the Commission put it. Yet, the reduction in the variety of ways in which relief could be offered did not mean that guidance was not needed. As Spicker suggests in his applying social policy text, '[w]herever there are rules, there have to be meta-rules'.[183] It is to these meta-rules that I will now turn, focusing on the decision-making of the Poor Law Commission, especially the policy-making they undertook in the aftermath of New Poor Law scandals.

## Notes

1    'Best practice' is a recently coined phrase, first used in 1984 in an accounting handbook. Whilst its usage is still rather confined to the world of business, it means (and will be used here to describe) 'the practice which is accepted by consensus or prescribed by regulation as correct; the preferred or most appropriate style'; *Oxford English Dictionary*.

2 An advert asking for offers for a contract to build a new workhouse at Alton; *Hampshire Chronicle*, 10 December 1792.

3 Alverstoke, Guardians' Minute Book, 26 November 1799, HRO PL2/1/1.

4 F.M. Eden, *The State of the Poor*, Volume 3 (1797, Bristol, 2001), pp. 716–18.

5 Alverstoke, Guardians' Minute Book, 9 November 1799, HRO PL2/1/1.

6 Alverstoke, Guardians' Minute Book, 26 November 1799, HRO PL2/1/1.

7 Brighton was under a Local Act by 1822, South Stoneham may have been under Gilbert's Act by 1822 (see Table 2.2 in Chapter 2) and the Newington mentioned here could have been Newington in either Oxfordshire or Kent.

8 Eden, 'Portsmouth', in *The State of the Poor*, Volume 2, p. 227.

9 Alverstoke, Guardians' Minute Book, 'Report of the Committee received at a public meeting of owners and occupiers [of] Alverstoke', 28 August 1822, HRO PL2/1/1.

10 Maidstone had a workhouse in operation from 1720; see T. Hitchcock, '*The English workhouse: a study in institutional poor relief in selected counties, 1696–1750*' (unpublished PhD thesis, University of Oxford, 1985), p. 267.

11 Alverstoke, Gilbert's Union Minutes, 28 August and 18 December 1822, HRO PL2/1/1.

12 Alverstoke, Gilbert's Union Minutes, 28 August 1822, HRO PL2/1/1.

13 T. Bush, J. Jones, Jr, T. Tugwell and W. Barker, 'Parochial regulations relative to the management of the poor of Bradford, Wilts; with notes, tendering to promote economy and comfort in the work-house' (Bristol, 1801), p. 37.

14 Millbrook, Vestry Minute, 11 June 1821, SCRO PR10/8/1.

15 Alverstoke, Guardians' Minute Book, 'Report of the Committee to the Parish in Vestry at Easter, 1803', HRO PL2/1/1.

16 For a summary of their Local Act, see 'Fourth Annual Report to The Right Honourable Lord John Russell', T.F. Lewis, J.G. Shaw Lefevre and G. Nicholls to Lord John Russell, 4 August 1838, *Fourth Annual Report of the Poor Law Commissioners* (London, 1838), pp. 18–19.

17 Alverstoke, Guardians' Minute Book, 19 March 1803, HRO PL2/1/1.

18 Alverstoke, Guardians' Minute Book, 29 September 1818, HRO PL2/1/2.

19 J. Rutter, *A Brief Sketch of the State of the Poor, and of the Management of the Houses of Industry; Recommended to the Consideration of the Inhabitants of the Town of Shaftesbury, and Other Places*, second edition (Shaftesbury, 1819), p. iv.

20 Rutter, *A Brief Sketch*, pp. 23–6.

21 Rutter, *A Brief Sketch*, pp. 23–4.

22 St Bartholomew Corsham, Select Vestry Order Book, 31 March 1826, W&SA PR/Corsham: St. Bartholomew/1812/9.

23 Another place may have been mentioned but this was illegible on the letter.

24 Also one unreadable address; Easebourne Union, Correspondence and proposals to farm the poor, 1818, PHA/10937.

25 Easebourne Union, Letters of application (some with testimonials) for the management of the poor, 1821, PHA/9638.

26 Quotation from William Ferrand, House of Commons, 17 May 1847, Hansard, vol. 92, col. 972. See A. Brundage, *The Making of the New Poor Law: The Politics of Inquiry, Enactment, and Implementation, 1832–1839* (London, 1978), p. 20; D. Green, *Pauper Capital: London and the Poor Law, 1790–1870* (London, 2010), pp. 98–9.

27 Alverstoke, Guardians' Weekly Report Book, 6 January 1825 and n.d., HRO PL2/1/3. It appears as though these contractors also contacted Alverstoke in 1823 about wanting to contract for the poor, although for eight years previously a man named Mr Millage maintained the poor; Alverstoke, Guardians' Minute Book, extract from vestry book dated 1 April 1823, HRO PL2/1/1.

28 K.D.M. Snell, *Annals of the Labouring Poor: Social Change and Agrarian England 1660–1900* (Cambridge, 1985), p. 106.

29 Sutton Union, Correspondence and proposals for farming the poor, 21 July 1793, PHA/6570. He took the position of contractor later that year; Sutton Union, Guardians' Minute Book, 2 December 1793, WSRO WG3/1/1.

30 Sutton, Guardians' Minute Books, 4 August 1794, WG3/1/2. By December, Richard Altrue and Elizabeth Matthews were appointed and given board in the house to superintend the sacking manufacture; Sutton Union, Guardians' Minute Book, 1 December 1794, WSRO WG3/1/2.

31 Sutton Union, Miscellaneous accounts and calculations, February 1795, PHA/6598.

32 Gilbert's Union, which consisted of Sidlesham, Selseam, Birdham, Itchenor and Appledram, Advert for contracting out the poor; *Hampshire Telegraph and Sussex Chronicle*, 4 February 1833.

33 For instance, the Burpham blanket charity started around 1840 when Mr Whieldon of Stanmore advanced the sum of £5 per annum for the purchase of blankets to be distributed to the poor of the parish; Burpham, Vestry Minute Book, 30 September 1844, WSRO Par31/12/1.

34 Easebourne, Easebourne Union, Letters concerning the establishment of a Sunday school, letter from E.M. (Poznty?) to Mr Tyler (Petworth), 26 November 1800, PHA/10940.

35 Easebourne, Letters concerning the establishment of a Sunday school, R. Lloyd (Midhurst) to Mr Tyler (Petworth), 14 November [no year], PHA/10940.

36  Bentley, Overseers' Account and Rate Book, 1 January 1798, HRO 1M80/PO2.
37  Sutton Union, Guardian's Minute Book, 21 May 1791, WSRO WG3/1/1.
38  Tyler received 10 guineas from the Sutton Board in 1791–92, 8 guineas a year in 1792–93, 12 guineas a year in 1793–94 and £20 in 1795–96; Sutton Union, Guardians' Minute Books, 6 February and 2 July 1792, 4 May 1795, WG3/1/2. For details on the forfeit for not attending a meeting, Sutton Union, Guardians' Minute Book, 3 November 1800, WSRO WG3/1/3.
39  The 'Petworth Poor' were maintained at 3s and 6d per head for 50 and subsidy for when wheat went above £16 per load, and the 'Sutton Poor' at 3s and 9d a head for 40 and subsidy when wheat went beyond £18 per load; Easebourne Union, Correspondence and proposals to farm the poor, 1818, PHA/10937.
40  S. Webster, 'Estate improvement and the professionalisation of land agents on the Egremont estates in Sussex and Yorkshire, 1770–1835', *Rural History*, 18 (2007), 57.
41  Webster, 'Estate improvement', p. 54. For more information about the tasks of other stewards in Sussex, see M. Lill, 'William Cooke, steward of the Sheffield Estate 1828–1832', *Sussex Archaeological Collections*, 144 (2006), 177–90.
42  G. Jacob, *The Compleat Parish-officer: Containing I. The Authority and Proceedings of High-Constables, … II. Of Churchwardens; … III. Of Overseers of the Poor, … IV. Of Surveyors of the Highways … To Which Are Added, the Statutes Relating to Hackney-Coaches and Chairs* (London, 1718).
43  See J.R. Poynter, *Society and Pauperism: English Ideas on Poor Relief 1795–1834* (London, 1969).
44  Poynter, *Society and Pauperism*, p. 106.
45  R. Cowherd, *Political Economists and the English Poor Laws: A Historical Study of the Influence of Classical Economics on the Formation of Social Welfare Policy* (Ohio, 1977), p. 17.
46  Poynter, *Society and Pauperism*, p. 106.
47  Bush *et al.*, 'Parochial regulations', p. 16.
48  J. Walter, T. Robbins and W. Gilpin, *An Account of a New Poor-House Erected in the Parish of Boldre: In New Forest near Lymington* (London, 1796). Also see G.S. Bowen, *The Reverend William Gilpin: Vicar of Boldre 1777–1804* (Lymington, 2004).
49  Rutter, *A Brief Sketch*, p. v.
50  Bush *et al.*, 'Parochial regulations', pp. 6–12.
51  Bush *et al.*, 'Parochial regulations', pp. 17–47.
52  Bush *et al.*, 'Parochial regulations', pp. 49–56.

53   Bush *et al.*, 'Parochial regulations', pp. 57–76.

54   Walter *et al.*, *An Account of a New Poor-House*, p. 3.

55   Walter *et al.*, *An Account of a New Poor-House*, p. 8.

56   Walter *et al.*, *An Account of a New Poor-House*, p. 22.

57   Walter *et al.*, *An Account of a New Poor-House*, pp. 23–5.

58   T. Ruggles, *The History of the Poor: Their Rights, Duties, and the Laws Respecting Them in a Series of Letters* (1793), 2 volumes. Further editions were produced throughout the 1790s.

59   Bush *et al.*, 'Parochial regulations', pp. 25–7; 'an interesting experiment' used to describe the manufactory is on p. 25.

60   Bush *et al.*, 'Parochial regulations', p. 37.

61   Bush *et al.*, 'Parochial regulations', pp. 46 and 44 respectively.

62   Poynter, *Society and Pauperism*, p. 88.

63   Poynter, *Society and Pauperism*, p. 87.

64   T. Gisborne, 'Extract from an account of a mode adopted in Staffordshire for supplying the poor with milk', article 23 in T. Bernard (ed.), *The Reports of the Society for Bettering the Condition and Increasing the Comforts of the Poor*, Volume 1 (London, 1798), pp. 129–34.

65   Poynter, *Society and Pauperism*, p. 91.

66   Gisborne, 'Extract from an account', p. 129.

67   Gisborne, 'Extract from an account', p. 130.

68   Bush *et al.*, 'Parochial regulations', p. 47.

69   Eden, 'Shrewsbury', in *The State of the Poor*, Volume 2, p. 622.

70   I. Wood, *Some Account of the Shrewsbury House of Industry, the Establishment and Regulations; With Hints to Those Who May Have Similar Institutions to View*, second edition containing 'The third edition of the bye-laws, rules, and ordinances, of the said house' (London, 1791); Eden, 'Shrewsbury', in *The State of the Poor*, Volume 2, pp. 622–41.

71   For more detail about the welfare system at Shrewsbury under the old poor laws, see S. Webb and B. Webb, *English Poor Law History, Part 1: The Old Poor Law* (1927, London, 1963), pp. 121–5; V. Walsh, 'Old and New Poor Laws in Shropshire, 1820–1870', *Midland History*, 2 (1974), 225–43.

72   Bush *et al.*, 'Parochial regulations', pp. 21, 44, 47 and 54.

73   The Bishop of Durham, 'Extract from the Rev. Mr. Gilpin's account of the new poor-house at Boldre, in Hampshire', article 32 in T. Bernard (ed.), *The Reports of the Society for Bettering the Condition and Increasing the Comforts of the Poor*, Volume 1 (London, 1798), pp. 174–82.

74   The Bishop of Durham at this time had previously held the position of Bishop of Salisbury; Bowen, *The Reverend William Gilpin*, p. 18.

75   Bought from the Earl of de la Warr.

76   J. Cannon, 'Holroyd, John Baker, first earl of Sheffield (1741–1821)', *Oxford Dictionary of National Biography* (Oxford, 2004; online edition, May 2012). Online: www.oxforddnb.com/view/article/13608 (last accessed 18 January 2016).

77   Printed poster announcing the near-completion of the Workhouse at Fletching and the detailed regulations to be observed in it, n.d., PHA/6075.

78   Proposal for the formation of a Gilbert Union to build a workhouse at Piltdown or Chelwood Common for the parishes of Newick, Isfield, Little Horsted, Ringmer, Uckfield, Framfield, Buxted, Maresfield, Fletching, Chailey, Lindfield and Horsted Keynes; n.d., ESRO, AMS4899/1. The failure of the plan is noted by an antiquarian and confirmed by further archival research. There is no indication why the plan did not come into fruition; Letter from H.D. Gilbert (Uckfield, Sussex) to Mr Bridges, 26 July 1959, with AMS4899/1.

79   Printed poster announcing the near-completion of the Workhouse at Fletching and the detailed regulations to be observed in it, n.d., PHA/6075.

80   The provision of relief had, however, been controversial between the years 1814 and 1818, when disputes occurred between Lord Sheffield and rival landowners (Sir Thomas Wilson, 7th Baronet and magistrate) and other magistrates who believed the poor had been ill-treated. These individuals were blamed for provoking the poor to rebel against the relief policy; see H. Rawlings, 'Lord Sheffield's last stand', *Danehill Parish Historical Society Magazine*, 4 (1993), 10–28.

81   Kingsclere Union, Minute Book, 13 December 1836, HRO PL3/11/1. It appears that this agreement continued into 1837; Kingsclere Union, Minute Book, 28 March 1837, HRO PL3/11/2. The Fareham Union Guardians decide to contact the Droxford Guardians; Fareham Union, Minute Book, 1 January 1836, HRO PL3/7/1. The Droxford Guardians accept the arrangement; Droxford Union, Minute Book, 19 February 1836, HRO PL3/7/1.

82   In 1831 it had a population of 4,951, and by 1841 it had 5,481; Dulverton Union, Minute Book, front page, n.d. (although the volume contains the minutes of meetings held between 1836 and 1842), SRO D\G\D/8a/1.

83   Dulverton Union, Minute Book, 7 September 1839, SRO D\G\D/8a/1; meeting of a Committee from each Board of Guardians held at the Tiverton Workhouse, Dulverton Union, Minute Book, 21 September 1839, SRO D\G\D/8a/1; minutes on the terms discussed, Dulverton Union, Minute Book, 19 October and 16 November 1839, SRO D\G\D/8a/1.

84 Dulverton Union, Minute Book, 30 November 1839, SRO D\G\D/8a/1.

85 Dulverton Union, Minute Book, 23 November 1844, SRO D\G\D/8a/1.

86 Clerk instructed to write to the Williton Union Guardians; Dulverton Union, Minute Book, 7 December 1844, SRO D\G\D/8a/1. A letter received from the Williton Union was read to the Board; Dulverton Union, Minute Book, 18 January 1845, SRO D\G\D/8a/2. The terms of the Williton Board were rejected and the Poor Law Commission notified of the proposed scheme; Dulverton Union, Minute Book, 1 February 1845, SRO D\G\D/8a/2.

87 A letter from the Poor Law Commission states that the scheme could not be legally entered into and the clerk was directed to write to the Williton Union informing them of the decision; Dulverton Union, Minute Book, 15 February 1845, SRO D\G\D/8a/2.

88 This culminated in a welfare scandal. See R. Wells, 'Andover antecedents? Hampshire New Poor-Law scandals, 1834–1842', *Southern History*, 24 (2002), 91–217; S.A. Shave, '"*Rascally handled": New Poor Law scandals and the working out of social policy*' (unpublished MSc dissertation, University of Southampton, 2006).

89 Droxford Union, Minute Book, 1 January 1836, HRO PL3/8/1.

90 Cranborne Union, Minute Book, 16 June 1836, DHC BG/WM A1/1.

91 Cranborne Union, Minute Book, 14 July 1836, DHC BG/WM A1/1; Cranborne and Wimborne Union, Minute Book (minutes of the Wimborne Union), 20 June, 14 July and 5 September 1836, DHC BG/WM A1/2. The first meeting of Guardians in the consolidated Union; Cranborne and Wimborne Union, Minute Book, 29 September 1836, DHC BG/WM A1/2.

92 Warminster Union, Minute Book, 29 February 1836, W&SA H15/110/1.

93 Mere Union, Minute Book, 11 December 1835, W&SA H12/110/1.

94 Clutton Union, Minute Book, 14 March 1845, SRO D\G\CL/8a/9.

95 Shaftesbury Union, Minute Book, 5 November 1838, DHC BG/SY A1/2.

96 Clutton Union, Minute Book, 27 April 1838, SRO D\G\CL/8a/3.

97 Clutton Union, Minute Book, 19 January and 2 February 1838, SRO D\G\CL/8a/2.

98 Wincanton Union, Minute Book, 13 January 1841, SRO D\G\WN/8a/4.

99 Bridgwater Union, Minute Book, 22 December 1837, SRO D\G\BW/8a/2.

100 Kingsclere Union, Minute Book, 23 and 30 May 1837, HRO PL3/11/2.

101 Shaftesbury Union, Minute Book, 12 November 1838, DHC BG/SY A1/2.

102 Cranborne and Wimborne Union, Minute Book, 28 December 1840 and 25 January 1841, DHC BG/WM A1/3.

103 'Circular Letter relative to Workhouse Dietaries', in *Second Report of the Poor Law Commissioners* (London, 1836), p. 63 (dietaries, pp. 64–6). The word 'model' has only been used by P. Higginbotham, *The Workhouse Cookbook* (Stroud, 2008), p. 51.
104 'General Report to Central Board, from Assistant Commissioners', Charles Mott Esq., in *Second Annual Report of the Poor Law Commissioners* (London, 1836), app. B.8, p. 355.
105 Clutton Union, Minute Book, 12 April and 20 April 1838, SRO D\G\CL/8a/3. They knew that both of the dietaries had received the sanction of the Commissioners; Reverend Henry (Hodges?) Mogg, Clerk (Clutton) to PLC, 12 May 1838, TNA MH12/10320.
106 In 1847 the Mere Union announced that it would adopt the dietary used in the Wincanton Union; Snook, Clerk (Mere) to PLC, 23 February 1847, TNA MH12/13820.
107 Beaminster Union, Minute Book, 13 April 1837, DHC BG/BE B3/1.
108 Clutton Union, Minute Book, 15 July 1836 and 22 July 1836, SRO D\G\CL/8a/1.
109 Kingsclere Union, Minute Book, 16 February 1836, HRO PL3/11/1.
110 Wincanton Union, Minute Book, 15 May 1844, SRO D\G\WN/8a/5.
111 'Letter to the Right Honourable Lord John Russell, on the subject of the Religious Instruction of the Inmates of Workhouses [from the Poor Law Commissioners]', in an annex to the letter is a copy of the 19th section of the Poor Law Amendment Act; *Second Annual Report of the Poor Law Commissioners* (London, 1836), p. 67.
112 Droxford Union, Minute Book, 13 August 1844, HRO PL3/7/3; Droxford Union, Minute Book, 10 December 1844, HRO PL3/7/4.
113 Clutton Union, Minute Book, 4 June 1841, SRO D\G\CL/8a/6.
114 The seven unions were Alton, Andover, Basingstoke, Hartley Wintney, Lymington, Romsey and Winchester; Fareham Union, Minute Book, 26 January 1844, HRO PL3/8/2.
115 Reverend G.H. Templer (Shapwick) to PLC, 12 June 1837, TNA MH12/10243. Position as a Guardian identified in Bridgwater Union, Minute Book, 12 May 1836, SRO D\G\BW/8a/1.
116 A. Brundage, *The English Poor Laws, 1700–1930* (Basingstoke, 2002), p. 71.
117 S. Webb and B. Webb, *English Poor Law History, Part 2: The Last Hundred Years* (1929, London, 1963), p. 113.
118 M. Rose, 'The allowance system under the New Poor Law', *Economic History Review*, 19 (1966), 607–20; N. Edsall, *The Anti-Poor Law Movement, 1834–44* (Manchester, 1971); J. Knott, *Popular Opposition to the 1834 Poor Law* (London, 1986); F. Driver, *Power and Pauperism: The Workhouse System 1834–1884* (Cambridge, 1993), pp. 112–30; D. Ashforth, 'The urban poor law', in D. Fraser (ed.), *The New Poor Law in*

*the Nineteenth-Century* (London, 1976), pp. 128–46; A. Digby, *Pauper Palaces* (London, 1978); A. Brundage, 'The landed interest and the New Poor Law: a reappraisal of the revolution in government', *English Historical Review*, 87 (1972), 27–48.

119  S. Haines and L. Lawson, *Poor Cottages & Proud Palaces: The Life and Work of the Reverend Thomas Sockett of Petworth 1777–1859* (Hastings, 2007), p. 169.

120  S. King, *Poverty and Welfare in England 1700–1850: A Regional Perspective* (Manchester, 2000), p. 227.

121  P. Harling, 'The power of persuasion: central authority, local bureaucracy and the New Poor Law', *English Historical Review*, 107 (1992), 53.

122  'Number of the Unions formed, with the Agency of each Assistant Commissioner; the Number of Parishes united; and the Average Amount of Poor's Rates', in *First Annual Report of the Poor Law Commissioners* (London, 1835), app. D.2, p. 406; BPP 1845 (41) Union workhouses. A return of all union workhouses under the Poor Law Amendment Act, in which the pauper inmates thereof are or have been employed in grinding or crushing bones [hereafter BPP 1845 (41) Return].

123  Copy of Minutes of Board of Guardians, South Molton Guardians (meeting held 9 December 1845), BPP 1846 (75) House of Commons Papers; Accounts and Papers. Poor law. Copy of any letter and general rule issued by the Poor Law Commissioners, relative to the employment of paupers in pounding, grinding, and otherwise breaking bones; &c. [hereafter BPP 1846 (75) House of Commons Papers], p. 12.

124  Fareham Union, Minute Book, 21 September 1838, HRO PL3/8/1a.

125  Various correspondence of A'Court July–September 1835 in TNA MH32/2; quotation from A'Court to PLC, 10 September 1835, TNA MH32/2.

126  'Statement of the Number of Unions Formed, with the Agency of each Assistant Commissioner; the Number of Parishes united; the Population; and the Average Amount of the Poor rates', in *Second Annual Report of the Poor Law Commissioners* (London, 1836), app. D.5, p. 570.

127  Tufnell (Shaftesbury) to PLC, 1 September 1835, TNA MH32/69.

128  There may have been more because the return was taken in 1844; BPP 1845 (41) Return.

129  Copy of Minutes of Board of Guardians, Stroud Union Guardians (meeting held 16 January 1846), BPP 1846 (75) House of Commons Papers, p. 46.

130  Letter from the Cranbrook Board of Guardians to PLC, 21 November 1845, BPP 1846 (75) House of Commons Papers, p. 31.

131  There are further examples. For instance, the South Molton Union (Devon) Guardians stated that 'the introduction of the bone-crushing

system was adopted in this union at the suggestion and on the recommendation of an Assistant Poor Law Commissioner'; Copy of Minutes of Board of Guardians, South Molton Guardians (meeting held 9 December 1845), BPP 1846 (75) House of Commons Papers, p. 12.

132 J. Boor, Clerk (Warminster Union) to PLC, 7 May 1836, TNA MH12/13863. A'Court's note on the back of the letter is dated 11 May 1836.

133 Cranborne and Wimborne Union, Minute Book (Wimborne Union minute), 13 June 1836, DHC BG/A1/2.

134 Bridport Union, Minute Book, 12 January 1842, BG/BT A1/2. 1840 start date in BPP 1845 (41) Return, p. 4.

135 Webb and Webb, *English Poor Law History, Part 2*, p. 179.

136 The 1844 returns were printed in BPP 1845 (41) Return.

137 Clutton Union, Minute Book, 24 February 1843, SRO D\G\CL/8a/7.

138 G. Nicholls, *History of the English Poor Law, Volume 2: 1714–1853* (London, 1898), p. 368.

139 George Nicholls, George Cornewall Lewis and Edmund W. Head (Poor Law Commissioners, Somerset House) to Sir George Gray Bart. MP, 18 September 1846 ('Statement of the manner in which the Business of the Commission is transacted', p. 42), TNA HO45/1682. There are nearly 17,000 volumes of letters in the record series TNA MH12.

140 G. Lefevre to G. Best, 23 November 1835, TNA MH12/11035.

141 Official Circulars of Public Documents and Information directed by the Poor Law Commissioners to be printed chiefly for the use of the Boards of Guardians and their officers (London).

142 Official Circulars, issue 1 May 1845, no. 47, pp. 65, 293.

143 Official Circulars, issue 1 December 1835, no. 54, pp. 177–92.

144 Full title: 'Employment of able-bodied paupers in the workhouse – best kind of mill to be used for', letter from PLC to Guardians of Bicester Union, 5 March 1842, in Official Circulars, issue 30 July 1842, no. 20, p. 298.

145 Nicholls, *History of the English Poor Law*, p. 368.

146 'As to the Employment of Able-Bodied Paupers. – Honiton Union', letter from PLC to Guardians of the Honiton Union, 18 February 1842, in Official Circulars, issue 13 February 1843, no. 23, pp. 42–3; Webb and Webb also notice this circular; *English Poor Law History, Part 2*, p. 179, fn 2.

147 Poor Law Commission to Samuel Cox, Clerk (Beaminster), 19 January 1844, TNA MH12/2707; Item V. 'Workhouse – Dietaries – Report of Mr. Parker, one of the Assistant Commissioners, pointing out the inconveniences and expense resulting from allowing the Inmates of Workhouses a certain number of ounces of Tea and Sugar, and suggesting a remedy', in Official Circulars, issue 1 May 1845, no. 47, p. 301.

148 Full title: 'Workhouse – Dietaries – Report of Mr. Parker, one of the Assistant Commissioners, pointing out the inconveniences and expense resulting from allowing the Inmates of Workhouses a certain number of ounces of Tea and Sugar, and suggesting a remedy', in Official Circulars, issue 1 May 1845, no. 47, p. 301.

149 The circular was issued by the Commission on 5 January 1844; J. Boor, Clerk (Warminster Union) to PLC, 9 January 1844, TNA MH12/ 13866.

150 'Order and regulations to be observed in the Workhouse of the – Union', in First Annual Report of the Poor Law Commissioners (London, 1835), app. A.9, pp. 96–110.

151 Report 'To the Right Honourable Sir James Graham, Bart., Her Majesty's Principal Secretary of State for the Home Department', G. Nicholls, G. Cornewall Lewis and E. Walker Head to Sir James Graham, 2 May 1842, Eighth Annual Report of the Poor Law Commissioners (London, 1842), pp. 12–13.

152 'General Order – Workhouse Rules', in Eighth Annual Report of the Poor Law Commissioners, articles 32 and 33, app. A.3, p. 85.

153 'General Order – Modifying Articles 32 and 33 of Workhouse Rules', 7 February 1843, in Ninth Annual Report of the Poor Law Commissioners (London, 1843), app. B.1, pp. 377–8.

154 4 & 5 Will. IV c.76, V. Also noted in Report 'To the Right First Honorable Lord John Russell, His Majesty's Principal Secretary of State for the Home Department', T. Frankland Lewis, J.G. Shaw Lefevre and G. Nicholls to Lord John Russell, 8 August 1835, in First Annual Report of the Poor Law Commissioners (London, 1835), p. 1.

155 Brundage, The Making of the New Poor Law, pp. 101–2.

156 A'Court (Wilton, leaving for Southampton) to PLC, 29 December 1836, TNA MH32/3; A'Court (Newport, Isle of Wight) to PLC, 23 February 1837, TNA MH32/4. In the following year A'Court provided the Commission with a list of unions and individuals who should be sent a copy, and obtained a few spare copies for his own distribution; A'Court (Southampton) to PLC, 8 October 1837, TNA MH32/4.

157 A'Court (Southampton) to PLC, 22 November 1838, TNA MH32/4.

158 Brundage provides the example of Lord Howick, who requested six copies; Brundage, The Making of the New Poor Law, p. 102. The First Annual Report is marked with a price of four shillings; First Annual Report of the Poor Law Commissioners (London, 1835).

159 Brundage, The Making of the New Poor Law, p. 99.

160 Webb and Webb, English Poor Law History, Part 2, p. 132.

161 Brundage, The English Poor Laws, p. 72.

162 B. Fletcher, 'The early years of the Westhampnett Poor Law Union 1835–1838' (unpublished MSc dissertation, University of Southampton, 1981), p. 90.
163 'Report from Henry Pilkington, Esq. to the Poor Law Commissioners for England and Wales', *First Annual Report of the Poor Law Commissioners* (London, 1835), app. B.9, p. 296.
164 Raper, Clerk of Westhampnett Union (Chichester) to Henry Pilkington, 22 July 1835, in 'Report from Henry Pilkington, Esq. to the Poor Law Commissioners for England and Wales', *First Annual Report of the Poor Law Commissioners* (London, 1835), app. B.9, quotations from pp. 296–7 and pp. 295–6, respectively.
165 'Report as to the Operation and Effects of the Poor Law Amendment Act, in the County of Sussex; by William Henry Toovey Hawley, Esq., Assistant Poor Law Commissioner', *Second Annual Report of the Poor Law Commissioners* (London, 1836), app. B.3, p. 239.
166 S.A. Shave, 'The welfare of the vulnerable in the late 18th and early 19th centuries: Gilbert's Act of 1782', *History in Focus*, 'Welfare' edition (2008). Online: www.history.ac.uk/ihr/Focus/welfare/articles/shaves.html (last accessed 11 December 2016); also see C. Choomwattana, *'The opposition to the New Poor Law in Sussex, 1834–1837'* (unpublished PhD thesis, Cornell University, 1986).
167 The radical newspaper, the *Brighton Patriot*, was eager to attack the Duke of Richmond (nicknamed 'Duky') for working with the Commissioners, whilst commending Lord Egremont for resisting change. Egremont, with the help of Thomas Sockett, was called 'a friend of the poor'; *Brighton Patriot and Local Free Press*, August 1836, cited in Haines and Lawson, *Poor Cottages & Proud Palaces*, p. 188.
168 Although in 1833 they appear to have implemented the 'workhouse test'; B. Fletcher, 'Chichester and the Westhampnett Poor Law Union', *Sussex Archaeological Collections*, 134 (1996), 185.
169 J. Boor, Clerk (Wimborne Union) to PLC, 31 January 1838, TNA MH12/13864; James Pratt, Clerk (Cricklade and Wootton Bassett Union) to PLC, 7 February 1838, TNA MH12/13720.
170 PLC to J. Boor, Clerk (Warminster Union), 5 February 1838, TNA MH12/13864; PLC to James Pratt, Clerk (Cricklade and Wootton Bassett Union), 13 February 1838, TNA MH12/13720.
171 'Third Annual Report to The Right Honourable Lord John Russell', T.F. Lewis, J.G. Shaw Lefevre and G. Nicholls to Lord John Russell, 17 July 1837, *Third Annual Report of the Poor Law Commissioners* (London, 1837), pp. 40–2.
172 Snook, Clerk (Mere Union) to PLC, 16 April 1845, TNA MH12/13820.

173 PLC to Snook, Clerk (Mere Union), 22 April 1845, TNA MH12/
13820; 'Eighth Annual Report, to the Right Honourable Sir James
Graham, Bart. Her Majesty's Principal Secretary of State for the Home
Department', G. Nicholls, G. Cornewall Lewis, E. Walker Head to
Sir James Graham, 2 May 1842, *Eighth Annual Report of the Poor Law
Commissioners* (London, 1842), pp. 38–9.

174 T. Blundell, Vicar, and John Ford, Churchwarden (Mere) to PLC, 24
April 1846, TNA MH12/13820.

175 The PLC told the Guardians to read pp. 37 and 38 from the *Eighth
Annual Report* and pp. 32 and 33 from the *Eleventh Annual Report*;
PLC to Guardians of Mere Union, 29 April 1846, TNA MH12/13820;
'Eleventh Annual Report to the Right Ho. Sir James Graham Bart.,
Her Majesty's Principal Secretary of State for the Home Department',
G. Nicholls, G. Cornewall Lewis, E. Walker Head to Sir James Gra-
ham, 1 May 1838, *Eleventh Annual Report of the Poor Law Commission-
ers* (London, 1845), p. 33.

176 King, *Poverty and Welfare*.

177 T. Bernard, 'Preliminary Address to the Public', in T. Bernard (ed.), *The
Reports of the Society for Bettering the Condition and Increasing the Comforts of the Poor*, Volume 1 (London, 1798), p. xii.

178 T. Hitchcock, 'Paupers and preachers: The SPCK and the parochial
workhouse movement', in I. Davison, T. Hitchcock, T. Keirn and R.B.
Shoemaker (eds.), *Stilling the Grumbling Hive: The Response to Social and
Economic Problems in England, 1689–1750* (London, 1992), pp. 146–66.

179 After being printed in the SBCP's publications, the reforms at Boldre
were sent to Philadelphia where it was reprinted for Philadelphian parishes; Bowen, *The Reverend William Gilpin*, p. 18.

180 Nicholls, *History of the English Poor Law*, p. 368.

181 W. Apfel and P. Dunkley, 'English rural society and the New Poor
Law: Bedfordshire, 1834–47', *Social History*, 10 (1985), 37–68.

182 Brundage, *The Making of the New Poor Law*, p. 99.

183 P. Spicker, *Policy Analysis for Practice: Applying Social Policy* (Bristol,
2006), p. 24.

# 5

# Policies from scandal

Why, Sir, until you passed this New Poor Law, the poor were ready to shed their blood to defend their country. They are now compelled to sacrifice their liberty to save their lives. William Ferrand MP, 1847

The Poor Law Commission was granted a five-year extension in 1842, but was left to expire in 1847. In its short life, the Commission was beset with countless problems, from poor administration to the abuse of the poor themselves. These were listed at length by opponents of the New Poor Law, including the Tory MP William Ferrand. During a marathon speech in the House of Commons he attempted to put the poor's horrific treatment centre-stage, and with it some context of the long-held rights of the poor to assistance, such rights being 'as sacred as the Monarch has to her Crown, the Peer to his palace, or any Member of this House to the coat which he wears upon his back'.[1] Yet his words, amongst others, were not enough to prevent the new Whig government from rebranding the Commission as the Poor Law Board and moving it closer to the heart of central government, from Somerset House to Whitehall.

As highlighted in Chapter 1, the Commission created a climate in which maltreatment, neglect and abuse were more likely to occur, not least through the implementation of the principle of less eligibility.[2] During and after the operation of the New Poor Law, scandals in particular – those abuses that heightened awareness in the public arena through media attention, government acknowledgement and inquiry – have come to represent the harsh system within which many people suffered. The power of scandals to end a fragile system has also been explored; the Andover Scandal was the catalyst to end a Commission in crisis. But this chapter presents us with a new direction. It seeks to shed light on the broader contexts and consequences of scandals to demonstrate how these moments influenced the development of pauper policies during the New Poor Law.

It is an approach influenced by the work of Butler and Drakeford, who demonstrate that scandals are important feedback mechanisms between the policy implementation and policy-making stages of the policy process. Scandals can make central welfare authorities review their policies and the ways in which they have been implemented. In consequence, authorities can revoke or change their policies or create new ones altogether.[3]

The two distinct case studies selected from the south of England, the Bridgwater (Somerset) and Andover Union (Hampshire) Scandals, impacted on the passage of new policies from the Poor Law Commission in the areas of medical relief policy and workhouse work policy respectively. Yet not all scandals in this period necessarily caused such a direct policy change. Butler and Drakeford note, 'to have an impact an individual scandal needs to take place at a time of policy strain … to be capable of catching a tide that is already beginning to run in a fresh direction'.[4] Each case study, its key events and repercussions, is presented in turn, but starts with an outline of the area of policy strain, namely medical relief and work in workhouses.

The final section of each case study underlines the creation of the new policies and the problems faced in unions to implement them. Perhaps unsurprisingly, the two General Orders created by the Commission as a consequence of the scandals were, akin to the General Outdoor Relief Prohibitory Order (1844), difficult to implement. In both cases, this was due to the circumstances of each individual union or the will of the Boards of Guardians to apply the policies issued to them. Although this approach highlights the long-term significance of each of the policies developed, it also casts some doubt on the effectiveness of these policies in the short term. Did policies developed as a consequence of scandal forge any immediate change in the experiences of relief claimants?

## Medical relief policy and the Bridgwater Scandal

*Medical relief provision*

The founding old poor law legislation, the Act for the Relief of the Poor 1601, did not make any explicit reference to medical relief. Subsequent legislation was also silent on the provision of medical relief, besides a couple of statutes passed during the early years of George III's reign, which permitted justices to order medical relief for indoor poor. As such, the provision of medical relief was not compulsory, relief being driven by custom rather than stipulation. Whilst, by the early nineteenth century, some parishes employed medical men, according to George Cornewall Lewis, appointed as a Poor Law Commissioner from 1839, such provision was not universal. Medical relief, he asserted, 'did not extend beyond the counties in the south, and east, and the centre of England'.[5] Although this is a narrow view of the geographical range of medical relief, there were no legally stipulated minimum standards and the actual standard of care varied from parish to parish and over time. In addition, parish-stipulated entitlement to medical relief varied. As the analysis of pauper letters shows, individual claimants detailed their ailments in different ways to secure a modicum of assistance in a context of 'uncertain and uneven entitlement to relief and medical intervention'.[6]

Medical relief was little alluded to in the 1834 report of the Royal Commission. The report simply concluded that medical relief was 'adequately supplied, and economically, if we consider only the price and amount of attendance'.[7] Unsurprisingly, then, the Poor Law Amendment Act contained only one reference to medical relief: section 54, which empowered magistrates to order medical attendance in an emergency.[8] To Michael Flinn, this is suggestive of the fact that medical relief under the New Poor Law was built on the 'foundations inherited' from what went before.[9] The Poor Law Commissioners acknowledged the long-held traditions of parish relief, noting in their First Annual Report the 'deficiencies' of medical relief under the old poor law.[10] The parish doctor had been employed at a small sum per year, on the 'condition that he should be allowed to make whatever charges he pleased for his attendance', whilst medicines were supplied 'at the highest rates'. Consequently, large profits, especially in more

'populous parishes', were being accrued by medical men and apothecaries. There were other 'evils', too. People in remote parishes 'had
no adequate protection', and any individual could be supplied with
'medicines considerably beyond what is required'.[11]

Although no statute in the Amendment Act directly stipulated
that medical relief should be provided, two further sections allowed
Boards of Guardians to appoint medical men. Section 46 permitted boards to appoint paid officers and section 109 noted that a
medical officer could be used to denote 'any ... Person duly licensed
to practise as a Medical Man'.[12] Medical officers were appointed
under these powers upon the establishment of unions throughout
England and Wales. For instance, at the first meeting of the Fareham
Union (Hampshire) the Guardians, in the presence of Assistant
Commissioner A'Court, divided the union into two medical districts.
The acreage and population of each district, taken by the Guardians
from the 1831 census, were not equal, however, so the Guardians set
different wages for each district and then appointed their medical
officers.[13] The administrative aspects of medical relief were, therefore,
forged under the guidance of the Commission. The lack of medical
relief stipulations and guidance beyond this point, however, resulted
in numerous difficulties. These centred on several fundamental, albeit
interrelated, themes: the qualifications and wages of medical officers,
to whom and what medical relief should be allocated, and the size of
medical districts. It is worth outlining these issues before providing
an account of the Bridgwater Scandal.

The position of medical officer could be given only to an individual 'duly licensed' to act as a medical man, although the Poor Law
Commission did not stipulate what qualifications or level of experience such a medical man should have. The quality of medical
relief could, therefore, vary greatly depending on whom Boards of
Guardians appointed. In their First Annual Report, the Poor Law
Commission was glad to announce that, as a check to the 'expense of
medical relief', they 'generally required that medical services should
be retained by contract and open tender'.[14] Medical men were paid on
a case-by-case basis or, as the Commissioners implied, in a lump sum
or at a rate per head of the population of the medical district, which
was set before the commencement of their appointment. Competitive
agreements were difficult to engineer in the latter case. In May 1836
the attention of Assistant Commissioner William Henry Toovey

Hawley was brought to the 'troublesome medical contracts' in his Hampshire unions. Of particular concern to Hawley was the eight shillings per head of population offered to the Hartley Wintney Guardians by the local medical men, a sum he thought too high.[15]

The Board of Guardians of the newly established Bridgwater Union had similar problems, which had far-reaching consequences. As Kim Price has highlighted in a new examination of medical officers under the New Poor Law, the position may have been stable at a time of economic instability when wages were low. Most 'were not well off', some were practising 'on a knife's edge of economic ruin'.[16] The financial preoccupations of the welfare authorities, according to Digby, meant that 'cost rather than adequate qualification became the driving force' for medical officers' appointments.[17]

Financial considerations also affected entitlement to medical relief. Writing in 1836, the Commissioners had already received queries from Boards of Guardians, asking to whom medical relief could be issued. Their response was that 'actual necessity or destitution is the condition on which all applications for relief, medical or otherwise, are to be decided'. Those in the workhouse had 'passed' the workhouse test and therefore were deemed to be sufficiently eligible for medical assistance. For those outside the workhouse, the situation was less clear-cut. Although individuals already in receipt of regular outdoor relief – on the 'list' – would have been entitled to medical relief, those who did not may have been asked to pay for their own medical assistance. The Commission also encouraged the formation of 'independent' sick clubs.[18] Even when an individual was 'entitled' to medical relief, judgements had to be made regarding what treatment would be offered. Medicines were expected to be supplied from the medical officers' own funds, whilst food, primarily consisting of meat and alcohol, was commonly allocated to the sick poor from union funds. It was unclear whether medical men should have to deliver children and undertake surgery, however, and they would often bargain for additional payments for such services. In practice, it was often the decision of the workhouse master and matron or the relieving officer (appointed to issue outdoor relief or send people into the workhouse throughout a number of parishes in a union) as to whether these procedures were required from a medical officer. Besides, other individuals, such as nurses and midwives, would often perform such tasks for lower wages.[19]

Another source of contention was the size of the medical districts. Doctors, who had previously served just one or two parishes, were now required to attend many parishes. This was problematic in rural unions, where large medical districts would 'make it insuperably difficult for even the most conscientious medical officer to operate efficiently'.[20] The medical officer would undertake rounds, visiting parishes on a regular basis. When medical relief was required outside these times, the poor had to search for their medical officer. In addition, it was assumed by the Commission that medical officers would secure the consent of a relieving officer before providing an individual with medical relief. This generated conflict. Medical officers thought that relieving officers were not capable of judging individuals' medical needs, and the relieving officers believed that medical officers were taking 'little account of the many moral and economic factors' surrounding relief provision.[21] This meant that the poor would have to obtain the attention of two officers, sometimes in different places. In the early years of the New Poor Law, much correspondence passed between the Guardians and the Commission containing details of those who had travelled vast distances to obtain assistance. Henry Williams's walk of 'several miles' to obtain outdoor relief within the confines of the Llantrisant Union, as detailed by Stewart and King, was far from unique. As Digby suggests, the outdoor poor, compared to those in the workhouse, suffered from a 'deterioration in the quality of care'.[22] Such problems were only brought to wider attention through a series of high-profile medical relief 'scandals' that exposed these deficiencies of medical provision.

*The Bridgwater Scandal*

The problems at the Bridgwater Union surfaced immediately after its formation by Assistant Commissioner Robert Weale in April 1836. The union encompassed 40 parishes in the north-west of Somerset covering parts of Exmoor and the Quantocks and had a low population density. The interests of all parishes were represented at the largest Board of Guardians in Somerset, made up of 48 elected members and 15 *ex officio* members.[23] Immediately after the formation of a union, it was a common practice to select existing workhouses to temporarily house the poor until a more substantial union workhouse was built. The Bridgwater and North Petherton houses were selected, with adults going into the former house and children into the latter. Both soon became overcrowded.[24] In the winter of 1836–37, one-third of the inmates died from enteric infection, the deaths mainly occurring in the Bridgwater parish workhouse, which accommodated 105 paupers during the winter.[25] Whilst overcrowding and unsanitary conditions were likely to have been the main cause of the deaths, the workhouse diet also received some blame. The Guardians chose to adopt dietary table number three, one of six dietaries designed by the Commission for implementation in every union workhouse. This table, akin to three other Commission-designed tables, contained the controversial foodstuff gruel that Abraham King, the workhouse medical officer, believed was the main cause of the sickness.[26]

Although rumours had spread amongst the Guardians about the overcrowding and sickness, it did not become general public knowledge until the following year. Still, Guardian William Baker, who had been appointed to the Visiting Committee, visited the Bridgwater poorhouse and advised the Guardians to change the inmates' diet and to stop sending paupers to the institution. He had little success.[27] John Bowen, Baker's friend and colleague, then intervened.[28] Bowen was a Tory and heavily involved in Bridgwater borough's politics.[29] He was a fierce opponent of the New Poor Law and frequently corresponded with the editor of *The Times*. In one such letter, Bowen expressed a dislike of the building plans for the Bridgwater Union workhouse, which were based on the Commission's approved Y plan designed by architect Samuel Kempthorne. With windows planned at six feet above the ground, Bowen claimed that the building would 'shut out … all enjoyment of the light of heaven' from the poor. The editor agreed, calling the building 'a nest of Kempthorne dungeons'.[30] After becoming aware of the article, Assistant Poor Law Commissioner Robert Weale wrote to the Commission, explaining that the old parish workhouse that Bowen called a 'palace' was, in fact, 'ten thousand times more worthy of the name of dungeon' compared to the planned new union workhouse.[31]

Regardless of the tension evident between Bowen and the Commission, Bowen wanted to become a member of the Bridgwater Board of Guardians. It was not his intention, though, to help administer the New Poor Law; on the contrary, he wanted access to information that would prove the Board's negligence. Bowen was elected in May 1837, and having the previous month visited the Bridgwater poorhouse and inspected the report book of the Visiting Committee, he immediately asked for a change of dietary and for better treatment of its inmates. He was ignored.[32] In July 1837 Bowen resigned and duly sent his notes to *The Times*.

Whilst the union evidently had problems caring for their indoor poor, their outdoor poor also suffered from a lack of adequate attention. Many of the medical relief problems derived from the board's desire to reduce associated costs. In the year before the formation of the union, medical salaries for the parishes totalled £577 per annum. After the formation of the union, seven large medical districts were created and seven medical officers were appointed to attend the poor. Their wages came to £363 per annum. The medical men in the Bridgwater area resented the reduction, but the chair of the board stressed that the first year was one of 'probation', implying that their wages would increase the following year.[33] When the year ended in May 1837, the board decided to discontinue the previous year's arrangements and proposed to create 12 medical districts, including one specifically for the workhouse. Details of these districts were circulated to the medical officers in the hope that they would respond to the proposal positively. By the following week, five of the medical men had replied. Although their comments cannot be found in the archive, their opinions clearly vexed the board and discussion was adjourned. On 18 May, a specially arranged meeting of the board called for another 'fresh Division of the Union', deciding to carve it into nine medical districts, including one for the attendance of the union workhouse.[34] The proposed salaries varied greatly because they were calculated on the basis of the population of each district. The medical men were then invited by the board to state their offers, which ranged from three pence and four pence per head in certain districts, and a flat rate of £50 was set for the workhouse district. Although, cumulatively, these proposed salaries were £50 below the medical costs before the union was established, their proposal was once again rejected by the board.[35]

The election of the medical officers to districts was to proceed on 16 June 1837, and the new allocations were to start a fortnight later. In the meantime, some members of the board were concerned that this would attract unskilled medical men to the union and argued that those appointed should possess specific medical qualifications. Anxious that *no* medical men would apply for the positions, overall the board rejected the idea. By early June the medical men were still in disagreement with the Guardians, writing a collective letter stating that 'they cannot with justice to the Poor, the Guardians, and themselves, continue their charge at the salaries proposed'.[36] The letter was written during a meeting of the Bridgwater Medical Association, formed of medical men from Bridgwater and the surrounding area, many of whom had previously acted as medical officers. By September 1838 it was documented as a branch of the Provincial Medical and Surgical Association (PMSA), one of the largest medical associations in Britain.[37] It was at such meetings that the medical men discussed their grievances and continued to exert pressure on the Guardians for fairer wages. Indeed, by June 1837 the medical men resorted to printing a handbill detailing their demands.[38] The public protest caused no material alteration in the views of the Guardians, who, whilst acknowledging the men's concern for the poor, were adamant that no change should occur to the proposed districts and salaries until 23 June when they would hold a meeting to appoint medical officers.[39]

Locked in a stalemate with the medical men, the board decided to contact Somerset House to request the Commissioners to recommend 'a candidate or two'.[40] The Commission, realising the magnitude of the problem, directed Weale to attend the next meeting of the Bridgwater Board.[41] Weale offered little advice, simply agreeing with the Board that the wages demanded by the medical men 'were more than adequate remuneration for their services and that they be not accepted'.[42] The board also decided that there should be only six districts, each covering a vast area of land. In consequence, just two of the medical men were allocated to districts, with the remaining vacancies advertised in the local and London press. One of the forthcoming candidates was unfamiliar with the area, whilst three local men took the remaining districts at the low rates offered by the board.[43] One of these individuals was apprehensive about taking such an expansive district, which was ten miles long and eight miles wide and contained 14 parishes.[44] After raising his concerns, he took the district alongside another local medical man. Overall, of the seven medical men appointed for the first year of the union, just four were re-employed, and on terms they found unsatisfactory.

During these extended negotiations and discussions, the old medical arrangements – in operation from May 1836 to May 1837 – had expired and a temporary medical service was established. Thinking on their feet, board members directed their medical officers to continue their services into July, but 'to attend the poor on the same terms as they did their private patients'. Mindful of the potential cost, the Guardians instructed the relieving officers 'to be sparing in their orders for medical relief'.[45] John Stagg, relieving officer for the Huntspill District, informed the medical officer of the district, William Lakin Caswell, that 'I am directed by the Board of Guardians to inform you that you are to discontinue your attendance on the under mentioned Paupers in Woollavington'.[46] A further four letters were sent to Caswell, directing him to stop attending four other paupers.[47] Caswell conformed to these orders reluctantly. On 2 July Caswell wrote in his notebook, 'in consequence of the Order of Mr. Stagg I have this Day been *reluctantly compelled* to refuse Medicine to George Reynold's Child, Kesia Coles, and Nancy Millard'. On 6 July Caswell wrote a letter to the Board of Guardians, arguing that they should not stop his attendance of the poor.[48]

For some of his patients, Caswell's protest was too late. Several paupers had been left without medical attendance, with devastating consequences. One case was that of 31-year-old Charlotte Allen, who lodged with Jane Fenn and Richard and Mary Date, a nurse, in the small parish of Nether Stowey.[49] A month before giving birth on 30 June 1837, Charlotte fell ill. She had no savings and was not able to draw on alternative sources of support.[50] As she approached motherhood, Charlotte received one shilling and sixpence and a loaf of bread every week from her relieving officer, James Franklin Waites. Thereafter, there was some confusion over who was going to deliver her child. Mary Date informed the relieving officer that Charlotte wanted Kitty Walker (Mary's sister) to act as her midwife, even though Charlotte had made no such request.[51] Mary Date had obviously abused her position and exploited the vulnerability of Charlotte to obtain employment for her sister. Nevertheless, Kitty Walker was a trained midwife with nine years' experience.[52] The birth of Charlotte's child was, however, difficult. Charlotte suffered from a laceration of the perineum during 'the violent Efforts of Labour', leading to a prolapsed womb.[53]

From this point, Charlotte should have been attended by a medical officer. Kitty thought there was nothing unusual with Charlotte's injuries and gave her castor oil, senna tea and some hot towels to aid her recovery. Charlotte was certain she should be seen by the medical officer and tried to relay her message to another person, Betty Woolley, who was going to see Waites for some bread.[54] Betty failed to pass on the details of Charlotte's illness, and Waites subsequently claimed it would be 'indelicate for me to ask Questions'. Waites suggested that Betty went to his wife to explain, after which Mary Waites and Betty went to see Charlotte.[55] In the meantime, Kitty spoke to Mr Waites, informing him that nothing was especially wrong with Charlotte, and so he did not send for a surgeon. Several days later, Charlotte sent another message from her bed, and a medical man, Richard Beadon Ruddock from Stowey, was finally sent. Ruddock visited Charlotte that Wednesday night, but he did not examine her until the following morning. It was only on this examination that Charlotte was told the extent of her injuries. Ruddock then notified Abraham King, another medical man, and from then on visited her regularly. This was because the womb needed to be constantly 'replaced', as it 'protruded by some little Exertion on her part'.[56] The type of injury sustained by Charlotte was fairly common, although it was rare for this injury to be so bad on the birth of a woman's first child. According to Charles Locock, another medical man, Charlotte was 'for many Months [after the birth] … constantly in pain, suffering from very distressing and painful Sensations'.[57]

Whilst Charlotte had sustained a lifelong, but not life-threatening, injury, there were two fatalities in the union. One of the four paupers Caswell was instructed not to attend, George Reynold's child, died.[58] Little information has been found about the circumstances surrounding his death; however, the fatality of young John Cook is well documented. John lived at Pig Cross and had been suffering from croup. One morning Lucretia Cook was anxious about her child's health and left the house to obtain an order. James Newman, the relieving officer, asked her about her circumstances, presumably to gauge her need for medical relief, and Lucretia explained that although her husband was a shoemaker, he did not always have work. Lucretia later stated, 'I recollect telling him … I was very poor, and in great Distress, and not able to pay a Doctor; and that I had before been attended by a Parish Doctor'. Newman informed her that she must pay for private medical assistance. Lucretia immediately pawned her son's jacket (for three shillings) and searched for King. He was not at home. When she did find him, he said he charged five shillings for a week's worth of attendance. Lucretia rushed to pawn a gun (for four shillings). At 11 o'clock, she saw James Coles Parker, a local medical man, and asked him to see her son. Parker gave her medicine, free of charge, and asked her to pass a note on to Newman.[59] The letter stressed that John was *'literally dying for want of surgical assistance'*.[60] Newman took the note to the Board of Guardians and told Lucretia to visit him half-an-hour later. After Newman had attended the board, Mrs Ware (Lucretia's neighbour) went to the 'Hall' (supposedly where the board had met) and had a note for Lucretia stating that King would attend John.[61] King finally arrived that afternoon and visited on several occasions. During this time John's illness had advanced, and he died that evening.[62]

The board's desire to keep the union purse strings tight had fatal consequences for the medical officers as well as medical relief claimants. After the medical officers had worked, temporarily, for the union for three weeks, their bills were sent in to the board. The Guardians decided not to keep to their word by paying the medical officers on a case-by-case basis, as had been agreed. On Friday 27 October, the board voted, by a majority of one, to pay a proportion of the bills based on their previous salaries, working out the cost of three weeks' pay.[63] It transpired that only a very small proportion of William Caswell's bill was reimbursed.[64] Some of the Guardians had anticipated the consequences of their actions and immediately declared that they would defend any legal actions brought against the board. The following week, Caswell was 'in a State of the greatest Excitement', believing that 'the Guardians had taken advantage of his Poverty'.[65] He could not afford to take legal action against them, being nearly bankrupt from attending more poor than he had intended to, a function of the size of his district, and also having worn out two horses in the process. Caswell took his own life; his body was found on 4 November.[66]

Caswell's suicide did not mark the end of the problems within the Bridgwater Union. A medical man appointed to attend the poor of the Bridgwater workhouse from July 1837, John Rodney Ward, had lied about his qualifications. He claimed he had obtained a qualification in the Netherlands at Leiden University, but it transpired that he had left before the course finished.[67] Unsurprisingly, in 1838 he was convicted at the Wells Assizes Court for botching a surgical procedure.[68] There was a similar trial in the Kingston Union (Surrey) but, according to Ruth Hodgkinson, such cases were rare, as medical men were usually only reprimanded by the Guardians.[69] That the

Bridgwater Medical Association was hostile towards Ward may have been a factor in his prosecution.[70] However, after the trial, Ward was, astonishingly, reappointed for a second year. When a 'more moderate' set of Guardians was elected in 1839, his contract was not renewed.[71]

*Inquiries and impacts*

The events at Bridgwater highlighted many of the fundamental problems with medical relief provision under the early New Poor Law. The competitive tendering desired by the Guardians and permitted by the Assistant Commissioners meant that a medical man's willingness to accept low wages, rather than his skills, was a prerequisite to his employment. This drive for economy led to temporary case-by-case payments, the hiring of unsuitable people to act as medical officers, the founding of large medical districts and, ultimately, the retrenchment of medical relief. As Butler and Drakeford have demonstrated, a scandal could not simply derive from such policies. A scandal *develops* from 'unanticipated exposure, followed by disapproval', after events created by policy decisions.[72] The events at Bridgwater were brought to light in a range of publications. In November 1837 the Bridgwater Medical Association wrote a pamphlet summarising their negotiations with the Board of Guardians and their subsequent broken promises. The medical men emphasised their inadequate pay, the temporary measures orchestrated by the board and the sufferings of the claimants: 'It is to such heart rendering cases as Charlotte Allen's, & Reynold's and Cook's, where the very bed clothes of the dying are stripped off and pawned to obtain relief, where immediate death or a life of torture are the consequences of the system acted on by the Board of Guardians'.[73] They detailed Charlotte's case, although the facts were exaggerated. Indeed, the pamphlet states that she was suffering from puerperal fever, although Charlotte herself did not acknowledge that she had suffered from the disease.[74] Just nine days after the pamphlet was published, it was reprinted in *The Times*.[75] News of the medical relief problems, combined with earlier news of overcrowding in the Bridgwater parish workhouse, led to greater awareness that Bridgwater had a troubled union.[76]

In March 1838 the Bridgwater Guardians sent a petition to the government expressing their support for the New Poor Law. Although this action was commended by the Poor Law Commission, it was unable to stop public curiosity.[77] It may have been in defence of the petition sent from the 'Bridgwater Members of College of Surgeons' to the House of Lords, deeply critical of the medical relief provided in the union.[78] So in March 1838, Lord Wharncliffe, a Tory, felt that it was time to investigate what he thought were unfounded allegations about the maladministration of the Amendment Act. There were several cases that had caught his attention, for which he thought papers should be requested and pursued. First, accusations had been made by General Johnson, a magistrate and *ex officio* Guardian, about the operation of the New Poor Law in the Bourne Union (Lincolnshire). Wharncliffe was angered that Johnson had 'take[n] facts on mere hearsay, and not to institute anything like a sufficient investigation'. Second, in the West Riding of Yorkshire, where there had been much 'violence and outrage', clergyman G.S. Bull had spoken at public meetings with stories of great cruelty resulting from the new welfare system. Whilst these two cases were not, as far as he was concerned, based on fact, Wharncliffe thought there were several other cases in which he 'did not think the working of the Poor-law was altogether satisfactory' and that perhaps 'some alteration should be made in the Act'. Knowledge of the events at Bridgwater had now reached parliament. According to Wharncliffe, two issues needed investigation: sickness in the poorhouse and the allocation of medical officers. Bowen and his writings were also mentioned. After the Poor Law Commission completed their own investigations, Wharncliffe thought that 'it was his duty to move their Lordships for a Committee to inquire into all those transactions', as both the circumstances of the Bridgwater Union and actions of the Commissioners appeared unsatisfactory. Lastly, he brought forward the case of a family who wanted to place their children in the Hungerford Union workhouse (Berkshire). Somerset House did not allow such an arrangement, as it was tantamount to relief in aid of wages, a position that Wharncliffe thought was most inflexible.

The Prime Minister, Viscount Melbourne, thought this an overreaction to several operational problems. Others saw it as a chance to push for the repeal of the Amendment Act itself; the Lords agreed for the papers to be requested. The Earl of Radnor moved for the papers relating to sickness and dietary in the Dudley Union to be examined, showing further support for the inquiries. This did not mean that the other House was not proceeding with its own investigations.

A Commons Select Committee was already underway, to 'Inquire into the Administration of the Relief of the Poor', but, according to Wharncliffe, it had done little more than collect minutes of evidence from the Poor Law Commissioners themselves.[79]

By the following May, a Select Committee was appointed in the House of Lords with Wharncliffe as chair, commencing its investigations in March 1838. Regardless of the fact that the inquiry was triggered by many different cases of maladministration, the majority of the committee's time was occupied with examining the events at Bridgwater; 787 pages of the 1,312-page report consisted of minutes of evidence taken from those involved. Key individuals, including Weale and Bowen, in addition to medical and relieving officers and relief claimants from the Bridgwater Union, were interviewed at length. It was only during these investigations that the full extent and state of medical administration in the union was revealed.[80] At the end of the investigations, the committee found the evidence to be inconclusive and did not allocate blame to any one party. Yet this did not mean the contents of the report were unimportant.

Bridgwater also featured in the 1837–38 Commons Select Committee, the committee about which Wharncliffe had previously been critical. Although the committee initially interviewed each of the Assistants on the implementation of the new welfare regime, it moved on to explore a number of policy themes.[81] According to the poor law Commissioners, medical relief was 'one of the most important subjects considered'.[82] The committee's 'Medical Inquiry', as they called it, began in July 1838, overlapping with the Lords' investigations into Bridgwater.[83] To gauge the opinions of those who had experience and knowledge relating to providing medical relief, the committee interviewed 'several gentlemen connected with that profession'.[84] These included the secretary of the PMSA, Henry Wyldbore Rumsey, and the president of the British Medical Association (BMA) and long-standing editor of *The Lancet*, Dr George Webster. Ten other men, who either represented medical men in local medical associations or had acted as medical officers, were also selected. It was no coincidence then that Jonathan Toogood, the chair of the Bridgwater Medical Association, was called on to give evidence.

Toogood was considered by the committee to be a man of 'great experience'.[85] He had been a surgeon all his professional life and had spent 20 years working in the Bridgwater Infirmary. He was also employed as a parish doctor prior to the formation of the Bridgwater Union. His opinions on the organisation and current state of medical relief were unsurprising, considering the recent events at Bridgwater. Toogood thought that allocating large medical districts was problematic.[86] He suggested that medical officers should reside near, or in, their districts and that medical officers should be familiar with the neighbourhood in which they practised. He also believed there should be 'a fixed salary for the fixed paupers' rather than any tendering or allowing payments 'per case'.[87] Toogood thus conveyed the views of the Bridgwater Medical Association at a national level. That they were similar to the national medical practitioners' associations, the PMSA and the BMA, must have helped his case. The national associations sent a joint petition to the Commons during the inquiry, asking for medical relief stipulations. The committee agreed with their analysis, positing that there were two main deficiencies in medical relief administration: 'that the medical districts, in some instances, seem to be inconveniently large ... and that the remuneration should be such as to insure the proper attention and the best medicines'.[88] Although the committee did not stipulate any particular policies, 'the introduction of these and other alterations' was left 'to the discretion of the Poor Law Commissioners'.[89] The Commission continued their tradition of fact-finding first, wanting to gather further information about the ways in which medical relief was provided before creating new policies.

The following year the Commission instructed the Assistant Poor Law Commissioners to make detailed reports about medical relief provision in their districts. The Assistants were directed to document how the medical officers were selected, whether they tendered for positions, how medical officers were paid, the size of each district, whether any dissatisfaction had arisen relating to medical relief and what types of individual or family were being provided with medical relief.[90] Bridgwater, unsurprisingly, did not receive a sparkling report. Bridgwater's new Assistant Commissioner, Daniel Goodson Adey, had already written to the Commission, explaining that 'the business of this Union appears to be done in a less satisfactory manner than *any* I've visited'.[91] Adey's district contained 35 unions, so clearly Bridgwater's medical relief provision was still flawed. This did not mean that everything was ticking over nicely in every other place under his superintendence. In ten of Adey's unions, medical officers were unhappy with the size of their medical districts, and the medical men of 14 unions were dissatisfied with their salaries. In addition, the Guardians of three unions and the poor of two were not satisfied with the attendance or efficiency of the medical officers.[92]

Before a deputation of men from the BMA had met with the Commission, similar reports were being drafted by the other Assistant Commissioners across England and Wales. The Commissioners gave the BMA representatives a copy of the survey recently issued to their Assistant Commissioners and asked them for any further thoughts they had on medical relief beyond those discovered in the 'Medical Inquiry'.[93] The following month another deputation of the association met with the Commissioners, this time to specifically complain that the system of tendering had continued. The Commission decided not to issue any immediate policies.[94] A couple of days later, the BMA president, Webster, presented a comprehensive 'Report and Plans for an Amended System of Parochial Medical Relief', which was soon to be discussed between the deputation, the Commissioners and the Home Secretary, Lord John Russell.[95] The recent medical relief problems, however, could not be forgotten by the Commission. During their meeting, members of the BMA drew on examples of bad practice from all over England and Wales to argue their points. Bridgwater featured at least twice. In relation to the objectionable practice of tendering and how, specifically, the lowest tender was taken in opposition to 'character, personal qualification, and residence', they referred to cases of maladministration at 'Aylesbury, Wallingford, Eastry, Hambledon, Ongar, Penshurst, Wheatenhurst, Leighton Buzzard, the Bridgewater [sic] and other Unions'. In relation to the inadequate skills possessed by men appointed by Boards of Guardians, the deputation made reference to the cases in the 'Bridgwater and Kingston Union[s], as evinced by actions at law and verdicts of juries'.[96]

Notwithstanding that summaries of the Assistants' reports were published at the end of 1839 in the Commission's *Report on the Further Amendment on the Poor Laws*, it took another two years for any policy stipulations to be enforced.[97] This delay was not in any way related to being unable to make policies, but was rather due to an anxiety on the part of the Commission not to dictate to the localities. In March 1840 the Commission issued a circular letter to Guardians, calling for 'their suggestions in this Report [*on the Further Amendment*]' to be considered.[98] The Commission, in their Seventh

Annual Report, pessimistically admitted that 'no extensive change in the existing [medical relief] arrangements were likely to originate with the Boards of Guardians'.[99] Much 'dissatisfaction continued to prevail amongst many members of the medical profession', and pressure on the Commission for reforms continued to be exerted.[100]

The Commission finally released compulsory and legally binding policies on 12 March 1842. It was known as the General Medical Order and took effect on 1 March 1843. There were seven main sections to the Order, each on different aspects of medical administration. The first addressed the problems of setting salaries, and made it unlawful for Boards of Guardians to invite tenders. Rather, if a vacancy arose for a medical officer in a union, the Board had to specify the salary he would receive alongside a list of the places he would have to visit. Any salary given to an officer in an alternative manner would be disallowed in the union accounts and the Guardians would personally become responsible for the cost. The Order also stipulated that the medical officers should have both medical and surgical qualifications. By Lady Day 1843 medical officers were not permitted to attend districts larger than 15,000 acres in size or containing populations of more than 15,000. A fourth theme in the Order set out a list of payments per case, but only for particular procedures. Medical officers could claim £5, in addition to their normal salary, for several types of operation, such as amputations. Medical officers would also receive an extra £3 per case for the treatment of simple fractures of the thigh or leg and just £1 for a fracture of the arm. For each case of midwifery, medical officers were to receive between 10 and 20 shillings, and £2 for difficult deliveries.[101]

The next section of the General Medical Order ensured that a union could check whether a patient had been visited and also that someone was always present to attend the sick within each district. Every officer was instructed to keep a weekly return, which should include the date of visits to paupers and their names. In addition, within 21 days of a new officer's appointment, he should provide the Guardians with the name of a substitute who would act on his behalf during absence or illness. Guardians were instructed to create a list of 'permanent paupers' every six months, including 'all such aged and infirm persons, and persons permanently sick or disabled, as may be actually receiving [outdoor] relief'. These poor could be issued with a ticket that allowed them to see a medical officer without gaining the prior permission of a relieving officer. The final theme of the Order related to the continuance of medical officers, indicating that they should only lose their positions if they resigned, became disqualified by the Commission or died.[102]

As Hodgkinson suggests, the policies closely follow the ideas of the medical men, and in particular Webster's report presented to the Commission in 1839.[103] The policies were inspired by and developed out of the medical relief problems experienced at the local level, including the events that culminated in the Bridgwater Scandal. These stipulations were evidently important in the development of medical relief during the New Poor Law, but adherence to the Order was another matter.

### The implementation of the General Medical Order

The fact that the Order had been issued did not mean that the practices altered instantaneously. Issued on 12 March 1842, the Order was supposed to take effect by Lady Day 1843, the Commission having factored in ample time to inform Boards of Guardians about its contents. One opportunity to inform the Guardians came when the Commission authorised the medical officer appointments in each year. For instance, in 1841 the Dulverton Guardians (Somerset) divided their union into only two medical districts. By the following year the union was redivided into three districts, but although these districts had very small populations, they far exceeded the maximum acreage stipulated in the Order.[104] The Commission therefore requested that the Guardians again redivide their union.[105] Whilst all unions had already received the documents containing the Order itself in 1842, the Commission was making sure that the stipulations of the Order had been read.

Although plenty of time had been allowed for the unions to adjust their practices, the General Medical Order had been applied with great difficulty and 'Guardians from all over the country demanded its suspension for their own Unions on one or several grounds'. According to Hodgkinson, between 20 and 30 unions obtained a suspension within the first year of the Order's implementation. Hodgkinson, drawing on the case of several northern towns and cities, thought that limiting the areas or population for the attendance of each medical officer was problematic, as there was ample charitable provision, including voluntary hospitals and dispensaries, to meet the needs of the poor. In addition, in such urban areas there was no point in limiting the population allocated to each officer because they 'resided so close to the poor'. The system of extras for surgical or midwifery cases was also ignored. Hodgkinson believes that the Guardians thought it had given medical relief recipients an unfair advantage over the independent labourer, deterring them from obtaining their own surgery and midwifery attendance. Sometimes there was simply a lack of resident medical officers, making the reduction of districts impossible. The ticket system did not work either. Referring to the Stepney Union in East London, Hodgkinson argues that some unions did not adopt the practice because there were simply 'numerous claims constantly being made for urgent and pressing cases'. In addition, ticket distribution gave individuals an entitlement to medical relief that apparently encouraged applications for help.[106]

There appear to have been three main problems with implementing the Order in rural unions. First, many unions had a low population density, meaning that the restriction of each medical district to 15,000 acres was problematic. The result would be a great number of medical officers, each one with a small wage, which was both unpopular with the medical men and inefficient for a union to administer. Some unions also contained vast expanses of unpopulated land, including woodlands and forests. The Wimborne and Cranborne Union (Dorset), for example, contained a segment of Cranborne Chase. The total area of the union was 78,358 acres, with a population of 15,793. Although the union was divided into four districts, each one exceeded the maximum acreage stipulated in the General Order. So eager were the Guardians to comply with the Order that they corresponded with their eastwardly neighbouring unions, Fordingbridge (made of parishes from Hampshire and Wiltshire) and Ringwood (Hampshire), asking whether they could take charge of medical attendance on the Chase.[107]

As Hodgkinson suggests, there was an increase in the number of medical officers 'by a few hundred every year' after 1843, which indicated 'the desired effect of diminishing the size of medical districts'.[108] Yet a lack of medical men in rural locations meant that large medical districts *had* to be accepted. One medical district in the Mere Union (consisting of parishes from Wiltshire, Dorset and Somerset), which had covered parts of the Wiltshire Downs, was large simply because there were no other resident medical men.[109] The Commission simply had to accept that, even if the district was divided in two, no one could fill the vacancy.[110] And, even if medical men were in residence, they were sometimes deemed unsuitable to perform the role of a medical officer. In 1844 the Commission heard how one medical officer, appointed by the South Stoneham Union (Hampshire), had practised for three years with just one of the two required qualifications.[111] The second problem with implementing the Order, therefore, was a lack of medical men, either in the right place or with suitable qualifications, to take up the positions available. Third, the ticket system did not always work because, rather than there being a plethora of cases to attend, as Hodgkinson found, there were sometimes too few and therefore such a system was deemed unnecessary. For instance, the Kingsclere Union Board of Guardians (Hampshire) reported that, as 'all the paupers here were known to the medical officers', the provision of tickets was futile.[112]

Although the Commission wanted all unions to follow the stipulations of the Order, they used their discretionary powers to sanction deviations where implementing the stipulations proved difficult. Whether these deviations were detrimental to the health of the medical claimants within these unions is, however, open to question. Nevertheless, for the first time in poor law history, medical relief standards had been set.

## Workhouse employment policy and the Andover Scandal

*Work in the workhouse and the controversy of bone-crushing*

A key component of the deterrent workhouse system was setting the poor to work. Initially, though, the Commission spent more of their time considering how unions should employ the poor *outside* the workhouse, rather than inside. Indeed, in 1835 they issued a circular letter to all unions containing 'Suggestions as to the most eligible Modes of providing Out-door Employment for Able-bodied Paupers'.[113] Such advice was needed for several reasons. Some unions, especially in Wales and the north of England, resisted building or expanding their workhouses on ideological or financial grounds.[114] The workhouse system did not suit, it was argued, the cyclical unemployment experienced in the industrial towns and cities.[115] Southern unions also lacked workhouses, but in unions such as Dulverton this was due to the low population rather than resistance to the New Poor Law. The Commission desired all unions to provide task-work that should 'discourage applications' and be free from corruption by local landowners and farmers.[116] Even in unions where the poor were accommodated within workhouses, the Guardians refused to employ the poor indoors. For instance, in the Huddersfield Union in 1843, the poor continued to work in stone quarries and on parish roads. According to Felix Driver, this reflected the 'localism' maintained by the Guardians, so the poor's labour would benefit the parish rather than the union as a whole.[117]

Gradually, unions with fully functioning workhouses were issued with 'Special Orders' prohibiting the provision of outdoor relief, and in 1844 the Outdoor Relief Prohibitory Order was released. Yet, important clauses or 'loopholes' remained to permit outdoor relief 'in cases of sudden and urgent necessity'.[118] Outdoor relief could legitimately continue under the authorisation of the Commission, and did so when many more people required relief than the union workhouse itself could accommodate. The slump in the stocking trade over the winter of 1837–38, for instance, forced the Commission to sanction outdoor relief in return for task-work on the roads in the Nottingham Union.[119] Hardship could also be caused by severe weather. In February 1840, for instance, wet weather flooded land in the parish of Tadley (Hampshire), leaving several families destitute and in need of poor relief.[120] A decade later, such exemptions led to the development of another order, the Outdoor Labour Test Order (1851), which formalised the process by which many unions had been providing outdoor relief alongside task-work. According to Brundage, it symbolised the Poor Law Board's belief that 'the "less eligibility" principle could be honoured without compelling' the labouring poor 'to enter the workhouse'.[121]

The Commission spent less time agonising over work provided within the workhouse, notwithstanding that a fundamental part of the workhouse regime was, as Brundage has asserted, the provision of 'monotonous and irksome tasks'.[122] This is not to say that the Commission did not promote the employment of inmates. In their 'Workhouse Rules', published in the First Annual Report, the Commission stipulated that work should benefit the union purse as a whole, that no inmate works 'on his own account', that work would be undertaken at particular times of the day, that no work 'except the usual household work and cooking' shall be undertaken on a Sunday and those who refused to work could be punished.[123] Although the domestic duties involved in running a workhouse were supposed to be 'performed by the female paupers', the Commission did not specify the other sorts of work the male poor should undertake.[124] As the Poor Law Commissioner George Nicholls recalled in his *History of the English Poor Law*, '[t]he kind of labour on which the inmates of the several workhouses should be employed, rested entirely with the boards of guardians'.[125] In consequence, the poor undertook a variety of tasks including stone-breaking alongside the lighter, but equally mundane, work of oakum-picking, although lighter tasks were usually saved for women and the elderly. A few Boards of Guardians encouraged 'local industries' in the workhouse: straw was plaited in Buckinghamshire and fruit punnets were made in Kent.[126] Even though the New Poor Law Union workhouse was used as deterrent to relief claimants, on paper the Commission was clear about the purpose of work in the workhouse. Whilst pauper labour could 'provide necessary articles for the workhouse', it was not supposed 'to be considered a punishment'.[127]

As the last chapter revealed, the Assistant Commissioners of the south of England recommended bone-crushing to Boards of Guardians. Bone-crushing was portrayed to these unions as a suitable employment in a number of ways. First, they believed it would deter individuals from entering the workhouse. As A'Court, writing to Somerset House regarding the recent increase in admissions in the Fareham Union workhouse, proclaimed: 'I am very sorry to hear … that the dread of the Workhouse House is wearing off! – I have suggested the immediate introduction of such irksome work as may make it a less desirable abode for such as ought to earn their maintenance elsewhere. We must have a mill – bone crushers &c. &c.'.[128] Boards of Guardians embraced this understanding too, claiming that the employment made the 'workhouse test' effective.[129] For instance, the Dorchester Union believed the employment deterred many vagrants who passed the workhouse whilst tramping on the adjacent 'high roads of communication'.[130] Second, bone-crushing did not, according to Tufnell, interfere with 'independent labourers' work', unlike '[s]tone breaking, faggot-making, and many other workhouse occupations'.[131] Later, this proved to be untrue, with Chadwick reporting that 'bone-dust is a regular article of manufacture and private com-merce'.[132] Third, the Assistants demonstrated that a profit could be made from bone-crushing. Using the example of Beaminster, Tufnell claimed that this could be up to 15 per cent over the cost of the raw materials.[133] Unions were clearly receptive to the economically minded arguments of the Assistants.

Bone-crushing was reserved for able-bodied men, male vagrants and the 'refractory'. Only the Andover Union is known to have also allocated the task to young boys.[134] It was undertaken in several dif-ferent ways. By far the most popular method was the iron rod and box, also referred to as a 'pestle and mortar' (Figure 5.1). The box was made of wood held together with iron brackets. The rod was either solid metal or had a metal end cast on a wooden handle.[135] One rod and box would be used by one inmate at a time. The number of boxes and rods purchased by Guardians therefore varied greatly from union to union. In some unions just a hammer was beaten against a 'block', an 'iron plate' or even on bare ground.[136] Inmates so engaged were directed to crush a certain weight of bones per day. Due to the range of abilities within the category 'able-bodied', men of differ-ing ability were not expected to crush the same weight of bones.[137] In Warminster (Wiltshire) the Guardians divided the men into two

**Figure 5.1** E. Carlton Tufnell's sketch of a box and rod for crushing bones.

classes, each grinding a different weight of bones. By the following year, three classes had been created.[138] The weight of dust to be crushed also depended on the size of the sieve holes.[139]

Bone mills were also procured by several unions in the region, including Alton and Droxford (Hampshire), Chertsey and Guildford (Surrey) and Westhampnett (west Sussex).[140] Groups of ten men would work the mill for 20 minutes at a time, whilst two employed men would embark on the dangerous task of supplying the mill with bones.[141] There were problems, though. Erecting a mill came at a 'very considerable expense', whilst the fact that several men had to turn the wheel troubled Tufnell because it was tricky to 'apportion' work to each individual.[142] Such thoughts were linked to the use of bone-crushing as a form of control in the workhouse, to punish those who were deemed as refractory. The Hartley Wintney Board believed that bone-crushing was a means 'of keeping the idle and disorderly paupers in order'.[143] The Epping Board in Essex thought bone-crushing was a useful task for the refractory inmates who were very 'difficult to deal with in the ordinary way'.[144] Although using work as punishment was in direct opposition to the wishes of the Commission on paper, the deterrent principle of the New Poor Law workhouse led to a system that legitimised the abuse of the poor through work.

Regardless of the supposed benefits of this employment, bone-crushing was a contentious practice from the start of the New Poor Law and was frequently condemned at a national level from the passage of the Amendment Act. In the House of Commons, anti-poor law speakers openly denounced this form of employment, such as Finbury's radical MP Thomas Wakley. An experienced surgeon and the founding editor of *The Lancet*, he was keen to expose 'a series of outrages' on the new system.[145] Indeed, in a House of Commons debate in 1841, he stated: '[t]he law had originated with a set of Utilitarians ... For them they would have gone on and ground the bones of the poor, and used them for manure if they thought it would enrich the soil'.[146] Whilst his words irritated pro-New Poor Law members sitting in that session, Wakley had described the workhouse system in a way that was hard to forget. This picture was also painted in the media, albeit several years later. When commenting on Lord John Russell's views that inmates who died within the workhouse could be buried on union land, *The Times* wrote: 'their bones might have been made as available as horse bones at Andover, thus completing the process of transmigration by an inexhaustible series of production, decomposition, and reproduction eternally revolving in the same circle'.[147] Evidently, bone-crushing was known to be an arduous task, and those who condemned it used it to symbolise the corrosive nature of the welfare system on the lives of workhouse inmates more generally.

Whilst bone-crushing had been linked to oppression by anti-poor law figures and anti-poor law media, it is clear that those who actually set to work on bone-crushing in southern England were also discontented. Four male paupers in the South Stoneham Union 'positively refused to do their appointed task of Bone crushing'. The Guardians decided to obtain a warrant against the men from the magistrate for 'disobedience of Orders'. In the following month another man who had refused to crush bones was similarly issued with a warrant.[148] In the Beaminster Union, the workhouse punishment book reveals a number of similar cases. Men refused to work, swore and annoyed their fellow inmates at work.[149] The most violent act of protest recorded came from James Spacklin, who, whilst working in the workhouse yard, picked up one of the bones and threw it at the infirmary window.[150]

Whilst the poor resisted bone-crushing, complaints would seemingly only echo within the workhouse walls. However, one individual's experiences of bone-crushing received national attention. In February 1842, Charles Brooker, who had stood as a Chartist parliamentary candidate for Brighton in the previous year, published an important pamphlet entitled 'The Murder Den, and Its Means of Destruction'. It examined the experiences of William Smith, an inmate who crushed bones in the Eastbourne Union (East Sussex).[151] Smith, a parishioner of Wilmington, entered the workhouse in May 1840 when he lost work for holding a Methodist prayer meeting at his cottage.[152] A year later he became very unwell and was hospitalised for a week. His illness was linked to his employment crushing bones in the workhouse. As detailed in the interview taken and transcribed by Brooker, many of the bones procured by the Guardians still had flesh on them and when crushed emitted a nauseous effluvium. Brooker argued: '[c]an any punishment; irrespective of any bodily pain or disease be contemplated as more dreadful; – and this as to other able-bodied workmen inmates – more horrible, than death by such a process as this?' He believed very firmly that the working classes 'have now become slave classes ... British liberty has now taken flight'.[153]

These views led to 'illegal chicanery', preventing him from sitting on the Eastbourne Board of Guardians.[154] Indeed, just like John Bowen in Bridgwater, Brooker wanted to sit on the board to more effectively campaign for the better treatment of the inmates. However, all was not lost. In the spring of 1842, the Brighton Whig MP, Captain George Pechell, took Brooker's concerns – and pamphlet – to the House of Commons. Pechell read out direct quotations, including one from Smith's interview: '[i]f I had stopped longer in the bone-house I should not have come out alive'.[155] Sir James Graham, appointed Home Secretary in September 1841, suggested that this was simply an 'unfortunate quarrel', and besides the Bill for continuing the Poor Law Commission soon to be passed would contain certain 'improvements'.[156] From that moment onwards it appears that Pechell had a personal mission: to make the government investigate work in workhouses.

Pechell's next chance to mention bone-crushing was in March 1843, after a motion made by William Ferrand, introduced at the beginning of this chapter, for a copy of the minutes of a recent meeting of the Halifax Guardians. Graham was not obliging, leaving Ferrand to wonder aloud, in his characteristically critical stance towards the New Poor Law, whether 'there was something behind the scenes' that he 'wished to conceal from the public'. The Prime Minister, Robert Peel, intervened, stating that the government had nothing to hide, and that they could move to get the requisite papers and 'also a copy of any resolution for the erection of a *rag-mill* made on that or any other day'.[157] Peel had been briefed before the session, as had Sir James Graham, who told the House he had already 'expressed a strong opinion to the Poor-law Commissioners' against the use of rag mills. Subsequently, the Commission informed the unions that 'such mills would not be used again'.[158] Pechell chipped in that he trusted a similar course would be pursued to put an end to bone-crushing.[159] But Pechell was again ignored, and Ferrand's request for papers was defeated. Just 11 MPs supported his request.[160]

It was not until the following year that Pechell mentioned bone-crushing again, during a debate concerning the 1844 Poor Law Amendment Bill. He reminded the House of the 'objection that was felt by paupers' to the work.[161] Graham then confirmed his dislike of bone-crushing as a workhouse employment and the conversation quickly returned to the intricacies of the Bill.[162] In the meantime, the Commission had instigated its own inquiries into whether the employment of crushing bones was unsuitable for the inmates of workhouses. In April every Board of Guardians was ordered to ask one of their medical officers, who attended the workhouse inmates, whether the employment was injurious to the inmates' health. The reactions varied – but not greatly. At Beaminster the medical officer claimed 'no case of disease has come under my observation, caused by the employment of crushing bones'.[163] The Warminster officer noted that some inmates had 'inflamed hand or fingers', but generally there was no 'risk to their health'.[164] The effluvia, reported many, had little adverse effect upon the health of the inmates or those within the workhouse grounds. Their symptoms clearly did not reach the severity of Smith's. The Commission seemingly had no cause for concern.

*Inquiries, the Andover Scandal and its impacts*

In July 1844, a frustrated Pechell moved for a return for information from all unions in England and Wales that had been using bone-crushing as a workhouse employment, including the date when crushing had commenced, the sums paid for bones and those received for the bone dust.[165] By February of the following year, Pechell complained that the returns had not been laid on the table of the House. The Commission, it was reported, had been engaged with other business, including assisting the Commons Select Committee on Gilbert's Act. Pechell and Graham locked horns once again. The Commission was, Graham believed, unable to impose a ban: 'if the Commissioners had had the power, they would have put an end to it instantly'. This was said regardless of the fact that, as the case of Halifax demonstrated, local practices could be amended and stopped altogether, and regardless of the explicit encouragement from the Assistant Commissioners to adopt bone-crushing. Graham stressed that the practice was 'persevered in by the local authorities'.[166] He contended that local adoption meant that only local-level powers could instigate change in policy, or national powers needed strengthening to overrule local autonomy. This provoked a sarcastic comment from Wakley that 'local interests are much stronger than I was at first inclined to believe'.[167]

The Commission finally provided the House with the returns in February 1845.[168] Not only did these provide a picture of how widespread the practice had become in the south, it illustrated that the work was unprofitable. In the meantime, however, the localities were certainly proving their independence. The Bolton Guardians declined to comply with the Order for information from the House, an issue that allowed Pechell to keep bone-crushing on the agenda throughout the spring.[169] Sir James Graham repeated himself. The powers of the Commission were set by the Amendment Act, and 'if any increase of them were desired, there must be an alteration of the law'.[170]

Soon, another disagreeable employment practice came to light in the Commons. On 1 August, another MP for Finsbury, radical Thomas Slingsby Duncombe, presented a petition from residents of Mansfield.[171] Here the vagrants of the union workhouse worked on a treadwheel that produced nothing.[172] When Duncombe asked Graham whether such an employment was suitable, his response indicated that the Commission already knew about the work and had sent out a 'peremptory order ... for its immediate discontinuance'.[173] Evidently, the government and Commission were able to assert some control over how Boards of Guardians were employing workhouse inmates. Straight after this discussion, another commenced on the topic of bone-crushing. Wakley stood to ask Graham whether he had heard from the Poor Law Commission of the 'practice which he understood to prevail in the Union of Andover'. Here the poor had been 'quarrelling with each other about the bones' from which they scavenged meat to eat.[174] Graham replied 'I will institute an inquiry this very night'.[175] Another New Poor Law scandal was brewing, as Commons attention created media attention, which in turn would inform the public about the problems in Andover. In order to understand how this developed, we need to understand the role of the Assistant Commissioner for Andover, Henry Parker, and the maltreatment experienced in the Andover workhouse.

Three days after Graham stated an inquiry would commence, Henry Parker arrived at the Andover Union workhouse to conduct some investigations.[176] After interviewing several of the inmates, he confirmed the accusations made in the Commons: 'it certainly appears to have been a practice with the inmates to pick out such bones and eat the marrow from them'. Parker also noticed that the food was 'unexceptional in quality' and that perhaps bread could be added to some of the meat- and potato-based dinners.[177] By mid-August, the

Commission directed Parker to make further enquiries, whilst also causing as 'little delay as possible'. As the historian Norman Longmate details, Parker was in an awkward situation: '[w]hen he tried to exclude irrelevant evidence, he was attacked in the press for planning to hush up injustice; when he granted a brief adjournment to allow more witnesses to be assembled, the Commissioners accused him of wasting time'.[178] Colin and Mary Ann McDougal, the workhouse master and matron, resigned their situations in September, not least because of the continuing inquiry and the threat of prosecution. Indeed their governance had resulted in more than hunger. They subjected the inmates supposedly in their care to horrifying physical and mental abuse – several female inmates were abused by the workhouse master himself.[179] Parker then made the mistake of recommending to the union a new master, a man who had managed the Oxford workhouse, only to discover he had been dismissed from a previous situation for misconduct.[180] Parker then suggested that the Commission should go ahead with the prosecution of the workhouse staff at Andover, but no legal action was decided upon.[181]

Press attention surrounding the events at Andover and in Somerset House escalated throughout the summer and autumn of 1845. Gossip included the scarring of inmate's faces from the fragments of bones flying out of the box, and the (unfounded) account of cannibalism whereby human bones from a local graveyard were added to the bones to be pounded that were then eaten by the starved inmates.[182] The Commission needed to demonstrate to the public and the government, quickly, that they acknowledged that the conditions in the Andover workhouse were abominable and that they were in control of the situation. These circumstances forced the resignation of Parker. Historians have been sympathetic towards Parker because his departure from the Commission was not entirely justified. Brundage, for instance, argues that although he could have noticed the problems at Andover before they had reached the Commons, 'the corps of assistants had been pared back from a high 21 to a mere 9, making meaningful inspections impossible'.[183] He was publicly named and shamed, not for his own deficiencies, but for the failings of the Commission. Parker did not remain silent, though. He released a 'torrent of abuse' upon the Commission in a pamphlet in which he outlined the trials he had encountered.[184] It gained support from the usual anti-New Poor Law crowd and garnered coverage in newspapers. At the same time,

William Day, another Assistant, had been asked to resign because of an illness, although the real reason stemmed from the resistance he had faced when trying to implement the New Poor Law in Wales.[185]

It was in this context that a ban on bone-crushing was issued. On 8 November a General Order was released banning 'the employment of Pauper Inmates of Union Workhouses in Pounding, Grinding, or otherwise Breaking Bones, or in preparing Bone Dust'.[186] The Commission did not, however, issue the ban on its own accord, not least because one of the three Commissioners, Nicholls, believed that there was no evidence to suggest that the work was improper. Indeed, he introduced the practice in the Southwell workhouse prior to 1834.[187] The government clearly had a direct influence on Somerset House, an influence for which Andover proved to be a catalyst. Graham recalled that it was 'owing to *that* case' he decided to direct 'his attention more earnestly and particularly to that subject'. After some 'investigation' he found that the Commissioners could issue a General Order and '*pressed* upon the Commissioners the expediency of issuing such an order'.[188] In the official report about the dangers of bone-crushing, written to justify the release of the Order, Chadwick focused on the offensive effluvia that arose from bone-crushing which was 'injurious' to the workers and other 'susceptible classes of inmates', and not the events at Andover.[189]

Nicholls recalled that 'under the excitement of the moment, bone-breaking was denounced as being an improper employment for the inmates of the workhouse'.[190] On one hand, he was correct – the Order was simply produced to show that the Commissioners were addressing 'the attacks made on bone crushing'.[191] On the other hand, Nicholls' claim was short-sighted. The practice had long been denounced as an improper form of employment and the Andover Scandal had simply tipped the balance, leading to a change in policy.

### The General Order prohibiting bone-crushing

Notice of the bone-crushing ban was made on Saturday 8 November 1845, and was to take effect by 1 January the following year.[192] However, 33 different Boards wrote to the Commission remonstrating with the ban on several grounds.[193] First, the Guardians could not understand why the ban applied to them, rather than to the Andover Union alone. The Maidstone Guardians expressed their regret that the Commission did not make inquiry into the employment in their workhouse, implying that it was completely sound compared to that at Andover.[194] Clearly, they were aware of the circumstances surrounding the ban. The Wareham and Purbeck Guardians expressed 'much regret that the public indignation, so naturally excited by the horrid details and gross mismanagement in the Andover Union, should have led to a sweeping order'.[195] Guardians associated the ban with this singular malpractice rather than the objectionable nature of the employment as a whole. Second, the Order was issued in the winter, a time of year when most workhouse populations increased. Without a deterrent, there were fears that workhouses would become overcrowded. Third, many Boards of Guardians had significant stocks of bones and had invested in crushing equipment.[196]

As a consequence of these complaints, 13 unions were granted a suspension of the Order until 1 April 1846. The Commission and Graham were unwilling to issue suspensions to many unions, prioritising those most in 'need'.[197] When the first suspension was issued, to the Wincanton Union, the Commissioners said they had been 'influenced by the special circumstances connected with the existing arrangements of the Board of Guardians for setting the Poor to work' in that union.[198] The Commission elicited the views of their Assistants as to the need for suspension. Tufnell, in response to the Commission's motion that the Melksham Union be suspended from the Order, highlighted the great stock of bones in the union and the pressure of able-bodied paupers in the winter, claiming that '[y]ou will observe that throughout the whole of the South of England, the first fortnight in February is the most pauperized part of the year'. As the Commission stated, 'looking to the special circumstances and upon the advice of the Assistant Commissioner, the Commissioners were prepared' to suspend the Order.[199]

Whilst it appears, as Graham stated, that each application was carefully considered before a suspension was issued, he and the Commission might have issued the suspensions with ulterior motives. Pechell, who was unwilling to let the suspensions go unchallenged, pointed out that unions granted a suspension 'had a large stock of bones', so the gruesome practice would, in some places, continue for longer than he had hoped.[200] His observation was, according to the correspondence received by the Commission from Boards of Guardians, largely true. The Commission and Secretary of State were, however, anxious that these final stocks would be worked on in the safest possible mode and even asked workhouse medical officers to carry out checks accordingly. The Guildford Union was allowed a suspension based 'on the understanding that the persons who are employed to feed the mill shall not be paupers, but paid servants of the workhouse'.[201] Such actions may have protected the Commission should another problem arise, but nevertheless Pechell wanted Graham to end the suspending order immediately.[202] Notably, these suspensions also caused tension between the Commission and some Boards of Guardians, but on the basis that there were not enough suspensions. The Frome Board (Somerset), for instance, wished the Commission had 'give[n] the same weight to the representations of this Board which they have given to the statements of other unions on the subject'.[203] The reply stated that the suspensions were issued to unions in 'special' circumstances.[204] Regardless of these complaints, bone-crushing was not illegal in *all* union workhouses until 1 April 1846.

Whilst the General Medical Order was impractical, it had not disrupted the operation of workhouses like the bone-crushing ban. All Boards were forced to find an alternative employment for their male residents, a task many Boards of Guardians thought was nigh on impossible to complete. The Beaminster Board stated that they could 'find no means of labour' for their poor.[205] The Commission started to recommend various employments, including stone-breaking, oakum-picking and a hand corn-milling.[206] This angered some Guardians, such as those at Cranbrook (Kent), who outlined why each of these employments was not applicable within their locality and within the pre-existing infrastructure of their workhouse. Stone for stone-breaking would have to be procured from Coxheath (12 miles away) and, they contended, there was no space for a hand corn-mill.[207] Of course, Somerset House could not rescind the Order, and had no desire to do so, not least because the Andover Scandal and its consequences had 'grown to be one of more than ordinary interest'.[208]

In the months, and years, that passed after the ban, the Guardians still struggled to find alternative employment. Some 16 months after the ban, Assistant Commissioner John Graves saw the men in the Cricklade and Wootton Bassett Union workhouse without work. The lack of employment, according to Graves, allowed the poor to enter and leave the workhouse as they pleased without working for the union in return. Graves recommended that the Guardians organise the poor to break stones and pick oakum.[209] Similarly, in late 1847, Edward Gulson, another Assistant Commissioner, noted that the Beaminster Union Guardians had established 'no work at which to employ this class of inmates'.[210] So bad was the problem in this union that parish officers evidently thought they could take matters into their own hands. The churchwardens of Netherbury, for instance, wanted to rent between 15 and 25 acres of land to employ their parishioners, an employment scheme that harked back to those implemented under the old poor laws.[211] Whilst this was not permitted by the Commissioners, as it was no longer supported by the poor laws, the Guardians were allowed to employ the poor on union land.[212] By the end of 1847, therefore, two-and-a-half acres of land opposite the workhouse had been reserved for the employment of the poor by the Guardians. In addition, the erection of a flour mill had been discussed, but not acted upon.[213] Boards of Guardians continued to drift along in this manner without a definite form of employment for many years.

The Andover Scandal had long-lasting repercussions for the Poor Law Commission at large, as well as the employment practices of their unions. A Select Committee investigation into the events at Andover was called for in January 1846 by the MP for Andover, Mr Etwall, and it was finally appointed in March. Fifteen members, including several anti-New Poor Law MPs, including Wakley, commenced their investigations a fortnight later.[214] Gradually, the full extent of the abuses at Andover unfolded, with each day of questioning being chronicled in *The Times*. Whilst the details from the Select Committee inquiry have been detailed at length elsewhere, it is worth noting that the master and matron had clearly behaved inappropriately in the performance of their duties.[215] They had siphoned off food from the prescribed dietaries, leaving the inmates hungry, and abused the poor physically and psychologically. As Wells concisely puts it, the Andover workhouse saw an eight-year-long 'regime of terror'.[216] Over the course of three-and-a-half months, the Committee held a plethora of interviews with a range of interviewees.[217]

The Andover inquiry, as Driver noted, became 'a trial of the central authorities rather than of the Guardians at Andover'.[218] It revealed, for instance, that the Commission had accidentally sanctioned an insufficient dietary table for use in the Andover workhouse. The Select Committee also showcased the disharmony amongst the

Commissioners and between the Commissioners and their Secretary, Chadwick, the inability of the Commission to recognise deplorable employments within workhouses and their harsh treatment of Assistant Commissioners such as Parker.[219] The Commission ended in 1847. Commentators at the time, as well as historians, agree that the Select Committee's findings had a large part to play in this. Yet, the New Poor Law itself was not scrapped. A Liberal government passed a reorganisation bill in 1847 that effectively removed some of the autonomy of the Commission by placing it within the responsibilities of four senior ministers, namely the Home Secretary, the Chancellor of the Exchequer, the Lord President and the Lord Privy Seal. The authority was renamed the Poor Law Board and its day-to-day management was headed by one president and two secretaries. The president and one of the secretaries were to sit in parliament. The whole organisation was removed from Somerset House and placed in Whitehall. This, as well as the reform in the management system, meant that the central welfare authority was under closer scrutiny from government. And the individual Boards of Guardians and union workhouses would come under closer scrutiny as well. The appointment of 'Inspectors' in lieu of Assistants reflected their primary responsibility of more thoroughly and frequently superintending the implementation of the New Poor Law within the localities.[220]

## Conclusion

As Butler and Drakeford suggest, welfare scandals have all the makings of a novel: 'all contain stock heroes and villains and many descend … to little more than morality plays'.[221] In the construction of these scandals, the Commission and Boards of Guardians remained remarkably silent. Indeed, why would welfare authorities draw attention to cases of cruelty and neglect, when it was not in their best interests to do so? Rather, there was another level – confined neither to the local or centre – of key actors and stakeholders who brought events to wider public attention. Without John Bowen's investigative reporting, news of Bridgwater's inept Board of Guardians would not have reached the press or received the attention of the House of Lords. Key actors were important in the genesis of the bone-crushing ban. The hype was first stirred up by a number of individuals, including Charles Brooker, in a context and on a topic where opponents of the New Poor Law were already vocal. William Smith's case alone did not result in a public inquiry but it had provided the Commons with a tangible story of why bone-crushing should be investigated and banned. Therefore, it helped to create 'policy strain' in the area of workhouse employments. Without the endeavours of these key actors, working between the Boards of Guardians and the governmental levels of administration, events occurring at the local level may not have reached the wider attention of the nation.

Key actors working at the national level had more power than those working within the middle strata. It was the decision of Lords and MPs on whether to instigate an inquiry into these local events or not. Indeed, Bowen's views on the problems at Bridgwater had caught the eye of Lord Wharncliffe. He wanted the government to ask: '[w]ere those stories of neglect true, or false?'[222] Pechell brought Brooker's pamphlet to the House of Commons and asked Graham whether something ought to be done about bone-crushing employment within the unions. Although Pechell constantly reminded Graham of the existence of the employment, Graham claimed that he was not willing to interfere with 'local practices', although, as detailed above, several other deplorable employments were reported, investigated and stopped. This matches Butler and Drakeford's observations that the exposure of one phenomenon 'produces further revelation in the same field'.[223] Pechell was able to stretch his powers further by moving for returns, which had added further 'strain' to the policy area before the news of Andover had broken. After the news, Graham then 'pressed' the Poor Law Commission for a ban. Evidently he could, one way or another, impose policy-making upon the Poor Law Commissioners.

Social policy analysts commonly view the policy-making process 'as an inescapably *political* activity into which the perceptions and interests of individual actors enter all stages'.[224] Stakeholders were also part of this political activity – united together to represent their own shared 'perceptions and interests'. This has been illustrated in the events that occurred after the neglect of medical relief claimants at Bridgwater. The Bridgwater Medical Association produced a pamphlet that was subsequently published in *The Times*, evidence that Wharncliffe used to call for an investigation. The House of Commons, aware of the trials of the local association, then interviewed its chairman to obtain an idea of what he thought were the deficiencies of medical relief policy. Thereafter the BMA and PMSA were in constant contact with the Poor Law Commission, which allowed them to showcase their policy ideas and exert pressure for change. By inviting representatives from the medical profession to Somerset House and corresponding with the national associations in a cordial manner, the Commission showed their ability to negotiate with stakeholders. What was evident during the end of bone-crushing practices was the willingness of anti-New Poor Law MPs to unite across political parties to repeatedly expose harsh treatments of the poor and create pressure for change. But regardless of this prodding, and regardless of a large cohort of opposition MPs, it was only when the Andover Scandal came to light that the Commission felt obliged to (re)act.

Although these cases highlight the processes through which policies were generated and were issued during the early years of the New Poor Law, they also demonstrate the different ways in which scandals impacted on this process. The Bridgwater Scandal fed into a wider understanding that medical relief policies were inadequate. The Andover Scandal had a more immediate impact by pushing the bone-crushing ban into force. Indeed, bone-crushing had been a controversial form of work within the workhouse for a long time prior to the news from Hampshire. This illustrates two very different types of 'policy strain' within medical relief and employment policy at the time. Medical relief policies were undeveloped in the Amendment Act, and as a consequence individuals and stakeholders demanded and set minimum standards. Employment policies were also undeveloped within the Amendment Act, but rather than there being a need to regulate employment per se, individuals and stakeholders wanted a ban on obnoxious employments.

Neither of the policies that developed after the scandals was easy to implement. The General Medical Order was released a year before it was to come into force, giving Boards of Guardians across England and Wales notice that they should adhere to its stipulations the next time the medical officers' contracts were set. The bone-crushing ban was released less than three months before it was implemented, and many Boards of Guardians were ill-prepared to provide alternative employment to their able-bodied male inmates. In the long term, bone-crushing came to an end, and was a much less complicated policy to implement than the General Medical Order. In both cases, however, it is difficult to tell how far these policies had a positive impact on the lives of relief claimants. For instance, alternative employments to bone-crushing, such as stone-pounding, may have been equally or more hazardous to inmates, whilst the General Medical Order simply reinforced district- rather than parish-based medical relief provision; the latter might have better served the needs of medical claimants.

## Notes

1   William Ferrand, House of Commons, 17 May 1847, Hansard, vol. 92, cols 985, 972.

2   Reading of Henriques by Bernard Harris, *The Origins of the British Welfare State: Social Welfare in England and Wales, 1800–1945* (Basingstoke, 2004), p. 50; U. Henriques, 'How cruel was the Victorian Poor Law?' *Historical Journal*, 11 (1968), 365–71.

3   I. Butler and M. Drakeford, *Scandal, Social Policy and Social Welfare*, revised second edition (Bristol, 2005).

4   Butler and Drakeford, *Scandal*, p. 238.

5   BPP 1844 (531) Report from the Select Committee on Medical Poor Relief, together with the minutes of evidence, appendix, and index, interview of George Cornewall Lewis, p. 1.

6   S. King, '"Stop this overwhelming torment of destiny": Negotiating financial aid at times of sickness under the English Old Poor Law, 1800–1840', *Bulletin of the History of Medicine*, 79 (2005), 234.

7   BPP 1834 (44), Report from His Majesty's Commissioners for Inquiring into the Administration and Practical Operation of the Poor Laws, 146, cited in M.W. Flinn, 'Medical Services under the New Poor Law', in D. Fraser (ed.), *The New Poor Law in the Nineteenth-Century* (London, 1976), p. 48.

8   Poor Law Amendment Act, 1834, 4 & 5 Will. c.76, s.54.

9   Flinn, 'Medical Services', p. 48.

10  'Instructional Letter Respecting the Formation of Independent Medical Clubs', in *Second Annual Report of the Poor Law Commissioners* (London, 1836), app. A.3, p. 50.

11  Report 'To the Right Honorable Lord John Russell, His Majesty's Principal Secretary of State for the Home Department', T. Frankland Lewis, J.G. Shaw Lefevre and G. Nicholls to Lord John Russell, 8 August 1835, *First Annual Report of the Poor Law Commissioners* (London, 1835), pp. 51–2.

12  Poor Law Amendment Act, 1834, 4 & 5 Will. c.76, s.109.

13  Fareham Union, Minute Book, 29 May 1835, HRO PL3/8/1.

14  'Lord John Russell', p. 52.

15  Hawley (Hartford Bridge) to Lefevre, 29 May 1836, TNA MH32/38.

16  K. Price, *Medical Negligence in Victorian Britain: The Crisis of Care under the English Poor Law, c. 1834–1900* (London, 2015), p. 37.

17  A. Digby, *Making a Medical Living: Doctors and Patients in the English Market for Medicine, 1720–1911* (Cambridge, 1994), p. 244.

18  'Instructional Letter', app. A.3, p. 50.

19  Flinn, 'Medical Services', p. 50.

20  Digby, *Making a Medical Living*, p. 244.

21  Flinn, 'Medical Services', p. 49.

22  J. Stewart and S. King, 'Death in Llantrisant: Henry Williams and the New Poor Law in Wales', *Rural History*, 15 (2004), 74; Digby, *Making a Medical Living*, p. 244.

23  Somerset contained a population of 28,566 in 1831 and was 10.5 miles in length and 15.5 miles in breadth; Schedule A: Summary of the Unions Formed by Robert Weale Esq., Assistant Poor Law Commissioner, 21 October 1837, TNA MH32/85. It was officially established on 16 April 1836.

24  C.A. Buchanan, 'John Bowen and the Bridgwater Scandal', *Proceedings of the Somerset Archaeological and Natural History Society*, 131 (1987), 185.

25  BPP 1837–38 (719) Report from the Select Committee of the House of Lords Appointed to Examine into the Several Cases Alluded to in Certain Papers Respecting the Operation of the Poor Law Amendment Act, and to Report thereon. With the minutes of evidence taken before the committee, and an index thereto [hereafter BPP 1837–38 (719), Bridgwater Inquiry], interview of William Baker, p. 967. Jonathan Toogood suggests that 40 per cent of their paupers in the union died; *The Times*, 26 January 1841.

26  Buchanan, 'John Bowen', 186; dietaries reproduced in P. Higginbotham, *The Workhouse Cookbook* (Stroud, 2008), pp. 53–5.

27  BPP 1837–38 (719), Bridgwater Inquiry, interview of William Baker, pp. 958, 965–6.

28  Baker had known Bowen for a number of years; they had also worked as overseers together in the town.

29  Buchanan, 'John Bowen', 187.

30  *The Times*, 12 October 1836.

31  Weale (Worcester) to PLC, 23 October 1836, TNA MH32/85.

32  Buchanan, 'John Bowen', p. 187.

33  'Report of the Poor-Law Committee, 1840', *Provincial Medical and Surgical Journal* [hereafter *PMSJ*], 1, 13 (1841), 212; The Medical Association, 'Facts Connected with the Medical Relief of the Poor in the Bridgwater Union', (Bridgwater, 13 November 1837) (hereafter Medical Association, 'Medical Relief'), p. 27; a copy can be found in Correspondence and documents received by the Home Office, TNA HO73/52/62.

34  Bridgwater Union, Minute Book, 12 and 15 May, 28 April 1837, SRO D\G\BW/8a/1.

35  'Poor-Law Committee', p. 212.

36  Bridgwater Union, Minute Book, 18 and 26 May, 2 June 1837, SRO D\G\BW/8a/1.

37  BPP 1837–38 (719), Bridgwater Inquiry, interview of Robert Young, pp. 676–7, 688–9. The PMSA was founded in 1832; the members were Abraham King, William Lakin Caswell, Baruch Toogood, Joseph Addison, Horatio Nelson Tilsley, John Evered Poole and Richard Beadon Ruddock, and their chairman was Jonathan Toogood; Bridgwater Union, Minute Book, 31 May 1836, SRO D\G\BW/8a/1; Medical Association, 'Medical Relief', pp. 4–5.

38  Handbill received by the PLC, 6 June 1837, TNA MH12/10243.

39  Bridgwater Union, Minute Book, 9 June 1837, SRO D\G\BW/8a/1.

40  George Warry (Shapwick, Glastonbury) to PLC, 17 June 1837, TNA MH12/10243.

41  Underdown to PLC, 16 June 1837, TNA MH12/10243; Lefevre to Weale, 22 June 1837, TNA MH12/10243.

42  Bridgwater Union, Minute Book, 23 June 1837, SRO D\G\BW/8a/1.

43  'Poor-Law Committee', pp. 212–13.

44  Medical Association, 'Medical Relief', p. 22.

45  Medical Association, 'Medical Relief', pp. 22, 16.

46  Medical Association, 'Medical Relief', p. 18. This letter was written on 1 July 1837.

47  This time sent from an overseer, John Knight; Correspondence and Documents, Copy of letter from Caswell (Huntspill) to the Board of Guardians of Bridgwater, 6 July 1837, sent by Weale to the PLC, December 1837, TNA HO73/52/62, pp. 463–4.

48  BPP 1837–38 (719), Bridgwater Inquiry, interview of Jonathan Toogood, pp. 751, 752.

49  Medical Association, 'Medical Relief', p. 16.

50  There was an established Women's Friendly Society based at Stowey, but, at the subscription rate of 20 shillings a year, Charlotte could not afford to join; see BPP 1834 (44), 31, Report from His Majesty's Commissioners for Inquiring into the Administration and Practical Operation of the Poor Laws, app. B 1, pt. 2, question 14, Nether Stowey (Somerset). The only possible alternative support for Charlotte was a small charity for regular church attendees, but this was unlikely to provide support to pregnant single women; R.W. Dunning (ed.), *The Victoria History of the Counties of England: History of the County of Somerset*, Volume 5 (Oxford, 1985), p. 200.

51  Correspondence and Documents received by the Home Office, Evidence of Mary Date sent by Weale to the PLC, December 1837, TNA

HO73/52/62, p. 456; BPP 1837–38 (719), Bridgwater Inquiry, interview of Mary Date, p. 855, interview of Charlotte Allen, p. 941.

52 Walker attended many members of the Stowey Female Friendly Soci-
ety; TNA HO73/52/62, Correspondence and Documents, Evidence of
James Franklin Waites and Kitty Walker sent by Weale to the PLC,
December 1837, pp. 443, 451.

53 BPP 1837–38 (719), Bridgwater Inquiry, interview of Charles Locock
MD (physician and accoucheur of Bridgwater), p. 981.

54 These were administered by her co-lodger and nurse, Mary Date; Correspondence and Documents, Weale to the PLC, December 1837,
TNA HO73/52/62; BPP 1837–38 (719), Bridgwater Inquiry, interview
of Charlotte Allen, p. 942; interview of Mary Waites, p. 449; interview
of Kitty Walker, p. 451.

55 BPP 1837–38 (719), Bridgwater Inquiry, interview of James Franklin
Waites, p. 772; Correspondence and Documents, Evidence of James
Franklin Waites sent by Weale to the PLC, December 1837, TNA
HO73/52/62, p. 444.

56 BPP 1837–38 (719), Bridgwater Inquiry, interview of Charles Locock,
p. 980.

57 Charles Locock said that medical men and midwives have 'met the
same Accident' on the birth of a woman's first child, 'though rarely to
this Extent'; BPP 1837–38 (719), Bridgwater Inquiry, pp. 981, 980.

58 Medical Association, 'Medical Relief', p. 18; Correspondence and Documents, Evidence of John Stagg, 1 December 1837, TNAHO 73/52/
62, p. 457.

59 BPP 1837–38 (719), Bridgwater Inquiry, copy of affidavit in interview
of Jonathan Toogood, p. 761.

60 Medical Association, 'Medical Relief', p. 10.

61 In the meantime, the relieving officer went into Cook's house, saw the
child and left without speaking to anyone, probably to assess John's need
for medical relief. This illustrates the Board of Guardians' inability to
trust Parker's opinion.

62 BPP 1837–38 (719), Bridgwater Inquiry, copy of affidavit in interview
of Jonathan Toogood, pp. 761–2.

63 Medical Association, 'Medical Relief', p. 24.

64 Caswell's bill was £92 and his payment was £40.

65 BPP 1837–38 (719), Bridgwater Inquiry, interview of Jonathan Toogood, p. 750.

66 He was married and had three children; 'Poor-Law Committee',
p. 213.

67 BPP 1837–38 (719), Bridgwater Inquiry, interview of John Rodney Ward,
pp. 1085–144. He was a licentiate of the Society of Apothecaries only.

68 'The case "Webber versus Ward'" and 'Western Circuit, Wells, Tuesday, August 7', *The Times*, 9 August 1838, cited in Buchanan, 'John Bowen', p. 188.

69 R.G. Hodgkinson, *The Origins of the National Health Service: The Medical Services of the New Poor Law, 1834–1871* (London, 1967), p. 26.

70 BPP 1837–38 (719), Bridgwater Inquiry, interview of Ward, p. 1101.

71 'Poor-Law Committee', p. 213.

72 Butler and Drakeford, *Scandal*, p. 223.

73 Medical Association, 'Medical Relief', p. 27.

74 Puerperal fever 'affected women within the first three days after childbirth and progressed rapidly, causing acute symptoms of severe abdominal pain, fever and debility'; C. Hallett, 'The attempt to understand puerperal fever in the eighteenth and early nineteenth centuries: the influence of inflammation theory', *Medical History*, 49 (2005), 1. Charlotte did not mention suffering from this disease in her Select Committee interview. She did, however, mention breastfeeding her child. It was uncommon for mothers suffering from the disease to breastfeed in case it passed onto the child. BPP 1837–38 (719), Bridgwater Inquiry, interview of Charlotte Allen, p. 944.

75 'Facts Connected with the Medical Relief of the Poor in the Bridgwater [*sic*] Union', *The Times*, 22 November 1837, reprinted in G.R. Wythen Baxter, *The Book of the Bastilles; or the History of the Working of the New Poor-Law* (London, 1841), pp. 477–80.

76 BPP 1837–38 (719), Bridgwater Inquiry, app. 5, 'Abstract of Petitions on the Poor Law Presented during Session 1837', see fifth division, p. 46.

77 Bridgwater Union, Minute Book, 23 March 1838, SRO D\G\BW/8a/2; Clerk (Bridgwater Union) to PLC, TNA MH12/10244, cited in Buchanan, 'John Bowen', p. 193.

78 BPP 1837–38 (719), Bridgwater Inquiry, app. 5, 'Abstract of Petitions on the Poor Law Presented during Session 1837', see fifth division, p. 46.

79 Lord Wharncliffe, House of Lords, 26 March 1838, Hansard, vol. 41, cols 1217–18, 1224–25, 1248–49.

80 This was the view of Jonathan Toogood; written 15 January, 'To the Editor of the Times', *The Times*, 26 January 1841.

81 This Select Committee produced a total of 49 reports.

82 'Letter Accompanying General Medical Order', Poor Law Commission to Clerk of the Guardians of Unions, 12 March 1842, *Eighth Annual Report of the Poor Law Commissioners* (London, 1842), app. A.6, p. 138.

83 The Bridgwater inquiry was held from March to July 1838; the medical inquiry was held from July 1838. BPP Forty-fourth, forty-fifth and forty-sixth reports from Select Committee on the Poor Law Amendment Act, with the minutes of evidence, and appendixes, 1837–38 (518), Medical Inquiry.

84  BPP 1837–38 (518), Medical Inquiry, 'Select Committee', p. 22.
85  BPP 1837–38 (518), Medical Inquiry, 'Select Committee', p. 23.
86  Districts of four or five miles in diameter were thought to be satisfactory by Jonathan Toogood; BPP 1837–38 (518), Medical Inquiry, interview of Jonathan Toogood, p. 367.
87  BPP 1837–38 (518), Medical Inquiry, interview of Jonathan Toogood, pp. 368–70.
88  BPP 1837–38 (518), Medical Inquiry, 'Select Committee', p. 25.
89  'Letter Accompanying General Medical Order', app. A.6, p. 138.
90  'Commissioners, Circular to Assistant Commissioners, Calling for Reports', Edwin Chadwick (PLC) to Assistant Poor Law Commissioners, 21 February 1839, *Report on the Further Amendment of the Poor Laws* (London, 1839), app. B.6, p. 157.
91  'Quarterly Summary of Unions Visited, &c. during the Quarter Ended 30th Day of December 1838' (emphasis mine), TNA MH32/6. The visit was on 16 November 1838. In another quarterly report on 30 July 1839, Adey notes that Bridgwater is 'still far from what is desirable', TNA MH32/6. For details about his district, see Adey to PLC, 4 October 1838, TNA MH32/6; 'Medical Relief: Reports of the Arrangements of Affording Medical Relief', 'Reports of Assistant Commissioners', 'D. G. Adey, Esq.: Counties of Somerset, Gloucester, Wilts, Dorset', in *Further Amendment*, app. A.6, p. 158.
92  'Medical Relief: Reports of the Arrangements of Affording Medical Relief', 'Reports of Assistant Commissioners', 'D. G. Adey, Esq.: Counties of Somerset, Gloucester, Wilts, Dorset', in *Further Amendment*, app. A.6, p. 159.
93  Edwin Chadwick, written 21 February, 'British Medical Association', *The Lancet*, 9 March 1839, p. 886.
94  'British Medical Association. Tuesday 26th March, 1839. Half-Yearly Meeting', *The Lancet*, 6 April 1839, pp. 90–1.
95  Article about the 'British Medical Association. Tuesday April 9th 1839 Meeting of Council', *The Lancet*, 13 April 1839, pp. 120–1.
96  'Communications from a Deputation from the Council of the British Medical Association', Letter British Medical Association (Dulwich) to PLC, 1 April 1839, in *Further Amendment*, app. B.6, pp. 281, 283. In the piece the BMA referred the Commissioners to the evidence given at the Medical Inquiry, and on p. 281 specifically a question answered by their president; BPP 1837–38 (518), Medical Inquiry, interview of Henry Wyldbore Rumsey, p. 36.
97  *Further Amendment*.
98  'General Medical Order', app. A.6, p. 138, circular letter dated 6 March 1841.
99  'General Medical Order', app. A.6, p. 139. Details of these responses can be found in 'Seventh Annual Report to the Most Noble Marquess

of Normandy, Her Majesty's Principal Secretary of State for the Home Department', J.G. Shaw Lefevre, G. Nicholls and G. Cornewall Lewis, 1 May 1841, *Seventh Annual Report of the Poor Law Commissioners* (London, 1841), pp. 8–14.

100 'Letter Accompanying General Medical Order', app. A.6, p. 139; 'Parochial Medical Relief', *PMSJ*, 1, 22 (1841), 361. Also, an association sent another petition to the government and details of medical relief sagas, including the Bridgwater Scandal, were published in the *PMSJ*; see 'Report of the Poor-Law Committee, 1840', 1, 10 (1840), 166–8; 1, 11 (1840), 184–7; 1, 12 (1841), 197–9; 1, 13 (1841), 209–13; 1, 14 (1841), 228–30.

101 'General Medical Order', app. A.5, *Eighth Annual Report of the Poor Law Commissioners* (London, 1842), pp. 129–35; for salaries to officers, see articles 1 and 2; for qualifications, see articles 3 and 4; for district sizes, see articles 6 and 7; for payments per case, see articles 10 to 13.

102 'General Medical Order', app. A.5, *Eighth Annual Report of the Poor Law Commissioners* (London, 1842), pp. 129–35; for weekly returns and substitutes, see articles 14 and 15; for the list of 'permanent paupers', see articles 16 and 17 (quotation in 16); for the continuance of medical officers, see article 20.

103 Hodgkinson, *National Health Service*, p. 14.

104 The districts were of 29,982 and 21,746 acres with populations of 2,805 and 2,222, respectively; TNA MH12/10346, Warren, Clerk (Dulverton Union) to PLC, 9 May 1842.

105 PLC to Warren, Clerk (Dulverton), 3 June 1842, TNA MH12/10346.

106 The towns and cities included Derby, Sheffield, Leeds, Manchester and Liverpool; see Hodgkinson, *National Health Service*, pp. 15, 14, 27.

107 Parker, Clerk (Wimborne and Cranborne Union) to PLC, 26 July 1843, TNA MH12/2913.

108 Hodgkinson, *National Health Service*, p. 15.

109 Snook, Clerk (Mere Union) to PLC, 15 February 1844, TNA MH12/13820.

110 PLC to Snook, Clerk (Mere Union) to PLC, 19 February 1844, TNA MH12/13820.

111 Stephen Stranger had only a Royal College of Surgeons qualification; Patterson, Clerk (South Stoneham Union) to PLC, 3 May 1844, TNA MH12/11037. The union obviously trusted him in his duties but realised he had only one of the qualifications the Commission desired, so the position was readvertised in local newspapers.

112 Holding, Clerk (Kingsclere Union) to PLC, 4 February 1845, TNA MH12/10854. The Commission, however, stipulated that tickets must be issued; see PLC to Holding, Clerk (Kingsclere Union), 12 February 1845, TNA MH12/10854.

113 'Suggestions as to the most eligible Modes of providing Out-door Employment for Able-bodied Paupers, in Cases where there is not an efficient Workhouse, and preparatory to the Establishment of the Workhouse System', 21 September 1835, *Second Annual Report of the Poor Law Commissioners* (London, 1836), app. A.1, pp. 45–8.
114 A. Brundage, *The English Poor Laws, 1700–1930* (Basingstoke, 2002), p. 79; N. Edsall, *The Anti-Poor Law Movement, 1834–44* (Manchester, 1971); G. Hagen, 'Women and poverty in South-West Wales, 1834–1914', *Llafur: Journal of Welsh Labour History*, 7 (1998–99), 21–33.
115 G. Boyer, *An Economic History of the English Poor Law, 1750–1850* (Cambridge, 1990), p. 261.
116 'Circular of Suggestions respecting the Employment of Able-bodied Paupers', *Second Annual Report of the Poor Law Commissioners* (London, 1836), app. A.1 p. 45.
117 F. Driver, *Power and Pauperism: The Workhouse System 1834–1884* (Cambridge, 1993), p. 141.
118 K. Williams, *From Pauperism to Poverty* (London, 1981), p. 64.
119 G. Nicholls, *History of the English Poor Law, Volume 2: 1714–1853* (London, 1898), p. 329.
120 Holding, Clerk (Kingsclere Union) to A'Court, 4 February 1840, TNA MH12/10853.
121 Brundage, *The English Poor Laws*, p. 91.
122 Brundage, *The English Poor Laws*, p. 80.
123 'Orders and Regulations to be observed in the Workhouse of the – Union', *First Annual Report of the Poor Law Commissioners* (London, 1835), app. A.9, pp. 96–110.
124 'Orders and Regulations to be observed in the Workhouse of the – Union', *First Annual Report of the Poor Law Commissioners* (London, 1835), app. A.9, pp. 103–4, section XXIV, which outlines the duties of workhouse matrons.
125 Nicholls, *A History of the English Poor Law*, p. 368.
126 M.A. Crowther, *The Workhouse System 1834–1929* (Athens, GA, 1981), p. 198.
127 Crowther, *The Workhouse System*, p. 197.
128 A'Court (Southampton) to the PLC (Sir), 17 January 1837, TNA MH32/4.
129 BPP 1846 (75) House of Commons Papers; Accounts and Papers. Poor law. Copy of any letter and general rule issued by the Poor Law Commissioners, relative to the employment of paupers in pounding, grinding, and otherwise breaking bones; &c. [hereafter BPP 1846 (75) House of Commons Papers], for instance, Copy of Stroud Union Minute, 8 November 1845, p. 45.

130  BPP 1846 (75) House of Commons Papers, Copy of Dorchester Union Minute, 24 December 1845, p. 39.
131  Tufnell to PLC, 21 February 1844, TNA MH12/71. A copy can also be found in the Select Committee Minutes of Evidence of the Andover Union Inquiry.
132  BPP 1846 (432) House of Commons Papers; Accounts and Papers. Bone-pounding. Copy of minute of the dissent of one of the Poor-Law Commissioners, on the subject of bone-crushing by paupers in workhouses; &c., 'Report of the Secretary of the Poor-Law Commissioners on Bone-Crushing' [hereafter BPP 1846 (432) House of Commons Papers], p. 10.
133  Tufnell to PLC, 21 February 1844, TNA MH12/71.
134  I. Anstruther, *The Scandal of the Andover Workhouse*, second edition (Gloucester, 1984), p. 119.
135  Tufnell to PLC, 21 February 1844, TNA MH12/71. The rod was also called a 'bar', 'crusher', 'stamper', 'champer', 'rammer', 'hammer', 'pounder' and 'bruiser'.
136  Block at Eastborne, Lewes, Newhaven and Petworth; iron plate at Thakeham and Uckfield; bare ground at Chipping Norton, Stafford, West Firle and St Albans.
137  At the Hartley Wintney Union, 'the labour is adapted according to age, strength, and constitution of the persons employed, it will be more beneficial than otherwise'; Copy of letter, Howard, medical officer (Hartley Wintney Union) to Guardians of Hartley Wintney Union, 12 January 1846, BPP 1846 (75) House of Commons Papers, p. 26.
138  Warminster Union, Minute Book, 3 June 1844, WRO H15/110/7.
139  Tufnell to PLC, 21 February 1844, TNA MH32/71.
140  Alton Union, Minute Book (minutes about getting the bone mill repaired) 2 September 1842 and 5 July 1844, HRO PL3/2/1, 31 October 1845, HRO PL3/2/2; (minute acknowledging the Commission's request for returns) 9 August 1844, HRO PL3/2/1; (minutes mentioning the sale of the bone mill) 3 and 6 April 1846, HRO PL3/2/2; copy of a letter, Bennett, Clerk (Mealbrook House, Alton) to PLC, 30 December 1845, BPP 1846 (75) House of Commons Papers, p. 19; Copy of letter, Smith, medical officer (Chertsey Union) to Guardians of Chertsey Union, 16 January 1846, BPP 1846 (75) House of Commons Papers, p. 28; Droxford Union, Minute Book (minutes about obtaining a bone mill) 23 and 30 January 1838; (minute about building a house for the bone mill) 20 March 1838, HRO PL3/7/2; (minute about purchasing four new plates for the bone mill) 3 March 1840, HRO PL3/7/3; Copy of a letter, Grenville Pigott (3 Upper Brook Street) to PLC, BPP 1846 (75) House of Commons Papers, p. 19; BPP 1846 (75)

House of Commons Papers, Copy of a letter, Raper, Clerk (Westhamp-nett Union, Chichester) to PLC, 22 December 1845, p. 9.

141 Copy of a letter, Grenville Pigott (3 Upper Brook Street) to PLC, BPP 1846 (75) House of Commons Papers, p. 45. The Chertsey Union oper-ated their mill in a similar way, with two men whose official duty it was to both 'feed the hopper of the mill, and to sift the ground bones'; Copy of letter, Smith, medical officer (Chertsey Union) to Guardians of Chertsey Union, 16 January 1846, BPP 1846 (75) House of Commons Papers, p. 28.

142 BPP 1846 (75) House of Commons Papers, Copy of a letter, Raper, Clerk (Westhampnett Union, Chichester) to PLC, 22 December 1845, p. 9. Examples include Fareham and Kingsclere: Fareham Union Min-utes, 3 February 1837, HRO PL3/8/1; 10 and 24 August 1838, 7 and 21 September and 5 October 1838, HRO PL3/8/1a; Kingsclere Union Minutes, 21 November, 5 December 1837 and 2 January 1837, HRO PL3/11/2; Tufnell to PLC, 21 February 1844, MH32/71.

143 Monk, Chairman (Hartley Wintney Union) to PLC, 3 January 1846, BPP 1846 (75) House of Commons Papers, p. 25.

144 Windus, Clerk (Epping Union) to PLC, 21 November 1845, BPP 1846 (75) House of Commons Papers, p. 56.

145 Article on bone-crushing, *The Times*, 3 October 1845.

146 T. Wakley, House of Commons, 28 September 1841, Hansard, vol. 59, col. 978.

147 Article on bone-crushing, *The Times*, 8 October 1845.

148 South Stoneham, Union Minute Book, 22 January and 18 March 1840, SCRO D/AGF 1 1/1.

149 Between 31 May 1842 (the start of a surviving punishment book) and the end of 1845 (the commencement of the bone-grinding ban), there were 18 recorded cases of paupers refusing to complete their 'task' or being disorderly at work; Beaminster Union, Pauper Offence Book, 31 May 1842–2 March 1869, DHC BG/BE B3/2.

150 Beaminster Pauper Offence Book, 24 June 1843, DHC BG/BE B3/2.

151 C. Brooker, 'The murder den, and its means of destruction; or, some account of the working of the New Poor Law in the Eastbourne Union, Sussex, etc' (Brighton and London, 1842).

152 Brooker, 'The murder den', pp. 21–2.

153 Brooker, 'The murder den', p. 8.

154 R. Wells, 'Resistance to the New Poor Law in the rural south', in J. Rule and R. Wells (eds.), *Crime, Protest and Popular Politics in Southern England, 1740–1850* (London, 1997), p. 113. Also see D. Jones, *Chartism and the Chartists* (Harmondsworth, 1975), p. 91; R. Wells, 'Popular pro-test and social crime: criminal gangs in southern England, 1790–1860',

*Southern History*, 13 (1991), 32–81; R. Wells, 'Southern Chartism', in Rule and Wells (eds.), *Crime and Protest*, pp. 127–51.

155 Captain Pechell, House of Commons, Hansard, 14 April 1842, vol. 62, col. 494. This quotation was taken directly from the interview; Brooker, 'The murder den', p. 20.

156 Sir James Graham, House of Commons, Hansard, 14 April 1842, vol. 62, col. 496.

157 Sir R. Peel, House of Commons, 15 March 1843, Hansard, vol. 67, col. 1070. These mills ground down rags into fibres that were either respun or used to make paper.

158 Sir James Graham, House of Commons, 15 March 1843, Hansard, vol. 67, col. 1071.

159 Captain Pechell, House of Commons, 15 March 1843, Hansard, vol. 67, col. 1071.

160 House of Commons, 15 March 1843, Hansard, vol. 67, col. 1072.

161 Captain Pechell, House of Commons, 18 July 1844, Hansard, vol. 76, col. 1050.

162 Sir James Graham, House of Commons, 18 July 1844, Hansard, vol. 76, col. 1051.

163 Cox, Clerk (Beaminster Union) to PLC, 22 April 1844, TNA MH12/2707.

164 Boor, Clerk (Warminster Union) to PLC, 23 April 1844, TNA MH12/13866.

165 House of Commons, 11 February 1845, Hansard, vol. 77, col. 304.

166 Sir James Graham, House of Commons, 11 February 1845, Hansard, vol. 77, col. 307.

167 Captain Pechell, House of Commons, 11 February 1845, Hansard, vol. 77, col. 309.

168 These were published on 18 February, BPP 1845 (41) Union workhouses. A return of all union workhouses under the Poor Law Amendment Act, in which the pauper inmates thereof are or have been employed in grinding or crushing bones.

169 Captain Pechell, House of Commons, 20 February 1845, Hansard, vol. 77, col. 827; House of Commons, 27 February 1845, Hansard, vol. 78, cols 118–19; House of Commons, 27 February 1845, Hansard, vol. 78, cols 118–19; see also copy of letter, Calthorpe, Clerk (Boston) to PLC, 18 January 1845, BPP 1846 (75) House of Commons Papers, p. 5.

170 Sir James Graham, House of Commons, 27 February 1845, Hansard, vol. 78, cols 118–19.

171 He supported Chartism and opposed the New Poor Law; see M. Lee, 'Duncombe, Thomas Slingsby (1796–1861)', *Oxford Dictionary of National Biography*, (Oxford, 2004; online edition, May 2005). Online: www.oxforddnb.com/view/article/8239 (last accessed 18 January 2016).

172 The petition was 'from Mansfield, for Removal of Treadwheel in Mansfield Union'; House of Commons, 8 July 1845, Hansard, vol. 82, col. 136.

173 Sir James Graham, House of Commons, 1 August 1845, Hansard, vol.
82, col. 1320.

174 Mr T. Wakley, House of Commons, 1 August 1845, Hansard, vol. 82,
cols 1320–1.

175 Sir J. Graham, *House of Commons, 1 August 1845, Hansard, vol. 82, col. 1321.*

176 N. Longmate, *The Workhouse: A Social History* (1974, London, 2003).

177 Parker (Andover) to PLC, 5 August 1845, TNA HO45/1031.

178 Longmate, *The Workhouse*, p. 126.

179 Anstruther, *The Scandal of the Andover Workhouse*, pp. 147–8.

180 Longmate, *The Workhouse*, p. 126; Anstruther, *The Scandal of the Andover
Workhouse*, p. 148.

181 Longmate, *The Workhouse*, p. 126.

182 Price, *Medical Negligence in Victorian Britain*, p. 56.

183 Brundage, *The English Poor Laws*, p. 88.

184 Driver, *Power and Pauperism*, p. 35.

185 Longmate, *The Workhouse*, p. 127.

186 A copy is in BPP 1846 (432) House of Commons Papers, pp. 1–5.

187 'Minute recording the Dissent of one of the Poor Law Commissioners
to the issue of the above Order of the Commissioners', BPP 1846 (432)
House of Commons Papers, p. 77. It was written by George Nicholls, 8
November 1845.

188 Sir J. Graham, House of Commons, 4 February 1846, Hansard, vol. 83,
col. 457 (my emphasis).

189 'Report of the Secretary of the Poor-Law Commissioners on Bone-
Crushing', BPP 1846 (432) House of Commons Papers, p. 7.

190 Nicholls, *History of the English Poor Law*, p. 369.

191 Longmate, *The Workhouse*, p. 127.

192 5 & 6 Vict. c.57, XVI states that General Orders could only take effect
after a minimum of period of 40 days had passed.

193 BPP 1846 (75) House of Commons Papers; 32 of these unions were
employing the inmates in bone-crushing work and one was just about
to commence.

194 Extract from Maidstone Union Minute Book, 27 November 1845, BPP
1846 (75) House of Commons Papers, p. 35. The Cranbrook Guardians
stated that the 'circumstances that took place at the Andover Union'
should not have influenced their General Order, Copy of Letter, Wilson,
Clerk (Cranbrook) to PLC, 28 January 1846, BPP 1846 (75) House of
Commons Papers, p. 34. The Stroud Guardians stressed that there had
been no fault in the operation of bone grinding in their union – just
some 'alleged abuse by others'; Copy of Letter, Crowdy, Clerk (Stroud)
to PLC, n.d. [before 17 January 1846, date of subsequent letter], BPP

1846 (75) House of Commons Papers, p. 71. The Bedford Guardians felt the same, as suggested in extract of minute book in a letter, Whig, Clerk (Bedford Union), 29 November 1845, BPP 1846 (75) House of Commons Papers, p. 36.

195 Copy of Letter Bartlett and Filliter, Clerks (Wareham and Purbeck Union) to PLC, 1 December 1845 (meeting and minute made 29 November 1845), BPP 1846 (75) House of Commons Papers, p. 35.

196 See various correspondence in BPP 1846 (75) House of Commons Papers.

197 5 & 6 Vict. c.57, XVI. According to the Amendment Act, the Secretary of State had to be notified of any deviation from a General Order.

198 Chadwick (PLC) to the under-secretary of the Home Secretary S.M. Phillips Esq. (Whitehall), 3 January 1846, TNA HO45/1031.

199 Extract of Tufnell's report in letter from Chadwick (PLC) to the under-secretary of the Home Secretary S.M. Phillips Esq. (Whitehall), 10 January 1846, TNA HO45/1031.

200 Captain Pechell, House of Commons, 4 February 1846, Hansard, vol. 83, col. 454. Pechell also believed that large stocks of bones had been accumulated when a 'Tariff had been passed, under which a reduction of the duty on bones had been made', cc 458.

201 Copy of letter, E. Chadwick (PLC) to Smallpiece Clerk (Guilford Union), 24 January 1846, BPP 1846 (75) House of Commons Papers, p. 20.

202 Captain Pechell, House of Commons, 4 February 1846, Hansard, vol. 83, col. 456.

203 Copy of minute, Frome Board of Guardians, 3 February 1846, BPP 1846 (75) House of Commons Papers, p. 42.

204 Copy of letter, E. Chadwick (PLC) to Hayley, Clerk (Frome Union), BPP 1846 (75) House of Commons Papers, p. 42.

205 Copy of letter and minute, Cox, Clerk (Beaminster) to PLC, 2 January 1846, BPP 1846 (75) House of Commons Papers, p. 43.

206 For example, PLC to Cranbrook Union Guardians, 13 January 1846, BPP 1846 (75) House of Commons Papers, p. 33.

207 Copy of letter, Wilson, Clerk (Cranbrook) to PLC, 28 January 1846, BPP 1846 (75) House of Commons Papers, p. 33.

208 Nicholls, *History of the English Poor Law*, p. 370.

209 Graves to PLC, 16 April 1847 (Report made on first visit, probably 16 April 1847), TNA MH12/13722.

210 Gulson to PLC, 10 November 1847 (Report made on visit of 28 October 1847), TNA MH12/2708.

211 John Udall (Bowood, Beaminster) to PLC, 8 May 1847, TNA MH12/2708.

212 This system was not permitted by the Commissioners as it was no longer supported in law; see PLC to Udall (Bowood, Beaminster), 10 May 1847, TNA MH12/2708.

213 Gulson to PLC, 10 November 1847 (Report made on visit of 28 October 1847), TNA MH12/2708.

214 Longmate, *The Workhouse*, p. 127; Brundage, *The English Poor Laws*, p. 88.

215 Anstruther, *The Scandal of the Andover Workhouse*; Longmate, *The Workhouse*, pp. 127–34.

216 R. Wells, 'Andover antecedents? Hampshire New Poor-Law scandals, 1834–1842', *Southern History*, 24 (2002), 91.

217 Longmate, *The Workhouse*, p. 127.

218 Driver, *Power and Pauperism*, p. 35.

219 Longmate, *The Workhouse*, pp. 133–5; Brundage, *The English Poor Laws*, p. 88.

220 Brundage, *The English Poor Laws*, pp. 88–99; S. Webb and B. Webb, *English Poor Law History, Part 2: The Last Hundred Years* (1929, London, 1963), pp. 185–8.

221 Butler and Drakeford, *Scandal*, p. 4.

222 Lord Wharncliffe, House of Lords, 26 March 1838, Hansard, vol. 41, col. 1224.

223 Butler and Drakeford, *Scandal*, p. 225.

224 I. Gordon, J. Lewis and K. Young, 'Perspectives on policy analysis', in M. Hill (ed.), *The Policy Process: A Reader* (Hemel Hempstead, 1993), p. 7.

# 6

# Conclusion: reform and innovation

The Introduction started with a letter from Ann Dunster, who was one of many thousands of individuals who wrote to their overseers for relief during the old poor laws. The letters reveal their everyday struggles and personal tragedies, but also a glimpse of hope – entitlement to poor relief. Robert Lacey, living in Bristol with little work, detailed his circumstances on paper and added: 'I hope that you will gave it to me', he explained, 'as every boddy have got it that have 4 Children'.[1] But as the economic and social depression took hold in the south of England, entitlement was already being replaced with work in return for relief, numerous restrictions on poor relief through select vestry policies, the hiring of assistant overseers and eventually a system that both incarcerated and threatened to incarcerate the poor. The result was an erosion of the long-held ideals of the Elizabethan Acts, for communities to look after their own poor. Many claim it was the Victorian workhouse system that dramatically changed poor relief in the south of England, as the architects of the Commission themselves believed.[2] Yet people were experiencing a reduction in their poor relief much earlier, and when the new workhouse system did commence, a refreshed eye on the financial costs of poor relief led to the catalogue of cruelties, abuses and neglects that came to symbolise the new system. The poor's entitlement to relief may have been diminished, but their voices were not silenced.

Throughout this period, many moral judgements were made about what to do with the 'problem' of the poor. This book has touched on many of the policy manifestations of such moral judgements: redrawing the categories of 'deserving' and 'undeserving' poor, setting everyone to work – not just the able-bodied – to better their morale and the parish purse, reforming the minds and habits of the unruly parishioners through institutionalisation, and the education of children. Behind this were ledgers, of every penny accounted for, each person inspected and the overseeing, overlapping stamps and initials of those in positions of power, including vestrymen, magistrates, Guardians, Commissioners and their assistants. This book was primarily concerned with the mechanisms at the heart of this system, those moments when the cogs and pistons creating, developing and implementing policies were in full motion.

By applying a policy process understanding of policy to the litera- ture on the poor laws, it became clear that many aspects of poor law administration had yet to receive systematic examination. Thereafter, the adoption of the policy process approach has enabled me to undertake a detailed examination of the different stages associated with the develop- ment, adoption and implementation of welfare policies in the final dec- ades of the old poor laws and the first few decades of the New. This was achieved by examining the adoption and implementation of two permis- sive Acts under the old poor laws and the nature and role of networks of policy exchange under both the old and New Poor Laws, and by explor- ing the development and impact of welfare scandals on individuals who needed relief and the shaping of the evolution of poor law policy after 1834. Enabling legislation was adopted and dropped at different times and implemented in diverse ways, policy transfer was important in the dissemination of best practice and early welfare scandals arose in areas of existing policy strain and influenced the New Poor Laws.

The wider implications of this nuanced picture of reform and inno- vation under the poor laws will be unpicked in three main sections in this final chapter. The first section outlines the implications of this research according to several different themes: local ideas and policy transfer, national legislation and, finally, policy-making. The second section provides an overview of the influences on the policy process under the poor laws, and the final section makes some suggestions for areas of further research using a policy process approach.

## The implications of a policy process approach

### Local ideas and policy transfer

Dorothy Marshall's observation on eighteenth-century legislation, 'that nothing was made legal by the authority of Parliament until it had become an established practice', was certainly true in the early nineteenth century, when it is evident that many de facto assistant overseers were engaged and select vestries in operation long before the passage of Sturges Bourne's Act.[3] The Poor Law Amendment Act was itself also influenced by local practices, not least the Nottinghamshire reforms led by George Nicholls. In Chapter 1, however, I argued that whilst we have a good understanding of how policies were made from the mid eighteenth century to the passage of the Amendment Act of 1834, we have little idea of how policies spread. In Chapter 4, I demonstrated that local innovations were not only important in the policy-making segment of the policy process, but they were also shared between welfare officials who assisted in the implementation of the poor laws. Officials under the old poor laws shared information through correspondence, visits, publications and third parties, including contractors, estate stewards and the time and money rich. The modes of disseminating information demonstrated that innovations not only influenced national policy-making on one hand, or remained confined within the parish boundaries, but also spread far and wide. As such, it was not just legislation, such as Gilbert's Act, that had breached the Elizabethan poor law 'central principle of "local problem – local treatment"'.[4] Local problems had stimulated local solutions, which, in turn, were shared between, and adopted beyond, individual parishes on an everyday basis.

These findings have two main implications for our current understandings of relief administration during the final decades of the old poor laws. First, there were common relief practices between neighbouring parishes, and often between parishes at some considerable distance from one another. Utilising social connections and networks, people informed each other about their policies and achievements, and visited each other's workhouses. The publication of pamphlets and edited collections, such as the SBCP's volumes, aided long-distance policy transfer, as did surveys, such as Eden's, which spread the word about successful reforms. It is these long-distance policy transfers that complicate the 'regional' analysis which Steven King advocates.[5] There was no overall regional picture of poor relief provision, just as there was never an overall national picture of poor relief in England. There were, conversely, islands of parishes dotted throughout England that were providing relief in similar ways. Furthermore, a more general point can be made about the topics of their publications. The age of 'debates, experiments and reforms', introduced in the Introduction and Chapter 1, has traditionally been perceived by historians as a time when Speenhamland-style scales and employment-linked relief schemes became popular, especially in the south and east of England.[6] Rather than exchanging information about outdoor relief schemes, however, they exchanged information about the management of workhouses. This suggests that, in the late eighteenth and early nineteenth centuries, the parish officials placed some of their efforts into providing indoor relief rather than, as our current understandings suggest, exclusively outdoor relief. Accordingly, parish officials were not simply concerned with assisting able-bodied males and labouring-class families through periods of depression, but they were also concerned with supporting those who required parish accommodation, typically children, the elderly and the infirm.

Such communications continued under the New Poor Law when Boards of Guardians exchanged information and even cooperated with each other in their attempts to implement the law. For instance, Guardians agreed to train each other's workhouse staff. There were, however, two general differences between the ways information was transferred under the old and new poor laws. Prior to 1834, policies and practices predominantly flowed between individuals vested with powers within the parochial welfare system, i.e. parish officials, the upper classes and the clergy. The creation of Boards of Guardians under the Amendment Act meant that local ideas were shared between groups of administrators, Guardians and *ex officio* members. Policy transfer, therefore, became a more formalised process, whereby individual unions rather than individual reformers were the source of information. There also appears to have been a shift in the types of place obtaining and providing information. Prior to 1834, policy transfer predominantly occurred between those individuals who had reformed or established a new workhouse or wanted to reform their local workhouse. After the creation of New Poor Law Unions, Boards of Guardians in places that had not previously managed large workhouses started to communicate. Evidently, the lack of experience in establishing and managing a workhouse in parts of the southern countryside, particularly in Dorset, Somerset and Wiltshire, meant that the welfare officials there were in greater need of advice than those Guardians who had run large institutions, notably welfare officials in the south of Hampshire, in previous years. The fact that many

of the enquiries from Boards of Guardians in Wessex focused on the
minutiae of furnishing and running the workhouse, such as what bed
frames, cooking apparatus, clothing, shoes, medical supplies and food
to buy for the workhouse, exposes these officials' lack of experience in
running an institution.

This 'horizontal' flow of knowledge between Boards of Guardians
was encouraged by the Poor Law Commission. The spread of bone-
crushing employment within New Poor Law Union workhouses was
a case in point. The Assistants played an active role in the uptake of
bone-crushing by informing Boards of Guardians about the employment. They also suggested that those Boards considering bone-
crushing should contact those Boards of Guardians that had already
implemented it, thereby encouraging the transfer of practices. The
Commission's regular publications then placed the ideas and endeavours of Boards of Guardians on a national stage. The extent to which
the Guardians followed the advice contained in these publications
is yet to be examined in detail. However, my analysis here suggests
that the implementation of the New Poor Law was not simply a top-
down process, but a process informed by local innovations.

The Poor Law Commission showed an active interest in disseminating advice based on successful local precedents. This understanding
adds further layers to our appreciation of the relationship between the
role of the central welfare authorities and the localities. The Webbs
thought the Commission was a centralised dictatorship whereby the
'Three Kings of Somerset House' had ended local autonomy over poor
relief policy.[7] In contrast, a later generation of historians highlighted
the extent to which relief practices survived the implementation of
the Amendment Act. In particular, they argued that Commissioners
could not control local landowners' interests enough to successfully
implement the Amendment Act.[8] Since then, more recent research
has examined the relationship between the central and local authorities. The work of historians, such as Dunkley, has demonstrated that
the Commission played a supervisory role in the implementation of
the Amendment Act and even made suggestions for the alleviation of
poverty during crises.[9] In addition, Harling argued that the Assistant
Commissioners, rather than the Commission itself, 'manage[d] to
mark out a circumscribed sphere of influence' over the localities.[10]
This research continued this trend by illuminating moments of cooperation and compliance between the centre and local authorities. The

Commission was not a dictatorship, nor was it powerless. Rather, it responded to the Guardians' queries and published Official Circulars, facilitating local authorities to decide how they were going to adhere to legislation. The Commission was attentive to the needs of each union and was diligent in recording ideas of best practice and disseminating them.

*National legislation*

Exploring a sample of parish records in Wessex archives has revealed many more adoptions of Gilbert's Act than has previously been acknowledged by historians. This work agrees with the perspective of other welfare historians, such as King, that there is a need for us to actually read legislation. This is because relief administration and relief practices were grounded and shaped through legislation.[11] The fact that Gilbert's Act permitted parishes to combine into unions or act alone to implement its provisions meant that Driver's distinction between 'Gilbert's Unions' and 'Gilbert's Parishes' has been very helpful in identifying adoptions here.[12] From this case study of Wessex, it is clear that the number of Gilbert's Act adoptions has been seriously underestimated throughout southern England, and possibly all of England, by welfare historians.

The fact that adoptions were sporadic throughout the region is not surprising, not least as we have known for a long time that the adoption of Gilbert's Act throughout England and Wales was geographically uneven. My findings have, however, shown that the perspectives of previous poor law historians are incorrect. Gilbert's Act appeared in the relief schemes in the south-central and south-western parishes of England, not just in the south-east, East Anglia, Midlands, Westmoreland, Yorkshire and also within both rural and urban settings.[13] Large market towns, such as Poole, Bradford-on-Avon and Gosport (in the parish of Alverstoke), all implemented the Act in Wessex, but so too did agricultural parishes across the Hampshire countryside and along the south coast. Rural adoptions of Gilbert's Act had, therefore, certainly existed outside East Anglia. Such a finding reminds us of the problems with relying too heavily on statistics in Parliamentary Papers, which – as is the case here – can only offer a snapshot of what policies were implemented at a fixed moment in time.

Whilst national figures on the adoption of Sturges Bourne's Act have been specified in particular years, and the decline in select vestries before 1830 has been noted, no one had examined the variations in adoption over time and within one region. My research demonstrates that although the south of England did generally reflect the national trends in the adoption of select vestries and assistant overseers, the two tools for reducing poor relief costs were more popular in some counties – such as Hampshire, Somerset and Sussex – than others – such as Dorset and Wiltshire. The spatial and temporal fluctuations in the adoption of enabling legislation are also interesting. In some instances, enabling legislation was simply suitable for a local context – a new workhouse regime was needed or an assistant overseer was required to collect rates and distribute relief in large parishes. Overwhelmingly, however, the adoption of enabling legislation came with an economic rationale. The large number of adoptees of Gilbert's Act in the 1790s, and the increasing number of parishes appointing select vestries and assistant overseers during years of acute economic strain, suggest that enabling legislation was used in the same way as other parish relief strategies under the old poor laws. This raises questions about people's intentions when adopting enabling legislation. In the case of Sturges Bourne's measures, the hope to reduce poor relief costs was key, as the legislation permitted parishes to implement measures that would restrict poor relief. However, the discourse of economy had also permeated the reasoning of vestrymen in adopting Gilbert's Act. Further questions could be asked in future research about people's rationales for adopting enabling legislation, whether these changed over time and how this impacted upon the ways in which enabling legislation was implemented. In-depth examinations of single parishes (or unions), similar to Wells' microstudies, could be usefully applied with these questions in mind.[14]

The abandonment of enabling legislation is also worthy of examination. Unlike Gilbert's Act, Sturges Bourne's Act required an annual vote of approval. As such, the archive better lends itself to an exploration of the abandonment of this legislation than Gilbert's. From the evidence analysed, it appears that legislation was not necessarily dropped due to an improving economic situation or a reduction in the rates. Enabling legislation proved to be difficult to implement in some localities. Sometimes this was the fault of the vestrymen themselves as they failed to attend select vestry meetings. This demonstrates the fragility of people's commitments to the stipulations of legislation, even when it was officially adopted. On other occasions, the legislation could not be adopted in the first instance. Indeed, Sturges Bourne's Act had proven to be controversial amongst some members of the magistracy. This all points to the multifarious reasons why there was such temporal and spatial variation in the adoption of enabling legislation.

Enabling legislation could also be implemented in a variety of ways. The inmates of different Gilbert's Act workhouses were treated differently depending on which workhouse they were accommodated within. For instance, children received structured schooling and training in some institutions and were put to work in others. Indeed, the most striking aspect of the implementation of Gilbert's Act was the importance of the role of work within the workhouse. Gilbert mentioned work in his plans, specifically how those who could work should do so for the benefit of the workhouse population as a whole. Yet, the eagerness of the Gilbert's Act committee members to obtain profits from the inmates' labour could have been to the detriment of those individuals whom the workhouse was supposed to shelter. Not only were there particular employments organised in the house, but contractors with specialist knowledge in profitable employments were hired. In addition, the widespread practice of admitting the able-bodied into the workhouse and setting them to work for local farmers ran counter to the stipulations of Gilbert's Act.

How parishes reduced relief provision under Sturges Bourne's legislation was not standardised. Outdoor relief list creation and review was common, but other parishes contacted employers for information about individuals' wages, restricted extras, established rules for keeping animals and created parish employment schemes. In a few parishes there was also a renewed interest in the provision of indoor relief. Inspecting the poor took different forms in different places. Some parishes instructed their assistant overseers to make enquiries into their resident and non-resident parishioners, whilst others made decisions based on local intelligence. Inquiring into the 'Character and conduct' of the poor, as Sturges Bourne's Act directed, was open to interpretation. Many parish officers in the post-Sturges Bourne period had returned to assess the 'deservingness' for relief based on similar criteria to those used by parish officers during the Elizabethan era. As Hindle argues, these included church attendance, industriousness, sobriety and deference.[15] Many parish vestries may have seen this as their chance to reform relief claimants' morals, as well as reduce relief bills. Clearly, many aspects of relief claimants' lives came under closer scrutiny after the passage of Sturges Bourne's Act. All such measures, regardless of variety, can only reinforce Wells' view that 'the rural poor bore the brunt of the discriminatory and punitive spirit of Sturges Bourne'.[16]

The various ways in which the enabling Acts were implemented is revealing in other ways. On one hand, their implementation confirms the view that the old poor laws offered a remarkably diverse set of ways of administering relief. Broad has argued that relief was provided flexibly under the old poor laws, through both charity and other parish-based funds, depending on what sorts of assistance could be funded.[17] I have argued elsewhere that parishes adopted various different policies and provided different types of relief depending on the need and character of each relief claimant.[18] This research adds evidence to the 'flexible old poor laws' perspective by demonstrating that non-compulsory legislation was adopted and implemented to suit local circumstances. One parish in Fareham noted that they should soon decide 'whether any and what of the plan' in Gilbert's Act would be adopted.[19] Enabling Acts were perceived as a strategy, with parishes considering adherence to only some of their provisions. On the other hand, the implementation of enabling Acts in such a diverse manner allows us to question the extent to which parishes were implementing relief under legislation in a different way from that intended by its makers. The timing of the adoptions of Gilbert's Act and the importance of work within Gilbert's Act workhouses suggests that economy may have been a more prominent motive for implementing the legislation than Thomas Gilbert himself had intended. The nuances in the ways in which enabling legislation was implemented therefore serve to act as a check to our generalisations about relief provision under enabling Acts. For example, King's description of the Gilbert's Act workhouse as 'a source of care, not deterrence' is far too simplistic.[20]

The ways in which knowledge was exchanged throughout this period, as examined in Chapter 4, also has repercussions for our understandings of national legislation. The fact that those who had established workhouses under Gilbert's Act were sharing and comparing their policies and practices with those who had established workhouses under Local Acts presents us with some interesting insights into the importance of legislation. The cross-fertilisation of knowledge between those managing institutions founded on different legislation suggests that, at least by the late eighteenth century, the Acts themselves were of a secondary concern. The Alverstoke Guardians did not ask the welfare officials managing workhouses which Act they were founded upon before obtaining information from them. Neither was this information recorded in their minute books. This is further demonstrated in the exchange of information via pamphlets. The pamphlet produced by Gilpin *et al.* about the reforms at Boldre had served as an inspiration for the reforms planned at Fletching. Yet, although Boldre was under Gilbert's Act, it was not mentioned in the pamphlet, the SBCP's publication or Fletching's poster. Rutter, in his desire to urge the parishioners of Shaftesbury to build a new workhouse, also drew upon workhouse reforms in places without mention of whether such institutions were established under particular pieces of legislation or not. Clearly, it was the building, management and running of workhouses that was of primary interest to the reformers and officials, not necessarily the underlying Acts upon which the institutions were founded.

The lack of attention paid by those exchanging information to the original Acts has important implications, especially for our understandings of the adoption of enabling legislation. Boldre's reforms spread far and wide, helped by the SBCP's publication of Gilpin *et al.*'s pamphlet. In consequence, parishes throughout the country might have followed the principles and practices of Gilbert's Act workhouses without formally adopting the legislation. Many more relief claimants might have experienced Gilbert's Act, or versions of it, than have hitherto been thought. It is worth mentioning here that other parishes in the south of England were influenced by Gilbert's reforms in a similar manner. An Assistant Commissioner informed the Royal Commission that Highworth (Wiltshire) acquired a Local Act in 1789, reporting that it was 'a modification of Gilbert's Act', altered only by the fact that there was no stipulation for an annual return to be made to the magistrates.[21] There is also evidence that Gilbert's Act had partially permeated into the Local Acts produced in Sussex. In 1812, three rural parishes in East Sussex passed their own Local Act, entitled, in Gilbert-style language, 'An Act for the Better Employment and Support of the Poor in the Parishes of

Westfirle, Beddingham, and Glynde, in the County of Sussex'.[22] The
Act contained statutes that we would associate with Local Acts (such
as the election of 'Directors' rather than Guardians) and the *practices*
of Gilbert's Act workhouses. Indeed, it permitted the union to provide one workhouse, within which any poor could enter as the parish
officers wished to nominate. The Directors were able to employ the
able-bodied and infirm inmates 'in such Manner as Churchwardens
and Overseers of the Poor are empowered to do by any Law now
being relating to the Poor, or in such other Manner ... [they] shall
think proper'.[23] Such a policy ensured that the officers had complete
flexibility over the employment of the poor, as practised in Sussex
and Hampshire Gilbert's Parishes and Unions. The way in which
the principles of Gilbert's Act, and the practices developed under
Gilbert's Act, influenced parish relief systems evidently requires further research.[24]

*Policy-making after 1834*

Scandals in the early years of the New Poor Laws profoundly impacted
upon policy-making. The policy outcomes of scandals do not simply
follow from scandals, but, as Butler and Drakeford write, '[t]o have
an impact an individual scandal needs to take place at a time of policy strain'.[25] The Bridgwater Scandal occurred when medical relief
arrangements were in dispute and the Andover Scandal was revealed
when bone-crushing employments were already controversial. In
the latter case, the commonly held view that the bone-crushing ban
was a scapegoat measure introduced during a crisis of confidence
in the Commission has been challenged. Tragic events occurred in
Bridgwater and Andover at times of policy strain, enabling them to be
constructed into scandals and subsequently to impact policy-making.
    Each scandal impacted upon the policy-making process in a dif-
ferent way. The Bridgwater Scandal was investigated in a Select
Committee initiated by the House of Lords, and then the chairman of the Bridgwater Medical Association attended the House
of Commons 'Medical Inquiry'. The events at Bridgwater reached
a national audience, but it was some years before a medical policy
was released. Indeed, policy-making was a matter of negotiation
between the Commission, national medical practitioners' associations
and Boards of Guardians. The news of the events at Andover caused

immediate change at a time when bone-crushing was already a topic of discussion in the Houses of Parliament and, therefore, controversial. It took the Home Secretary, though, to persuade the Commission that it needed to ban the practice. This builds upon Butler and Drakeford's work by demonstrating that although a scandal must occur during a time of policy strain in order to penetrate into policy-making and thereby influence policy outcomes, each scandal impacted upon the policy-making process at different times and with different results.

These two cases also illustrate how the actual 'facts' of neglect and abuse cases can become exaggerated and lost in the very policy-making process they influence. For instance, Charlotte Allen's illness was exaggerated in the Bridgwater Medical Association's pamphlet. Clearly, different key actors and stakeholders would use and twist the 'facts' of the abuses to support their own ends. This perspective has some currency: what is called 'claims-making' by social constructionists.[26] The medical associations wanted regulations that provided medical claimants with a minimum standard of assistance, but, at the same time, these regulations also confined the duties of and created fair wages for medical men. The 'facts' of cases can also become watered down. Events would be referred to in correspondence and administrative paperwork very generally, without mentioning any details of the abuses that could potentially provoke a sense of shame. For example, Boards of Guardians, in their correspondence to the Commission, wrote that the bone-crushing ban was unfair as they perceived it as a reactionary measure brought in after the events that occurred in the 'Andover Union' or even 'another union'. Such vagueness, intentional or otherwise, demonstrates a distancing from the Andover Scandal itself.

The fact that many of the stories that reached the newspapers during this period were false or half-truths, as illustrated by Roberts, is hardly surprising.[27] But rather than wanting to secure policy outcomes, most people who brought cases of neglect and abuse to national attention did so in order to expose the deficiencies of the New Poor Law. Their efforts had been achieved to some extent in the Commission's replacement by the Poor Law Board in 1847, as explained in Chapter 5. Yet, the very existence of a central welfare authority meant that local abuses could receive national attention, as the Commission, and later the Board, became accountable for maladministration and maltreatment in the relief system across England and

Wales. This perspective offers a significant advance on those offered in the Roberts–Henriques debate. Roberts argued that the abuses symbolised people's hatred of the Amendment Act and Henriques suggested that it was the Amendment Act itself that created 'a climate of opinion in which abuses were more likely to occur'.[28] I argue that the anti-New Poor Law feeling and the existence of the central welfare authority made abuses more likely to reach a national audience and therefore obtain redress. Although there is no way of knowing how many abuses happened under the old compared to the New Poor Law, stronger accountability created by the Amendment Act enabled cases of maladministration to reach the ears of national policy-makers.

Both of these scandals revealed that the Commission had only a partial knowledge of how the Amendment Act was being implemented, and often lacked adequate powers to enforce change. What those opposed to the passage of the Amendment Act failed to realise, however, was that their endeavours had actually assisted the central welfare authorities in identifying areas of policy strain. This allowed the central welfare authorities to implement new policy interventions in areas where only modest rules had previously been put in place, namely workhouse employment and medical relief. These policies had ultimately extended both the power of the central welfare authorities over the localities and the scope of relief offered by local welfare authorities. Scandals, overall, acted as an important feedback mechanism, between policy implementation and policy-making, during the early years of the New Poor Law.

Scandals are followed by examinations of how welfare authorities implement policies, but these examinations arise suddenly. How did the central welfare authorities evaluate their own progress in implementing the New Poor Law? Did they set targets? When these were not met, did they alter or issue new policies? Although the Commission's resources may have 'always been too small for the task in hand', by scratching the surface of the paperwork created by the authorities, there is evidence that the Commission was monitoring and evaluating the progress in the implementation of the New Poor Law.[29] The Annual Reports contained regular surveys of the numbers of unions formed in each county, the numbers of unions with adequate workhouses (built, purchased and enlarged), tables of old parish properties sold and figures of poor relief expenditure. Other, less frequently published, returns included the numbers of people who emigrated, and the sums that the Commissioners raised or borrowed to enable this. Accounting practices under the poor laws, Walker argues, had 'functioned as a tool of social management as well as financial control'.[30] Yet how were these figures monitored and in what ways were they used as cues for policy developments? Future research could address these questions, providing more insights into the operation of the Commission. Of course, although the Commission assumed power over poor law policy across the regions, the influences on the policy process were diverse, just as they had been in the final decades of the old poor law. This will be explored in the next section.

## Influences on the policy process under the poor laws

This book has illustrated how individuals and groups played their part in the policy-making process, during the adoption, development and implementation of policy, and during policy transfer. The administration of the poor laws was more 'pluralist' than has hitherto been acknowledged. 'The central feature of pluralist theory', according to Bochel and Bochel, 'is its contention that, in western industrialised societies … power is widely distributed among different groups'. The distribution of power amongst groups creates a 'multiplicity of channels of influence' whereby 'no one group is dominant in the decision-making process'.[31] Although the power in the administration of the poor laws was far from even, it is worth considering the contribution these 'channels of influence' made to the policy process.

Under the old poor laws there was a wide variety of different stakeholders and key actors, each with different roles in the policy process. Vestrymen and local landowners were integral to the adoption, implementation and transfer of policy. There appears to have been a strong correlation between places adopting Gilbert's Act and the presence of large landowners. It is little surprise then that the most detailed set of records I found on the adoption and implementation of this enabling Act were in Lord Egremont's collection. Great landowners' influence persisted in the policy process under the New Poor Law, as others, including Driver and Song, have already identified.[32] Under the old poor laws, however, there appears to have been a multitude of other individuals involved in the policy process. Contractors could change the management of workhouses and also dictate the size of Gilbert's

Unions. The gentry and nobility suggested changes to relief provision. Parish vestries were, however, only semi-autonomous authorities and had to adhere to magistrates' stipulations as guardians of the law. In addition, magistrates also recommended reforms for particular parishes. Yet, as revealed in Chapter 3, just as Sturges Bourne's Act reforms were supported by some magistrates, others refused to sanction the policy or undermined it once it was in operation. Magistrates were, therefore, not always supportive of parish policy reform.

The clergy could also impact on the policy process, especially in transferring information to parish officials seeking reform. Their influence was itself helped along by groups that sought to place the interests of the poor at the forefront of society's concerns, such as the Society for Bettering the Condition and Increasing the Comforts of the Poor (SBCP). The Bishop of Salisbury had the power to select reforms such as those at Boldre for the SBCP publications, however. The fact that the bishop knew Gilpin indicates that social connections had also played a part in the policy process. This organisation and others also impacted on other types of relief policies being adopted in parishes. For instance, the SBCP, Labourer's Friend Society and the Agricultural Employment Institution influenced the uptake of allotment policies before 1834.[33]

Although landowners' influence remained under the New Poor Law, some of the stakeholders and key actors had changed. No longer were the vestry or the magistrate of such importance to the policy process, as powers to administer relief became vested in individual Boards of Guardians and the Commissioners at Somerset House. The cases used in Chapters 4 and 5 showed that Boards of Guardians in the south were not always willing to comply with the stipulations and views of the Commission. Boards informed the Commission when they released policies that they regarded as inappropriate. These communications were effective – the Commission changed or compromised their policies in consequence. This was best illustrated when the Commission allowed women with illegitimate children to leave the workhouse to attend local churches and chapels and secured 13 extensions in the bone-crushing ban. This showed that Guardians too were important stakeholders, playing an active role in the shaping and making of policies.

The policy process was further complicated under the New Poor Law by key actors and stakeholders who had either worked *between* the local and national welfare authorities or represented the interests of individuals on the national stage, as demonstrated in Chapter 5. In the first instance, Assistant Commissioners superintended the implementation of the New Poor Law. Their role was similar to that of magistrates under the old poor laws, not least because they oversaw the implementation of national legislation and recommended and discouraged the adoption and implementation of specific policies and practices. Assistant Commissioners, however, were civil servants whose investigations, reports and opinions about local phenomena fed back to the Commission. Ultimately, power was vested with the Commission alongside the Home Secretary, who intervened to insist on the release of national policies. As such, stakeholders and key actors who represented individuals' interests on a national stage were used to exert their influence on the policy process at the national level. MPs, representing their constituents, and Lords had brought cases of neglect and abuse to the Houses of Parliament. New pressure groups, such as the Provincial Medical and Surgical Association and British Medical Association, brought the demands of medical officers to the Commissioners and Parliament.

Poor law historians have tended to criticise the focus on an administrative history of the poor laws at the expense of efforts to (re)construct the lived experience of welfare claimants. I argued that this is a false dichotomy, not least because their perspective fails to take into account, amongst other things, the ways in which relief recipients themselves could influence administration. The medical relief claimants of Bridgwater, William Smith's grievances in Sussex and the hunger-induced bone scavenging at Andover attest to this importance. It must be noted, though, that in order to have any influence on the subsequent reforms developed by the Commission, their experiences were carried to policy-makers at the national level by those who already had a degree of power in the established channels. Had I investigated the treatment of claimants under the old poor laws, it is quite possible that a similar series of events would have been revealed, albeit apparent to a more localised audience. Individuals' cases of neglect and abuse would have been championed by the local press, clergy and magistrates before impacting upon local relief regimes.[34] My research here has been assisted by the new accountability of both local authorities to a centralised welfare authority and the central welfare authority's accountability to the state, both of which resulted in a substantial amount of formal paperwork being produced. More archival evidence and the linkage of more disparate data from locally created documents would be needed to bring in the voices of the poor into the policy process under the old poor laws.

## The policy process: a malleable approach

This research has exposed how a policy process approach to understanding the poor laws can advance our knowledge of poor law reform and policy innovation over a long period of time, over a large expanse of the south of England. Would the influences upon the policy process be similar elsewhere, considering that here I have focused upon an area of England that suffered severely from the post-1815 economic depression? A similar approach could be deployed to examine the administration of the poor laws in other parts of England, such as the far south-western counties of Devon and Cornwall. We have also tended to place our analysis of the poor laws in rural England in agricultural areas, rather than coastal settlements that depended on fishing and associated industries to make a living. Studies, therefore, of the poor laws in these counties and along shorelines would redress this balance. The dynamics of the policy process may have also been different in the rapidly urbanising areas of this region, such as Bath and Weymouth, and cities such as Southampton and Portsmouth, but also in the growing industrial towns and cities of the Midlands and the north of England. Wales is also of interest, especially because of the low population densities that presented challenges to policies drawn up in Somerset House with numerical requirements: for instance, regarding the size of medical districts. It is clear from the section above that pauper policies were influenced by a broad range of information and ideas from a much wider area than the counties in focus. Studies that take on board a policy process approach in other areas also need to be very aware of these patterns and, therefore, to be outward-looking.

The policy process approach can also be applied to understand reform and innovation in wider public policy of the past, too. From the early nineteenth century, Britain witnessed greater state intervention in many areas of people's everyday lives, including education, employment and health. Alongside new legislation came central government agencies, including the Privy Council Committee on Education and the General Board of Health, which, like the Poor Law Commission, were responsible for the implementation and the development of new policies.[35] The reforms in the poor laws in the nineteenth century, and the reforms in education, factories, public health, vaccination, lunacy, emigration, charities, prisons, juvenile reformatories and various employments, all permitted the government to appoint inspectors, leading to an increasing inspectorate.[36] This was the 'age of the inspector'.[37] Although, for instance, public participation in the making of the early Factory Acts has already been examined, a policy process approach would reveal more about how policies were made, implemented, evaluated and changed, and how policies and practices transferred amongst and between local and central authorities.[38]

## Notes

1   Robert Lacey to Sir [Overseers] (Cannington), 10 September 1820, Cannington Overseers' Correspondence, SRO D\P\Can13/13/6.
2   G. Nicholls and G. Cornewall Lewis (PLC, Somerset House) to Sir George Grey, 11 December 1846, Home Office Registered Papers, Poor Law: Method of carrying on work of the Commission, 1846, TNA HO45/1682, p. 28.
3   D. Marshall, *The English Poor in the Eighteenth Century: A Study in Social and Administrative History* (London, 1926), p. 128.
4   S. King, *Poverty and Welfare in England 1700–1850: A Regional Perspective* (Manchester, 2000), p. 25.
5   King, *Poverty and Welfare*.
6   A. Brundage, 'Debates, experiments, and reforms, 1800–1832', in *The English Poor Laws, 1700–1930* (Basingstoke, 2002), pp. 37–60.
7   S. Webb and B. Webb, *English Poor Law History, Part 2: The Last Hundred Years* (1929, London, 1963), p. xi.
8   For instance, A. Digby, *Pauper Palaces* (London, 1978).
9   P. Dunkley, 'The "Hungry Forties" and the New Poor Law: a case study', *Historical Journal*, 17 (1974), 329–46.
10  P. Harling, 'The power of persuasion: central authority, local bureaucracy and the New Poor Law', *English Historical Review*, 107 (1992), 53.
11  For instance, King, *Poverty and Welfare*, p. 24.
12  F. Driver, *Power and Pauperism: The Workhouse System 1834–1884* (Cambridge, 1993), p. 45.
13  S. Webb and B. Webb, *English Poor Law History, Part 1: The Old Poor Law* (1927, London, 1963), p. 275; P. Mandler, 'The making of the New Poor Law redivivus', *Past and Present*, 117 (1987), 133.

14   R. Wells, 'Poor-law reform in the rural south-east: the impact of the "Sturges Bourne Acts" during the agricultural depression, 1815–1835', *Southern History*, 23 (2001), 52–115.

15   S. Hindle, 'Civility, honesty and the identification of the deserving poor in seventeenth-century England', in H. French and J. Barry (eds.), *Identity and Agency in England, 1500–1800* (Basingstoke, 2004), pp. 38–59.

16   Wells, 'Poor-law reform in the rural south-east', p. 91.

17   J. Broad, 'Parish economies of welfare, 1650–1834', *Historical Journal*, 42 (1999), 985–1006.

18   S.A. Shave, 'The dependent poor? (Re)constructing the lives of individuals "on the parish" in rural Dorset, 1800–1832', *Rural History*, 20 (2009), 67–97.

19   St Peter and St Paul Fareham, Vestry Minute Book, 17 April 1793, PCRO CHU43/2B/1.

20   King, *Poverty and Welfare*, p. 25.

21   BPP 1834 (44) XXVIII, Report from His Majesty's Commissioners for Inquiring into the Administration and Practical Operation of the Poor Laws. Appendix A. Reports from Assistant Commissioners. Part 1. Report 2. D.O.P. Okeden, Esq. (Second Report), p. 8.

22   52 Geo. III c.12.

23   52 Geo. III c.12, II and XLVIII.

24   Digby also found that the Buxton Incorporation (Norfolk) had started as a Gilbert's Union in 1801 before enlarging and uniting again under a Local Act in 1806. 'Its indeterminate character', Digby notes, 'means that it is equally valid to describe it as a Gilbert Union under local act or as a local incorporation under Gilbert's Act'; Digby, *Pauper Palaces*, p. 47.

25   I. Butler and M. Drakeford, *Scandal, Social Policy and Social Welfare*, revised second edition (Bristol, 2005), p. 238.

26   Butler and Drakeford, *Scandal*, p. 226.

27   D. Roberts, 'How cruel was the Victorian Poor Law?', *Historical Journal*, 6 (1963), 97–107.

28   Reading of Henriques by Bernard Harris, *The Origins of the British Welfare State: Social Welfare in England and Wales, 1800–1945* (Basingstoke, 2004, p. 50; U. Henriques, 'How cruel was the Victorian Poor Law?', *Historical Journal*, 11 (1968), 365–71; Roberts, 'How cruel was the Victorian Poor Law?'.

29   King, *Poverty and Welfare in England*, p. 228.

30   S. Walker, 'Expense, social and moral control: accounting and the administration of the old poor law in England and Wales', *Journal of Accounting and Public Policy*, 23 (2004), 123. For a similar analysis of the New Poor Law accounting practices, see S. Walker, 'Accounting, paper

shadows and the stigmatised poor', *Accounting, Organizations and Society*, 33 (2008), 453–87.

31 C. Bochel and H. Bochel, *The UK Social Policy Process* (Basingstoke, 2004), p. 50.

32 Digby, *Pauper Palaces*; B.K. Song, 'Continuity and change in English rural society: the formation of poor law unions in Oxfordshire', *English Historical Review*, 114 (1999), 314–89.

33 R. Wells, 'Historical trajectories: English social welfare systems, rural riots, popular politics, agrarian trade unions, and allotment provision, 1793–1896', *Southern History*, 25 (2003), 100–5; J. Burchardt, *The Allotment Movement in England: 1793–1873* (Woodbridge, 2002), pp. 9–97.

34 See, for instance, P. Henvill, *A Brief Statement of Facts; Wherein, Several Instances of Unparalleled Inhumanity, Oppression, Cruelty, and Neglect, in the Treatment of the Poor in the Parish of Damerham South, in the County of Wilts, Are Considered and Exposed* (Salisbury, 1796).

35 Harris, *Origins of the British Welfare State*, p. 36.

36 P.W.J. Bartrip, 'British Government inspection, 1832–75: some observations', *Historical Journal*, 25 (1982), 607, cited in R. Jones, *People/State/Territories: The Political Geographies of British State Transformation* (Oxford, 2007), p. 122.

37 Jones, *People/State/Territories*, p. 111. Also see the collection of essays in R. MacLeod (ed.), *Government and Expertise: Specialists, Administrators and Professionals, 1860–1919* (Cambridge, 1988).

38 J. Innes, 'Legislation and public participation 1760–1830', in D. Lemmings (ed.), *The British and Their Laws in the Eighteenth Century* (Woodbridge, 2005), pp. 102–32.

# Appendix

Further details of identified Gilbert's Act Parishes and Unions in Table 2.2.

(a) Earliest evidence for identified adoptions

| County | Name of Gilbert's Parish or Union | Evidence |
| --- | --- | --- |
| **Dorset** | Cranborne | BPP 1834 (44) XXVIII, Report from His Majesty's Commissioners for Inquiring into the Administration and Practical Operation of the Poor Laws. Appendix A. Reports from Assistant Commissioners. Part 1. Report 3. D.O.P. Okeden, p. 18. |
| | Poole | Poole St James Vestry Minutes, Churchwardens Accounts and Vestry Minutes, 20 April 1813, DHC PE/PL/CW1/1/4. |
| **Gloucestershire** | Cheltenham | C. Seal, 'Poor relief and welfare: a comparative study of the Belper and Cheltenham Poor Law Unions, 1780 to 1914' (unpublished PhD thesis, University of Leicester, 2010), p. 41. |

| County | Name of Gilbert's Parish or Union | Evidence |
|---|---|---|
| | Westbury-on-Trym | Westbury-on-Trym, Overseers' Accounts and Poorhouse Documents, Agreement to Erect Poorhouse, 6 and 21 August and 5 October 1802, BCRO P/HTW/OP/2(c). |
| **Hampshire** | Alverstoke | Alverstoke, Guardians' Minute Book, 9 November 1799, HRO PL2/1/1. |
| | Bishopstoke | A'Court's correspondence, 'Notes on every Parish in the Winchester Division', 'Bishop Stoke', November 1834, TNA MH32/1. |
| | Boldre | A'Court's correspondence, 'Notes on the Parishes in the Lymington Division', 'Boldre', 3 December 1834, TNA MH32/1. |
| | Farnborough | Farnborough, Workhouse Account Book, 1794–1822, HRO PL2/2/2. |
| | Froyle | A'Court's correspondence, 'Notes on the magisterial division of Alton', 'Froyle', 23 February 1835, TNA MH32/2. |
| | Headley | Headley account book started in 1795 entitled: An Account of Money expended in the House of Industry belonging to the united parishes of Bramshott, Headley & Kingsley'; Headley Account Book 1795–1852, HRO 57M75/PO16. |
| | Hordle | A'Court's correspondence, 'Notes on the Parishes in the Lymington Division', 'Hordle', 3 December 1834, TNA MH32/1. |

| County | Name of Gilbert's Parish or Union | Evidence |
|---|---|---|
| | Hursley | Hursley, Vestry Minute Book, 23 February and 16 March 1829, HRO 39M69/PV1. |
| | Lymington | Lymington, Vestry Order Book, 13 April 1809 notice (meeting held 28 April), HRO 42M75/PV9. |
| | Medstead | A'Court's correspondence, 'Notes on the magisterial division of Alton', 'Medstead', 23 February 1835, TNA MH32/1. |
| | Micheldever and East Stratton | Micheldever, Parish Vestry Minutes, 28 December 1826, HRO 7M80 PV1; and (although containing no exact date) A'Court's correspondence, 'Notes on every Parish in the Winchester Division', 'East Stratton', November 1834, TNA MH32/1. |
| | Milford [on Sea] | Milford, Book of Vestry Resolutions, 6 June 1816, HRO 31M67/PV1. |
| | [New] Milton | A'Court's correspondence, 'Notes on the Parishes in the Lymington Division', 'Milton', 3 December 1834, TNA MH32/1. |
| | Otterbourne | A'Court's correspondence, 'Notes on every Parish in the Winchester Division', 'Otterbourne & Boyatt', November 1834, TNA MH32/1. |
| | Selbourne | A'Court's correspondence, 'Notes on the magisterial division of Alton', 'Selbourne', 23 February 1835, TNA MH32/1. |

| County | Name of Gilbert's Parish or Union | Evidence |
|---|---|---|
| | South Stoneham | South Stoneham, Disbursements and Parish Treasurer Accounts, 5 March 1792, SCRO PR9/15/10. |
| | Winchester | BPP 1834 (44) XXXV, Report from His Majesty's Commissioners for Inquiring into the Administration and Practical Operation of the Poor Laws. Appendix B.2. Answers to the Town Queries in Five Parts. Part 2. Question 15. Winchester, St. Thomas & St. Clement (United Parishes). |
| **Hampshire and Surrey borders** | Aldershot and Bentley | Bentley, Overseers' Account Book, 26 October 1818, HRO 1M80/PO3; Bentley, Receipted bill of expenses incurred by Thomas Clement for the Guardians of the parishes of Aldershot and Bentley, 1824–25, HRO 1M80/PO43. |
| | Ash | From at least 1801 it appears united with Seal, Puttenham and Ash, Long Sutton, Vestry Minute Book, HRO 78M72/PV1, yet the formal agreement to unite was 19 April 1806; see The Workhouse website, compiled by P. Higginbotham. Online: www.workhouses.org.uk/Ash/ (last accessed 11 December 2016). |
| **Surrey** | Cranleigh | Agreement to provide relief according to Gilbert's Act; Surrey Quarter Session Bundles, Midsummer Sessions 1793, SHC QS2/6/1793/Mid/31. |

| County | Name of Gilbert's Parish or Union | Evidence |
|---|---|---|
| | Ewhurst | Agreement to provide relief according to Gilbert's Act and provide a workhouse, Surrey Quarter Session Bundles, Midsummer Sessions 1799, SHC QS2/6/1799/Mid/33. |
| | Farnham | Advert asking for offers for a builder to contract for building of a workhouse with a capacity to accommodate 200 people; *Hampshire Chronicle*, 1 February 1790. |
| | Frensham | Agreement to provide a workhouse and appoint Guardians according to Gilbert's Act, Surrey Quarter Session Bundles, Easter Sessions 1795, SHC QS2/6/ 1786/Mid/36. |
| | Frimley | n.d., SHC catalogue. |
| | Godalming | Agreement to provide a workhouse according to Gilbert's Act; Surrey Quarter Session Bundles, Midsummer 1786, SHC QS2/6/1786/ Mid/36. |
| | Hambledon | The expansion happened in two phases, in 1789 and 1792. An agreement of 1789 stated that the parishes of Bramlet, Chiddingfold, Dunsford, Hambledon and Hascombe had united for the relief and employment of the poor in a 'house … already … built for that purpose at |

| County | Name of Gilbert's Parish or Union | Evidence |
|---|---|---|
| | | … Wornley Heath'; Surrey Quarter Session Bundles, Midsummer Sessions 1789, SHC QS2/6/1789/Mid/25. In 1792 Haslemere, Elstead, St Martha's and Shalford were added; Surrey Quarter Session Bundles, Midsummer Sessions 1792, SHC QS2/6/1792/Mid/13. |
| | Reigate | Agreement of the parishes of Borough and Foreign parishes of Reigate, with Horley, Nutfield and Headley to provide relief according to Gilbert's Act; Surrey Quarter Session Bundles, Midsummer Session 1795, SHC QS2/6/1795/Mid/9. An agreement of the same five parishes to provide a workhouse at Horley in 1795; Surrey Quarter Session Bundles, Michaelmas Session 1795, SHC QS2/6/1795/Mic/36. |
| **West Sussex** | Arundel | BPP 1834 (44) XXXVI, Report from His Majesty's Commissioners for Inquiring into the Administration and Practical Operation of the Poor Laws. Appendix B.2. Answers to the Town Queries in Five Parts. Part 4. Question 43. Arundel. |

| County | Name of Gilbert's Parish or Union | Evidence |
| --- | --- | --- |
| | Easebourne | Seal of the union stating it was established in 1792 accidentally used on a Sutton contract; Contracts between Mary Bryan and Daniel Bryan of Petworth [to 1803] or Daniel Bryan [1804 on], and the Visitor and Guardians of Sutton United Parishes for the Governorship of the Workhouse, and the care, feeding, clothing etc. of the poor; with bonds, contract of 1803, PHA/6515. |
| | East Preston | East Preston Union, Treasurer's Book, 1791–1814, WSRO WG2/1; East Preston Union, Treasurer's Book and Guardians' Agreement and Forfeit Book, 1791–1832, WSRO WG2/2. |
| | Petworth | Date of establishment unknown but existence acknowledged in R. Wells, 'The Poor Law 1700–1900', in K.C. Leslie and B. Short (eds.), *A Historical Atlas of Sussex* (Chichester, 1999), p. 71. |
| | Sidelsham | Consists of Sidlesham (where meetings were held), Appledram, Birdham, Itchenor and Selsey; from advert for contracting out the poor, *Hampshire Telegraph and Sussex Chronicle* 4 February 1833. They particularly wanted a couple to contract the poor to have been involved in sacking manufactory. |

| County | Name of Gilbert's Parish or Union | Evidence |
|---|---|---|
| | Sutton | Sutton Union, Guardians' Minute Book, 21 May 1791, WSRO WG3/1/1. |
| | Thakeham | Thakeham Union, Guardians' Minute and Account Book, 16 February 1789, WSRO WG4/1. |
| | Westhampnett | Date of establishment unknown but existence acknowledged by R. Wells, 'The Poor Law 1700–1900', in K.C. Leslie and B. Short (eds.), *A Historical Atlas of Sussex* (Chichester, 1999), p. 71. |
| | Yapton | Date of establishment unknown but existence acknowledged by R. Wells, 'The Poor Law 1700–1900', in K.C. Leslie and B. Short (eds.), *A Historical Atlas of Sussex* (Chichester, 1999), p. 71. |
| **Wiltshire** | Devizes | Devizes Union, Proceedings of a meeting held to combine the parishes of St John's and St Mary's Devizes, to provide a joint parochial workhouse, 27 June 1796, W&SA H7/110/1. |
| | Mere | Agreement at a local meeting, to adopt the provisions of the 1782 Act of Parliament for the better relief of the poor, 10 and 28 April 1814, W&SA 438/38. |

(b) Parishes that formed the identified Gilbert's Unions

| County | Name of Gilbert's Parish or Union | Eventual number of parishes | Parishes within Gilbert's Union |
|---|---|---|---|
| **Hampshire** | Farnborough | 4 | Eversley<br>Farnborough<br>Hartley Wintney<br>Yateley |
| | Headley | 3 | Bramshott<br>Headley<br>Kingsley |
| | Micheldever and East Stratton | 2 | East Stratton<br>Micheldever |
| | Winchester | 2 | St Thomas Winchester<br>St Clement Winchester |
| **Hampshire and Surrey borders** | Aldershot and Bentley | 2 | Aldershot (Surrey)<br>Bentley (Hampshire) |
| | Ash | 5 | Ash (Surrey)<br>Frimley (Surrey)<br>Long Sutton (Hampshire)<br>Seal (Surrey)<br>Puttenham (Surrey) |
| **Surrey** | Hambledon | 9 | Bramley<br>Chiddingfold<br>Dunsfold<br>Elstead<br>Hambledon<br>Hascombe<br>Haslemere<br>St Martha-on-the-Hill [Chilworth]<br>Shalford |
| | Reigate | 5 | Headley<br>Horley<br>Nutfield<br>Reigate Borough<br>Reigate Foreign |

| County | Name of Gilbert's Parish or Union | Eventual number of parishes | Parishes within Gilbert's Union |
|--------|-----------------------------------|------------------------------|----------------------------------|
| **West Sussex** | Easebourne | 16 | Bepton |
| | | | Chithist |
| | | | Cocking |
| | | | Easbourne |
| | | | Harnhurst |
| | | | Iping |
| | | | Linchmere |
| | | | Lodsworth |
| | | | Lurgashall |
| | | | Selham |
| | | | Stedham |
| | | | Tillington |
| | | | Trayford |
| | | | Trotton |
| | | | Woolbedding |
| | | | Woolavington |
| | East Preston | 19 | Amberley |
| | | | Angmering |
| | | | Broadwater |
| | | | Burpham |
| | | | Climping |
| | | | Durrington |
| | | | East Preston |
| | | | Ferring |
| | | | Ford |
| | | | Goring by Seas |
| | | | Houghton |
| | | | Lancing |
| | | | Littlehampton |
| | | | Lyminster |
| | | | Poling |
| | | | Rustington |
| | | | Tortington |
| | | | West Tarring |
| | | | Wiggenholt |
| | Sidelsham | 5 | Appledram |
| | | | Birdham |
| | | | Itchenor |
| | | | Selsey |
| | | | Sidelsham |
| | | | Barlavington |

| County | Name of Gilbert's Parish or Union | Eventual number of parishes | Parishes within Gilbert's Union |
|---|---|---|---|
| | Sutton | 17 | South Berstead<br>Bignor<br>Burton<br>Bury<br>Clapham<br>Coates<br>Coldwaltham<br>Duncton<br>Egdean<br>Fittleworth<br>Greatham<br>Heyshott<br>Patching<br>Slindon<br>Sutton<br>Warningcamp |
| | Thakeham | 6 | Ashington<br>Findon<br>Sullington<br>Thakeham<br>Washington<br>Wiston |
| | Westhampnett | 11 | Barnham<br>Binderton<br>Boxgrove<br>East Dean<br>Eartham<br>Graffham<br>East Lavant<br>Mid Lavant<br>Singleton<br>West Stoke<br>Westhampnett |
| | Yapton | 3 | Felpham<br>Walberton<br>Yapton |
| **Wiltshire** | Devizes | 2 | St John's Devizes<br>St Mary's Devizes |

# Select bibliography

Anstruther, I., *The Scandal of the Andover Workhouse*, second edition (Gloucester: Geoffrey Bles, 1984).

Apfel, W. and P. Dunkley, 'English rural society and the New Poor Law: Bedfordshire, 1834–47', *Social History*, 10 (1985), 37–68.

Baldock, J., N. Manning and S. Vickerstaff (eds.), *Social Policy*, second edition (Oxford: Oxford University Press, 2003).

Bartrip, P.W.J., 'British government inspection, 1832–75: some observations', *Historical Journal*, 25 (1982), 605–26.

Baugh, D.A., 'The cost of poor relief in south-east England, 1790–1834', *Economic History Review*, 28 (1975), 50–68.

Bettey, J., *Rural Life in Wessex 1500–1900* (Bradford-on-Avon: Moonraker Press, 1977).

Bettey, J., *Wessex from AD 1000* (London: Longman, 1986).

Blaug, M., 'The myth of the Old Poor Law and the making of the New', *Journal of Economic History*, 23 (1963), 151–84.

Blaug, M., 'The Poor Law Report re-examined', *Journal of Economic History*, 24 (1964), 229–45.

Boulton, J. and J. Black, 'Paupers and their experience of a London workhouse: St-Martin-in-the-Fields, 1725–1824', in J. Hamlett, L. Hoskins and R. Preston (eds.), *Residential Institutions in Britain, 1725–1970: Inmates and Environments* (London: Pickering & Chatto, 2013), pp. 79–91.

Boulton, J. and L. Schwarz, '"The comforts of a private fireside"? The workhouse, the elderly and the poor law in Georgian Westminster: St Martin-in-the-Fields, 1725–1824', in J. McEwan and P. Sharpe (eds.), *Accommodating Poverty: The Housing and Living Arrangements of the English Poor, c. 1600–1850* (Basingstoke: Palgrave Macmillan, 2013), pp. 221–45.

Boyer, G., *An Economic History of the English Poor Law, 1750–1850* (Cambridge: Cambridge University Press, 1990).

Boyer, G., 'Malthus was right after all: poor relief and the birth rate in southeastern England', *Journal of Political Economy*, 97 (1989), 93–114.

Broad, J., 'Housing the rural poor in southern England, 1650–1850', *Agricultural History Review*, 48 (2000), 151–70.

Broad, J., 'Parish economies of welfare, 1650–1834', *Historical Journal*, 42 (1999), 985–1006.

Brundage, A., *The English Poor Laws, 1700–1930* (Basingstoke: Palgrave, 2002).

Brundage, A., 'The landed interest and the New Poor Law: a reappraisal of the revolution in government', *English Historical Review*, 87 (1972), 27–48.

Brundage, A., *The Making of the New Poor Law: The Politics of Inquiry, Enactment, and Implementation, 1832–1839* (London: Hutchinson, 1978).

Buchanan, C.A., 'John Bowen and the Bridgwater Scandal', *Proceedings of the Somerset Archaeological and Natural History Society*, 131 (1987), 181–201.

Burchardt, J., *The Allotment Movement in England: 1793–1873* (Woodbridge: Boydell Press, 2002).

Burchardt, J., 'Rural social relations, 1830–50: opposition to allotments for labourers', *Agricultural History Review*, 45 (1997), 165–75.

Butler, I. and M. Drakeford, *Scandal, Social Policy and Social Welfare*, revised second edition (Bristol: Policy Press, 2005).

Charlesworth, L., *Welfare's Forgotten Past: A Socio-Legal History of the Poor Law* (Abingdon: Routledge, 2010).

Checkland, S.G. and E.O.A. Checkland (eds.), *The Poor Law Report of 1834* (1834, Harmondsworth: Penguin, 1974).

Coats, A.W., 'Economic thought and poor law policy in the eighteenth century', *Economic History Review*, 13 (1960), 39–51.

Crowther, M.A., *The Workhouse System 1834–1929* (Athens, GA: University of Georgia Press, 1981).

Digby, A., 'The labour market and the continuity of social policy after 1834: the case of the eastern counties', *Economic History Review*, 28 (1975), 69–83.

Digby, A., *Making a Medical Living: Doctors and Patients in the English Market for Medicine, 1720–1911* (Cambridge: Cambridge University Press, 1994).

Digby, A., *Pauper Palaces* (London: Routledge & Kegan Paul, 1978).

Digby, A., *The Poor Law in Nineteenth-century England and Wales* (London: Historical Association, 1982).

Driver, F., *Power and Pauperism: The Workhouse System 1834–1884* (Cambridge: Cambridge University Press, 1993).

Dunbabin, J., *Rural Discontent in Nineteenth Century Britain* (London: Faber, 1974).

Dunkley, P., 'The "Hungry Forties" and the New Poor Law: a case study', *Historical Journal*, 17 (1974), 329–46.

Dunkley, P., 'Paternalism, the magistracy and poor relief in England, 1795–1834', *International Review of Social History*, 24 (1979), 371–97.

Dunkley, P., 'Whigs and paupers: the reform of the English Poor Laws, 1830–1834', *Journal of British Studies*, 20 (1981), 124–49.

Eastwood, D., *Governing Rural England: Tradition and Transformation in Local Government 1780–1840* (Oxford: Clarendon Press, 1994).

Eastwood, D., 'The republic in the village: the parish and poor at Bampton, 1780–1834', *Journal of Regional and Local Studies*, 12 (1992), 18–28.

Edsall, N., *The Anti-Poor Law Movement, 1834–44* (Manchester: Manchester University Press, 1971).

Englander, D., *Poverty and Poor Law Reform in Nineteenth Century Britain, 1834–1914* (Harlow: Longman, 1998).

Fletcher, B., 'Chichester and the Westhampnett Poor Law Union', *Sussex Archaeological Collections*, 134 (1996), 185–96.

Floud, R. and D. McCloskey (eds.), *The Economic History of Britain since 1700*, Volume 1, second edition (Cambridge: Cambridge University Press, 1994).

Fowler, S., *Workhouse: The People, the Places, the Life behind Doors* (Kew: National Archives, 2007).

Fraser, D., *The Evolution of the British Welfare State*, third edition (Basingstoke: Palgrave Macmillan, 2003).

Fraser, D. (ed.), *The New Poor Law in the Nineteenth-Century* (London: Macmillan, 1976).

French, H., 'An irrevocable shift: detailing the dynamics of rural poverty in southern England, 1762–1834 – a case study', *Economic History Review*, 68 (2014), 769–805.

French, H., and J. Barry (eds.), *Identity and Agency in England, 1500–1800* (Basingstoke: Palgrave Macmillan, 2004).

Gestrich, A., E. Hurren and S. King (eds.), *Poverty and Sickness in Modern Europe: Narratives of the Sick Poor 1780–1938* (London: Continuum, 2012).

Gestrich, A., S. King and L. Raphael (eds.), *Being Poor in Modern Europe: Historical Perspectives 1800–1940* (Oxford: Peter Lang, 2006).

Gordon, I., J. Lewis and K. Young, 'Perspectives on policy analysis', in M. Hill (ed.), *The Policy Process: A Reader* (Hemel Hempstead: Prentice-Hall, 1993), p. 7.

Gray, P., *The Making of the Irish Poor Law, 1815–1843* (Manchester: Manchester University Press, 2009).

Green, D., *Pauper Capital: London and the Poor Law, 1790–1870* (Farnham: Routledge, 2010).

Green, D., 'Pauper protests: power and resistance in early nineteenth-century London workhouses', *Social History*, 31 (2006), 137–59.

Griffin, C.J., 'Parish farms and the poor law: a response to unemployment in rural southern England, c.1815–35', *Agricultural History Review*, 59 (2011), 176–98.

Griffin, C.J., *Protest, Politics and Work in Rural England, 1700–1850* (Basingstoke: Palgrave Macmillan, 2014).

Griffin, C.J., *Rural War: Captain Swing and the Politics of Protest* (Manchester: Manchester University Press, 2012).

Haines, S. and L. Lawson, *Poor Cottages & Proud Palaces: The Life and Work of Reverend Thomas Sockett of Petworth 1777–1859* (Hastings: Hastings Press, 2007).

Hammond, J.L. and B. Hammond, *The Village Labourer* (1911, London: Longman, 1978).

Harley, J., 'Material lives of the poor and their strategic use of the workhouse during the final decades of the English Old Poor Law', *Continuity and Change*, 30 (2015), 71–103.

Harling, P., 'The power of persuasion: central authority, local bureaucracy and the New Poor Law', *English Historical Review*, 107 (1992), 30–53.

Harris, B., *The Origins of the British Welfare State: Social Welfare in England and Wales, 1800–1945* (Basingstoke: Palgrave Macmillan, 2004).

Harris, B. and P. Bridgen (eds.), *Charity and Mutual Aid in Europe and North America since 1800* (London: Routledge, 2007).

Hay, D., P. Linebaugh, J.G. Rule, E.P. Thompson and C. Winslow (eds.), *Albion's Fatal Tree: Crime and Society in Eighteenth-Century England* (London: Allen Lane, 1975).

Healey, J., 'The development of poor relief in Lancashire, c. 1598–1680', *Historical Journal*, 53 (2010), 551–72.

Healey, J., *The First Century of Welfare: Poverty and Poor Relief in Lancashire, 1620–1730* (Woodbridge: Boydell Press, 2014).

Henriques, U., 'How cruel was the Victorian Poor Law?', *Historical Journal*, 11 (1968), 365–71.

Higginbotham, P., *The Workhouse Cookbook* (Stroud: The History Press, 2008).

Hill, M., *The Policy Process in the Modern State*, third edition (Hemel Hempstead: Prentice-Hall, 1997).

Hilton, B., *The Age of Atonement: The Influence of Evangelicalism on Social and Economic Thought, 1795–1865* (Oxford: Clarendon Press, 1988).

Hindle, S., 'Civility, honesty and the identification of the deserving poor in seventeenth-century England', in H. French and J. Barry (eds.), *Identity and Agency in England, 1500–1800* (Basingstoke: Palgrave Macmillan, 2004), pp. 38–59.

Hindle, S., 'Dependency, shame and belonging: badging the deserving poor, *c.* 1550–1750', *Cultural and Social History*, 1 (2004), 6–35.

Hindle, S., *On the Parish? The Micro-Politics of Poor Relief in Rural England c.1550–1750* (Oxford: Clarendon Press, 2004).

Hitchcock, T., *Down and Out in Eighteenth Century London* (London: Hambledon Continuum, 2004).

Hitchcock, T., 'A new history from below', *History Workshop Journal*, 57 (2004), 294–8.

Hitchcock, T., 'Paupers and preachers: the SPCK and the parochial workhouse movement', in I. Davison, T. Hitchcock, T. Keirn and R.B. Shoemaker (eds.), *Stilling the Grumbling Hive: The Response to Social and Economic Problems in England, 1689–1750* (London: Alan Sutton, 1992), pp. 145–66.

Hitchcock, T., P. King and P. Sharpe (eds.), *Chronicling Poverty: The Voices and Strategies of the English Poor, 1640–1840* (Basingstoke: Palgrave Macmillan, 1997).

Hitchcock, T. and R. Shoemaker, *London Lives: Poverty, Crime and the Making of a Modern City, 1690–1800* (Cambridge: Cambridge University Press, 2015).

Hobsbawm, E. and G. Rudé, *Captain Swing* (London: Lawrence & Wishart, 1969).

Hodgkinson, R., *The Origins of the National Health Service: The Medical Services of the New Poor Law, 1834–1871* (London: Wellcome Historical Medical Library, 1967).

Hufton, O.H., *The Poor of Eighteenth-Century France 1750–1789* (Oxford: Clarendon Press, 1974).

Humphries, J., *Childhood and Child Labour in the British Industrial Revolution* (Cambridge: Cambridge University Press, 2010).

Huzel, J.P., 'Malthus, the poor law, and population in early-nineteenth century England', *Economic History Review*, 22 (1969), 430–52.

Innes, J., *Inferior Politics: Social Problems and Social Policies in Eighteenth-Century Britain* (Oxford: Oxford University Press, 2009).

Innes, J., 'Legislation and public participation 1760–1830', in D. Lemmings (ed.), *The British and Their Laws in the Eighteenth Century* (Woodbridge: Boydell Press, 2005), pp. 102–32.

Jones, P., 'Clothing the poor in early-nineteenth-century England', *Textile History*, 37 (2006), 17–37.

Jones, P., '"I cannot keep my place without being deascent": pauper letters, parish clothing and pragmatism in the South of England, 1750–1830', *Rural History*, 20 (2009), 31–49.

Jones, P., 'Swing, Speenhamland and rural social relations: the "moral economy" of the English crowd in the nineteenth century', *Social History*, 32
(2007), 271–90.

Jones, R., *People/State/Territories: The Political Geographies of British State
Transformation* (Oxford: Blackwell, 2007).

Keith-Lucas, B., *The Unreformed Local Government System* (London: Croom
Helm, 1980).

Kidd, A., *State, Society and the Poor in Nineteenth Century England* (Basingstoke: Macmillan Press, 1999).

King, S., '"It is impossible for our vestry to judge his case into perfection
from here": managing the distance dimensions of poor relief under the
old poor Law', *Rural History*, 16 (2005), 161–89.

King, S., *Poverty and Welfare in England 1700–1850: A Regional Perspective*
(Manchester: Manchester University Press, 2000).

King, S., 'Reconstructing lives: the poor, the poor law and welfare in Calverley, 1650–1820', *Social History*, 22 (1997), 318–38.

King, S., 'Regional patterns in the experiences and treatment of the sick poor,
1800–40: rights, obligations and duties in the rhetoric of paupers', *Family
and Community History*, 10 (2007), 61–75.

King, S., '"Stop this overwhelming torment of destiny": negotiating financial
aid at times of sickness under the English Old Poor Law, 1800–1840',
*Bulletin of the History of Medicine*, 79 (2005), 228–60.

King, S. and A. Tomkins (eds.), *The Poor in England, 1700–1850: An Economy
of Makeshifts* (Manchester: Manchester University Press, 2003).

Knott, J., *Popular Opposition to the 1834 Poor Law* (London: Croom
Helm, 1986).

Lane, P., N. Raven and K.D.M. Snell (eds.), *Women, Work and Wages in England, 1600–1850* (Woodbridge: Boydell Press, 2004).

Lees, L.H., *Solidarities of Strangers: The English Poor Laws and the People,
1700–1948* (Cambridge: Cambridge University Press, 1998).

Lemmings, D. (ed.), *The British and Their Laws in the Eighteenth Century*
(Woodbridge: Boydell Press, 2005).

Levene, A., *The Childhood of the Poor: Welfare in Eighteenth-Century London*
(Basingstoke: Palgrave Macmillan, 2012).

Levene, A. (ed.), *Narratives of the Poor in Eighteenth-Century Britain*, 5 volumes (London: Pickering & Chatto, 2006).

Levene, A., 'The origins of the children of the London Foundling Hospital,
1741–1760: a reconsideration', *Continuity and Change*, 18 (2003), 201–35.

Levene, A., T. Nutt and S. Williams (eds.), *Illegitimacy in Britain, 1700–1920*
(Basingstoke: Palgrave Macmillan, 2005).

Longmate, N., *The Workhouse: A Social History* (1974, London: Pimlico, 2003).

Lubenow, W., *The Politics of Government Growth: Early Victorian Attitudes toward State Intervention 1835–1838* (Newton Abbot: David & Charles, 1971).

MacLeod, R. (ed.), *Government and Expertise: Specialists, Administrators and Professionals, 1860–1919* (Cambridge: Cambridge University Press, 1988).

Mandler, P., 'The making of the New Poor Law redivivus', *Past and Present*, 117 (1987), 131–57.

Mandler, P., 'Tories and paupers: Christian political economy and the making of the New Poor Law', *Historical Journal*, 33 (1990), 81–103.

Marshall, D., *The English Poor in the Eighteenth Century: A Study in Social and Administrative History* (London: Routledge, 1926).

Marshall, D., 'The Nottinghamshire reformers and their contribution to the New Poor Law', *Economic History Review*, 13 (1961), 382–96.

Neuman, M., *The Speenhamland County: Poverty and the Poor Laws in Berkshire, 1782–1834* (New York: Garland Publishing, 1982).

Neuman, M., 'A suggestion regarding the origin of the Speenhamland Plan', *English Historical Review*, 84 (1969), 317–92.

Nicholls, G., *History of the English Poor Law, Volume 2: 1714–1853* (London: P.S. King and Son, 1898).

Ottaway, S.R., *The Decline of Life: Old Age in Eighteenth-Century England* (Cambridge: Cambridge University Press, 2004).

Parsons, W., *Public Policy: An Introduction to the Theory and Practice of Policy Analysis* (Cheltenham: Edward Elgar, 1995).

Poynter, J.R., *Society and Pauperism: English Ideas on Poor Relief 1795–1834* (London: Routledge & Kegan Paul, 1969).

Price, K., *Medical Negligence in Victorian Britain: The Crisis of Care under the English Poor Law, c. 1834–1900* (London: Bloomsbury, 2015).

Randall, A., *Before the Luddites: Custom, Community and Machinery in the England Woollen Industry, 1776–1809* (Cambridge: Cambridge University Press, 1991).

Randall, A. and E. Newman, 'Protest, proletarians and paternalists: social conflict in rural Wiltshire, 1830–1850', *Rural History*, 6 (1995), 205–27.

Reay, B., *Microhistories: Demography, Society and Culture in Rural England, 1800–1930* (Cambridge: Cambridge University Press, 1996).

Reay, B., *Rural Englands: Labouring Lives in the Nineteenth Century* (Basingstoke: Palgrave Macmillan, 2004).

Reed, M. and R. Wells (eds.), *Class, Conflict and Protest in the English Countryside, 1700–1880* (London: Frank Cass and Company Limited, 1990).

Richmond, V., *Clothing the Poor in Nineteenth-Century England* (Cambridge: Cambridge University Press, 2013).

Richmond, V., '"Indiscriminate liberality subverts the morals and depraves the habits of the poor": a contribution to the debate on the poor, parish clothing relief and clothing societies in early-nineteenth century England', *Textile History*, 40 (2009), 51–69.

Roberts, D., 'How cruel was the Victorian Poor Law?', *Historical Journal*, 6 (1963), 97–107.

Roberts, D., *The Victorian Origins of the Welfare State* (New Haven: Yale University Press, 1960).

Rose, M., 'The allowance system under the New Poor Law', *Economic History Review*, 19 (1966), 607–20.

Rose, M., 'The Anti-Poor Law Movement in the North of England', *Northern History*, 1 (1966), 70–91.

Rose, M., *The English Poor Law 1780–1930* (Newton Abbott: David & Charles, 1971).

Rule, J. and R. Wells (eds.), *Crime, Protest and Popular Politics in Southern England, 1740–1850* (London: Continuum, 1997).

Sharpe, P., *Adapting to Capitalism: Working Women in the English Economy, 1700–1850* (London: Macmillan, 1996).

Shave, S.A., 'The dependent poor? (Re)constructing the lives of individuals "on the parish" in rural Dorset, 1800–1832', *Rural History*, 20 (2009), 67–97.

Shave, S.A., '"Immediate death or a life of torture are the consequences of the system": the Bridgwater Union Scandal and policy change', in J. Reinarz and L. Schwarz (eds.), *Medicine and the Workhouse* (Rochester, NY: University of Rochester Press, 2013), pp. 164–91.

Shave, S.A., 'The impact of Sturges Bourne's Poor Law reforms in rural southern England', *Historical Journal*, 56 (2013), 399–429; Corrigendum, 57 (2014), 593.

Shave, S.A., 'The welfare of the vulnerable in the late 18th and early 19th centuries: Gilbert's Act of 1782', *History in Focus*, 'Welfare' edition (2008). Online: www.history.ac.uk/ihr/Focus/welfare/articles/shaves.html (last accessed 11 December 2016).

Slack, P., *The English Poor Law, 1531–1782* (1990, Cambridge: Cambridge University Press, 1995).

Snell, K.D.M., *Annals of the Labouring Poor: Social Change and Agrarian England 1660–1900* (Cambridge: Cambridge University Press, 1985).

Snell, K.D.M., 'Belonging and community: understandings of "home" and "friends" among the English poor, 1750–1850', *Economic History Review*, 65 (2012), 1–25.

Snell, K.D.M., *Parish and Belonging: Community, Identity and Welfare in England and Wales 1750–1950* (Cambridge: Cambridge University Press, 2006).

Sokoll, T. (ed.), *Essex Pauper Letters, 1731–1837* (Oxford: Oxford University Press, 2001).

Song, B.K., 'Continuity and change in English rural society: the formation of poor law unions in Oxfordshire', *English Historical Review*, 114 (1999), 314–89.

Spicker, P., *Policy Analysis for Practice: Applying Social Policy* (Bristol: Policy Press, 2006).

Thompson, S.J., 'Population growth and corporations of the poor, 1660–1841', in C. Briggs, P.M. Kitson and S.J. Thompson (eds.), *Population, Welfare and Economic Change in Britain 1290–1834* (Woodbridge: Boydell Press, 2014), pp. 189–225.

Tomkins, A., *The Experience of Urban Poverty: Parish, Charity and Credit, 1723–82* (Manchester: Manchester University Press, 2006).

Tomkins, A., 'Self presentation in pauper letters and the case of Ellen Parker, 1818–1827', *Women's History Notebooks*, 6 (1999), 2–7.

Verdon, N., 'Hay, hops and harvest: women's work in agriculture in nineteenth-century Sussex', in N. Goose (ed.), *Women and Work in Industrial England: Regional and Local Perspectives* (Hatfield: Local Population Studies, 2007), pp. 76–96.

Verdon, N., *Rural Women Workers in Nineteenth-Century England: Gender, Work and Wages* (Woodbridge: Boydell Press, 2002).

Walker, S., 'Accounting, paper shadows and the stigmatised poor', *Accounting, Organizations and Society*, 33 (2008), 453–87.

Walker, S., 'Expense, social and moral control: accounting and the administration of the old poor law in England and Wales', *Journal of Accounting and Public Policy*, 23 (2004), 85–127.

Webb, S. and B. Webb, *English Poor Law History, Part 1: The Old Poor Law* (1927, London: Frank Cass, 1963).

Webb, S. and B. Webb, *English Poor Law History, Part 2: The Last Hundred Years* (1929, London: Frank Cass, 1963).

Webb, S. and B. Webb, *The Parish and the County* (1906, London: Frank Cass, 1963).

Webster, S., 'Estate improvement and the professionalisation of land agents on the Egremont estates in Sussex and Yorkshire, 1770–1835', *Rural History*, 18 (2007), 47–69.

Wells, R., 'Andover antecedents? Hampshire New Poor-Law scandals, 1834–1842', *Southern History*, 24 (2002), 91–217.

Wells, R., 'Historical trajectories: English social welfare systems, rural riots, popular politics, agrarian trade unions, and allotment provision, 1793–1896', *Southern History*, 25 (2003), 85–245.

Wells, R., 'The poor law 1700–1900', in K.C. Leslie and B. Short (eds.), *A Historical Atlas of Sussex: An Atlas of the History of the Counties of East and West Sussex* (Chichester: Phillimore, 1999), pp. 70–1.

Wells, R., 'Poor-law reform in the rural south-east: the impact of the "Sturges Bourne Acts" during the agricultural depression, 1815–1835', *Southern History*, 23 (2001), 52–115.

Wells, R., 'Popular protest and social crime: criminal gangs in southern England, 1790–1860', *Southern History*, 13 (1991), 32–81.

Wells, R., 'Resistance to the New Poor Law in the rural south', in J. Rule and R. Wells (eds.), *Crime, Protest and Popular Politics in Southern England, 1740–1850* (London: Continuum, 1997), pp. 91–125.

Wells, R., 'Southern Chartism', in J. Rule and R. Wells (eds.), *Crime, Protest and Popular Politics in Southern England, 1740–1850* (London: Continuum, 1997), pp. 127–51.

Wells, R., *Wretched Faces: Famine in Wartime England 1763–1803* (Gloucester: Alan Sutton, 1988).

Williams, K., *From Pauperism to Poverty* (London: Routledge & Kegan Paul, 1981).

Williams, S., 'Earnings, poor relief and the economy of makeshifts: Bedfordshire in the early years of the New Poor Law', *Rural History*, 16 (2005), 21–52.

Williams, S., 'Malthus, marriage and poor law allowances revisited: a Bedfordshire case study, 1770–1834', *Agricultural History Review*, 52 (2004), 56–82.

Williams, S., *Poverty, Gender and Life-Cycle under the English Poor Law, 1760–1834* (Woodbridge: Boydell Press, 2011).

Wood, P., *Poverty and the Workhouse in Victorian Britain* (Stroud: Alan Sutton, 1991).

Wrightson, K., 'The politics of the parish in early modern England', in P. Griffiths, A. Fox and S. Hindle (eds.), *The Experience of Authority in Early Modern England* (Basingstoke: Palgrave Macmillan, 1996), pp. 10–46.

# Index